The Erotic Whitman

The Erotic
Whitman

Vivian R. Pollak

UNIVERSITY OF CALIFORNIA PRESS
Berkeley · *Los Angeles* · *London*

I acknowledge with appreciation the University of
Iowa Press for permission to reprint chapter 6, an
earlier version of which appeared in *Walt Whitman:
The Centennial Essays,* edited by Ed Folsom. I also
acknowledge Oxford University Press for permission to reprint chapter 7, an earlier version of which
appeared in *Breaking Bounds: Walt Whitman and
American Cultural Studies,* edited by Betsy Erkkila
and Jay Grossman. Finally, I am grateful to the
William R. Perkins Library of Duke University for
permission to quote from manuscript materials in
the Trent Collection.

University of California Press
Berkeley and Los Angeles, California

University of California Press, Ltd.
London, England

Library of Congress Cataloging-in-Publication Data

Pollak, Vivian R.

The erotic Whitman / Vivian R. Pollak
    p.   cm.
Includes bibliographical references and index.
ISBN 0-520-22189-3 (alk. paper)—
ISBN 0-520-22190-7 (pbk. : alk. paper)
    1. Whitman, Walt, 1819–1892—Criticism and
interpretation.   2. Whitman, Walt, 1819–1892—
Knowledge—Sex.   3. Sex in literature.   4. Homosexuality, Male, in literature.   5. Homosexuality
and literature—United States—History—19th
century.   I. Title.
PS3242.S47 P65   2000
811'.3—dc21   00-022229
                                                          CIP

Manufactured in the United States of America

09 08 07 06 05 04 03 02 01 00

10 9 8 7 6 5 4 3 2 1

The paper used in this publication meets the
minimum requirements of ANSI/NISO Z39.48-1992
(R 1997) (*Permanence of Paper*). ∞

For Steve and Jill and Julia and Ed and Fi

Contents

Illustrations follow page 80

Acknowledgments

Writing this book over the course of more years than I care to remember, I've incurred many pleasurable debts: so many, in fact, that I can't be sure I'm recollecting all of them at this moment. First and foremost, to my students: for their enthusiasm and skepticism and shades of thought and emotion in between. First and foremost, too, colleagues and friends: for their conversations, their readings, their own modeling of the thinking life. And for phone calls, faxes, letters, e-mails, lunches, coffees, dinners, drinks—all those tokens of connectedness which Whitman in some sense inspires. In no particular order, here's an expandable catalogue of scholars who contributed to the progress of this venture, a list which has to include C. Carroll Hollis, Carolyn Allen, Gay Wilson Allen, Paula Bennett, Margaret Dickie, Tenney Nathanson, Betsy Erkkila, Jay Grossman, Jerome Loving, Carol J. Singley, anonymous readers for California University Press, Elizabeth (Sue) Avery, Kenneth M. Price, David Reynolds, Geoffrey Sill, David Leverenz, Bob Milder, Dana D. Nelson, Ed Folsom, Sandra Gilbert, Calvin Bedient, Carter Revard, Naomi Lebowitz, Steve Zwicker, Paul Crumbley, Adam Sonstegard, Bethany Reid. And then there are the institutions that hold our books and manuscripts and photographs and other valuables and the people who make them work. Alice Birney at the Library of Congress, the librarians at the University of Pennsylvania, the University of Washington, Washington University in St. Louis, Duke University, the Harry Ransom Humanities Center at the University of Texas (Austin),

Yale University, Bryn Mawr and Haverford Colleges, the Houghton Library at Harvard. To my former chairs Dick Dunn and Tom Lockwood and Joe Loewenstein and Dan Shea, to Ed Pollak for a timely bit of research assistance, to various other research assistants including Carolyn Klumpar and Christy Auston and Loretta Clayton. To the University of Washington in Seattle and to Washington University in St. Louis for invaluable research leaves. To the National Endowment for the Humanities for a six month Fellowship for University Teachers in the last stages of the project. To my editors at the University of California Press, Linda Norton and Scott Norton (no relation), along with Damion Searls, whose meticulous attention saved me from many errors. And to Bob Pollak for being there on the ground, so to speak: for participating actively in the daily ins and outs, the minutiae and larger visions which have finally in some fashion come together. I'll say nothing of his computer expertise. To the other members of my family and to personal friends. Thanks to one and all for helping me on my way, even when, especially when, we didn't see eye to eye about Walt Whitman and why he matters.

Citation Note

Works by Walt Whitman and frequently cited collections of source material are referred to parenthetically in the text with the following abbreviations:

CH   *Walt Whitman: The Critical Heritage.* Ed. Milton Hindus. New York: Barnes and Noble, 1971.

Corr   *The Correspondence of Walt Whitman.* Ed. Edwin Haviland Miller. 6 vols. New York: New York University Press, 1961–77.

DBN   *Daybooks and Notebooks.* Ed. William White. 3 vols. New York: New York University Press, 1978.

DT   *Drum-Taps and Sequel to Drum-Taps.* Ed. F. DeWolfe Miller. Gainesville, Fla.: Scholars' Facsimiles and Reprints, 1959.

DV   *Democratic Vistas,* in *Walt Whitman: Complete Poetry and Collected Prose.* Ed. Justin Kaplan. New York: Literary Classics of the United States, 1982.

EPF   *The Early Poems and the Fiction.* Ed. Thomas L. Brasher. New York: New York University Press, 1963.

LG   *Leaves of Grass: Comprehensive Reader's Edition.* Ed. Sculley Bradley and Harold W. Blodgett. New York: New York University Press, 1965.

LG 1855   *Leaves of Grass: The First (1855) Edition.* Ed. Malcolm
           Cowley. New York: Viking, 1959.

LG 1856   *Leaves of Grass: Facsimile of 1856 Edition.* Intro. Gay
           Wilson Allen. Folcroft, Pa.: Norwood, 1976.

LG 1860   *Leaves of Grass: Facsimile Edition of the 1860 Text.* In-
           tro. Roy Harvey Pearce. Ithaca: Cornell University Press,
           1961.

NUPM   *Notebooks and Unpublished Prose Manuscripts.* Ed. Ed-
           ward F. Grier. 6 vols. New York: New York University
           Press, 1984.

SD   *Specimen Days,* in *Walt Whitman: Complete Poetry and
           Collected Prose.* Ed. Justin Kaplan. New York: Literary
           Classics of the United States, 1982.

UPP   *The Uncollected Poetry and Prose of Walt Whitman.* Ed.
           Emory Holloway. 2 vols. Garden City, New York: Dou-
           bleday, Page, 1921. Rpt. Peter Smith, 1972.

WWWC   Horace Traubel. *With Walt Whitman in Camden.* 9 vols.
           Vol. I (Boston: Small Maynard, 1906); II (New York:
           D. Appleton, 1908); III (New York: Mitchell Kennerly,
           1914); IV (Philadelphia: University of Pennsylvania Press,
           1953); V and VI and VII (Carbondale: Southern Illinois
           University Press, 1964 and 1982 and 1992, respectively);
           VIII and IX (Oregon House, Calif.: Bentley Books, 1996).

Preface

This book links Whitman's critique of American sexual ideology and practice to the underlying anxieties of his personal life. That Whitman *was* highly anxious socially during his most deeply innovative years as a writer is perhaps my major contention and one that runs counter to many of his most notable self-representations across a range of genres. I show how Whitman refashioned intimate fears and fears of intimacy into a complex critique of gender and sexuality as it had been articulated up to his time. In Whitman's reading of American culture, fear of sexual intimacy and fear of male social and political aggression were virtually indistinguishable.

Making his sexually marked body public in the first (1855), second (1856), and third (1860) editions of *Leaves of Grass* was Whitman's way of seeing how much physical, social, and psychological closeness he and others could bear. In 1855, he began to distinguish sexualized emotion from familiar object choice; he emphasized this process of defamiliarization in 1856; and in 1860 he privileged love between men. In challenging traditional heterosexual norms, Whitman was in part seeking to undo the seemingly fatal consequences of his social isolation. This isolation was not always apparent to those around him—to readers, for example, whom he first addressed as mere "outlines" and then as cherished "brothers and sisters" in the 1855 *Leaves of Grass* (p. 85)—yet it was none the less generative for its lack of "understanders." On the contrary. Had there been better readers of his submerged sexual and (anti)social narrative, there might have been no need for his book.

Whitman's determination to write his sexed body into history emerged out of a lack of psychological intimacy with what he understood as his "real" self, and one of the issues I deal with throughout the book is Whitman's understanding of the real. There are times when he uses this term approvingly to mean a coherent and necessary subordination of the thinking self to some originary power, such as nature, or history. There are other times when greater fluidity and freedom and decentering produce the results he desires. This fundamental contradiction in Whitman's understanding of personhood also informs his understanding of democracy, which remains, at best, a slippery term in his analysis. Without minimizing the ideological inconsistencies of his project, I try to describe a historically situated response to the literary politics of his time that seems to me persuasive. I see Whitman as having internalized the fierce antagonisms of his age and as fighting himself, among others, to create a more authentically "friendly" nature.

In this inner civil war, whose terms were not always constant or apparent, Whitman looked to strangers, and to poets and readers of the future, to clarify his sexual, social, and psychological confusions. But intellectual clarity was ultimately less important to Whitman than emotional honesty, notwithstanding his extraordinary penchant for revising text and self. In examining the pattern behind these revisions, I focus on Whitman's struggle to deprivatize his experience of male-homoerotic desire. My approach to Whitman's development is not rigorously chronological, however, since I use later texts and events to illuminate earlier times. Moreover, I hope to add something to current debates about Whitman and the national war, which strengthened his understanding of the power of nonhegemonic love and of its limitations.

Once he had emerged from his literary apprenticeship and transformed himself from Walter to Walt, discarding a promising career as a fiction writer along the way, Whitman vehemently criticized the power of a domesticating culture to repress women and children, to separate the sexes from each other, and to silence his story of male-male love. These attacks on repressive social structures were linked to others: for example, attacks on political and religious leaders, on greed itself, and on racial injustice. Thus his "faith in sex" was part of a complicated negotiation with other faiths, including a feminine-identified cult of domesticity, whose exclusionary, middle-class values he purported to despise. Yet discarding exclusionary, middle-class values while appealing to a middle-class audience was easier said than done. The Whitman I de-scribe represented himself as a sexual iconoclast, but he also wanted to refresh the public sphere by infusing it with the compassion he associ-ated with an archetypal and nonspecific family life. As the nation's lover and perfect equal, he thus distanced himself from an actual family his-tory and from friendships that were significantly more complex.

Whitman's critique of culture, the "savage" freedoms of his personal life, and their dynamic interrelationship immediately commanded the attention of the first startled reviewers of *Leaves of Grass*. And rightly so. For the Whitman who promised to speak out where others were silent represented himself as the teacher of new forms of erotic plea-sure previously unexplored (at least in literature and by him). Though he staunchly declared himself no "sentimentalist," the emerging poet suggested in 1855 that to read *Leaves of Grass* was to experience hith-erto undreamed-of happiness. Disciplinary structures of domination be-longed to the past, he argued; he himself had once battled with vague yet powerful adversaries, whom he called "linguists and contenders." But now, in his own words, "I witness and wait" (*LG* 1855, p. 28). What-ever his missionary ambitions, Whitman's sex project, social philosophy, and literary style were intended to legitimate and/or reduce the extrava-gant tensions of his inner life. In proposing to heal national ills, he was trying to heal inner tensions as well. Throughout the book, then, I explore a psychological project designed to produce something like "happiness" or "form" or "union" or "plan" for Whitman as well as his readers (*LG* 1855, p. 85). Though I hope not to reduce Whitman's rich literary achievement to the sum of his insecurities, I *do* hope to dem-onstrate that his insights into "the problems of freedom" (*LG* 1860, p. 349) were always conditioned by the "chaos" that he himself had encountered.

As much recent criticism has demonstrated, Whitman's writings do not fully effect the visionary affiliations he proposes as his ideological goal. His gender and sex democracy remains unachieved; public dis-course and private need are not identical; he is less generous and more aggressive than he purports to be. The self-reflexive intellectual who represents himself as friend, father, brother, and lover is flawed. Never-theless, as gender and other social roles are renegotiated in contempo-rary culture, the example of Whitman's prescient struggle with domi-nant forms of love and desire in nineteenth-century America has much to teach us.[1] That he does not always live up to his own high ideals is human; that his ideals are not always perfectly coincident with our own is inevitable. Whitman used poetry to create a daring sexual persona, but he also used the persona's aggressions and inhibitions to justify a complex erotic life. How, then, are we to understand the consistency of his project?[2]

Whitman's poetry establishes emotional intimacies that, for multiple reasons, are quickly broken. It emerges out of a life about which a great deal is known, but which refuses to reveal its final secrets. "Encompass worlds, but never try to encompass me," he wrote in "Song of Myself" (*LG* 1855, p. 51), and the warning should not be overlooked. When Whitman promises to provide constant companionship, this promise is not sustained. How could it be? What common bond would justify the kind of unswerving loyalty he seems to offer? Ideological consistency, perhaps, but Whitman associates such consistency with emotional repression. Thus, at the end of the "Preface" to the 1855 *Leaves of Grass*, he remarks, "The proof of a poet is that his country absorbs him as affectionately as he has absorbed it." This statement revises the fear of habitual association expressed in the "encompass[ing]" image of the earlier, more obviously wary warning.[3] However much the new crowd of friends and lovers Whitman dreamed up absorbs the strangeness of his *dis*affections, the imagined audience for *Leaves of Grass* is based on the fallible and at times desperate people he knew. This limited personal audience included women as well as men. For example, it included his childless sister Hannah, whose disastrous marriage informed Whitman's understanding of romantic obsession and of gendered physical and psychological abuse. And from beginning to end, it included his mother.

Most consistently, Whitman set out to challenge misogynist and homophobic literary codes that violated his experience of a more sexually fluid self. He also observed that the sexed body signifies in relation to other culturally marked identities: that no social identity is purely "natural." Since American authorship has traditionally been equated with the phallus—with the power to initiate change in the public sphere and to privilege the problems of masculinity—Whitman was understandably reluctant to divest himself of its imperial trappings. In fact, he described himself in an early notebook entry, without apparent irony, as "the phallic choice of America," who "leaves the finesse of cities" and all the "achievements of literature and art" to "enjoy the breeding of full-sized men, or one full-sized man or woman, unconquerable and simple" (*NUPM* 4:1303–4). Nevertheless, he associated "the artist race" with his own feminization, an association that was to some extent neutralized

by his "rough," hypermasculine persona. I discuss this co~~n~~
virilization throughout the book.

During the late 1840s and early 1850s, as Whitman the fic~~tional~~
and journalist became increasingly absorbed by his search ~~new~~
forms of less gendered self-representation, he identified certain currents
of affection as crucial to a regenerated national life. These included but
were not restricted to currents of affection between men. How was
Whitman able to convert his fear of erotic intimacy—for such it appears
to have been—into a poetics of national closeness? Was Whitman's fear
of intimacy a defense against an overcrowded erotic history? What are
the sources of this crowding? By 1842, his semiautobiographical hero
Franklin Evans was characterizing himself as fickle. Was this true of
Whitman? If so, what connections can be established between Whitman's experience of social arrangements in flux and his understanding
of a nation without a soul? If we assume that Whitman's left-leaning
politics were conditioned by his membership in an erotic minority of
same-sex lovers, how can we reconcile the lyric poet's need to tell a limited story with the social reformer's need to locate a more comprehensive and impersonal point of view? Until quite recently, as Kerry C. Larson reminds us, Whitman's democratic idealism "has been commonly
thought to be at best a subsidiary concern marginal to his true achievement as a poet and at worst a product of megalomaniacal fantasies
hopelessly out of touch with the social and political complexities of
his day."[4] That is, his sexual idealism has too often been treated as a
purely personal matter. But in the past decade or so, culturally oriented
critics such as Larson, George B. Hutchinson, Betsy Erkkila, M. Jimmie
Killingsworth, Michael Moon, Robert K. Martin, Tenney Nathanson,
Bryne R. S. Fone, Karen Sánchez-Eppler, and David S. Reynolds have
begun to connect Whitman's sexual idealism to other elements of his
democratic project. The time is therefore right, I hope, for a more prob-
ing consideration of what Larson further describes as a poetry combin-
ing "impossible demands for intimacy with equally impossible demands
for absolute equality."[5]

Whitman's ideal of sexual democracy theoretically equalizes all vari-
eties of desire and resists none. This goal remains imperfect in his textual practice, which liberates some forbidden voices and silences others.
Some emancipations demonstrably matter more to Whitman than others, as do some persons. Sexism, racism, classism, homophobia: these
pernicious attitudes crop up not only in Whitman's journalism and pub-

lished essays but also in *Leaves of Grass*—early, middle, and late. Consequently, I locate the erotic Whitman within rather than above the literary history whose political legacy contemporary poets continue to challenge, a legacy of cultural elitism which has perpetuated various forms of material, emotional, and intellectual impoverishment in our time. Still, I hope not to lose sight of the broadly inclusive Whitman who suggested, with some measure of sincerity, that to the fatherless he would be a father, to the motherless a mother, to the lovelorn a lover, to the friendless a friend, to the voiceless a voice, to anyone what he or she was seeking. Capitalizing on personal and national loneliness, this poet who believed that moral curiosity begins at home, with the self, willed himself to see beyond contemptible dreams. The Whitman who matters most to me never claimed perfect knowledge of his own emotional and intellectual needs. Rather, he honored the erotic tensions which had first shaped his quest for new forms of intimate affiliation. How Whitman developed the vision that propelled him into our future forms no small part of my theme.

In trying to recuperate the Whitman who lived powerfully in his imagination, though not always as fully in the social, political, and literary worlds as he wished to do, I draw on the recent Anglo-American tradition of historically based feminist criticism which, in treating women writers, has successfully deconstructed the universalized male subject. This interdisciplinary tradition challenges the concept of an essential, unchanging, and fundamentally unchangeable (hetero)sexual self. Consequently, I locate the erotic Whitman by tracing the development of his subjectivity as it emerged, fraught with contradiction, from and within a very particular social context, the Whitman family, which, like other families, united individuals whose precise material and emotional needs did not always coincide. In chapter 1 and throughout the book, I seek to recover the intimate, intersubjective context that shaped the gender politics of Whitman's literary imagination. I show that Whitman's critique of the American moral imagination, and of the sexual binaries on which it has traditionally depended, was grounded in desires that were themselves dynamic and diverse, both attainable ambitions and phantasmal dreams.

Examining Whitman's attitudes toward women as a crucial element of his poetic identity, I read back through the mother, as historical person and as psychologically powerful trope. Eventually a fierce proponent of sexual egotism as well as a touchingly dutiful son and brother, the poet idealized his "perfect" mother, Louisa Van Velsor Whitman, and suggested that from her strength and wisdom, he derived his own. This fundamental life-relation, part love affair, part unacknowledged burden—he identified her with a "law of nature"—was central to his sexual politics, which in turn are central to *Leaves of Grass*. Yet as I show in my concluding chapter, Whitman's understanding of the emotional, educational, political, and legal needs of nineteenth-century American women was self-interested and incomplete. He admired women in their maternal social roles and sought to affirm the potential of nurturance to dissolve social differences. But in so doing Whitman mythologized the cultural isolation of the American woman, exaggerated the degree to which most nineteenth-century American women had come to hate their own bodies, and, when psychologically pressed, tended to fall back on the white, middle-class doctrine of separate spheres which restricted women's authority to the home, exaggerated the distinction between the home and the marketplace, and denied women access to the public sphere. The gender bending in which Whitman engaged did not go as far as it could have, in both directions: he claimed the authority to voice female desire and to appropriate the intimate stories of women's lives without suggesting that women (or, more crucially, women writers) possessed comparable representational power over his. Thus he contributed to the dominant culture that publicly silenced Emily Dickinson, while also indirectly facilitating her reception as an experimental poet in the 1890s. I discuss this matter more fully in chapter 7.

Whitman, however, wrote *Leaves of Grass* not only to guide and gain power over others but also to affirm and reintegrate himself. In so doing, he held out the promise of a transformed present for men and women who had been alienated from conventional models of community as workers in the public sphere and as lovers in the house of friends. The sources of Whitman's early and enduring *dis*affection are overdetermined. In chapter 1, I describe Whitman's alienation from conventional models of manliness, including the model offered by his all-but-silenced father, Walter Senior. This discussion of "The Erotics of Youth" draws on "proof[s]" of affection and disaffection (*LG* 1855, p. 24) such as Whitman's variously dated notebooks and prose, together with letters written by his mother during the 1860s and 1870s. I pay close attention to those turning points in the family narrative where communication breaks down, and I offer a reading of "The Sleepers" that leans on a line beginning, "Now I tell what my mother told me" (*LG* 1855, p. 110). This chapter approaches the relationship between Whitman's family identifications and disidentifications without drawing on an oedipal model of sexual development. Instead, I concentrate on a less universalizing approach, one designed to recreate the particular social anxieties to which Whitman responded courageously and carefully in his time.[6]

In subsequent chapters, I examine the relationship between Whitman's imaginings of collective others and his desire to animate the "morbid" and "unmanly" discourses of what seemed to him an unreal (in the bad sense) erotic tradition. Never marrying and by more than one account never "bothered up by a woman,"[7] Whitman was powerfully attracted to barely literate young men whose various powers of encouragement and resistance are difficult to assess. Sometimes there was parental interference, as when Whitman the teenage country schoolmaster was reproved by a vigilant farmer-father for making a "pet" of his son.[8] More often, the young men whom the more mature Whitman saw and admired in public places in Brooklyn and New York City during the 1840s, 1850s, and early 1860s were eager for some version of his attention. One such eager person was Fred Vaughan, a Broadway stage driver whose relationship to Whitman has been the subject of much speculation. "Remember Fred Vaughan," Whitman cautioned himself in 1870, when his relationship with Peter Doyle was most unhappily unsettled, and in chapter 4, I look closely at what Whitman might have been remembering.

Nevertheless, we are unlikely ever to know definitively what happened in Whitman's bedroom or in any of the other places where his rendezvous were appointed, and I do not claim to have fully resolved what Louis Crompton describes as "the central issue confronting gay studies," which he calls "'the friendship problem.'" Crompton asks,

> If a novel, poem, or essay describes or expresses ardent feelings for a member of the same sex, when are we to interpret these as homosexual and when are we to regard them merely as reflections of what is usually called romantic friendship? We may be genuinely perplexed by Shakespeare's sonnets, by Montaigne's account of his love for Etienne de La Boëtie, or by Mary Wollstonecraft's novels, Melville's stories, and Emily Dickinson's poems. In Byron's day there was a popular cult of romantic friendship to which Byron as a boy had wholeheartedly responded. Many of his early poems were certainly inspired by it. But he also went beyond this by falling in love with boys and (at least during part of his early life) by becoming a homosexual lover in the physical sense.[9]

We do not know for certain that Whitman became a homosexual lover in the physical sense, though this seems highly likely. We *do* know that Whitman wrote most compellingly out of his search for a lover who was not a mere outline, and out of his inability to find such a person—except, perhaps, in his mother. The poet's insights into love and aggression and their interrelationship made him wary of sustained erotic intimacy. "There is something fierce and terrible in me, eligible to burst forth," he wrote in one of the *Calamus* poems (*LG* 1860, p. 374). And he meant it. "The embrace of love and resistance" described in the 1855 poem "I Sing the Body Electric," "The upperhold and underhold—the hair rumpled over and blinding the eyes" (*LG* 1855, p. 117), was played out in his relationships with younger men; there was love, but there was also resistance, and the excess of love could prove blinding. He understood heterosexual partnerships as no less aggressive, if anything more so. "Thruster holding me tight and that I hold tight!" he wrote in the long 1855 poem later titled "Song of Myself," "We hurt each other as the bridegroom and the bride hurt each other" (*LG* 1855, p. 45). Such lines, which construct any form of sexual initiation as punitive, are scattered throughout his most vital books.

Certainly we would like to know what male-homoerotic actions Whitman considered excessive. When he encouraged himself to "depress the adhesive nature," writing in a famous notebook entry in July 1870, "It is in excess—making life a torment" (*NUPM* 2:889), what was his norm? Something or nothing? A lot or a little? We may never know how much male-male sexual passion Whitman considered "diseased, feverish, disproportionate" (*NUPM* 2:890), although Section 26 of "Song of Myself" provides a clue. At first sexual passion inspires him, but when passion deprives him of agency, a loss of power he likens to dying, Whitman disengages. Turning lovers into "objects"—that is, symbols—he is then able to lead them "harmlessly" through himself, rather than being led by them to the brink of destruction. As a student of the grand opera, he knows romantic thralldom when he sees it and when he feels it. For, as he emphasizes, *his* is no callous shell. In 1855, 1856, and 1860, Whitman's paradoxical critique of American sexual ideology and practice reflected his fear of passion, as well as his more self-evident "faith in sex." Thus I refute or qualify the extravagant narratives constructed by some recent sexual historians, who mythologize the homosexual Whitman as a boundlessly energetic performer.[10] I also refute the lurid, panicked tradition which suggests that Whitman was tarred and feathered for sodomy during his schoolteaching days on Long Island.[11] Instead, I emphasize that Whitman lived at home in Brooklyn during his most productive years as a poet; that during part of that time, he shared a small bedroom with his retarded and crippled brother, Ed; and that his complex, interlineated devotions to family, to nation, to permeable and impermeable psyches, prepared him for his subsequent role as "wounddresser" during the Civil War, as well as for his (re)production of that role in poetry. Whitman had begun to visit young men in hospitals before the war, but in Washington the prolonged strain of caring for wounded and dying soldiers—caring for them physically and emotionally—overwhelmed him. This is the more understandable since he fell in love with several soldiers who recovered and moved on. When successful, his nursing undid those intimate, indestructible and yet liberating relationships he was trying to develop. In going home to recuperate from "spells of deathly faintness" and other attendant disorders in late June 1864 (*Corr* 1:231), Whitman was following the advice of his physicians. He stayed in Brooklyn for the next seven months and, despite some evidence to the contrary, a domesticated cautiousness was one of his leading traits.[12]

To recapitulate. Until a fortuitous move to Washington, D.C., in December 1862, when Whitman was forty-three, a move precipitated by the search for his brother George, who had been wounded in battle, Whitman appears to have enjoyed *transitory* sexual relationships with men—especially men who were poorer, less well educated, and significantly younger than himself. We do not know whether these relationships included anal penetration, an activity Whitman probably considered constitutive of homosexual identity, as did the British homosexual rights advocates, whom he was beginning to influence as early as the mid-1860s.[13] Though these "fluid" relationships did not last, they shaped his understanding of desire and of a potentially democratic politics of love. (Whitman was also part of an unofficial drinking club, the "Fred Gray Association," which gratified his need for more recognizably elite male companions.) Important recent discussions of male-male friendship and of homosexual desire in Whitman's project have tended to describe their collective political value.[14] I have tried to enrich this conversation and to make it more real (in the good sense) by appealing to the biography, to the prose, and to the poems. The three overlap, though in some instances they are clearly distinguishable.

In the winter of 1865–66, however, when he met the ex–Confederate soldier Peter Doyle on a Washington streetcar, the poet began to live out the domesticated "Calamus" fantasy of a continuous, cooperative erotic life that he had anticipated before the war in the 1860 *Leaves of Grass*. Whitman and Doyle did not actually make a home together—Doyle lived with his mother—but Whitman did not rule out this possibility in the summer of 1869, when Pete was depressed and needed extra help. "I have had this in my mind before," Whitman wrote to his "dearest boy," who thought he had contracted syphilis and was threatening to kill himself, "but never broached it to you" (*Corr* 2:84). After the crisis passed, these loving comrades continued to see each other almost daily.[15] Yet the emotional security Whitman derived from this (open) relationship should not be exaggerated. There were times when he was tormented by jealousy, especially since Doyle made no secret of his (hetero)sexual conquests.[16] As a defense against this torment, Whitman attempted to expand his erotic circle. Thus shortly after writing to Pete, "I don't know what I should do if I hadn't you to think of & look forward to" (*Corr* 2:47), and shortly after signing himself "Yours for life, dear Pete, (& death the same)" (*Corr* 2:58), the anxious lover stepped up his correspondence with another "loving boy," John (Broadway Jack) Flood, Jr., a New York streetcar conductor whom he had seen during his recent vacation in Brooklyn. "Whether we are indeed to have the chance in future to be much together & enjoy each other's love & friendship," he wrote, "—or whether worldly affairs are to separate us—I don't know. But somehow I feel (if I'm not dreaming) that the good square love is in our hearts, for each other, while life lasts" (*Corr* 2:74).[17] Where is Pete? For Whitman, *one* streetcar conductor, even if that conductor was "Pete the Great," was not enough.[18]

Following Whitman's move to Camden for reasons of health in 1873, when he retreated to the home of his brother George and sister-in-law Lou, Whitman and Doyle wrote to each other regularly for several years. They were rarely able to meet in person.[19] By 1876, the recuperating poet had entered into a new relationship with Harry Stafford, a farm boy, though that love affair was even stormier.[20] Thus Whitman's subsequent narrative of his emotional life, which emphasizes the transforming power of the war itself, is also, in many respects, the one I adopt, but I shift the focus from overt national politics to a covert politics of love. Whitman found that a clearly focused historical crisis enabled him to respond less anxiously to other men. Some recent discussions of war and gender have suggested that military conflict provides an occasion for society to remasculinize itself.[21] Happily, for Whitman, this was not the case.

Creating such new connections as were possible in the remarkably resilient language of his time and life, Whitman engaged in powerful repressions of his personal past and mythologized an untroubled self that never was. But he also insisted on the psychological necessity of his project. Thus, in "A Backward Glance O'er Travel'd Roads," he described *Leaves of Grass* as an "attempt, from first to last, to put *a Person,* a human being (myself, in the latter half of the Nineteenth Century, in America,) freely, fully and truly on record" (*LG,* pp. 573–74). Despite the radical simplicity of this statement, I have tried to take the poet at his word. To the extent that he put himself "freely, fully and truly on record," Walt Whitman recorded his hesitations as well as his daring, his sadness as well as his verve. In so doing, he clarified and remystified the experience of living. His was a deeply personal poetry: nothing if not a literary performance, and nothing if nothing more.

ONE

The Erotics of Youth

Late in the day on August 9, 1888, a "gradually sinking & dissolving" Whitman began to talk about his mother to his note-taking friend and neighbor Horace Traubel. Reminiscing in his cramped, paper-strewn bedroom on Mickle Street in Camden, New Jersey, the poet exclaimed,

> How much I owe her! It could not be put in a scale—weighed: it could not be measured—be even put in the best words: it can only be apprehended through the intuitions. Leaves of Grass is the flower of her temperament active in me. My mother was illiterate in the formal sense but strangely knowing: she excelled in narrative—had great mimetic power: she could tell stories, impersonate: she was very eloquent in the utterance of noble moral axioms—was very original in her manner, her style. (*WWWC* 2:113–14)[1]

Often described by himself and others as a reluctant talker, Whitman proved "garrulous to the very last" (*LG*, p. 536) with the right person. In his final years, the right person was Traubel, who was helping to manage his affairs and who, as Whitman explained in recommending him for a job to his own Philadelphia publisher, was "of liberal tendencies and familiar with printing office matters and the run of books" (*WWWC* 1:171). Traubel, who was nearly forty years Whitman's junior, visited the semiparalyzed poet every day, sometimes more than once, assiduously recording their conversations in "condensed longhand." To date, nine volumes of these interview-like conversations have been published, and they show this invaluable young friend prompting Whitman to make sense of the great labor of his life and of the paper "raw product" he was still producing, though at a sadly reduced pace (*WWWC* 2:110).

When Whitman began to talk about his mother, he had recently had a series of small strokes that nearly killed him, and the following day, Traubel noted that the invalid poet, though clearheaded, sometimes suffered from a sort of aphasia—"can't get his words without a search" (*WWWC* 2:115). On the August evening in question, however, Whitman spoke fluently, moving from a meditation on the Tyrolean Alps, to the natural wonders of the American continent, to the thought that beauty exists where we least expect to find it, to the idea that the formally uneducated Louisa was "responsible for the main things . . . in Leaves of Grass" (*WWWC* 2:113). He had sounded this note before, though never so emphatically. Not surprisingly, Traubel was skeptical. Where was the proof that "the reality, the simplicity, the transparency" of the poet's mother's life could have been responsible for a project of such demonstrable magnitude and complexity? Where were the documents?

Five months later, Traubel encouraged an even more debilitated Whitman to admit that *none* of the people in his own family, including his mother, had understood *Leaves of Grass*. Whitman explained that he had always felt like "a stranger in their midst" and that his faithful mother, who believed in *him,* had been thoroughly baffled by his poetry (*WWWC* 3:525–26). Whitman allowed his anger to show and this version of events was flattering to Traubel's self-esteem.[2] Clearly, the bookish young man was more eager to hear about the influence of the *literate* people in Whitman's life, and when Whitman talked about *Leaves of Grass* as "the flower of her temperament active in me," Traubel did not know how to respond. Consequently, he said nothing and Whitman changed the subject and produced documents. Compliments were exchanged, Traubel kissed him good night, and left the room.

Reversing a critical tendency to ignore Whitman's "illiterate" mother as a powerful influence on *Leaves of Grass,* in the first section of this chapter I look further at Louisa, who subtly encouraged Whitman to rewrite the conventional history that excluded both her and him and their intersubjective realities. Following in the Traubel tradition of nonresponse, critics such as Quentin Anderson have suggested that his mother's alleged perfection "doesn't account for the poems, nor does it qualify the poems," and I agree.[3] I propose, however, to deidealize Louisa. Her dissatisfactions with the experience and institution of motherhood in nineteenth-century America informed the poet's critique of domesticity in literature and to some extent inspired the gender democracy of the poems. In the chapter's second section, I look at the gender-divided Brenton family in which Whitman lived briefly as a young journalist and stranger, a discussion that has the effect of deidealizing the early Whitman as a democratic equalizer. And in the third section, I look at the emerging poet's attempt to move beyond a critique of domesticity into a loving and ambitious male friendship community which excludes women. Throughout the chapter, I trace the relativity of Whitman's understanding of happiness, which circles back again and again to his need to rewrite a gradually sinking and dissolving family scene. As son and poet, Whitman had absorbed the thwarted dreams of his story-telling mother. Who would comprehend the form-defying anxieties of his own?

FAMILY FACES

Memorialized in a late poem as "the ideal woman, practical, spiritual, of all of earth, life, love, to me the best" (*LG,* p. 497), Louisa Van Velsor Whitman was born on September 22, 1795, near Cold Spring Harbor, Long Island. Little is known of her rural youth beyond such fragmentary descriptions as Whitman provides in poems, in *Specimen Days,* in an obscure early "Fact-Romance," and in the notebooks which served as sources for his writing.[4] In one of these notebook entries, he recalls how her father gallantly defied the British during the American Revolution. When a raiding party invaded his stable, Major "Kell" held his ground. Eighteen-year-old Cornelius was acting as a private citizen; the title, bestowed later, was honorific. "As usual," Whitman wrote, "great courage, will, and coolness, stood him in hand. The swords flourished and flashed around his head—the women were in tears, expect'g he would be killed; but he held on to the mare, and the upshot of it was, the British rode away without her" (*NUPM* 1:19). After this inspiring beginning, "Kell" settled down to an unremarkable career as a farmer whose passion was horse breeding. The heroic beginning was not fulfilled and Walt Whitman bore the burden, transmitted to him by his mother, of exemplifying the great courage, will, and coolness exhibited by her father in his only notable moment of glory.[5] This, then, was manliness: courage, will, and coolness. But was it his mother or his father who exhibited these characteristics? Louisa, remember, could "impersonate."

Whitman's maternal grandmother Amy Van Velsor presided efficiently over the family hearth, welcoming visitors and then generally receding into the background of a hospitable home. Probably she is the prototype of the elderly woman in "The Sleepers," who carefully darns her grandson's stockings, while sitting "low" in a straw-bottomed chair (*LG* 1855, p. 108). Humble, serviceable Grandmother Amy might have been a Quaker, had she not married out of the faith. She was Quakerish in her style of dress, or at least in the style of her cap. Accounts vary.[6] Grandmother Amy is also a likely model for Whitman's nostalgic portrait of "The justified mother of men!" which he uses to conclude the turbulent 1855 poem "Faces." "Behold a woman!" the speaker commands, averting his gaze from more disturbingly modern sights,

> She looks out from her quaker cap. . . . her face is clearer and more
>   beautiful than the sky.
>
> She sits in an armchair under the shaded porch of the farmhouse,
> The sun just shines on her old white head.
>
> Her ample gown is of creamhued linen,
> Her grandsons raised the flax, and her granddaughters spun it with the
>   distaff and the wheel.
>
> The Melodious character of the earth!
> The finish beyond which philosophy cannot go and does not wish to go!
> The justified mother of men!
>   (*LG* 1855, pp. 127–28)[7]

Using his grandmother Amy Van Velsor to repair the ravages of a later time, Whitman shows us a "clear" face unmarked by history. But this optimistic portrait of a woman at peace with herself and her surroundings has no depth. The emphasis is on costume, as though all the figures were intent on impersonating a happy family.[8]

Grandmother Amy as the "Faces" Quakeress leads the peaceful life that Whitman wished could have been his own mother's—a life in which no stoically philosophizing son would need to justify the maternal presence. However, we encounter a significantly less tranquil image of the Van Velsors together in a piece of ephemeral journalism published when Whitman was in his mid-twenties. The story beginning "When my mother was a girl" first appeared in the *Aristidean* in December 1845. As editor, Whitman reprinted it in the *Brooklyn Daily Eagle* in December 1846, under the title "An Incident on Long Island Forty Years Ago." Here an older Cornelius Van Velsor is depicted as insensitive to the fears of his wife and daughter and as more concerned with his horse than with their well-being. As the slyly humorous narrative ends, his wife almost chokes him to death "in good earnest" (*EPF* 325–26). The story initially pivots on Kell's untimely absence from home. Whitman labeled it a "Fact-

Romance," while mocking anyone who might purport to be "an authentic biographer."

The domestic confrontation of the "Incident" repeats an underlying motif of the notebook entry describing "Major Kell" as a fearless if minor hero of the American Revolution. In both episodes, Kell alarms the women in his family, but in the earlier episode, the anxiety he causes is justified. The civilian sketch presents a coarsened Kell—he is described as red-faced, laughing, and bluff-voiced. The Revolutionary Kell arouses pride as well as fear, but the civilian Kell is a lout. In both episodes, Cornelius Van Velsor makes women feel anxious, and Grandmother Amy makes Grandfather Kell feel—but how does he feel? At this point Whitman's 1845–46 story ends and the notebook entry written in the 1860s does not attempt to probe Kell's inner life. In both episodes, the women are invested in Kell; they care enough to cry about him. In the "Incident," however, this care is not reciprocated and Kell's favorite horse is called "Dandy—a creature he loved next to his wife and children—he rode away to attend to it."

The story reworks a number of urgent family themes, including the anger shared by Whitman and his mother at his grandfather's untimely death. For the historical rather than the fantasized Cornelius Van Velsor seems to have been a stabilizing influence in Walt's uncertain youth and an obvious contrast to Walt's hard luck father. Then, too, hospitable and useful Grandmother Amy died when Walt was about seven and Louisa about thirty. From their mutual perspective, the replacement stepgrandmother was not "a very good investment" (*NUPM* 1:7 n. 30). Relations between the two families were less close after that time. The Major died in 1838 before Walt was twenty and so far as we can tell the Whitmans inherited nothing from his estate.[9] Memorializing him late in his own life, Whitman presents Cornelius Van Velsor as a "solid" role model. But there is a disquieting conclusion when he describes the trips they often took together up and down the Island. Despite their physical proximity, no words are exchanged, no feelings acknowledged. In this account, Kell's old-fashioned "ease" once again did not translate into sensitivity to the dis-ease of others.

> Major Van Velsor was a good specimen of a hearty, solid, fat old gentleman, on good terms with the world, and who liked his ease.—For over forty years, he drove a stage and market wagon from his farm to Brooklyn ferry, where he used to put up at Smith & Wood's old tavern on the west side of the street, near Fulton ferry.—He was wonderfully regular in these weekly trips; and

in those old fashioned times, people could almost tell the time of day, by his stage passing along the road—so punctual was he.—I have been up and down with him many times: I well remember how sick the smell of the lampblack and oil with which the canvass covering of the stage was painted, would make me. (*NUPM* 1:6–7)

Weaving memories of his childhood and personal and family fortunes in and out of his published and unpublished poetry and prose, Whitman returned again and again to the woman he idealized as a model of familial steadiness and domestic self-control. After her death, he wrote about the "calm benignant face fresh and beautiful still," but this was the face, too, that drew him into "the coffin" of convulsive, sexualized feelings he could not control. Whitman lived beyond the morbidity of his 1881 "monumental line," but he continued to turn to thoughts of "the divine blending, maternity" to fuse his various irreconcilable moods (*LG*, p. 497). This process of idealistic fusion, abetted by culturally encouraged images of mother-worship, had begun early. So too had the inevitable counter-response, the movement away from the coffin out into the sunlight, away from convulsive kisses and toward a more artfully individuated masculine self. In the Long Island "Incident" of 1845, with its undercurrent of free-floating malice, Whitman characteristically describes Louisa as doing her best to soothe her frightened mother, and her cheerfulness is a consistent theme in his various accounts of her reassuring nature. Others found her less cheerful, especially once old age and loneliness had begun to depress her. But whether or not she was *always* calm and compassionate, stoical and capable, generous and loving— whether or not she was the consistently noble and flowering mother of the Whitman myth—Louisa Van Velsor Whitman was an unusually dependable worker in a world where much was undependable. In this, she was like her father with his market wagon: the wagon that for Whitman served to isolate as well as to provide.

Physically active and proud of her physical and mental endurance, Louisa was generally able to suppress whatever anger she felt toward the men in her life, including the husband who was less steady emotionally than she. At least, there is no record of any mock-murderous outburst on her part such as Whitman attributes to Grandmother Amy after she had been deserted and humiliated by Grandfather Kell. When provoked, however, Louisa was tart-tongued, and one of the ways in which she defended herself against outrageous fortune was by treating young Walt as her confidant. "In the observation of the drama of human nature," he later wrote, in one of his fabulous self-reviews, "if, indeed, 'all the world's a stage'—Walt Whitman has had rare advantages as auditor, from the beginning" (*UPP* 2:58–59). "My dear mother possessed the story-telling faculty," he recalled more simply, "whenever she had been anywhere she could describe it, tell me all about it." Despite her "happy-tending natural disposition" (*Corr* 3:366), which Walt at times claimed to have inherited, in later years Louisa's outspoken catalogue of complaints, however erratically spelled and punctuated, was weighty and long.

In a photograph taken in 1855, Louisa Van Velsor Whitman's mobile expression is difficult to decode. She is simply dressed. The strings of her white ruffled cap hanging down Quaker style, her deep-set eyes do not quite meet the camera's gaze. Looking slightly to one side, she appears alternately grim and amused. Either she is smiling slightly, her thin-lipped mouth closed, or she isn't. Her straight, darkish hair is mostly covered by her cap. She looks strong, intelligent, self-possessed, but there is little trace of the physical beauty Walt proudly ascribed to her. Probably the photograph is unflattering, as is the single portrait we have of her husband, in which he looks angry and desperately unkempt. With her athletic body—like all the Whitmans except Eddy she was "good-sized"—Louisa was able to do more housework than many other women. And while Walt's brother Jeff complained of her stinginess at table, Walt adored her cooking. Louisa was tall for a woman of her time, and when he was searching for mother-surrogates to pull him out of his unusually prolonged depression in the 1870s—a depression precipitated by ill health and by feelings of repressed hostility toward the lost mother he had consciously adored—he took pleasure in the company of Susan Stafford, a "good-sized" farm woman whose welcoming home at Timber Creek helped to turn him back from death toward life. "*Shape-first, face afterward,*" he explained jocularly to her son Harry, Harry himself being part of the cure (*Corr* 3:361).

Meeting Walt's mother in November 1855, Bronson Alcott described Louisa Whitman as "a stately sensible matron, believing in Walter absolutely and telling us how good he was and wise as a boy, how his four brothers and two sisters loved him, and how they take counsel of the great man he is grown to be now." [10] But the numbers don't add up. Jesse (b. 1818), Walt (b. 1819), Mary (b. 1821), Hannah (b. 1823), Andrew (b. 1827), George (b. 1829), Jeff (b. 1833), Eddy (b. 1835). Including Walt, there were six Whitman brothers. Assuming Alcott remembered correctly, which one of her sons was Louisa eliminating? Her oldest, Jesse, irritable and unstable, who wouldn't listen to Walt? Or her youngest, Ed, mentally feeble and physically lame? Did Walt learn from her his ability to fold disturbing particulars into a larger, nobler scheme? Is that one of the ways in which "Leaves of Grass is the flower of her temperament active in me?" And to what extent did this proud habit encourage self-isolation, rather than producing the desired sociable effect? John Burroughs, meeting Walt's mother in 1868, called her a "spry, vivacious, handsome old lady."[11] Like other members of the Whitman circle, he accepted her uncritically as the fond mother of a fond son. "My mother was a Van Velsor," Whitman subsequently explained to Traubel. "I favor her: 'favor' they call it up on Long Island—a curious word so used, yet a word of great suggestiveness" (WWWC 2:280). On Long Island, where they remembered her as a young woman, people commented on the similarity of their features, their gait, their voice.

Despite her great pride in Walt, and his in her, Louisa's was a hard life, its pleasures far from obvious. Losing her husband in 1855, she continued to yearn for a secure home of her own and was only too dependent on her grown sons, including Walt, for handouts. Here is a letter from her later years, written after she had had too much family company for too long. Her son Jeff, his wife Mattie, and their two young daughters were visiting from St. Louis in the fall of 1868. Mattie arrived in mid-October with the girls, Jeff joined them on November 20, and they left in mid-December. Louisa was seventy-three and complaining as usual about the stinginess of her relatives. "O Walt," the letter begins, using the plaintive "o" that figures so prominently as an emotive signal in his poems,

> haint i had a seige they pretended to live up stairs but the provisions was prepared down . . . they have never paid a cent of rent nor a cent of gas bill nor give me a dollar when they went away they gave me an allapaca dress when they came and Jeff bought me a little mite of a castor that is all about three weeks ago george [another son] bought 20 lb of butter and they have used out of it ever since and matty borrowed 50 dollars of george but jeffy dident settle it they had plenty of money as Jeffy drawed that out of the bank i really think they had ought to give me some but let everything go but i would ask more than 100 to go through the same again burn this letter[12]

Obviously, Walt did not comply. Louisa's emphasis on pretense is especially interesting given that Walt himself was in Providence, Rhode Island, during part of this time, and writing to Peter Doyle about his success "in the midst of female women" as a "gay deceiver" (Corr 2:62). If Leaves of Grass "is the flower of her temperament active in me," one element of this temperament was the desire to keep up appropriately gendered appearances—as Louisa, for all her dissatisfactions as a mother, mother-in-law, grandmother, and hostess, was attempting to do.

To say this is not to deny the genuineness of the compassion that Louisa, like Walt, could feel for others. Louisa could direct pity outward as well as in, but it was Walt who needed to mythologize the constancy of this element of her character. Thus when the besieging and borrowing Mattie died of lung cancer in February 1873, only several months before Louisa's own death, Louisa explained with pity first for her daughter-in-law and then, increasingly, for herself,

> poor matt i feel so bad about her i cant keep her out of my mind
> (*February 27, 1873*)
>
> poor dear Matt i think of her day and night but i very seldom mention her name walt matt was a kind daughter to me i have cause to regret her death
> (*March 21, 1873*)
>
> O i think sometimes if i could see matty once more as i used to and tell her all my ups and downs what a comfort it would be to me i never had any one even my own daughters i could tell every thing to as i could her when you get old like me Walt you feel the need of such a friend
> (*Spring 1873*)[13]

This indirect recrimination may not have hurt, since Walt probably accepted the fact that close friendships among women were the norm. An intimate mother-daughter relationship was to be expected, though here too Louisa describes herself as shortchanged. Louisa's letter suggests that confidences are gendered and that she longed for specifically female companionship, for the empathic discourse of a "female world of love and ritual."[14] Geographically separated from her own daughters, and perhaps emotionally separated as well, Louisa did what she could to cultivate daughter substitutes. One of them, Josephine Barkeloo, wrote to her in October 1872, "it is my bed hour. Good night, you are in your dreams, and I am kissing you in imagination you half awaken and say 'Is that you—Walter?' but you are mistaken it was—Yours truly, Joe."[15] It would be nice to think that close friendships with younger women made Louisa's later life bearable, but Joe Barkeloo suggests that Louisa's primary identification was with "Walter," the name shared by father and son. In this context, "Walter" is Walt, and "Joe" was right. Although she respected the demands of his career, Louisa preferred to have Walt by her side.

Here is another of Louisa's letters, written in December 1865. George Whitman, a former prisoner of war, had been living at home since the preceding March, and Louisa, perplexed and depressed by his uncharacteristic stinginess, turned to Walt for emotional and financial relief.

> Dear Walt i have got in the habit of writing to you every sunday so i thought
> i wouldent break through to day) i received your letter yesterday after look-
> ing all day for one i was glad to have the letter and glad to have the 2 dollars
> at noon i hadent one cent and i asked georgee to give me 50 cents and after
> looking for a considerable time he laid me down 50 cents well Walt i felt
> so bad and child like i cried because he dident give me more if i had got
> the 2 dollars [sent by Walt] a little sooner i should not have asked i have got
> along very well up to about 2 weeks ago and since that time george has been
> moody and would hardly speak only when i spoke to him well of course you
> will say mother put the worst construction on it well walt i did not the first
> few days i thought perhaps something had gone wrong in his business af-
> fairs but up to day he has been so different from what he was ever since i
> have been home but to day he is more like himself well Walt i thought of
> every thing sometimes i would think maybee he is tired of having me and
> Edd and then i would think george is too noble a fellow for that to be the
> cause and i knew that i had not or he had not been to more expence than if
> he paid his board Jeffy told me to have a talk with george and ask him what
> made him so but i dident like to i would ask him if he wasent well and so
> on but i doo hope it will go over i acted just the same as if i did not notice
> any change but i felt awful bad and what has made him act so god only
> knows but i believe it runs in the Whitman family to have such spells any
> how i hope they wont come often. . . . well walt next sunday when i write
> maybe it will be more cheerful i wish walt you will send me ten dollars not
> all at one time but if you can send me 5 at the next writing my shoes is
> rather bad for cold weather i have some mind to not send this letter now
> i have wrote it if you write any thing about it put it in a separate peice.
>   L Whitman

Casting about late in life for a satisfactory myth of origins, Whitman hit on his mother's "Hollandish" and Quaker inheritance. He emphasized her sunny temperament, which shone the brighter in contrast to his father's dour English disposition. Yet there were gaps in the family narrative that genetic or racial discourse was inadequate to explain. If Walt described himself as in certain senses "a stranger in their midst," Louisa, too, suffered from social isolation. In the letter quoted above, for example, she encodes a double message. On the one hand, she craves sympathy and needs to talk; on the other, her pride prevents her from expressing her hurt to her son George, by whom she feels cruelly rejected. Turning to Jeff for advice, she ignores it. Instead, she carries on as usual, speculating to herself about "what has made him act so," which has the effect of further isolating both herself and George. Hopelessly, she concludes "god only knows" and fatalistically interprets her son's punishing

silence as a Whitman family trait. To the extent that there is a spiritual dimension to this interaction—for Walt called his ideal woman "spiritual"
as well as "practical"—the spirituality consists in turning inward. Louisa
turned inward to avoid confrontations she was afraid of losing. The strat-
egy was practical, in that it salvaged what remained of her self-esteem.

Several months before he received the tearful letter quoted above,
Whitman, who was visiting in Brooklyn, had written to Nelly O'Connor
about his mother's "splendid condition" (*Corr* 1:270). Undoubtedly
Louisa was *more* splendid because Walt was in the house, but he had always tried to protect her and did his best, even as a child, not to burden
her with his troubles. "He was a very good, but very strange boy,"
Mrs. Whitman explained to a chance visitor, after her son had become
famous.[16] Did she mean that he was always studying or that he so rarely
asked anything for himself, especially since some of the others were so
much more demanding? The myth that Whitman was an idler during his
youth is just that. As Sandra Tomc has suggested in her analysis of "literary leisure," writers other than Whitman "insisted on their exemption
from the modern rhythms of labor and accumulation." She traces the
deployment of an "idleness ethic from the early republican to the antebellum periods," using Nathaniel Parker Willis as her prime example of
a conflicted relationship to the middle-class marketplace.[17] Whitman,
too, sought to uncouple the relationship between class status and the
aristocratic fantasy of leisure. But we should not be fooled. During his
youth, Walter Whitman Junior, like his mother, was notably hardworking. Louisa recognized as much and was not one of those persons who
called him "lazy."

In any event, the conflicted psychological community formed by Whitman and his mother was written into the fiction published by Walter
Whitman Junior in the 1840s. At this time Walter Senior, with his "sound
strong body heredity," was still working and well,[18] but Whitman most
memorably represents his fictional mother as a widow, and he represents
himself as her only son. At some level this exclusionary fantasy would
have been gratifying to Louisa. At some level, too, Whitman's transformative narratives expressed their shared, mutually reinforcing ambivalence not only toward Walt's father, but toward some of his brothers.
For example, both Louisa and Walt had to contend with the firstborn
Jesse, who, in addition to being highly intelligent, was passionate from
birth and subject to violent outbursts. Jesse's lack of self-control reinforced the young Whitman's tendency to withdraw into himself; he was
never known as a glib talker.[19]

Walt and Louisa were probably both relieved when as a teenager Jesse ran away to sea, but he suffered a severe head injury in an accident or brawl during the late 1840s, which ended his life as a merchant marine. He drifted during the 1850s, still thinking of the sea, and, according to Jeff, living with an Irish whore.[20] By March 1860, he was working in the Brooklyn Navy Yard "again" and wanted to come home "again," as he seems to have done in the recent past. But Louisa, having rented out part of the house, explained to Walt, "I told him he would have to hire board somewhere as I had hired out so much of the house I had no place for him to sleep" (March 30, 1860). Jesse continued to work at the Navy Yard, and in the summer of 1861 he was working there every day (*Corr* 1:56). However, when Walt committed Jesse to the Kings County Lunatic Asylum in December 1864, the record of admission stated, "He has been considered somewhat insane by his friends [that is, family] for the last four years."[21] This opinion was shared by Louisa, who in 1863 considered him "deranged," but no more so than he had been for the last three years. Much about Jesse's "dissipated" history is vague, but at some point after April 29, 1860, when Fred Vaughan visited the Whitmans in Brooklyn, Louisa had "again" found room for Jesse in her crowded home.[22] More constantly, she was burdened by her youngest, Ed, who was lame and "weak brained" and institutionalized only after her death.[23] The aging Louisa was faced with "two [cases] of grown helplessness," as Walt called them, and during the Civil War he wrote that her bravery was "beyond the heroisms of men" (*Corr* 1:183). So why *should* we expect Louisa to be a stranger to jealousy and bitterness? Given the limited control she had over her life, she had a great deal to be jealous and bitter *about*.

In the many letters she sent Walt during her later years (1863–73), Louisa Van Velsor Whitman represented herself as chronically impoverished. When she had five hundred dollars in her bank account she was afraid to use it, since her children supported her and she experienced her lack of financial independence as infantilizing. While Jeff, for one, thought she exaggerated her poverty, it is easy to understand why she felt forced to hoard and scrimp and save, and to charge her grown children board money when they wanted to come visit—even if those visits were rare, and even if the occasion was a wedding. "When I get desperate I write[,] commit it to paper[,] as you literary folk say," she explained in November 1863, shortly before describing the heartrending "particulars of Andrew's death."[24] (Her son Andrew died of tuberculosis complicated by alcoholism at the age of thirty-six.) Walt, by then living in Washington, D.C., was her "good old standby." Such a role took its toll on him; he suffered a nervous breakdown when his mother died in May 1873. This followed his stroke in January, from which he had only just begun to recover. "My only torment," he explained to Emerson when he first arrived in Washington, in December 1862, "family matters" (*Corr* 1:60).

As we have seen, Louisa Van Velsor Whitman was semiliterate; she could read and write, but her formal schooling was extremely limited. Time permitting, in later years she enjoyed reading newspapers and magazines and reading and writing letters. She followed the ups and downs of Walt's literary career with great interest and once wrote him that she read a little in his *Drum-Taps* every night before going to sleep.[25] She also enjoyed his poems "Whispers of Heavenly Death" and "Proud Music of the Storm." As a literary critic, she was strong on family loyalty, commenting to her untalkative, unimaginative son George in 1855 that if Longfellow's *Song of Hiawatha* was poetry, then maybe so was *Leaves of Grass*.[26]

According to Walt, Louisa was a daring and spirited rider in her youth, of which no further accomplishments have been noted.[27] On June 8, 1816, when she was twenty, she married Walter Whitman Senior, six years older than she, whose family lived only several miles away. They moved into a nearby house that her husband had built. He earned a meager living as a carpenter, building houses and barns when he could get the work.[28] Their promising first child, Jesse, who disappointed them all, was born about March 2, 1818. Some fifteen months later, "on the last day of May 1819," Walt was born, as he tells us in "Who Learns My Lesson Complete?"—the 1855 poem that alludes to his mother's womb as the source of his identity, while omitting any mention of his father's role in this presumably immaculate conception. After Walt's birth, there was a child almost every other year, including a male infant who died still unnamed in 1825. The last child, Edward, born in 1835 when Louisa was forty, was, as I mentioned earlier, lame and mildly retarded.

Married for thirty-nine years but virtually silent in her letters on the subject of her feelings about her husband, Louisa was increasingly dependent on her growing children both for material and for emotional support. Two of them, Jeff and Walt, plainly adored her, though Jeff commented ruefully, "Work and worry she will and I dont think the power of man can prevent it."[29] Work also emerges as a central issue in the short but powerful "fact-romance" in the 1855 *Leaves of Grass,* which presents itself as the story of Louisa's young womanhood as told to Walt, and as told by him to us:

> Now I tell what my mother told me today as we sat at dinner together,
> Of when she was a nearly grown girl living home with her parents on the
>   old homestead.
>
> A red squaw came one breakfasttime to the old homestead,
> On her back she carried a bundle of rushes for rushbottoming chairs;
> Her hair straight shiny coarse black and profuse halfenveloped her face,
> Her step was free and elastic. . . . her voice sounded exquisitely as she
>   spoke.
>
> My mother looked in delight and amazement at the stranger,
> She looked at the beauty of her tallborne face and full and pliant limbs,
> The more she looked upon her she loved her,
> Never before had she seen such wonderful beauty and purity;
> She made her sit on a bench by the jamb of the fireplace. . . . she cooked
>   food for her,
> She had no work to give her but she gave her remembrance and fondness.
>
> The red squaw staid all the forenoon, and toward the middle of the
>   afternoon she went away;
> O my mother was loth to have her go away,
> All the week she thought of her. . . . she watched for her many a month,
> She remembered her many a winter and many a summer,
> But the red squaw never came nor was heard of there again.
>
> (*LG* 1855, pp. 110–11)

Whether or not this episode ever happened we shall probably never know. There were remnants of native peoples living on Long Island in Louisa's youth; some of them were itinerant weavers and we have already seen Whitman's reference to his grandmother Amy's straw-bottomed chair—like the one Whitman himself eventually occupied during his paralytic days. But whether or not it happened, this beautiful and disturbing episode presents a strong-willed Louisa for whom the past is more real than the present. The Indian woman by whom Louisa is permanently captivated comes to her looking for work and leaves her looking for work elsewhere. Though her step is described as "free and elastic," and though "her voice sounded exquisitely as she spoke," the beautiful stranger cannot accept "remembrance and fondness" for pay. As her letters amply demonstrate, Louisa herself was not satisfied with emotion as remuneration. In a particularly self-expressive letter, she complained to Walt, "i think sometimes i wish i was a hundred miles off." [30] Ironically, in "The Sleepers" the vanishing Indian woman represents the physical and social mobility the white woman covets. Romantic racialism? Yes. But the point is not that the historical Louisa envied an impoverished Indian squaw. Rather, as romanticized by her poet-son, Louisa held firm to the dreams of her young womanhood, idealized the beautiful stranger, and did not willingly let her go. Writing as his mother's biographer, Whitman fuses his story with hers. There is forbidden same-sex love, an unremitting search for remunerated work, and the appeal of the open road. Why should we doubt that like her Dutch ancestor, "Old Salt Kossabone," Louisa often yearned to be "free—[to be] on her destination" (*LG*, p. 522)? Despite her oppressively domestic context, she successfully transmitted this love of freedom to her poet-son. Whatever else she accomplished, she accomplished this.

And what of George Washington, the father of his country, whose story precedes Louisa's in "The Sleepers"? What binds "Washington" to Louisa? Nothing, it seems, except the poet's imagination. In Whitman's account, both Washington and Louisa are reluctant to let go of the past and both are defined through a combined logic of fact and romance. In repeating the homosocial elements of Washington's well-known story in Louisa's unofficial homoerotic narrative, however, Whitman heightens the effect. And he has made no attempt to represent himself as Washington's intimate. Instead, he has located the official male tradition further back in time and in public places. Thus the speaker has no privileged access to Washington's history, as he had to his mother's. As befits the sentimental mode, Whitman's Washington weeps copiously. His feelings are expressed through his body. While he encourages physical expressiveness in others, the importance of conversation is correspondingly diminished.

> The same at last and at last when peace is declared,
> He stands in the room of the old tavern. . . . the wellbeloved soldiers all
>   pass through.
>
> The officers speechless and slow draw near in their turns,
> The chief encircles their necks with his arm and kisses them on the cheek,
> He kisses lightly the wet cheeks one after another. . . . he shakes hands and
>   bids goodbye to the army.
>
> > (*LG* 1855, p. 110)[31]

In describing both "the defeat at Brooklyn" and Washington's farewell to his men at Fraunces Tavern, the poet emphasizes that even the father of his country is unable to preserve the intense homosocial bonds generated by war. Similarly, Louisa is unable to preserve the female world of love and ritual associated with a romantic and racialized peace. Following his mother's story, to which he does not respond, there is a violent break in narrative structure, and the speaker describes himself as "Lucifer's sorrowful terrible heir." That is, he does the structural equivalent of getting up and leaving the table since his identification with his mother's erotic defeat has made him deeply anxious. To control this anxiety, he initiates a heterosexual romance. Now, however, the Luciferian Whitman has no one to kiss or weep with, as did Washington, and no son to feed with tales of her lost loves, as did Louisa. Instead, the "confused . . . pastreading" speaker has a clearly designated antagonist, a traitorous Judas figure who "informs against my brother and sister and takes pay for their blood." This stage villain "laughs when I look down the bend after the steamboat that carries away my woman" (*LG* 1855, p. 111). Impersonating an enraged slave, Whitman melodramatically links the heterosexual present with other oppressions and martyrdoms, drawing as well on the background of Shakespearean revenge tragedy, as in Hamlet's "How all occasions do inform against me" (III, iv). The poem's coherence is strained to the breaking point in this episode, which links slavery and heterosexual desire. But it now appears that romance constitutes subjectivity and that the failure of romance, for whatever reason, destroys the man and creates the beast. Do we believe the speaker, whoever he is? Is he serious, or camping?

Despite the stylistic breaks in the poem's structure, which are intended to open the door to the future, the compulsions of the past linger on. The most emphatic of these breaks occurs as the speaker turns to "an amour of the light and air," representing himself as both "jealous *and* overwhelmed with friendliness" (*LG* 1855, pp. 111–12; italics mine). Normally, these emotions are incompatible, though the word "overwhelmed" rationalizes their union. "Friendliness" is a quality we may feel or receive; Whitman's language does not distinguish between being overwhelmed by his own desire and being overwhelmed by someone else's. This fusion of subject and object is a problem for the poet who possesses a sympathetic imagination and for an actual self in the feeling world. "Friendliness" is also oddly paired with love, though "an amour of the light and air" may provide exactly the kind of inconsequential diversion he needs if he is to extricate himself from the identity confusions that haunt both his waking and his sleeping hours. Finally, the speaker continues to fear too much of a good thing, the good thing identified at the poem's conclusion as a symbolization of maternal presence. Following a diversionary passage, in which all sufferings and sicknesses are charmingly relieved but in which no one speaks to anyone else, the poet expresses his wariness of the night, which he equates with the unconscious and with the chaotic feminine element in his psyche. "Why should I be afraid to trust myself to you?" he asks. But now, we understand. Still looking for that perfect place where "The father holds his grown or ungrown son in his arms with measureless love. . . . and the son holds the father in his arms with measureless love," where "The white hair of the mother shines on the white wrist of the daughter," but in which no mother tells heartrending tales to her son, Whitman has not clarified his gender sympathies and confusions (*LG* 1855, p. 114). Though he has affirmed the value of love between men, love between women, and love between men and women, he has not settled on a "fact-romance" for himself. An "amour of the light and air" sounds good. But what will it mean?

In analyzing "The Sleepers" from the perspective of Whitman as a psychologically attentive and internally conflicted poet and son, I have suggested that there were times during his youth and subsequently when Whitman viewed both of his parents as heroic victims of circumstance, though in the end he sat down at the table with his mother, while his father remained somehow isolated on a high hill and beyond the lines. Louisa, whose official and unofficial story it is possible to follow in greater detail, may have wished to preserve her ties to the past, but her own mother died when Louisa was little more than thirty and the step-grandmother, as we have seen, was not a "good investment." For most of her married life, therefore, Louisa was unable to depend on a traditional kinship network. She was also unsustained by a religious community or the power of religious belief—though she occasionally uses the word "god" in her letters. Thus at the time of the death of her son Andrew in 1863, she wrote Walt, "i am composed and calm would not wish him back to suffer poor soul i hope he is at rest." There is no suggestion of an afterlife for the third son of whom she had recently written to Walt, "you know Andrew always was testy and jelous" (November 1863). "he died like any one going to sleep without a struggle sensible to the last," Louisa wrote. "just before he died he turned his head and looked at your and georges pictures for some time and then shut his eyes god grant i may never witness another" (December 18, 1863). "i pity Andrew very much," she wrote, "but i think sometimes how much more those poor wounded and sick soldiers suffer with so much patience poor souls i think much about them and always glad to hear you speak of them i dont think walt after you being amongst them so long you could content yourself from them it becomes a kind of fasination and you get attached to so many of the poor young men" (November 1863). Meanwhile, Jesse was raging, but she quelled him with a word. "i said jesse your brother lies up stairs dead he calmed down immediately and is very good natured." [32]

Faulknerian in its intensity of family distress, as young children provoke and as brother turns insanely against brother—Andrew himself had threatened to break his niece's neck—Louisa's unsentimental narrative is framed by requests for and complaints about money. Throughout her life, her physical and social aspirations were chronically compounded by her lack of financial independence, which, as we have seen, to a woman of her high spirit was galling indeed. Notably, too, there is only one place in her letters where she appears to be quoting *Leaves of Grass*. In June 1867, she suggested to Walt that George, the ex-soldier, tired by an overly long walk to and from work and handicapped by lameness in his legs, felt as if "he would like to loaf and live at his ease," a phrase which echoes the famous opening of "Song of Myself" ("I loafe and invite my soul / I lean and loafe at my ease observing a spear of summer grass").[33] As Louisa was quick to point out, George refused to take her advice, returning to work earlier in the afternoon than she deemed necessary. Thus, though she describes herself as having "to work so very hard i feel when i lie down at night as if i should not be able to get up in the morning," she was judgmental about the hard work of others, including her daughter-in-law Mattie, whose "working on the [sewing] machine so steady hurt her."

There are many widely dispersed sources for Walt's "lazy" poetic persona, including his own "Sun-Down Papers from the Desk of a Schoolmaster" (1840), in which he asserts, mock humorously, "All the old philosophers were loafers," and "For my part, I have had serious thoughts of getting up a regular ticket for President and Congress and Governor and so on, for the loafer community in general. I think we loafers should organize" (*UPP* 1:44, 45).[34] But surely one source of Walt's loaferish bachelor persona—his sexy dreamer, his "rough" of leisure—was his identification with a mother who, despite her surface cheerfulness ("i feel quite smart considering i have to work so very hard"), was a chronic struggler for success in the form of physical comfort, which she felt had eluded her. Anticipating yet another move in her early seventies, "well Walt," she wrote, "here we are yet in the same old place but i doo want to get out of it very much indeed there is so many children and not the best i ever see but a continual traveling up and down from morning till night one good thing their dog is dead he filled the house with fleas so maybe we shall get clear of them now." [35]

Whatever the difficulties of recovering the "original" and "strangely knowing" Louisa who "excelled in narrative" and had "great mimetic power," who loved to tell stories, impersonate, and circulate noble advice, the blooming Louisa whose self-confidence in some measure inspired *Leaves of Grass* and who inspired the poet's lifelong devotion, it is even more difficult to recapture the voice of Whitman's all-but-silenced father. For example, there are no letters from *any* period that enable us to piece together the "minute particulars" of Walter Senior's life story as told by himself. Instead, there are stray tags filtered through others, which comprise the barest outlines of a life full of struggle and flux, but not without ambition, however imperfectly realized, and not without goodness. "Good luck to you walter dear," Louisa wrote wistfully to Walt on February 17, 1868. "Dont you remember your poor old father always wished that wish to every one." But luck was precisely what Walter Senior did not have.

As Louisa reported and as Walt duly noted, this skilled craftsman "would sometimes lay awake all night planning out some unusually difficult plan in his building arrangements" (*NUPM* 1:24). Yet despite his "extraordinary ability as a natural mechanic, [who was] noted for the strength and symmetry of his work," Walter Senior was a poor businessman, and late in life Walt was still angry at the conniving Methodist elder, a consummate hypocrite, who had nearly swindled his "poor straightforward father . . . out of his boots" (*WWWC* 1:256).[36] "My old daddy used to say it's some comfort to a man if he must be an ass anyhow to be his own kind of an ass," Whitman reported to Traubel (*WWWC* 2:41). But *some* comfort turned out to be not enough, and it was "in the Whitman breed" to take disappointment hard (*WWWC* 4:473).

To Traubel, Whitman recalled his father's humor as sardonic and self-deprecating. "My father used to say, a good time to pay your debts is when you have the money. And I can't suggest an improvement over that" (*WWWC* 7:439). "My father used to say to me in his funny way, 'Always pay your small debts, whatever you do with your large!'" (*WWWC* 7:57). Self-deprecating or not, Walter Senior had it in him to assert himself forcefully, as a loner would. Thus, after meeting a "hunted & tormented" soldier from Tennessee in a hospital in 1863, a *Union* soldier ostracized by his Confederate neighbors who had spent ten months in Southern prisons and who had "suffered every thing but death," Whitman explained to Louisa, "He is a large, slow, good natured man (somehow made me often think of father), shrewd, very little to say—wouldn't talk to any body but me." The soldier "had stuck to his convictions like a hero," even though he had been "hung up by the heels, head downwards" (*Corr* 1 : 107, 147). In this revealing comparison, Walter Senior, who could be stubborn and uncommunicative, reemerges as a man of principle, "firm as a rock," while Walt is transformed at one remove into his intimate, as he had never been in life: "Wouldn't talk to any body but me." But "what has made him act so god only knows," Louisa commented about one of her son George's punishing silences, in a memorable passage already quoted: "i believe it runs in the Whitman family to have such spells" (December 1865).

As he continued to describe his interaction with the soldier, Whitman suggested to Louisa that there was a fanatical quality to the Tennessee Unionist's resistance, and that his rigidity could be viewed as self-destructive and malevolent:

> I asked him once very gravely why he didn't take the southern oath & get his liberty—if he didn't think it was foolish to be so stiff &c—I never saw such a look as he gave me, he thought I was in earnest—the old devil himself couldn't have had put a worse look in his eyes— (*Corr* 1 : 147)

Shrewd and good natured or foolish and stiff? Where should we place the emphasis? Did Whitman conclude that he was questioning the old devil himself or a rock-firm hero? He could never be sure.

In a later and equally revealing comparison, Whitman identified his father with Elias Hicks, the incendiary Quaker preacher, whose biography he hoped to write but was never able to complete. In *November Boughs* (1888), Whitman therefore included the following anecdote.

> Though it is sixty years ago—and I was a little boy at the time in Brooklyn, New York—I can remember my father coming home toward sunset from his day's work as carpenter, and saying briefly, as he throws down his armful of kindling-blocks with a bounce on the kitchen floor, "Come, mother, Elias preaches tonight." Then my mother, hastening the supper and the table-cleaning afterward, gets a neighboring young woman, a friend of the family, to step in and keep house for an hour or so—puts the two little ones to bed— and as I had been behaving well that day, as a special reward I was allow'd to go also.[37]

Hicks was famous and Walter Senior obscure, but both men had been raised on rural Long Island farms and both had been carpenters' apprentices. Both men were fighting a rearguard action against changing economic times. Both were married, both had sons. Here the analogy breaks off, however, since as a young man Hicks experienced a "moral and mental and emotional change," after which, as he wrote in his autobiography, "light broke forth out of obscurity, and my darkness became as the noon-day." [38] Walter Senior experienced no such emotional resolution to the anxieties he faced, and despite the possibly manic energy that kept him up all night planning for new buildings, he was prone to depression. That, at least, is the legend that has come down to us: there was a "disheartened" father who took his "emotional entities hard" (*Corr* 1:72 n, *WWWC* 4:473).

There is some question as to whether Whitman's "Come, mother" anecdote reflects a fact or a "fact-romance," but in any event Walter Senior was not usually able to facilitate his son's entry into the swanky interior of a Morrison's Hotel, where Hicks was speaking, in a "large, cheerful, gay-color'd room, with glass chandeliers bearing myriads of sparkling pendants, plenty of settees and chairs, and a sort of velvet divan running all round the side-walls," "a handsome ball-room . . . used for the most genteel concerts, balls, and assemblies." [39] Walt's father was born in the simple West Hills farmhouse near Huntington, Long Island, where "his and his and his were born and lived" (*WWWC* 7:108), where "books were scarce," and where "the annual copy of the almanac was a treat" (*SD* 695). He spent his early youth "near enough to the sea to behold it from high places, and to hear in still hours the roar of the surf." On one side of the farmhouse in West Hills, with its "great heavy timbers, low ceilings, upper chambers," and "long kitchen," there was a "beautiful grove of black-walnuts" and "locusts," and "in the rear a small peach orchard." Unfortunately, when Walt visited as a little boy summer after summer, "All was in great neglect" (*NUPM* 1:21). Grandfather Jesse Whitman was long since dead and grandmother Hannah Brush Whitman, despite her "great solidity of mind" (*SD* 695), could not prosper without him.

Walter Senior was barely into his teens when his own father died. He was then apprenticed to a cousin as a carpenter, an apprenticeship completed in New York City when he was about fifteen (*NUPM* 1:23).[40] He spent the next three years boarding in the city and working at his trade, before returning to Long Island. M. Wynn Thomas explains,

> The urban artisan class was that section of the American population which, during Whitman's formative years, was most dramatically affected by the transition to a new stage of capitalism, and especially by the far-reaching social and political consequences of this transition. . . . Whitman's father was fairly typical of the disoriented artisan of this period, struggling to adjust to the new capitalist conditions. By turns a small-scale employer and a wage earner, he worked only fitfully while alternating between the kind of morose sense of

isolation that drove many of his class to drink and the "rudimentary class awareness and sense of solidarity" that produced the working-class movements of the late twenties and early thirties, stimulating the passion for education and self-improvement that was evident in his young son.[41]

Walt Whitman was proud of his father's "democratic and heretical tendencies" (*NUPM* 1:6)—his enthusiasm for Hicks; his subscription to the *Free Enquirer,* a newspaper edited by the utopian socialists Robert Dale Owen and Frances Wright; perhaps even his affinity for Constantin Volney's *The Ruins, or Meditations on the Revolutions of Empires,* an anticlerical work on which Whitman took copious notes (*NUPM* 5:2024–27) and on which, as he explained to the agnostic Traubel, "I may be said to have been raised" (*WWWC* 2:445).[42] Whitman was also proud of his father's mechanical intelligence and physical strength. For much of his adult life, however, Walter Whitman was haunted by the specter of economic disaster. For part of it, he was "addicted to alcohol," and according to one account, Whitman wondered whether this addiction might have been responsible for the physical and mental defects of his youngest brother, Eddy.[43] He was often morose and cynical. His youthful dreams, he felt, had not been realized.

Because of the family's precarious economic circumstances, none of the Whitman children had much formal schooling. Walt, after spending six years in the absurdly overcrowded and rigidly regimented Brooklyn public schools, went to work as an office boy for two prominent lawyers when he was eleven.[44] Fortunately, the Clarkes, father and son, interested themselves in furthering his education. Edward Clarke, the son, helped him with his handwriting and composition and subscribed to a circulating library for him, so that Whitman was able to revel in "romance-reading of all kinds," including the patriotic romances of Sir Walter Scott, which he devoured "one after another, and his poetry" (*SD* 699). This "Arabian Nights" abundance was short lived, for after an intervening stint in a doctor's office of unknown duration, the twelve-year-old Whitman found himself employed in the printing office of the Long Island *Patriot,* to which his father subscribed. "There," according to Gay Wilson Allen, "he became interested in journalism, which in turn aroused literary ambitions."[45]

Perhaps in the summer of 1831, the precocious Whitman began to contribute "sentimental bits," now lost, to the *Patriot.* And there too, he learned to set type from the venerable William Hartshorne, whom Whitman subsequently immortalized in his *Brooklyniana* essays of 1861–

62 as the "veteran printer of the United States" and as an ideal, perhaps *the* ideal, father surrogate. "He remembered well," Whitman wrote of Hartshorne, "and has many a time described to the writer hereof (who listened with a boy's ardent soul and eager ears,) . . . the personal appearance and demeanor of Washington, Jefferson, and other of the great historical names of our early national days" (*UPP* 2:246–47). Even more than his maternal grandfather Major Van Velsor, Hartshorne seemed to Whitman an important link to a heroic past. On the verge of his teens, he was already beginning to glimpse the possibility of substituting a national family romance for a less glamorous private inheritance. Along with several other apprentices, Whitman boarded with Hartshorne's granddaughter; his parents and brothers and sisters lived some ten or eleven blocks away.[46]

While Whitman was learning the printer's trade in Brooklyn and New York City, his father continued to pursue his trade as carpenter and builder, "with varying fortune" (*SD* 700). He built heavily mortgaged houses, and the Whitmans continued to move.[47] During some or most of this unsettled period, Walt was living in boarding houses, an arrangement that freed him from his parents' control but which he subsequently described as injurious to young apprentices such as himself. By May 1833, Walter Whitman had moved his family back to the region of West Hills, and by 1834, after another move, the family was living at Norwich. Louisa Whitman, pregnant with the grandly named Thomas Jefferson, was "very ill for a long time" (*SD* 700). As an apprentice printer and then as a journeyman, Walt continued to publish occasional pieces, now lost, in the local newspapers, and to benefit from access to his employers' circulating libraries. He also got free theater tickets and was an insatiable playgoer. "At first, I remember [he wrote, using the family pseudonym Velsor Brush], I used to go with other boys, my pals; but I afterward preferred to go alone, I was so absorbed in the performance, and disliked anyone to distract my attention."[48] These teenage "Illusions of youth! Dreams of a child of the Bowery!" were curtailed in the spring of 1836 when an out-of-work Whitman—he turned seventeen in May—was forced to join his family in Hempstead, where his father was farming on land that he did not own.[49]

Moving from the city to the country apparently felt like a terrible defeat, and Whitman later recorded his reaction to this involuntary rustication in the semiautobiographical story "The Shadow and the Light of a Young Man's Soul." "When the young Archibald Dean went from the city," Whitman wrote,

> (living out of which he had so often said was no living at all)—went down into the country to take charge of a little district school, he felt as though the last float-plank which buoyed him up on hope and happiness, was sinking, and he with it. But poverty is as stern, if not as sure, as death and taxes, which Franklin called the surest things of the modern age. And poverty compelled Archie Dean. (*EPF* 327)

In the country, "pent up . . . among a set of beings to whom grace and refinement [were] unknown," Archie Dean consoles himself by writing long confessional letters, "outpourings of spleen," to his widowed mother, who, "strange as it may seem to most men, . . . was also his confidential friend" (*EPF* 328). But we have no record of correspondence between Whitman and Louisa, who was busy with her growing family.[50] Instead, we see an irritable Walter Junior struggling to maintain his equanimity on the edge of other people's lives and to establish some kind of career.[51] He was physically large—misleadingly so, he thought, since his emotional life remained cramped and undeveloped—and he was intellectually ambitious. But as he explained to a young friend many years later, "The time of my boyhood was a very restless and unhappy one: I did not know what to do."[52]

BOARDING AT THE BRENTONS

As a teacher in at least eight different one-room schoolhouses on eastern Long Island between 1836 and 1841, Whitman received mixed reviews from his pupils and their parents. Some praised his gentleness and innovative methods; others considered him too self-absorbed and dreamy. "Shall I become old without tasting the sweet draught of which the young may partake," he asked in the first of his "Sun-Down Papers from the Desk of a Schoolmaster," which was printed in the Hempstead *Inquirer* on March 14, 1840. "Silently and surely are the months stealing along.—A few more revolutions of old earth will find me treading the paths of advanced manhood.—This is what I dread: for I have not enjoyed my young time. I have been cheated of the bloom and nectar of life.—Lonesome and unthought of as I am, I have no one to care for, or to care for me." Even after we allow for the fashionable melancholia of Whitman's lonesome bachelor pose, the self-pity seems genuine, the loneliness real.

Whitman's mystic reveries served to carry him "far, far away" from his "then and there existence." Almost forgotten landscapes resurfaced and, as in a dream, lost companions reappeared, causing him to wonder at the apparent randomness of his waking thoughts. Comparing himself to "some expert swimmer, who has tired himself, and to rest his limbs, allows them to float drowsily and unresistingly on the bosom of the sunny river," Whitman, already developing trance-like powers of concentration, was nevertheless afraid to yield himself fully to this condition in which "Real things lost their reality":

> Like a long forgotten dream, a day of childhood was distinct to me.—I saw every particular tree, and hill, and field, my old haunts. Then leaping off again, remembrance carried me a few years farther on the path; and I was surrounded with the intimates of more advanced youth—young companions to whom I long since gave "good bye." It is strange how a train of thought will carry a person onward from period to period, and from object to object, until at last the subject of his cogitations bears no affinity to what he first started from.[53]

Forced to teach school because of economic hard times that severely affected the printing industry in New York City, Whitman had taken up schoolteaching in the country almost as a last resort. Like Archie Dean, he missed the excitement of the city and considered schoolteaching beneath him. Moreover, despite the impression that Whitman sometimes created of detachment and aimlessness (his enemies called him *lazy*), he had already conceived the desire to distinguish himself, perhaps by writing a sociological treatise, a "wonderful and ponderous book."[54] As one of the first steps toward the realization of his dream of celebrity, he joined the Smithtown Debating Society in the fall of 1837, was promptly elected secretary, and "associated with some of the most prominent men of the town, including two judges, a congressman, a member of the New York legislature, two physicians, two justices of the peace, a dentist, several businessmen, and some prosperous farmers."[55] In the spring of 1838, he started a newspaper, *The Long Islander,* in Huntington, where he lived over the print shop with his eight-year-old brother George. "I went to New York," he explained many years later, "bought a press and types, hired some little help, but did most of the work myself, including the presswork. Everything seem'd turning out well (only my own restlessness prevented me gradually establishing a permanent property there)" (*SD* 919).

In May 1839, Walt's physical and mental restlessness caused him to sell the paper, along with the horse he used to deliver it; he was fond of the horse, a white mare called Nina. By August, he was back in the village of Jamaica working for James J. Brenton, a newspaper publisher and a leader of the Queens County Democratic party. Brenton had already reprinted several of Whitman's prose pieces from the *Long Islander*, along with his first known poem, "Our Future Lot"—a lugubrious meditation on powerlessness with an affirmative ending along conventional religious lines:

> Mortal! and can thy swelling soul
>   Live with the thought that all its life
> Is centred in the earthly cage
>   Of care, and tears, and strife?
>
> Not so; that sorrowing heart of thine
>   Ere long will find a house of rest;
> Thy form, re-purified, shall rise,
>   In robe of beauty drest.
>
> The flickering taper's glow shall change
>   To bright and starlike majesty,
> Radiant with pure and piercing light
>   From the Eternal's eye!
>   (EPF 28–29)

Whitman liked the poem well enough to revise and reprint it in the 1842 New York *Aurora* under the title "Time to Come." The reworked poem is more successful in evoking the vague and "unrequited cravings," "the alternate throbs" of hope and fear that define the overly solemn speaker's "brain, and heart." Yet despite some willingness to open up his rhymes, and despite the parodic openings provided by his humor—as, for example, in "Young Grimes," a satire on the dullness of rural family life—throughout this early period Whitman had trouble using the conventional-looking (and -sounding) poems he was writing to express anything other than received opinions in which he himself hardly believed. Though unlike Young Grimes he was refusing to be "a chip of the old block" (*UPP* 1:2), and more specifically to celebrate the patriarchal family as the foundation of social order, the sense of entrapment expressed in "Our Future Lot" was genuine, but formal solutions continued to elude him. "O, Death!" he wrote in the revised version in 1842, "a black and pierceless pall / Hangs round thee, and the future state; / No eye may see, no mind may grasp / That mystery of Fate."

> This brain, which now alternate throbs
>   With swelling hope and gloomy fear;
> This heart, with all the changing hues,
>   That mortal passions bear—

This curious frame of human mould,
    Where unrequited cravings play,
This brain, and heart, and wondrous form
    Must all alike decay.

The leaping blood will stop its flow;
    The hoarse death-struggle pass; the cheek
Lay bloomless, and the liquid tongue
    Will then forget to speak.

The grave will tame me; earth will close
    O'er cold dull limbs and ashy face;
But where, O, Nature, where shall be
    The soul's abiding place?

Will it e'en live? for though its light
    Must shine till from the body torn;
Then, when the oil of life is spent,
    Still shall the taper burn?

O, powerless is this struggling brain
    To rend the mighty mystery;
In dark, uncertain awe it waits
    The common doom, to die.

                       (*EPF* 27–28)

Striving for Bryantesque sublimity and not reaching it, lapsing into McDonald Clarke melancholy and looking for a way out of it, Whitman announced in "Sun-Down Paper" number seven, published in September 1840, that he planned to survey "the nature and peculiarities of men" in his "wonderful and ponderous book" (*UPP* 1:37).[56] As a political philosopher, however, Whitman disclaimed all knowledge of *woman* because, as he explained, "it behoves a modest personage like myself not to speak upon a class of beings of whose nature, habits, notions, and ways he has not been able to gather any knowledge, either by experience or observation." Whitman went on to ask, "Who should be a better judge of a man's talents than the man himself? I see no reason why we should let our lights shine under bushels. Yes: I *would* write a book! And who shall say that it might not be a very pretty book? Who knows but that I might do something very respectable?" The rest of the essay is a disquisition on the theme, "I have found out that it is a very dangerous thing to be rich."

Though uncertainly cadenced, the "Sun-Down Papers" reflect the emerging Whitman's suspicion of the "pleasures of dollars and cents." Serious and jeering, earnest and campy, they move nervously from subject to subject, as the speaker attempts to formulate a program for personal and professional success. "Nobody, I hope, will accuse me of conceit in these opinions of mine own capacity for doing great things," he wrote. "In good truth, I think the world suffers from this much-bepraised modesty" (*UPP* 1:37). Scorning the "cold and heartless limits of custom," Whitman was already beginning to distinguish "the sickly sentimentality which is so favorite a theme with novelists and magazine writers" from "an affectionate tenderness, and warm-heartedness" which enables him to be "affectionate and gentle to all men." This distinction between appropriate and inappropriate sentimentality allows him to impute social significance to "the kiss of a sister or a brother," to "our arms clasp[ing] the form of a friend," and to "our lips touch[ing] the cheek of a boy or girl whom we love" (*UPP* 1:47–48). "Sickly sentimentality" makes men vulnerable to rejection, whereas these healthier, more fully embodied affections never replicate the male-male animosity of the fractious, money-making family.

In Jamaica, in the summer and fall of 1839, Whitman boarded with the Brentons, an experience that brought him into contact with a woman who failed to appreciate his ostentatiously disengaged, loaferish point of view. According to her daughter-in-law, Orvetta Hall Brenton, whose account is long, but well worth reading,

> My mother-in-law, Mrs. Brenton, was a practical, busy, New England woman, and very obviously, from her remarks about Whitman, cared very little for him and held him in scant respect. He was at that time a dreamy, impracticable youth, who did very little work and who was always "under foot" and in the way. Except that he was always in evidence physically, he lived his life very much to himself. One thing that impressed Mrs. Brenton unfavorably was his disregard of the two children of the household—two small boys—who seemed very much to annoy him when they were with him in the house.
>
> Mrs. Brenton always emphasized, when speaking of Whitman, that he was inordinately indolent and lazy and had a very pronounced disinclination to work! During some of the time he was in the household, the apple trees in the garden were in bloom. When Whitman would come from the printing office and finish the mid-day dinner, he would go out into the garden, lie on his back under the apple tree, and forget everything about going back to work as he gazed up at the blossoms and the sky. Frequently, at such times, Mr. [Brenton] would wait for him at the office for an hour or two and then send the "printer's devil" up to the house to see what had become of him. He would invariably be found still lying on his back on the grass looking into the tree entirely oblivious of the fact that he was expected to be at work. When spoken to, he would get up reluctantly and go slowly back to the shop. At the end of such a day, Mr. Brenton would come home and say, "Walt has been of very little help to me to-day. I wonder what I can do to make him realize

that he must work for a living?" and Mrs. Brenton would remark, "I don't see why he doesn't catch his death of cold lying there on the ground under the apple tree!"

Whitman was such an annoyance in the household that Mrs. Brenton was overjoyed when he finally decided to leave the office of the *Democrat*. Mr. Brenton, however, was sorry to have him go, for, even in those early days, he showed marked ability as a writer and was of great value to the "literary" end of the newspaper work. How long he was in Jamaica, or what salary he received, I do not know. Of course, in those days, a considerable part of the salary consisted in "board and lodgings"....

Another detail comes to mind in regard to his behavior in the house. He cared nothing at all about clothes or his personal appearance, and was actually untidy about his person. He would annoy Mrs. Brenton exceedingly by "sitting around" in his shirt sleeves, and seemed much abused when she insisted on his putting on his coat to come to the family table. While she would be setting the table for meals, Whitman was always in her way in the dining room. His favorite seat was in the dining room near the closet door where Mrs. Brenton had to pass him every time she wished to get the dishes and stumble continually over his feet. He would never think to remove his feet from the pathway until requested definitely to do so, nor would he move at all out of the way unless he was told to.

I am sorry I cannot tell you more. My impression has always been of a dreamy, quiet, morose young man, evidently not at all in tune with his surroundings and feeling, somehow, that fate had dealt hard blows to him. I never heard him spoken of as being in any way bright or cheerful. I cannot see how he could have been an interesting or successful teacher because of his apparent dislike of children at the time we knew him. I never heard a word against his [sexual] habits. He spent most of the time off duty reading by the fire in the winter or out of doors dreaming in the summer. He was a genius who lived apparently, in a world of his own. He certainly was detached enough from the Brenton household at Jamaica.[57]

Evidently, Whitman's self-proclaimed respect for women was a later phase of his development; the sexual symbolism of those provokingly outstretched feet is hard to miss. James Brenton, on the other hand, continued to wish Whitman well and to publish his poetry and prose. "May the smiles of fortune ever attend Walt in all his peregrinations," he wrote in 1849, a year when he also included Whitman's morbid story "Tomb Blossoms" in *Voices from the Press: A Collection of Sketches, Essays, and Poems* honoring "practical printers" from Franklin to the then present (*EPF* 88–89 n).[58] (Set in a rural cemetery, "Tomb Blossoms" features a widow with a French-sounding name who tends two graves, since she cannot be sure in which grave her husband is buried. This odd behavior permits the narrator to flirt with a transgressive subplot, in which monogamous marriages are destabilized and men's bodies are thrown

together in death, if not in life.)⁵⁹ James Brenton was a family man with
a business to run, but he knew that his readers enjoyed Whitman's various voices, including the anti-dollars-and-cents voice freeing bodies
from the usual constraints of gender. Furthermore, Whitman and Brenton shared a common bond, Democratic party politics, from which
Mrs. Brenton was mostly excluded.

The polarization of the Brentons' responses to their intrusive (to her)
but useful (to him) boarder suggests that Whitman's imitation of the
ethic of idleness described by Sandra Tomc in her study of literary leisure
was more acceptable to men than to women. Men such as James Brenton understood the dangers of overworking outside the home and could
romanticize emotional leisure, as well as the privileges of indiscriminate
male bonding beyond and beneath the marketplace. But women such
as his wife who were confined to their homes and isolated from other
women, with children and boarders to care for, could not afford the lux-
ury of loafing and inviting their souls. Male economic nonproductivity
was threatening to her and to most American women. A coatless, man-
nerless man who would not work probably caused his wife or mother or
housekeeper or sister or daughter to work harder. Whether or not this
is the case—Ellen Moers, for example, has suggested that women novelists romanticize wealth precisely because they have had so little experience of it—⁶⁰ on at least one count Mrs. Brenton was dead wrong. For
all his social dissatisfaction and satirical self-absorption, moody young
Whitman was not as friendless as she believed him to be.

A FIRST FRIENDSHIP

Unlike Mrs. Brenton, Whitman's Jamaica friend Abraham Paul Leech
appreciated his style. He managed to save the nine letters Whitman wrote
him beginning in the summer of 1840, most of them from Woodbury,
where Whitman was again teaching school. They are primarily diatribes
against the stupidity, rough manners, and execrable taste of the local
people with whom Whitman was forced to associate and with whom he
boarded, along the following lines:

> I believe when the Lord created the world, he used up all the good stuff,
> and was forced to form Woodbury and its denizens, out of the fag ends,
> the scraps and refuse: for a more unsophisticated race than lives hereabouts
> you will seldom meet with in your travels.—They get up in the morning,
> and toil through the day, with no interregnum of joy or leisure, except
> breakfast and dinner.—they live on salt pork and cucumbers; and for a

delicacy they sometimes treat company to rye-cake and buttermilk.—Is
not this enough to send them to perdition "uncancelled, unanointed, unan-
nealed?"—If Chesterfield were forced to live here ten hours he would fret
himself to death: I have heard the words "thank you," but once since my
sojourn in this earthly purgatory.

Starved for intelligent companionship, Whitman kept up an unremitting litany of complaints. "Send me something funny," he implored in
the same letter of July 1840, "for I am getting to be a miserable kind of
a dog":

> I am sick of wearing away by inches, and spending the fairest portion of
> my little span of life, here in this nest of bears, this forsaken of all God's
> creation; among clowns and country bumpkins, flat-heads, and coarse
> brown-faced girls, dirty, ill-favoured young brats, with squalling throats
> and crude manners, and bog-trotters, with all the disgusting conceit, of
> ignorance and vulgarity.—It is enough to make the fountains of good-
> will dry up in our hearts, to wither all gentle and loving dispositions,
> when we are forced to descend and be as one among the grossest, the
> most low-minded of the human race.—Life is a dreary road, at the best;
> and I am just at this time in one of the most stony, rough, desert, hilly,
> and heart-sickening parts of the journey.—[61]

Several weeks later, the future celebrant of the democratic open road
was complaining of sunburn after a "huckleberry frolick" with the "ladies and gentlemen of this truly refined place." Dating his letter "Devil's
den, Tuesday, Aug. 11," Whitman inveighed against "these contemptible ninnies, with whom I have to do, and among whom I have to live."
Additionally, he was angry with Leech for having disappointed him.
"Why the dickins didn't you come out to the whig meeting at the court
house, last Saturday week?" the letter opens. "I went there, with the hope
of seeing you and one or two others, as much as for any thing else." Describing himself as "an evil spirit" wandering "over hills and dales, and
through woods, fields, and swamps," he exclaimed,

> O, damnation, damnation! thy other name is school-teaching and thy resi-
> dence Woodbury.—Time, put spurs to thy leaden wings, and bring on the
> period when my allotted time of torment here shall be fulfilled.—Speed, ye
> airy hours, lift me from this earthly purgatory; nor do I care how soon ye
> lay these pudding-brained bog-trotters, amid their kindred earth.—I do not
> believe a refined or generous idea was ever born in this place; the whole con-
> cern, with all its indwellers, ought to be sunk, as Mosher says, "to chaos."
> Never before have I entertained so low an idea of the beauty and perfec-
> tion of man's nature, never have I seen humanity in so degraded a shape,
> as here.—Ignorance, vulgarity, rudeness, conceit, and dulness are the reign-
> ing gods of this deuced sink of despair.—The brutes go barefoot, shave once

in three weeks, call "brown cow" "*bre*own *ke-ow;*" live on sour milk, rye bread, and strong pork; believe L. I. sound and the south bay to be the ne plus ultra of creation; and the "gals" wear white frocks with red or yellow waist-ribands.—

Think, my friend, think on all this; and pray nightly for my deliverance from this dungeon where grace or good-breeding never were seen, and from whence happiness fled shrieking twenty years ago.—Farewell—and may the blessings of hope and peace, the sunshine of a joyous heart, never be absent from you.—May the bloom of health glow on your features, the tide of joy swell in your heart, and care and grief be strangers to your dwelling.[62]

A week or so later, things were no better, as Whitman continued his diatribe against the disgusting material and mental culture he associated with Woodbury and its inhabitants. Leech, a genial and lighthearted correspondent, teased Whitman about his dire fantasies and urged him to return to Jamaica, where they both belonged to a debating society that argued such questions as "Are the British justified in blockading the Chinese ports?" and "Would the establishment of manual labor schools be desirable?" In addition to their mutual acquaintances, the two friends shared a substantial and combative interest in politics: Leech was a Whig, Whitman a Locofoco, or radical Democrat. Mainly, however, Whitman would not be deflected from his sexual and economic critique of "Woodbury," which he expressed most forcefully in gastronomical terms. *Food* forms the focal point of many of these letters to Leech. In his letter headed "Purgatory Fields, Wednesday Aug 19," for example, Whitman wrote,

> I have eaten my dinner since the last line over leaf was written; but I don't know that I felt any the better as to good-humour.—What do you think I had for dinner?—Guess, now.—Beef?—no.—Mutton?—No.—Pot-pie?—No.—Salad and iced champagne?—No, no, no.———I'll tell you in the order that it was put up, or rather put down.—Firstly, two cold potatoes, with the skins on, one of said potatoes, considerably nibbled in a manner which left me in doubt whether it had been done by the teeth of a mouse or the bill of a chicken; secondly three boiled clams, that had evidently seen their best days;—thirdly a chunk of molasses cake made of buckwheat flour;—fourthly, a handful of old mouldy pot-cheese, with a smell strong enough to knock down an ox;—fifthly, and lastly, two oblong slats of a mysterious substance, which I concluded, after considerable reflection, must have been intended for bread;—this last would undoubtedly [have] been very interesting either to a Grahamite, or to one fond of analyzing and studying out the nature of the *mineral* kingdom.—Was n't this a feast for an Epicure?—Think, O thou banquetter on good things, think of such an infernal meal as that I describe, and bless the stars that thy lot is as it is.—Think, moreover that this diabolical compound was wrapped up in

[a] huge piece of brown paper, and squeezed into a little tin pail, which said pail, being minus in the matter of a handle or bail, had to be carried by a tow string instead!—Imagine to yourself, now, that you see me toting along with such an article as I [have] been describing.—Don't I cut a pretty figure? O, ye gods, press me not too far—pour not my cup too full—or I know what I shall do.—Dim and dreadful thoughts have lately been floating through my brain.—The next you hear of me, I may possibly be arraigned for murder, or highway robbery, or assault and battery, at the least.—I am getting savage.—There seems to be no relief.—Fate is doing her worst.—The devil is tempting me in every nook and corner, and unless you send me a letter, and Brenton remits me an armful of news, there is no telling but what I shall poison the whole village, or set fire to this old school-house, and run away by the light of it.—[63]

Cutting a pretty "figure," Whitman now resisted metaphor, as if to show that Woodbury, with its disastrous matter of fact, inhibited unusual connections. When Henry James came to review Whitman's posthumously published letters to Peter Doyle in 1898, he observed that

There is not even by accident a line with a hint of style—it is all flat, familiar, affectionate, illiterate colloquy. If the absolute natural be, when the writer is interesting, the supreme merit of letters, these, accordingly, should stand high on the list (I am taking for granted, of course, the interest of Whitman.) The beauty of the natural is, here, the beauty of the particular nature, the man's own overflow in the deadly dry setting, the personal passion, the love of life plucked like a flower in a desert of innocent, unconscious ugliness. . . . Whitman wrote to his friend of what they both saw and touched, enormities of the common, sordid occupations, dreary amusements, undesirable food. . . .[64]

Whitman's letters to Leech are more self-consciously literary than his later letters to Doyle, but James's remarkable analysis reminds us of the ways in which men can be stranded together, bound by narratives that pivot on the threat or the reality of "undesirable food." In the early letters, we see the beginnings of a symbolic language and a private code, and the "Purgatory Fields" letter concludes with a plea, "for pity's sake," for "something or other . . . in the shape of mental food" from his friend. But it is a code that cannot quite believe in its own powers of association. The setting is still too powerful, the man too full of fury.

In what he called his next "epistolary gem," however, Whitman equates food with affection and affection with language. "Dearly beloved," the letter begins, an opening that Arthur Golden describes as an "ironic play on . . . the marriage ceremony from the Book of Common Prayer." [65] "You must by this time have become accustomed to the semi-weekly receipt of these invaluable morsels; and therefore to deprive you of the usual gift, would be somewhat similar to sending a hungry man to bed without his supper." Extending the banal metaphor, Whitman added a coarse anatomical flourish: "Besides, conscience spurs me to a full confession; which generally operates on me like a good dose of calomel on one who has been stuffing immoderately, making a clear stomach and comfortable feelings to take the place of overburdened paunch and rumbling intestines.—Excuse the naturality of my metaphor." The formalities over, Whitman launched into another smear campaign against the rural Long Island domestic scene: "families of fourteen or fifteen, in these parts, have but one *head* amongst them."[66] And so on. In fact, Whitman associated bad food with middle-class family life.[67]

Apart from Whitman's two brief letters to his family during his trip to New Orleans in 1848, Leech is Whitman's only known personal correspondent before 1857.[68] And in addition to saving Whitman's letters, Leech saved several drafts of his side of the correspondence. As a bookkeeper, he must have had some formal education, and he seems to have sensed the possibility of a book in the making.[69] "A most miraculous production," he wrote, "a clever piece of intellectual fabric inwrought with blooming flowers from the productive garden of your fruitful imagination." For his part, Leech was seeking to convert Whitman to Whig politics, though not to the hard cider with which the Harrison campaign was associated. He reminded Whitman to "be a good boy," and cast him as the more impulsive of the two friends. "Fie upon you boy," Leech's draft of a letter to Whitman reads. "You are out of your senses. Much learning (no, not learning but wine) hath made you mad. But I do not intend to preach a temp [temperance] discourse on the occasion." Evidently, Leech saw a freer side to the Whitman who had recently explained in print, "The excessive use of tea and coffee, too, is a species of intemperance much to be condemned."[70]

Whatever Leech's reservations about Whitman's politics, his emotional stability, or his drinking habits, he urged him to return to Jamaica so that they might again enjoy their moonlit walks.[71] From darkest Woodbury, the histrionic Whitman created the impression that his life was a battle (as undoubtedly it was). From sunnier Jamaica, Leech observed with some degree of satisfaction, "In our part of the country we have no huckleberry frolicks, no bussing matches, no fights terminating in scratched faces and broken combs. As we were when you was here so are we still—a peaceable amicable friendly, loving affectionate kind of people."

In the fall of 1840, Whitman was rescued from classroom drudgery by the Democrats of Queens County, who employed him as a propagandist in the presidential campaign. His spirits improved. In the winter and spring of 1841, he was again teaching, happily for the last time. By March 25, in another letter to Leech—their correspondence having been interrupted by Whitman's return to Jamaica during the campaign—Whitman was again harping on the deprivations of his former life, albeit in a comparatively good humored, self-parodic way. "You no doubt remember those precious missives that sprang almost diurnally from my teeming hand at Purgatory Place," he wrote from his new locale, Whitestone,

> But that *Place!* O, it makes my nerves quiver as I think of it.—Yes, anathema! anathema, curse, curse, upon thee thou fag end of all earthly localities, infernal Woodbury! But I fear I am getting warm.—Let me push the subject no farther.—The fact is, the most distant mention of that diabolical region, that country of buckwheat dough-nuts, and pot-cheese, and rye sweet-cake, always makes me fall a swearing.—Faugh!

Though Whitestone was far from perfect—Whitman disliked the "money making spirit" of its leading citizens and hinted broadly at their adulteries—he declared himself "quite happy here," and refused to succumb to the "splenetic, fault-finding current, on which those Woodbury documents were set afloat."

> Of course, I build now and then my castles in the air.—I plan out my little schemes for the future; and cogitate fancies; and occasionally there float forth like wreaths of smoke, and about as substantial, my day dreams.—But, take it all in all, I have reason to bless the breeze that wafted me to Whitestone.

After an enthusiastic description of the shipping traffic and "fortification under weigh" on Long Island Sound, Whitman introduced an apparently casual erotic fantasy:

> My quarters are quite satisfactory too as regards boarding.— One of the windows of my room commands a pleasant view of the sound.—Another looks to the east and the great round face of the sun; he comes along in the morning, almost seems to kiss me with a loving kiss.—I am generally dressed and ready to receive him at this first appearance.—This said room of mine is something that I much value.—It is my sanctum sanctorum, which profane foot invadeth not.—Its hallowed precincts are forbidden ground to every she in the house, except for absolutely necessary entrances, which concern the vital well-being of its lord.—
>   I hope this will find you enjoying health and peace.—O that I were Napoleon that I might load the heads of my friends with golden coronets.—

My best wishes I waft to you, wrapped up and sealed with a wafer,—May your shadow never be less.—Adieu

Walter Whitman[72]

A room with a view. A room without women. A relationship with the sun, who "almost seems to kiss me with a loving kiss." A vision of political and military might as generosity, as shared wealth. Himself as Napoleon, so that he might "load the heads of my friends with golden coronets." Adequately nourished by surroundings in which fantasy could triumph over reality, Whitman wound down his correspondence with Leech. There were several more letters and some further meetings. The letters were perfunctory. Perhaps the meetings were too. In Whitestone, Whitman may have found a new friend. "*We* are close on the sound," Whitman wrote. "*We* hear the busy clink of the hammers at morn and night, across the water; and sometimes take a sail over to inspect the works, for you know it belongs to the U.S." (emphasis added). The editorial We? Or Whitman and his new companion? Whether or not such a person actually existed, by the end of the school term in the spring, New York beckoned. Whoever "we" was, it was time for the confused, idealistic, and angry young exile in the provinces to move on.

,

TWO

Why Whitman Gave Up Fiction

Between August 1841 and June 1848, Walter Whitman published twenty-three short stories and a temperance novel that he subsequently described as "damned rot—rot of the worst sort—not insincere perhaps, but rot, nevertheless" (*EPF* 124 n. 1). Shortly after its publication in November 1842 as *Franklin Evans or The Inebriate: A Tale of the Times,* Whitman's novel sold over 20,000 copies as a softcover pamphlet. It was commissioned and distributed by the *New World* under the editorship of Park Benjamin, who was apparently inclined to forgive his enemies for the sake of a sale; Whitman, an ex-employee, had recently savaged him in print as a fraud and a foreigner.[1] As for the 20,000 copies selling at twelve and a half cents each, certainly no single edition of *Leaves of Grass* approached the size of this readership before Whitman's death in 1892. And it is likely that *all* the editions of *Leaves of Grass* combined did not sell 20,000 copies during Whitman's lifetime. Whatever the financial arrangements—Whitman later said that he had received one hundred and twenty-five dollars for writing *Franklin Evans,* seventy-five dollars "cash down" and an additional fifty dollars two or three weeks later because the book sold so well—had Whitman wished merely to be a *popular* writer of fiction, he was on his way to success by the end of 1842. Moreover, eight of his short stories had been published in the *Democratic Review,* the most prestigious American literary magazine of the day. (The *Review* published work by Hawthorne, Poe, Whittier, Longfellow, Lowell, and Bryant, among others.)[2]

True, the *Review* is unlikely to have paid Whitman very much for
such stories as "Wild Frank's Return," "Bervance: or, Father and Son,"
or "The Child-Ghost; a Story of the Last Loyalist"—fast-paced melo-
dramas which James Russell Lowell once characterized as "*à la* Hawthorne."[3] On January 9, 1843, for example, Sophia Hawthorne observed that "The Democratic Review is so poor now that it can only
offer twenty dollars for an article of what length soever . . . and besides
it is sadly dilatory about payment."[4] As the *Review*'s premier short story
writer, Hawthorne undoubtedly commanded considerably higher prices
than did Whitman, who tried unsuccessfully to sell "The Angel of Tears"
to the *Boston Miscellany of Literature and Fashion* for eight dollars, in
June 1842. Several months later this story of fratricide and repentance,
complete with supernatural machinery, appeared in the *Review*. Perhaps
the *Review* paid Whitman less than the eight dollars he had been hoping to get for it in Boston.[5] But I shall be assuming that financial con-
siderations alone could not have caused Whitman to abandon fiction.
Fiction writing, however poorly paid, was more lucrative than the writing of nonnarrative, experimental poetry, to which he eventually turned.
Rather, I shall be arguing that the psychological urgency of these slippery fictions was incompatible with the inner serenity he was attempting to cultivate. Talking to Horace Traubel in 1888, more than four
decades later, the very memory of this obsessive project, as exemplified
by *Franklin Evans,* rekindled his rage. Whitman abandoned fiction primarily, I believe, because he was not yet ready to claim the unconventional sexual desires that his narratives had begun, furtively, to uncover.
Grounded in an overarching vision of dysfunctional family life, these
stories unsettled Whitman on a variety of fronts. As self-representations,
they were imperfect. As guides for living, they were mainly ineffectual.
Yet they emerged out of a powerful need to redefine gendered morality,
even if these "queer" fictions were the children of an imagination, and a
sexual identity, still in search of a stylistic home.[6]

Some of the commentary on Whitman's fiction stresses its awfulness;
some of the psychoanalytic criticism stresses its obsessiveness.[7] In certain respects, the fiction *is* awful and awfully obsessive, in its need to ex-
pose and correct patriarchal abuses of power: whether, as in "The Last
Loyalist," the patriarch is King George and the cowardly child-abuser
who supports his corrosive practices; or whether, as in "Wild Frank's
Return," the patriarch is a simple Long Island farmer who tragically
mismanages his "domestic government" and who invests his eldest son
"with the powers of second in command" (*EPF* 62). The story's passion-

ate, liberty-loving hero, "Wild Frank," refusing to submit to father *and* brother, is forced to flee. But this fiction is also uncannily compelling, teachable (many students like it), and surprisingly rich in its variations on the organizing abuse-of-patriarchal-power theme. If we grant that Whitman's stories are rushed and painfully earnest, they still command considerable interest for their value as social history and even greater interest as quirky documents in the history of his unsettled consciousness.

Whitman, as we shall see, racializes this antipatriarchal fiction with some persistence. Although he associates himself with the imperial project that organizes national manhood around the construction of racialized and gendered otherness, he is even more powerfully identified with those enraged others who threaten white men. Sporadic acts of violence fascinate him, yet the only *woman* who commits a "crime" in these stories is the ex-slave Margaret, one of the many women scorned in *Franklin Evans*. Margaret murders to preserve her marriage and her victim is the white woman who is her erotic rival, rather than Evans, the man who betrays her. There is a sense, then, in which the light-skinned Margaret murders because she aspires to whiteness, which is associated in the novel with domesticity and with middle-class norms of erotic fidelity. Nevertheless, Whitman's sympathy with Margaret's rebellion against those norms fragments the structure of his narrative, undermining its official racial binaries. There is wisdom in her unwisdom. Enraged Indians, too, refuse to vanish from Whitman's fictionalized landscape of desire, and as we might expect, he is both fascinated and repelled by their cruelty. My point, then, is not that Whitman dispenses with racialized and gendered stereotypes but that he begins to inhabit them. In so doing, he derationalizes himself.

However identified he may be with enraged, racialized victims of either gender, in rescripting national manhood Whitman is primarily concerned with abuses of power by white, native-born American men. As representatives of the dominant culture, they are driven by economic greed and introduce the competitive tensions of the marketplace into white family life, which they chronically disrupt. Yet traditional, father-centered white family life has already been disrupted before most of these plots are set in motion, for the situation that captured Whitman's deepest attention is the following, in which race is elided and whiteness assumed as the norm. A poor widowed mother depends on her only child, an adolescent son, for emotional and financial support. There are no happy memories of the dead father. The story of the failure of love between men is then told from the point of view of a materially and emotionally impoverished son who must find his way in an indifferent or actively hostile masculine world that seems determined to thwart his desire for happiness. In variations on this theme, traditional masculine occupations are associated with the desire to dominate others; material greed is associated with moral corruption; male-male rivalry at home and in the marketplace leads to male-male victimization in both public and private life.

This tale of the perils young men face in a society dominated by self-interest is based on the assumption that mothers, however weakened by their lack of money-making power, are potentially if not actually calming influences. Consequently, the greatest male-male violence erupts in families where no mother is present. In "Bervance: or, Father and Son," for example, a widower deliberately drives his son mad; in "The Last Loyalist," an abusive uncle beats his motherless ward to death; in "A Legend of Life and Love," a dying grandfather attempts to blight the lives of his two beautiful grandsons by endowing them with his own suspicion of "natural feelings." In "The Angel of Tears," the story of a latter-day Cain and Abel, we encounter neither Adam nor Eve; the plot depends instead on an "Almighty" and his ambiguously gendered angel-emissaries to rescue "the imprisoned fratricide." But there is no human or supernatural presence to teach brotherly love in "Wild Frank's Return," where a mother who plays favorites is unable to temper her husband's harshness. "Oh, it had been a sad mistake of the farmer," Whitman explains, "that he did not teach his children to love one another . . . sweet affection, gentle forbearance, and brotherly faith, were almost unknown among them" (*EPF* 64). Interestingly, Whitman's novelette, *The Half-Breed: A Tale of the Western Frontier,* violates most of the patterns I am describing. In this early fiction, "situated on one of the upper branches of the Mississippi," an Irish refugee-adventurer turned priest sets out to redeem his hateful and "passionate" half-breed son, whom he first viewed as a "monstrous abortion" (*EPF* 272). However, the story allows us to feel little sympathy for the son, who is genuinely vengeful. Instead, Whitman asks us to sympathize with his victims, who include members of both races. Unlike the marriage of a luxuriantly-locked Indian maiden and a luxuriantly-bearded trapper subsequently idealized in "Song of Myself," the pseudo-marriage of Father Luke and his hot-blooded Indian lover has led to moral and physical deformity. Despite the fact that "in the West, all men are comrades" (*EPF* 257), the demonized bad son Boddo—a thief, a liar, a hunchback, and a half-breed—exists almost beyond the pale of human affection. To be sure, it could be argued that Father Luke is not fully white because he is an Irishman, and furthermore that this good but ineffectual priest functions as a mother, if we accept the notion that mothers nurture and fathers beat or cheat. Racial ambiguity aligned with Roman Catholicism on the frontier thus has the power to trouble gender.[8] But it takes a lot to do it. Sometimes a cheating *is* a beating, as in "One Wicked Impulse," a tale which asks the question, "When is patricide justified?" As these descriptions may suggest, sometimes the wicked patriarch is an uncle or a guardian, rather than a biological father.

A classic example of Whitman's generationally coded abuse-of-power theme, which also presents a poor widow and her (one is tempted to say) suicidally helpful son, is "Death in the School-Room (A Fact)." So far as is known, this contribution to the contemporary discipline-in-the-schools debate was Whitman's first published fiction when it appeared in the *Democratic Review* in August 1841.[9] "Death in the School-Room" describes the brutality of a schoolmaster who falsely accuses a thirteen-year-old boy of being a thief. In fact the boy, Tim, has an unusually vivid conscience; he "would not steal,—hardly to save [himself] from starving" (*EPF* 56). An only child who suffers from a mysterious, congenital malady, "Tim's pleasant disposition had made him many friends in the village." One of these friends, young farmer Jones, frequently presents him with surreptitious gifts of food; these small gifts embarrass Tim's mother, who is deeply ashamed of her poverty. Jones is not a wealthy man, but rather a "young farmer . . . who, with his elder brother, work'd a large farm in the neighborhood on shares." This elder brother is "a parsimonious, high-tempered man;" he "had often said that Tim was an idle fellow, and ought not to be help'd because he did not work." Since both Tim's mother and his benefactor prefer the cover of darkness, the boy feels doubly obligated not to reveal to his teacher and classmates that he and his mother have been the objects of petty charity. Unfortunately, however, on the night in question, Tim is seen struggling under his load of a bag of potatoes while an actual theft is being committed from another neighbor's more luscious garden. Much of this background information about the theft itself is presented retrospectively and awkwardly. Initially, Whitman concentrates on the monstrous schoolmaster, Lugare. "He was the terror of the little world he ruled so despotically," we are informed. "Punishment he seemed to delight in" (*EPF* 58).

When Lugare questions Tim in front of the entire class,

> The boy look'd as though he would faint. But the unmerciful teacher, confident of having brought to light a criminal, and exulting in the idea of the se-

vere chastisement he should now be justified in inflicting, kept working himself up to a still greater and greater degree of passion. In the meantime, the
child seem'd hardly to know what to do with himself. His tongue cleav'd to
the roof of his mouth. Either he was very much frighten'd, or he was actually
unwell.

"Speak, I say!" again thunder'd Lugare; and his hand, grasping his ratan,
tower'd above his head in a very significant manner.

"I hardly can, sir," said the poor fellow faintly. His voice was husky and
thick. "I will tell you some—some other time. Please let me go to my seat—
I a'n't well." (*EPF* 57)

Tim's Billy Budd–like inability to speak when questioned by the vicious schoolteacher spells his doom, not because Lugare flogs him to
death, but because Tim's mysterious, congenital malady causes his heart
to stop beating during the hour that Lugare gives him to confess. When
the hour is up, Tim is found slumped over his desk; Lugare thinks he is
pretending to be asleep. Narrative time seems to stop, as Whitman, a
former schoolmaster, lingers with loving horror on Lugare's sadism, and
then on his utter humiliation by Tim, an apparently powerless person:

> Quick and fast, blow follow'd blow. Without waiting to see the effect of the
> first cut, the brutal wretch plied his instrument of torture first on one side of
> the boy's back, and then on the other, and only stopped at the end of two or
> three minutes from very weariness. But still Tim show'd no signs of motion;
> and as Lugare, provoked at his torpidity, jerk'd away one of the child's arms,
> on which he had been leaning over the desk, his head dropp'd down on the
> board with a dull sound, and his face lay turn'd up and exposed to view. When
> Lugare saw it, he stood like one transfix'd by a basilisk. His countenance
> turn'd to a leaden whiteness; the ratan dropp'd from his grasp; and his eyes,
> stretch'd wide open, glared as at some monstrous spectacle of horror and
> death. The sweat started in great globules seemingly from every pore in his
> face; his skinny lips contracted, and show'd his teeth; and when he at length
> stretch'd forth his arm, and with the end of one of his fingers touch'd the
> child's cheek, each limb quiver'd like the tongue of a snake; and his strength
> seemed as though it would momentarily fail him. The boy was dead. He had
> probably been so for some time, for his eyes were turn'd up, and his body was
> quite cold. Death was in the school-room, and Lugare had been flogging A
> CORPSE. (*EPF* 59–60)

If, as David Leverenz has suggested, buried fears of male rivalry structured the literary imagination of manhood in the American Renaissance,
perhaps some of the enduring fascination of Whitman's brutal tales
emerges from the fact that, in many of them, buried fears of male rivalry
are not all that buried. Take "The Child's Champion," for example,
which was published in the *New World,* in November 1841. Surely it ex-

emplifies Leverenz's belief that "in very different ways, American Renaissance writers try to disorient and convert their readers, especially male readers, from one style of manhood to another."[10] Subsequently retitled "The Child and the Profligate" and heavily revised, the story extends the covert sexual symbolism of "Death in the School-Room" to suggest, somewhat more overtly, an attempted homosexual rape. As the story opens, the abused child of the title, a bruised, thirteen-year-old apprentice, is being ruthlessly exploited by a farmer for whom he works overly long hours in the blazing sun. An only child, he parts tearfully from his mother, a poor widow. She works hard for a bare living and is unable to rescue him from his economic bondage. Tormented by helplessness, she urges him not to run away from "the hard rule" of his employer, "a soulless gold-worshipper" (*EPF* 70).

Following this pathetic opening scene, the boy passes a tavern. He lingers to listen and watch. In the barroom, heavy-drinking sailors are having a good time. The music, the black musician, the laughter and talk and dancing—all contribute to the apparent good cheer of male fellowship. Wistfully, Charles (as he is now called) looks in on this scene through an open casement window. Whitman explains,

> But what excited the boy's attention more than any other object was an individual, seated on one of the benches opposite, who, though evidently enjoying the spree as much as if he were an old hand at such business, seem'd in every other particular to be far out of his element. His appearance was youthful. He might have been twenty-one or two years old. His countenance was intelligent, and had the air of city life and society. He was dress'd not gaudily, but in every respect fashionably; his coat being of the finest broadcloth, his linen delicate and spotless as snow, and his whole aspect that of one whose counterpart may now and then be seen upon the pave in Broadway of a fine afternoon. (*EPF* 71–72)

This superior young man, who sounds like a stand-in for Whitman himself, is the Profligate. Though he participates in smutty jests "by no means distinguish'd for their refinement or purity," though he drinks too much, though he has no steady employment and has not been making the most of the superior educational opportunities afforded him by his family's class privilege (he could have been a physician), though he has been keeping low company, and though he is "a dissipated young man—a brawler," known to the New York police, Langton is also a Christian gentleman with a good heart who is possessed of "a very respectable income" and a house "in a pleasant street on the west side of the city" (*EPF* 76–77).

An orphan himself, albeit a grown one, Langton has been living "without any steady purpose" or anyone "to attract him to his home." He finds the purpose and the person in young Charles. After rescuing Charles from a vicious assault on his emerging manhood, Langton also rescues both Charles and Charles's mother from penury. Could there be a happier ending? In saving a child, he saves himself. Charity redeems the redeemer. Actually, however, the story has *two* endings. Following Charles's rescue from a drunken sailor who "seized the child with a grip of iron; he bent Charles half way over, and with the side of his heavy foot gave him a sharp and solid kick," Langton and Charles, in the story's original *New World* version, spend the night together in the same bed.

> It was now past midnight. The young man told Charles that on the morrow he would take steps to have him liberated from his servitude; for the present night, he said, it would perhaps be best for the boy to stay and share his bed at the inn; and little persuading did the child need to do so. As they retired to sleep, very pleasant thoughts filled the mind of the young man; thoughts of a worthy action performed; of unsullied affection; thoughts, too—newly awakened ones—of walking in a steadier and wiser path than formerly. All his imaginings seemed to be interwoven with the youth who lay by his side; he folded his arms around him, and while he slept, the boy's cheek rested on his bosom. Fair were those two creatures in their unconscious beauty—glorious, but yet how differently glorious! One of them was innocent and sinless of all wrong: the other—O to that other, what evil had not been present, either in action or to his desires! (*EPF* 76 n. 38)

This scene is blessed by an angel enabler, who legitimizes sundrenched kisses, and Charles's unspecified "beautiful visions" while dreaming. Yet Whitman's extravagant allegory evades the subversive political implications of the new style of male bonding he is depicting:

> No sound was heard but the slight breathing of those who slumbered there in each others arms; and the angel paused a moment, and smiled another and doubly sweet smile as he drank in the scene with his large soft eyes. Bending over again to the boy's lips, he touched them with a kiss, as the languid wind touches a flower. He seemed to be going now—and yet he lingered. Twice or thrice he bent over the brow of the young man—and went not. Now the angel was troubled; for he would have pressed the young man's forehead with a kiss, as he did the child's; but a spirit from the Pure Country, who touches anything tainted by evil thoughts, does it at the risk of having his breast pierced with pain, as with a barbed arrow. At that moment a very pale bright ray of sunlight darted through the window and settled on the young man's features. Then the beautiful spirit knew that permission was granted him: so he softly touched the young man's face with his, and silently and swiftly wafted himself away on the unseen air. (*EPF* 78 n. 43)

In revising this well-received story, which was also one of his personal favorites—it was the only story he further revised when he included it in *Collect*—Whitman eliminated the homoerotic idyll in the scene just quoted. In all versions, including those in the 1844 *Columbian* and the 1847 *Eagle*, Whitman asks, when Langton is first moved to intervene after the one-eyed sailor forces Charles to swallow a large glass of strong brandy,

> What was there in the words which Charles had spoken that carried the mind of the young man back to former times—to a period when he was more pure and innocent than now? "*My mother has often pray'd me not to drink!*" Ah, how the mist of months roll'd aside, and presented to his soul's eye the picture of *his* mother, and a prayer of exactly similar purport! Why was it, too, that the young man's heart moved with a feeling of kindness toward the harshly treated child? (*EPF* 73–74)

But in the *New World* version, Whitman further asks,

> Why was it that from the first moment of seeing him, the young man's heart had moved with a strange feeling of kindness toward the boy? He felt anxious to know more of him—he felt that he should love him. O, it is passing wondrous, how in the hurried walks of life and business, we meet with young beings, strangers, who seem to touch the fountains of our love, and draw forth their swelling waters. The wish to love and to be loved, which the forms of custom, and the engrossing anxiety for gain, so generally smother, will sometimes burst forth in spite of all obstacles; and, kindled by one, who, till the hour was unknown to us, will burn with a lovely and pure brightness. No scrap is this of sentimental fiction; ask your own heart, reader, and your own memory, for endorsement to its truth. (*EPF* 74 n. 23)

Already, then, in 1841 Whitman was writing himself into a vision of male bonding that was prophetic for him and, he dared to hope, for American literature. "Death in the School-Room" describes the collapse of a meaningful moral community; "The Child and the Profligate" describes another version of this collapse. In the former instance, the solution to the problem is nominally linked to educational reform; in the latter, to the temperance movement. Langton gives up drinking; Charles never drinks voluntarily. Implicitly, however, Whitman already functions as "The Child's Champion" in "Death in the School-Room," though the specifically erotic component of his role is less pronounced. Drawing back from the gender-exclusive implications of this eroticism in revising his story, Whitman, even in the original *New World* version, carefully locates Langton years later as the head of a family of his own, shuddering "at the remembrance of his early dangers and his escapes." As a married man, he is able to sustain his friendship with Charles, which "grew not slack with time" (*EPF* 79).[11]

In Whitman's composite master narrative, then, social reform is linked to the spontaneous creation of a generationally coded city or country of friends. Consequently, his positive, functional model of family life, which excludes biological fathers, is less the mother-centered, middle-class home than an affective union between men that, whatever its other functions, must resolve the economic and vocational anxieties of the younger of the two. Finally, this master narrative begs the question of the role of women within it. As mothers, women are to benefit from the friendships of their sons. But they are also marginalized by the greater social, economic, and political power of the new man whose healing presence redefines the meaning of family life. This marginalization of women is especially clear in "The Child and the Profligate," but even in "Death in the School-Room," the emphasis is less on Tim's closeness to his widowed mother (at best she is a shadowy figure) than on the peculiar disadvantages under which the boy labors as a fatherless son. Within Whitman's paradigm, there is no possibility of reempowering the mother as mother. His poor widows never inherit a fortune, nor do they become housekeepers in middle-class families, nor do they set up cent shops or become teachers or journalists or novelists. Once impoverished, mothers never earn enough money to recoup their losses and are thus unable to defend their pathetic Tims or Charleys against cruel father-surrogates such as Lugare, the "soulless gold-worshipper," or against the fluid-spilling one-eyed Sailor.[12] As weak havens in a heartless world, these women demand the care of their sons, rather than the other way around. Poverty eviscerates their maternal function. What Tim needs, then, is a father-surrogate such as the farmer who is strong enough to protect him against the Lugares produced by early industrial capitalism, those omnipresent loaded guns waiting to shoot down ineffectual young men. In Whitman's narrative, the farmer, however, is himself in bondage to his insensitive older brother, so that the only father-surrogate the story admits is the narrator, who, with his language-weapon, takes sadistic pleasure in his role as Lugare's flogger. Given the force of Whitman's language-whip, a misdirected gun such as Lugare does not stand a chance.

The combination of liquor, music, and sex that was so potent in unleashing violent passions in "The Child and the Profligate" proves equally irresistible in Whitman's temperance novel *Franklin Evans*.[13] As a defense against these threats, he of course counsels abstinence, but he also counsels marriage. "I would advise every young man to marry as soon as possible, and have a home of his own," Whitman's hero confides at the conclusion of the novel that bears his name. Franklin Evans remarks smugly,

> Boarding-houses are no more patronized by me. The distaste I formed from them in my memorable search for quarters, when I first came to New York, was never entirely done away with. The comforts of a home are to be had in very few of these places; and I have often thought that the cheerless method of their accommodations drives many a young man to the barroom, or to some other place of public resort, whence the road to habits of intoxication is but too easy. Indeed, the thought has long been entertained by me, that this matter is not sufficiently appreciated. (*EPF* 236)

From time to time Evans acknowledges his character flaw, his want of "resolution," but in general he scapegoats others, especially his former friend Colby, whom he blames for having introduced him to alcohol and to sexual entertainment in the musical saloons. In the course of this discussion, then, we will look a little more closely at the boarding houses patronized by Evans before his two marriages and before he inherits from a virtual stranger the modest fortune that rescues him from his problems, characterological and otherwise, at the story's end.[14]

An orphan who has been reared by an uncle to whom he has been apprenticed, the twenty-year-old Evans sums up his background as follows:

> My father had been a mechanic, a carpenter; and died when I was some three or four years old only. My poor mother struggled on for a time—what few relations we had being too poor to assist us—and at the age of eleven, she had me apprenticed to a farmer on Long Island, my uncle. It may be imagined with what agony I heard, hardly twenty months after I went to live with my uncle, that the remaining parent had sickened and died also. . . .
>   I continued to labor hard, and fare so too; for my uncle was a poor man and his family was large. In the winters, as is customary in that part of the island, I attended school, and thus picked up a scanty kind of education. The teachers were, however, by no means overburthened with learning themselves; and my acquirements were not such as might make any one envious. (*EPF* 147)

After introducing a more extensive genealogy to motivate his departure from "an obscure country town," Evans says nothing further about his somewhat kindly but impoverished uncle, his aunt, his cousins, or his dead father and mother, to say nothing of the few other relatives who were too poor to help him. At the story's conclusion, however, a better-connected Evans remarks,

> My country relations were not forgotten by me in my good fortune. The worthy uncle, who had kindly housed and fed me when I was quite too small to make him any repayment for that service, received in his old age the means to render his life more easy and happy. My cousins too, had no reason to be sorry for the good-will which they had ever shown toward me. I was never the person to forget a friend, or leave unrequited a favor, when I had the payment of it in my power. (*EPF* 234–35)

Presumably his aunt shares in his uncle's good fortune, yet Evans's failure to include her in his list of beneficiaries is significant. Franklin Evans, as we shall see, is a lady-killer. He marries twice and is responsible for the deaths of both of his wives, together with the death of a third woman whom he perhaps wishes to marry. Strangely, though, Evans has a knack for rescuing distressed mothers. His eventual good fortune depends on this talent. Even in the opening chapters he has demonstrated it, or attempted to—thereby *almost* attracting the favorable attention of a model gentleman, "the Antiquary," who turns out to be his great benefactor.

Arrived in Brooklyn from the country, Evans spends his first night away from "home" at an undisclosed location. The next morning, after breakfast, he takes the ferry to New York, buys a newspaper, and reads the ads. Feeling sorry for himself and feeling, too, that the world owes him if not a living then at least a room of his own, Evans is put off by the inflated language of the boarding house advertisements and further provoked to discover that some boasted there were " 'no children in the house.' " Although he rarely praises himself, Evans observes on a false note, "I loved the lively prattle of children, and was not annoyed as some people pretend to be, by their little frailties." Consequently, he neurotically eliminates any place that excludes children and proceeds to investigate his shortlist.

> The first place that I called at was in Cliff-street. A lean and vinegar-faced spinster came to the door, and upon my inquiring for the landlady, ushered me into the parlor, where in a minute or two I was accosted by that personage. She was as solemn and sour as the spinster, and upon my mentioning my business, gave me to understand that she would be happy to conclude a bargain with me, but upon several conditions. I was not to stay out later than ten o'clock at night—I was to be down at prayers in the morning—I was never to come into the parlor except upon Sundays—and I was always to appear at table with a clean shirt and wristbands. I took my hat, and politely

informed the lady, that if I thought I should like her terms, I would call again. (*EPF* 149–50)

Not about to subject himself to strict supervision (and from a vinegar-faced woman at that), Evans moves on. In the next house, a sort of dormitory or "open attic" arrangement, the landlady has no pretensions to gentility and makes no attempt to control his manners or morals, but, Evans remarks, "I did not like the look of the woman, or the house. There was too little cleanliness in both; so I made the same remark at parting, as before." For undetermined reasons, houses numbers three and four are unacceptable as well. Number five is eliminated because "all the boarders were men" and, Evans remarks genteelly, "I desired to obtain quarters where the society was enlivened with ladies." At house number six, somewhat anticlimactically, Evans signs on, at three and a half dollars a week, for "a snug little room in the attic, exclusively for my own use," after meeting the landlady—"an intelligent, rather well-bred woman, and the appearance of the furniture and floors quite cleanly." Now all this makes some kind of sense as a temperance novel, except that before Evans can suffer any of the boarding house loneliness that supposedly leads to alcoholism, he seeks out his "gay" friend Colby, who agrees to spend the evening with him.[15] Furthermore, he gets an interesting lead on a promising job opportunity that same day, returns to dinner at his boarding house "with some twenty well-bred ladies and gentlemen," and holds his own as to table manners, "though many of the observances were somewhat new to me, and one or two of my nearest neighbors, plainly saw, and felt amused, at my unsophisticated conduct in some respects; I believe I came off upon the whole, with tolerable credit" (*EPF* 152). His disintegrating country morals are another matter.

Four chapters later, Evans has had his first hangover, gotten a job, had a brief infatuation with a fashionable actress, gotten an even better job, and, under Colby's auspices, started on "the downward career of a drunkard" (*EPF* 159). He has also moved to a more expensive boarding house in a better neighborhood. When Evans loses his new job because he spends the night carousing with Colby and his set rather than delivering an urgent message for his employer, he is forced to find cheaper quarters. Here the full ludicrousness of Evans's critique of boarding houses emerges. Remember that Evans urges his young male readers to marry as soon as possible to escape the loneliness of boarding house life. The rootlessness of boarding house life is presumed to precipitate alcoholism. In the case of Evans, however, boarding house life leads to marriage, which leads to guilt, which leads to alcoholism. For Evans, as it turns out, marries his landlady's daughter. He explains,

> My landlady was a widow, with only one child, her daughter Mary. She was a modest, delicate, sweet girl, and before I had been in the house a week, I loved her. I do not choose to dwell upon the progress of our affection, for it was mutual. The widow knew nothing of my former intemperance—in fact, I had desisted during my residence with her, from any of my dissolute practices.

The self-centered Evans, who wants to enjoy all the comforts of home without being bothered by female-imposed responsibilities, is now fortunately situated:

> Six months passed away. I had obtained employment soon after taking up my abode there, in a factory not far from the house; where, though I was forced to labor, and my remuneration was moderate, because I did not understand the business well at first, I was in a fair train for doing better, and getting higher wages. The widow grew sick. She was of the same delicate temperament which her daughter inherited from her, and in less than a fortnight from the commencement of her illness, she left the world for ever.

All to the well and good, of course, from Evans's point of view. Almost inconsolable in her grief, poor Mary turns to Evans for support, and he turns to her "as the only resource from utter *friendliness*" (*EPF* 173; italics mine).

What kind of woman would marry the seemingly irresolute yet secretly determined Evans? Mary, we are told, is industrious, prudent, affectionate. Although neither an heiress nor the possessor of a fashionable education, "she had a gentle, kindly heart; she had good temper; she had an inherent love of truth, which no temptation could seduce aside, and which she never failed to put in practice; she had charity, a disposition to look with an eye of excuse on the faults of her fellow-creatures, and aid them as far as she could in their poverty, and console them in their griefs." But Mary, "a *good woman*, if ever God made one," cannot earn a dime. Supposedly the marriage goes well for the young couple until Evans succumbs to the temptation to buy a lot and build a house on it. As Whitman's father appears to have done with some consistency, he loses the property and is forced to abandon the venture, which is mortgaged to the hilt.[16] Whitman/Evans adds, "I was half crazed with mortification and disappointment" (*EPF* 173–74). At this point, for comfort in his sorrows, Evans again turns to drink. Mary, who has known nothing of his former "weakness," is unable to cope. Isolated in his suffering, Evans continues to drink. His business goes from bad to worse and not long thereafter, the neglected and agonized Mary dies of a broken heart.

Crazed with guilt, Evans, after an unbelievable series of adventures, ends up in the South, in Virginia, partly on business and partly for pleasure. There, he marries his second wife, and again marriage proves disastrous to his self-esteem and fatal to his wife. The circumstances are as follows. Evans has settled into a comfortably dissolute life with a French-born planter called Bourne, who takes the position that slavery in the New World is a "merely nominal oppression" when compared to the "stern reality of starvation and despotism in the [Old]" (*EPF* 202). Whitman/Evans seems to endorse this view. The amiable Bourne then encourages Evans's desire to marry his Creole slave by offering to free her as a courtesy to his friend. Under the influence of alcohol, Evans weds the beautiful Margaret. He likes the fact that she needs "a defender and advocate—perhaps one whose word would be effectual," as well as the fact that she has rebuffed the attentions of a lascivious overseer, using a farm tool to fell him "with a heavy blow" (*EPF* 205). Sober, he is horrified to discover that he has bound himself to a former bondswoman and proceeds to treat her so callously that Margaret, now crazed with jealousy, contrives the murder of her blond-haired, blue-eyed, white, northern rival. Successful in her plot, Margaret pays a high price for revenge—losing her sanity, her beloved younger brother, whom she has corrupted, and her life. Boarding house life has, of course, nothing to do with Evans's second marriage, or with the marriage he might have liked to contract with the heartless flirt, Mrs. Conway, who is much less sympathetically portrayed than Whitman's passionate and, within the limits of her situation, powerful Creole.

When Whitman revised his temperance novel for republication in the *Brooklyn Daily Eagle* in 1846, he eliminated several of the more egregious digressions and condensed the episodes between Evans's break with his second employer, the munificent merchant Stephen Lee, and his departure for the South. He thereby eliminated Evans's first marriage and caused Lee to rehire Evans almost immediately after firing him. He further revised the novel so as to eliminate Evans's *marriage* to Margaret, though Margaret remains an important character, as does Bourne, whom Evans admires and seeks to emulate. In both versions, Lee dies quickly and fortuitously as soon as Evans returns to New York, making Evans the beneficiary of his considerable fortune. In both versions,

Evans ends up rich, healthy, and unencumbered by the "blessings" of
home. "So, at an age which was hardly upon the middle verge of life,"
he remarks smugly,

> I found myself possessed of a comfortable property; and, as the term is "un-
> incumbered" person—which means that I had no wife to love me—no chil-
> dren to please me, and be the recipients of my own affection, and no domes-
> tic hearth around which we might gather, as the center of joy and delight. My
> constitution, notwithstanding the heavy draughts made upon its powers by
> my habits of intemperance, might yet last me the appointed term of years,
> and without more than a moderate quantity of the physical ills that man is
> heir to. (*EPF* 232)

In all these changes, Whitman further emphasized the importance of male
bonding, even eliminating the crucial episode in which Evans endears
himself to the wealthy Lucy Marchion, when he saves her little girl from
drowning. And he deemphasized the positive value of marriage. Far
from demonstrating that boarding house life drives men to drink and
that the comforts of home provide an effective barrier to alcohol, *Franklin Evans* demonstrates that there *are* no happy marriages. Stephen Lee's
wife, for example, turns out to have been a drunkard whose neglect of
their children has caused their death. In adopting Evans as his heir, Lee
carries out the novel's deepest impulse, which is toward male bonding
and the prior exclusion of women on which the perpetuity of male community depends. Perhaps that is why Evans, who is normally a pacific person, whatever his faults, attempts to strangle Colby. Colby, we remember, first introduced Evans to liquor and to women. In *Franklin Evans,*
at least, the combination is fatal, not because it leads away from marriage but because it leads toward it.

In one of his *Aurora* essays, Whitman asserted that half the population
of New York City lived in boarding houses. "English travellers sometimes characterise the Americans as a 'trading, swapping, spitting race,' "
he wrote. "Others again consider our most strongly marked features
to be inquisitiveness, public vain glory, and love of dollars. If *we* were
called upon to describe the universal Yankee nation in laconic terms,
we should say, they are 'a boarding people.' " In this 1842 *Aurora* essay,
which antedates by a number of months the composition of *Franklin Evans,* Whitman observed somewhat plangently, "We have taken up quarters in all the various kinds [of boarding houses], and therefore 'speak
from experience.' " [17]

Speaking from experience, Whitman discovered in writing fiction the
slippage between his desire to uphold the institution of the family,

whether patriarchal or matriarchal, and his more urgent need to celebrate, however obliquely, the love of comrades. In advising young men
to marry as soon as possible, he was not really trying to rescue them
from boarding house life, which, as the *Aurora* essay suggests, readily
accommodated married couples, though he was certainly trying to rescue them from loneliness. In later years, he liked to deflect attention
from his only full-length novel by claiming that he wrote it in three days
of constant work "with the help of a bottle of port or what not," adding,
"It was not the business for me to be up to. I stopped right there: I never
cut a chip off that kind of timber again." But as Thomas L. Brasher
notes, "Perhaps Whitman had forgotten that he had begun the publication of another temperance novel—*The Madman*—about two months
after the appearance of *Franklin Evans*" (*EPF* 124–25 n. 1).

The Madman, of which only two short chapters survive (more may
never have been written), was published in a New York temperance
newspaper, the *Washingtonian and Organ,* in January 1843. The two
extant chapters are exclusively concerned with a friendship between two
sympathetically presented young men. "The Madman" is presumably a
third character, as yet unknown to them, who violates their code of conduct, or one of the original characters transformed. When he stopped
writing the novel, Whitman had not decided whether the two friends,
Richard Arden and Pierre Barcoure, were to share equal status in the
narrative, and he probably had not made up his mind as to the identity
of the Madman. The more seductive of the two main characters—Whitman calls him a "strange and dreamy creature" (*EPF* 243)—is clearly
modeled after *Franklin Evans*'s Bourne and shares his French ancestry.
Like Bourne, he has a freethinking immigrant father, but in this northern urban setting, his politics are more attractively portrayed. Bourne,
after all, was a slaveholder, whereas Pierre Barcoure is "imbued with
that fierce radicalism and contempt for religion which marked the old
French revolution" (*EPF* 243). The less romantic of the two heroes,
Arden, shares some of Franklin Evans's traits, such as his irresolution,
his (Benjamin) Franklinesque desire to rise in the world, and his poverty. The two friends meet, amid the clatter of knives and forks, in a
realistically depicted restaurant on upper Fulton Street, and by "The
next week, they were on the footing of intimacy and familiarity" (*EPF*
242). So ends chapter one. In the very brief second chapter, Whitman
explains,

> So these two—Pierre and young Arden—became near and dear to one an-
> other.

> Their friendship was not of that grosser kind which is rivetted by intimacy in scenes of dissipation. Many men in this great city of vice are banded together in a kind of companionship of vice, which they dignify by applying to it the word which stands second at the beginning of this paragraph. How vile a profanation of a holy term!
>
> (To be continued.) (*EPF* 243)

And there the novel ends.

To conclude. In the early 1840s Whitman was not ready to develop homoerotic themes in fiction, though such themes increasingly dominated his literary imagination. He associated intemperance with the loss of conventional sexual and social identity, including whiteness, as *Franklin Evans* richly demonstrates. He also associated alcohol with daydreams and "a species of imaginative mania" (*EPF* 220) whose structure of desire anticipates a poetics that includes male-homoerotic love. Whitman continued to publish short stories off and on until the spring of 1848, when he returned with his brother Jeff from New Orleans. But he never repeated the concentrated effort that ended with the collapse of *The Madman* in early 1843.

His shift toward poetry was not a sudden one. As he explains in "The Shadow and Light of a Young Man's Soul," the last of his stories that can be effectively dated, "few great changes are" (*EPF* 330). Fiction writing continued to remain an option for Whitman in the mid-1840s and off and on for the rest of his life. In late June 1859, for example, after he had given up the editorship of the *Brooklyn Daily Times,* when his financial fortunes were at a low ebb and when he was writing the *Calamus* sequence, he reminded himself, "It is now time to *Stir* first for *Money* enough *to live and* provide for M—*To Stir*—first write Stories, and get out of this Slough" (*NUPM* 1:405). So far as we know, those stories were never written, and "M—" has never been conclusively identified.[18] Though Whitman considered writing more stories after publishing the first edition of *Leaves of Grass* in 1855 and may even have considered writing "Song of Myself" as a spiritual novel,[19] by the time he declared himself the "poet of slaves and of the masters of slaves" (in his famous notebook entry of about 1848) he had also reached the conviction that "Every soul has its own language" and that "Every soul has its own individual language, often unspoken" (*NUPM* 1:67, 65, 60). For Whitman, the soul's language was figurative and therefore untranslatable into what he understood as the more socially disciplined language of prose.[20]

In his fiction of the 1840s, Whitman was already beginning to write against the compulsory heterosexuality of the traditional love plot—the aristocratic love plot, as he liked to call it subsequently in such poems as "Song of the Exposition," when his discourse of class privilege was more pronounced. He stopped writing fiction when the conflict between his desire to uphold the heterosexual values of middle-class family life and his desire to undermine those values in print could no longer be ignored. Male bonding, as he was coming to understand it, exploded the domestic myths on which popular prose representations of well-regulated passion depended. Writing antipatriarchal poetry (in the main—I consider this multiply complicated issue further in subsequent chapters), Whitman needed a more individualized language in which, as he later explained to John Addington Symonds, he could let the "spirit impulse . . . rage" (*Corr* 5:73). Consequently, Whitman's projected New York romance of proud Antoinette, the unhappy prostitute, would have to remain unwritten (*NUPM* 1:401–2).[21] For while "the intellect . . . delights in detachment or boundary," as Emerson remarked in a revised version of the lecture heard by Whitman in March 1842, six months before the publication of *Franklin Evans,*[22] in the formally fluid poetry he created in the 1850s Whitman could descend into an ecstatic world virtually devoid of limited human agency. In this sexually fluid world beyond gendered moral convention, the delight is in the hitherto forbidden attachment, as when

> The cloth laps a first sweet eating and drinking,
> Laps life-swelling yolks. . . . laps ear of rose-corn, milky and just ripened;
> The white teeth stay, and the boss-tooth advances in darkness,
> And liquor is spilled on lips and bosoms by touching glasses, and the best
> liquor afterward.
>
> (LG 1855, p. 108)

The true poet, "the man without impediment," as Emerson called him, rejoices unambiguously in connection, which is perhaps why Whitman, writing to Emerson in 1856, claimed never to have found him.[23] In making this claim, he was not only following Emerson's lead—Emerson, too, looked for his true poet in vain—but also telling us something important about his imagination of himself as a democratic lover. In the next chapter, we will look further both at Whitman's need to turn himself into an erotic authority for modern times and at the internal and external impediments he encountered along the way.

Interleaf

From Walter to Walt

He is wisest who has the most caution,
He only wins who goes far enough.
      "Debris" (LG 1860, p. 421)

Some time after he had decided to become the *Leaves of Grass* poet, Whitman reminded himself, "I want something to offset the overlarge element of *muscle* in my poems—it must be counterpoised by something to show I can make perfect poems of the graceful, the sweet, the gentle, the tender—I must show perfect blood, the great heroic gentleman" (*NUPM* 1:386). Whitman's aspirations to gentility were admittedly cleverly disguised by his iconoclastic textual persona as "one of the roughs" in 1855, and still further screened by his bland, post–Civil War incarnation as the "good gray poet." But his early desire to be and to be considered a gentleman—expressed in his fiction, in his journalism, and in his dandyish 1840s man-about-town persona, the latter captured in a memorably awkward photograph—never entirely disappeared.[1] During the "long foreground" that so fascinated Emerson, Whitman worked to fuse his contradictory self-imaginings into a broadly inclusive social role. Having in his own eyes "split the earth and the hard coal and rocks and the solid bed of the sea," having gone down "to reconnoitre there a long time," Whitman, ever the faithful journalist, brought back "a report" on what he had seen (*NUPM* 1:69), in which he described his struggle with naturalized traditions of language that split body from soul, men from women, men from men. Having seized, he dared to hope, the "passkey" to hearts (*LG* 1855, p. 130), and armed with this token of his struggle, Whitman determined to transform those others, including the "gentleman of perfect blood," who normally resisted his advances.

Whitman, then, used poetry to create a comprehensive persona and to answer to his historically particular needs. The rough was not only a recognizable social type but a figure from within; so too was the bachelor gentleman, who surfaces briefly in the untitled 1855 poem later called "Song of the Answerer," in response to the poet's desire to be loved and to receive the honor that is his due. Together, the democratic poet and the gentleman of perfect blood absorb those recalcitrant others who impede their progress toward happiness, an ill-defined but no less tantalizing goal.

> The gentleman of perfect blood acknowledges his perfect blood,
> The insulter, the prostitute, the angry person, the beggar, see themselves
>   in the ways of him. . . . he strangely transmutes them,
> They are not vile any more. . . . they hardly know themselves they are so
>   grown.
>
> (*LG* 1855, p. 131)

Although most criticism has ignored Whitman's perfect gentleman, preferring instead to focus on the rough as an exuberant manifestation of the poet's democratic ideology, the "gentleman" expresses Whitman's fastidious recoil from social outcasts and from his "vile" imagination of himself as one of them. Both the muscular New York rough and the sweet and tender gentleman are impervious to criticism: the rough because of his hypermasculine coarseness, the gentleman because of his class-based access to tradition. Both are armored as Whitman was not. Or rather, he wrote most movingly out of that part of himself that needed protection from the distant ironical echoes and indecipherable messages that already haunt the 1855 volume, littering it with debris.

"Apart from the pulling and hauling stands what I am," the poet notes with a superb touch of aristocratic hauteur in Section 4 of "Song of Myself,"

> Stands amused, complacent, compassionating, idle, unitary,
> Looks down, is erect, or bends an arm on an impalpable certain rest,
> Looking with side-curved head curious what will come next,
> Both in and out of the game and watching and wondering at it.
>
> Backward I see in my own days where I sweated through fog with linguists
>   and contenders,
> I have no mockings or arguments, I witness and wait.
>
> (*LG*, p. 32)

The rough fights anybody who gets in his way; the gentleman fights nobody, he doesn't need to. Evidently the perspective from above is the gentleman's, whereas the social and psychic underworld belongs to the rough. Both of these figures depend on each other for definition: the rough is hypermasculine; the bachelor gentleman, a "sentimentalist," is more ambiguously gendered. Whereas the rough is part of a "gay gang of blackguards" (*LG* 1855, p. 107) and the gentleman is more of a loner, the Whitmanic poet sees the interconnections between them as they themselves do not. He speaks for both figures, and for the embattled ego as well.

Divergent and differently marked voices haunt the 1855 *Leaves of Grass,* as in some measure they continue to haunt subsequent books. Even as he strove for unity, consecutiveness, ensemble, Whitman mainly produced a poetry of disunion, gaps, and indirection. Despite the generosity and amplitude of his vision, few of the poems of the first three editions were psychologically complete, and Whitman looked to readers to complete the task that he himself had only begun. Although "launched from the fires of [him]self," "*too personal,*" and "too emotional" (*Corr* 3:307), the *Leaves of Grass* project was grounded in "unconscious, or mostly unconscious intentions," as the poet himself freely acknowledged (*LG*, p. 562).

Drawing on the fierce energies of his discontents, the poet who sought to deflect criticism by writing his own self-reviews both entered into and withdrew from the American literary scene in 1855; its battles were his and not his, just as his book was both published and privately printed; it was commercially distributed by Fowlers and Wells, yet he paid for its publication himself. Despite his intense fear of criticism and failure, Whitman tried to recount his emotional battles to an audience he might trust even as he sought to defend himself against predictably hostile, skeptical, or indifferent responses to his literary ambitions, whether they were muscular, graceful, sweet, gentle, tender, heroic, or bloody. As he explained mock-humorously in "Song of Myself," "To touch my person to some one else's is about as much as I can stand" (*LG* 1855, p. 53), a statement that captures perfectly both the intensity of his desire to be loved and the suspiciousness of his intellectual stance. Though famously singing the body electric, he thoroughly distrusted those "instant conductors" which alerted him to his own tactile vulnerability, finding it difficult to imagine that in seizing "every [erotic] object" he might lead it "harmlessly" through himself. Objects needed to be neutralized, as did people. And people needed to be objectified, to be transformed into characteristic and harmless types.

This ability to read people (including himself) as types apparently deserted Whitman in 1859 while he was writing the poem originally called "Bardic Symbols" and later retitled "As I Ebb'd with the Ocean of Life," in which he looked back disdainfully on his earlier work and disowned it.

> O baffled, balk'd, bent to the very earth,
> Oppress'd with myself that I have dared to open my mouth,
> Aware now that amid all that blab whose echoes recoil upon me I have not
>   once had the least idea who or what I am,
> But that before all my arrogant poems the real Me stands yet untouch'd,
>   untold, altogether unreach'd,
> Withdrawn far, mocking me with mock-congratulatory signs and bows,
> With peals of distant ironical laughter at every word I have written,
> Pointing in silence to these songs, and then to the sand beneath.

Following this appealingly agitated passage, the poet casts about for redemption which, to say the least, does not come quickly or easily. After an unsatisfactory encounter with a silently rejecting father, he turns in desperation to a mother so caught up in her own troubles that she has no time for him: a "fierce old mother . . . hoarse and angry," bemoaning her losses, the "castaways" of her dead dreams. Out of this emotional and rhetorical impasse Whitman writes bitterly to his fierce and tender muse, "We, capricious, brought hither we know not whence, spread out before you, / You up there walking or sitting, / Whoever you are, / We too lie in drifts at your feet" (*LG*, pp. 254, 256). Self-convicted for his arrogance, on which almost all the early reviewers remarked, the self-estranged Whitman of "As I Ebb'd" did not boast of the contrary contractile impulse which he expressed through such figures as the hermit thrush in "When Lilacs Last in the Dooryard Bloom'd," the "shy and hidden bird . . . withdrawn to himself, avoiding the settlements," who "Sings by himself a song" (*LG*, p. 330).

For the Whitman of the 1855 *Leaves of Grass,* who was not only recording his experience but creating it, the expression of sexual desire could precipitate physical and emotional crises whose outcome was desperately uncertain. "You villain touch!" the speaker exclaims operatically about midway through "Song of Myself," "what are you doing?. . . . my breath is tight in its throat; / Unclench your floodgates! you are too much for me" (*LG* 1855, p. 54). Contextually free-floating even as the speaker is pinned down, "touch" is responsible for those fitful acts of aggression by which Whitman's speaker is brutally and irrationally possessed. Such initially destructive but (he hopes) ultimately creative losses of self-possession invade the hero's gendered self-consciousness; they strain the udder of his ungendered heart for its withheld drip, whether milk or semen he cannot tell. Such solitary sexual spasms violate the class-marked ideal of "perfect blood" to which Whitman alludes in the notebook entry quoted above. There is thus no security in solitude, since it is dangerous to be alone. Marked by engorged muscle and imperfect blood both in the notebook entry and in the poem, the Whitmanic speaker seeks to draw back from the insane edge, even as he is lured toward the abyss by phantoms and phantom caresses.

In the first three editions of *Leaves of Grass,* Whitman sought to make a virtue of the "roughness" that he distrusted in himself and in his society. Embracing the social violence and psychological vulnerability that he could not extirpate, he folded these fateful forces into a larger rhetorical scheme. Balancing muscle with tenderness, invoking not only the genital "meat of a man or woman" but also "the meal pleasantly set," "the meat and drink for natural hunger," this orally aggressive poet masked the "occult convolutions" of his brain with blandnesses, such as the soothing thought that "All truths wait in all things" (*LG* 1855, pp. 54, 42, 49, 54). Yet this same self-disguising and deeply divided poet also asserted that "Logic and sermons never convince, / The damp of the night drives deeper into my soul" (*LG* 1855, p. 54). Thus Whitman created his own organic logic and endorsed a daring doctrine of sexual candor, despite the formidable codes of rhetorical and emotional caution to which he also resorted. The risk-taking sexual persona was born out of roughnesses inflicted on and internalized by the man. The fitful identification with "Blind loving wrestling touch! Sheathed hooded sharptoothed touch!" (*LG* 1855, p. 54) was genuine, but so too were the "occult convolutions" of a calculating, highly disciplined emotional intelligence which sought out unequal power relations in the erotic sphere. Making textual sex emerged as Whitman's solution to psychological, social, and political dilemmas he could not resolve in life. As Richard Rorty remarks, "Whitman wanted the struggle for social justice to be the country's animating principle, the nation's soul." [2] But what if he could not exemplify this struggle in his own innermost person? What if his "blood" was not "perfect"?

During the 1830s, 1840s, and 1850s, the Whitman who distrusted the privacy of the bedroom lived much of his dream life, which he folded into his professional life as a writer, in urban public places.[3] Our premier walker in the city, he browsed storefronts and bookstores and art galleries and concert halls and phrenological cabinets and Crystal Palaces; he famously loved operas and plays and photographic exhibits; he responded passionately to the faces in the Manhattan crowds as they swirled by him, losing himself in "those neverending human currents" (*SD* 701). And good reporter that he was, he kept track of notable achievers, seeing on Broadway alone "Andrew Jackson, Webster, Clay, Seward, Martin Van Buren, filibuster Walker, Kossuth, Fitz Greene Halleck, Bryant, the Prince of Wales, Charles Dickens, the first Japanese ambassadors, and lots of other celebrities of the time" (*SD* 701). Even before the Civil War, however, Whitman had begun his distinguished and psychologically imperative career as a hospital visitor. Fascinated by James Fenimore Cooper, whom he saw "in a court-room in Chambers street, back of the city hall, where he was carrying on a law case . . . a charge of libel he had brought against someone"; fascinated by Edgar Allan Poe, with whom he had a "short interview . . . in his office, second story of a corner building . . . very kindly and human, but subdued, perhaps a little jaded"; fascinated, as he recalled from his early youth, by John Jacob Astor, the richest man in America—"a bent, feeble but stout-built very old man, bearded, swathed in rich furs, with a great ermine cap on his head, led and assisted, almost carried, down the steps of his high front stoop (a dozen friends and servants, emulous, carefully holding, guiding him) and then lifted and tuck'd in a gorgeous sleigh, envelop'd in other furs, for a ride" (*SD* 702)—Whitman the fascinated observer/manipulator of his own inner life was so drawn to scenes of suffering, to sick and injured Broadway stage drivers, for example, that the doctors with whom he socialized, themselves drawn to Whitman as a celebrity and humanitarian, also thought that he was a "crank."

"No one could see him sitting by the bedside of a suffering stage driver without soon learning that he had a sincere and profound sympathy for this order of men," recalled the distinguished eye surgeon Dr. D. B. St. John Roosa, who had known Whitman in the late fifties when he was a young member of the House Staff of the old New York Hospital on Broadway. Roosa also observed Whitman in more relaxed settings. Accompanied by other physicians, they went to Pfaff's "rather famous cellar restaurant" in the afternoons and shared lager beer and "Schweitzer kase, schwartz brod, Frankfurter wurst, and even sauerkraut," at a time when these ordinary German foods were still exotic entries on the North American table. Yet despite this *gemütlich* atmosphere of male camaraderie, much of it occurring in the house doctor's combined bedroom and office, its walls ornamented with an 1855 *Leaves of Grass* self-portrait donated by Whitman, Roosa recalled that "he seemed to live above the ordinary affairs of life. I do not remember—and I saw him at least fifty times—ever having heard him laugh aloud, although he smiled with be-

nignancy. He did not make jokes or tell funny stories. We always wondered why he was interested in the class of men whom he visited." In
these vivid if partial reminiscences, which were published shortly after
Whitman's death, Roosa further recalled that

> He was not interested in the news of everyday life—the murders and acci-
> dents and political convulsions—but he was interested in strong types of hu-
> man character. We young men had not had experience enough to understand
> this kind of a man. It seems to me now that we looked at Whitman simply as
> a kind of crank, if the word had then been invented. His talk to us was chiefly
> of books, and the men who wrote them—especially of poetry, and what he
> considered poetry. He never said much of the class whom he visited in our
> wards, after he had satisfied himself of the nature of the injury and of the pros-
> pect of recovery. He gave me a copy of "Leaves of Grass," and he was ap-
> parently very proud of his achievements in verse. I must confess that I did not
> understand them then, any more than I understood the character of the man
> who wrote them. (*NUPM* 2:527–28)

Like his character Langton in "The Child and the Profligate," who
had turned aside from a vaguely defined career in medicine, and like the
psychiatrist friend of his later years, Richard Maurice Bucke, Whitman
needed to feel needed. But what kind of sexual life emerged from his emblematic interactions with vigorously virile Broadway stage drivers, with
these same young men humbled into working-class patienthood, and
with the more privileged male physicians whose combined office and bedroom was "the hiding place of many a secret, and the source of no in-
considerable brief authority" (*NUPM* 2:527)? The 1855 "Preface" had
noted that "The old red blood and stainless gentility of great poets will
be proved by their unconstraint" and that "A heroic person walks at his
ease through and out of that custom or precedent or authority that suits
him not" (*LG* 1855, p. 13), but unconstraint did not come easily to
Whitman. He was too aware of the "cruel inferiorities" of American
life to abandon himself outside of literature to the class-defying, male-
homoerotic orgies of which he dreamed. So while the American bard
was no "irresolute or suspicious lover," Whitman appears to have been
just that (*LG* 1855, p. 11). Before the Civil War, he lived most of his sexual life (to the extent that it was not primarily autoerotic) as a man of
the crowd, drawing on the energies of the modern city and using "the energy of his sexuality to formulate a utopian image of social harmony."[4]
Whitman identified with young, working-class men such as the drivers
he visited in New York Hospital because they exemplified the cruelty
and threatened social death he himself feared, and the pain of representational exclusion permeates the 1855 *Leaves of Grass*. Whitman dra-

matized this pain mainly by creating a cast of suffering, angry, alienated, or disempowered character types other than himself. These selves-in-crisis are variously feminized, since the poet alone has access to dominant modes of discourse and vision.

In 1855, Whitman spoke boldly of his own sexual confusion in a number of the most radically innovative sections of his book-in-process, such as the famous "villain touch!" passage discussed above. And he returned obsessively to the reassuringly common pleasures of the body, of which he could not get enough. Even when sexually marked as male, or female, or both, the body-in-process became his symbol of democratic community, and of our humanly undifferentiated, all-too-common fear of death. Whitman hoped that his body-worship would enable him to penetrate his neighbor's otherwise incomprehensible dress and dreams, and in some measure to descend into the chaos of his own (*DBN* 3:765–66). Embracing the double-life magnetisms of day and night, the poet explored both his need for relational self-definition and his need to flee from the limitations of the flesh into the freer languages of fantastic mélanges. These two projects were not mutually exclusive, since Whitman knew almost too well that relationships may be mainly fantasy, and that freedom and limitation were not easily differentiated from each other. Despite his claims to know the meaning of freedom, sexual freedom in particular remained difficult to specify.

Considering his neighbor's dreams, Whitman understood them from different vantage points. Though fundamental, sexuality was read in and through other categories of subjectivity, such as race and education and age and athleticism and beauty and social class. In his apostrophe to touch, for example, Whitman draws on various vocabularies to suggest that he is many people flooded with multiple sensations: burning, etherized, electrified, scalped, suffocated, and so on. Given the productive violence of such multiplicity, ordinary language categories which ask us to distinguish between various forms of sexual experience are revealed as ineffective. Whitman writes those new words which are still not in any book. In his own terms, as he explained in his 1856 open letter to Emerson, he was "wording the future" (*LG*, p. 740).

To say this is not to deny that Whitman was ambivalent as well as occasionally complacent about resolving the very real contradictions of feeling and principle which informed his life and his texts. He believed that the personal was political, but his project was not truly argumentative and dialectical, as Rorty contends, since he was constantly defining the boundaries of the personal. The self as Whitman understood it was an elusive concept, especially if the self in question was an author. To be an author was to escape from those selfish origins that limited, and Whitman was a master at doing so. As a personality, he saw health and sanity in "being one of the mass" (*LG* 1855, p. 15), while at the same time seeing disease and insanity in excessive individualism. Despite Rorty's claim that "Whitman wanted competition and argument between alternative forms," it was unclear how differences could be negotiated when public opinion alone would not do.[5] Whitman distrusted paper laws, and as a political journalist, he had been too hot for some and not hot enough for others. Moreover, as Dana Brand further suggests, the Knickerbocker New York journalists with whom Whitman had been associated—not the morally earnest and politically engaged Horace Greeleys but the bland and amusing Nathaniel Parker Willises—were, as a group, prone to moral complacency. Adopting a tone of superficial geniality which erased the incoherent threat of the modern urban scene, the affable Knickerbocker journalists could say with Whitman, "Do I contradict myself? / Very well then. . . . I contradict myself; / I am large. . . . I contain multitudes" (*LG* 1855, p. 85). Writing

> This is the city. . . . and I am one of the citizens,
> Whatever interests the rest interests me. . . . politics, churches, newspapers, schools,
> Benevolent societies, improvements, banks, tariffs, steamships, factories, markets,
> Stocks and stores and real estate and personal estate.
>
> (*LG* 1855, pp. 73–74)

Whitman does not really represent himself as a political poet fearing the impending threat of national disunion. Rather, he portrays himself as an amiable gawker who delights in the haphazard material and social abundance of an urbanized landscape to which he thoroughly belongs, owning both the reassuring transparency of the place and of himself. This is the spectatorial Whitman who cruises store windows during his 1860 visit to Boston, noting "fine stores on Wash st. (Jones, Ball & Co Rich Ornamental goods & Jewelry (Williams & Everitts, Pictures & Rich engravings)," finding on Washington Street fine trees and hot air furnaces and "Wentworth & Bright Carpets / John Collamore China &c also the adj building on the corner / iron front building of Parker, Towle & Sons Corner of Wash also iron front building Am Tract Society toward foot of Washn st / Oliver Brewster's cor State st gray granite / Codman Buildings gray granite / Wash st Warren & Co Chickering, pianos very good" (*NUPM* 1:426, 424–25). This noncontroversial Whitman might have recorded what Emerson said to him at this time, which we would all like to know. But instead he spotted a painting by his brother-in-law in the window next to one by Martin Johnson Heade. His brother-in-law's painting was a "real Yankee farm scene, July hay-cutting, the hay-cocks, the loading, one horse grazing, a part of the field not yet mowed, &c / Meadow fine clouds" (*NUPM* 1:427).[6]

Of course, there were more serious issues that commanded his attention in Boston in 1860, a Boston which was like, yet different from New York. "BLACKS," he wrote, in a passage filled with extraordinary modulations of tone,

> You see not near as many black persons in Boston, as you would probably expect; they are not near as plenty as in New York or Philadelphia. Their status here, however, is at once seen to be different. I have seen one working at case in a printing office, (Boston Stereotype Foundry, Spring lane,)—and no distinction made between him and the white compositors. Another I noticed, (and I never saw a blacker or woolier African,) an employee in the State House, apparently a clerk or under-official of some such kind. At the eating-houses, a black, when he wants his dinner, comes in and takes a vacant seat wherever he finds one—and nobody minds it. I notice that the mechanics and young men do not mind all this, either. As for me, I am too much a citizen of the world to have the least compunction about it. Then the blacks here are certainly of a superior order—there is a black lawyer, named Anderson (a resident of Chelsea) practising here in Boston, quite smart and just as big as the best of them. / and in Worcester, they are now put on the jury list, two of the names put on being black men, one of them a fugitive slave who has purchased his freedom. (*NUPM* 1:422–23)

Whitman encompasses all these voices, which also correspond, I am suggesting, to various sexual attitudes: naive, sophisticated, eager, indifferent. "No one will perfectly enjoy me who has not some of my own rudeness, sensuality and hauteur," he remarked in another one of those notebook entries which survived his 1874 bonfire (the first of several) and which sound as though they were written with an eye to being read (*NUPM* 3:380). But how are these three terms related? Is to be rude to be sensual and arrogant? Or does the finer politeness, the greater heroism and moral elegance, consist precisely in the willingness to sacrifice conventional models of social consideration to a higher duty which consists in acknowledging one's own roughness? To what extent can the great heroic gentleman violate codes of conduct that the ordinary gentleman respects?

Wrestling with these issues in the publicity he generated for the 1855 *Leaves of Grass,* Whitman approached them both directly and indirectly.

"Self-reliant," he wrote of himself in the *United States Review,* "with haughty eyes, assuming to himself all the attributes of his country, steps Walt Whitman into literature, talking like a man unaware that there was ever hitherto such a production as a book, or such a being as a writer." "Every move of him has the free play of the muscle of one who never knew what it was to feel that he stood in the presence of a superior," he continued. "Every word that falls from his mouth shows silent disdain and defiance of the old theories and forms" (*CH* 35). For the Whitman who felt that he had circumvented the gendered, initiatory rites of an emerging capitalist culture, "muscle" was a thrilling and terrorizing syn-ecdoche for the virile, working-class male body.[7] "Muscle" offered the promise of unmediated presence. Theoretically, at least, "muscle" could speak itself. "Loves the streets," Whitman wrote about himself in another defensive and snobbish self-review, this one appearing in the *Brooklyn Daily Times* in September, 1855, as he persisted in his spectatorial fan-tasies of sexual, racial, and social slumming,

> loves the docks—loves the free rasping talk of men—likes to be called by his given name, and nobody at all need Mr. him—can laugh with laughers— likes the ungenteel ways of laborers—is not prejudiced one mite against the Irish—talks readily with them—talks readily with niggers—does not make a stand on being a gentleman, nor on learning or manners—eats cheap fare, likes the strong flavored coffee of the coffee-stands in the market, at sunrise— likes a supper of oysters fresh from the oyster-smack—likes to make one at the crowded table among sailors and work-people—would leave a select soi-ree of elegant people any time to go with tumultuous men, roughs, receive their caresses and welcome, listen to their noise, oaths, smut, fluency, laugh-ter, repartee—and can preserve his presence perfectly among these, and the like of these. (*CH* 46)

Although there is no persuasive evidence that a working-class male lover or a series of such lovers transformed the class conscious Walter of the fiction, the journalism, and the dandyish 1840s man-about-town photograph into the democratic Walt of the 1855 *Leaves of Grass*—and I am arguing that this progressive transformation was never completed— Whitman certainly used poetry to reduce the conflict between his uto-pian imagination of the sexually open road and his dystopian experi-ence, as a bachelor-intellectual, of a sexually confining literary tradition that privileged white, heterosexual, middle-class norms. Whether or not Whitman's sexual experience during his twenties and thirties was a combination of autoeroticism and casual homoeroticism—and there is reason to think that it was—during the period 1848–55, as his life-circumstances became more than ordinarily fixed—fixed, that is, in relation to the volatility of his desire, which could never be adequately contained, it then seemed to him, within a single gender, sexuality, class, race, ethnicity, age, or social role—Whitman's struggle to recreate himself in opposition to genteel literary norms and to free language of its perniciously pre-existing meanings began to take on a life of its own.

Conscious that the full flush of youth had now passed him by and that he was unlikely ever to perpetuate himself except through language—no biological children for him—the Whitman who, so far as we can tell, never committed himself to an extended relationship with a male lover during the 1850s committed himself instead to sustaining his quarrel with oblivion. Whether or not he was to command a sufficiently responsive audience during his lifetime, "One world is aware, and by far the largest to me, and that is myself," he explained confidingly in "Song of Myself,"

> And whether I come to my own today or in ten thousand or ten million
>   years,
> I can cheerfully take it now, or with equal cheerfulness I can wait.
>
> My foothold is tenoned and mortised in granite,
> I laugh at what you call dissolution,
> And I know the amplitude of time.
>
> (LG 1855, p. 44)

As an artist-survivor intermittently buoyed up by his faith in a deferred or even posthumous audience, Whitman reveled in his freedom from the seminal conventions of poetic time as it had traditionally been expended. And the outrageous humor which had been singularly missing in his fiction and journalism bubbled up from the float now. No deadlines, he proclaimed. NO DEAD LINES. No man nor woman shall see the end. As writing became a form of erotic roving, he hoped that his words would endure like granite. And he could cheerfully compare his seemingly effortless craft to the family business, the builder's trade. His faith in *some* enduringly responsive erotic community, he seemed to be saying, was graved in adamant. Refusing to be snuffed out by his father, or like him, "I know this orbit of mine cannot be swept by a carpenter's compass," he wrote. "I know I shall not pass like a child's carlacue [curlicue] cut with a burnt stick at night." Experiencing himself as threatened, perhaps castrated, he also experienced himself as "august" (*LG* 1855, p. 44). Most modern individuals, he felt, were beset by comparable "natural" contradictions.

By 1854, then, Whitman was discovering a new solution to his sexual, gender, and class anxieties along the following lines. He would him-

self become the infinitely self-revising alter ego his readers needed if they
were to free themselves from the falsely unitary promises of American
life. In addition to releasing readers from the discipline of compulsory
heterosexual monogamy—"The novels and plays are always based on
passionate love of man for woman & vice versa," he noted confidentially
somewhat later, while praising the Damon-and-Pythias model of male-
homoerotic friendship (*NUPM* 3 : 1269–70)—Whitman would dismantle the hereditary basis of class privilege by shifting the national conversation toward a politics of the cooperative rather than the competing
body; toward a conversation in which, theoretically, all persons might
equally share. In so doing, he would be fighting "nature," history, and
literary history by demonstrating, as politics could not, the compassionate power of a determined poet's love. Thus, like his Romantic predecessors, Whitman set himself the task of defamiliarizing "nature" and of
expanding its claims, so as to empower those whom traditional societies
habitually persecuted or ignored. To put the matter in these terms, however, is to underestimate the zeal of Whitman's language experiment.
Determined as he was to reenfranchise not only slaves and privy clean-
ers but beetles rolling balls of dung (in long-range ethical spirit if not in
immediate political fact), Whitman sought to transform himself by radically revising literary history. The process of writing poetry had the power
to integrate Whitman spiritually. It did for him what neither religion nor
drink nor work had been able to do for his father. This fitful process,
which embraced multiplicity and contradiction, enabled him to move beyond gender binaries and to speak as the self-compassionating *Calamus*
lover whose emerging story we shall consider in later chapters.

Following his return from New Orleans in 1848, political events he
could not control caused Whitman the reform journalist to view himself
as professionally marginalized. He spent part of the summer relaxing on
the beach, but he was also elected as one of fifteen delegates representing Kings County at the convention which formed the Free-Soil Party in
Buffalo in early August. Living in the deep South had strengthened Whitman's antagonism to the spread of slavery, even if, as we have seen, it
had not purged his vocabulary of the word "nigger." By September 9,
1848, he had published the first issue of the *Weekly Freeman*. That night,
fire struck and his office was destroyed. Undaunted, he resumed publication by November 1 and was able to convert the paper into a successful
daily in the spring of 1849. When the so-called "Barnburners," the radi-

cal Democrats who had bolted the party and who supported the Free-Soil movement, returned to the Democratic fold in the late summer, joining forces with the "Hunker" conservatives, Whitman's local base of financial support collapsed. He resigned from the paper in disgust, announcing on September 11 that

> After the present date, I withdraw entirely from the Brooklyn Daily Freeman. To those who have been my friends, I take occasion to proffer the warmest thanks of a grateful heart. My enemies—and old hunkers generally—I disdain and defy just the same as ever.[8]

Called the "Abdiel of his party" by the *Brooklyn Star,* Whitman was taunted as "a very crying child" by the *Eagle,* which noted that "Like Oliver Twist, he was always asking for 'more.'"[9]

Although he continued to engage sporadically in freelance journalism and held at least one other short-lived editorial post, Whitman was becoming thoroughly disenchanted with the scurrilous attacks to which he was subjected as a political journalist, as well as increasingly frustrated by the dependency of his profession on the whims of others.[10] Poetry was beginning to seem to him the more radical and uncontaminated medium.[11] Meanwhile, on the personal front he had already begun to act out the reparenting comedy he was later to write, admittedly on a larger and more fantastic scale. His hair had turned prematurely gray, he considered his siblings "My Boys and Girls,"[12] he was ardently attached to his younger brother Jeff, whom he had taken with him to New Orleans, and he was looking for ways to transform himself from Walter to Walt. *Walter,* his father's name, suggested a certain woodenness, tension, and reserve. The comradely *Walt* hinted at relaxation and a continuous, self-inscribed present. "Likes to be called by his given name, and nobody at all need Mr. him," he had written in the *Brooklyn Daily Times* review. "Can laugh with laughers."

At what point, then, did *Walter* become *Walt?* What caused him, like so many other male writers of the American Renaissance—Emerson, Thoreau, Hawthorne, Melville, Poe, Douglass—to alter his name? Richard Maurice Bucke's 1883 biography, which was partially written by the poet himself, addresses this issue in an early footnote: "At home, through infancy and boyhood, he was called 'Walt,' to distinguish him from his father 'Walter,' and the short name has always been used for him by his relatives and friends."[13] Whether or not Whitman was the source of this note, in some sense he approved of its publication. At the

very least, he let it pass. Yet in early correspondence, Whitman is invariably called Walter, not Walt. Writing from New Orleans in March 1848,
for example, Whitman's fourteen-year-old brother Jeff observed,

> You need not be alarmed about the yellow fever as that gentleman will (the
> folks think) not visit this place this summer. The reason they give for that is
> this. It does not come but once in three or four years, and last season it was
> very hard and killed a great many persons (I mean it does not come but once
> in three or four years in such a shape). Besides it is a great humbug, most
> every one in our office has had (some of them have had it twice) and got
> well. It is caused mostly (I think all of it) by the habits of the people, they
> never meet a friend but you have to go drink and such loose habits.
>
>   You know that *Walter* [emphasis added] is averse to such habits, so you
> need not be afraid of our taking it. (*Corr* 1:31)

Whitman himself signed all his pre–*Leaves of Grass* correspondence either with his initials or as Walter. And Helen Price, who knew the family beginning in 1857, remarked that she never heard his mother call him
Walt. To her, he was always *Walter*.[14] By 1860, however, his mother had
begun to call him Walt in her letters, while also continuing to address
him, often within the same letter, as Walter.[15] Thus, despite the possibility that the Whitmans operated at two levels, oral and written, or that
his mother began to call him Walter only after his father's death in July
1855, it seems highly unlikely that Whitman was consistently called
Walt during his childhood to distinguish him from his father. In short,
there is no known use of the name "Walt" before its appearance in the
first *Leaves of Grass*,[16] where it figures in Section 24 of "Song of Myself" as textual proof of Whitman's erotic availability. Describing himself as a revolutionary poet who "make[s] short account of neuters and
geldings, and favor[s] men and women fully equipped, / And beat[s] the
gong of revolt, and stop[s] with fugitives and them that plot and con-
spire," Whitman further names himself as

> Walt Whitman, an American, one of the roughs, a kosmos,
> Disorderly fleshy and sensual. . . . eating drinking and breeding,
> No sentimentalist. . . . no stander above men and women or apart from
>   them. . . . no more modest than immodest.
>
>   (*LG* 1855, pp. 47–48)

Hypervirile. No sentimentalist. No sissy. Breeding negations which are
also affirmations. But of what? And what kind of drinking is he talking
about? Is this the kind of drinking in which Franklin Evans engaged after meeting his friend Colby in New York City?

"But come," said he, "this is dull fun here. Let us go out and cruise a little, and see what there is going on."

"Agreed," said I. "I shall like it of all things."

So we took our hats and sallied forth from the house. (*EPF* 152)

Turning, however, to the letters written to Walt by his brother Jeff during the post–*Leaves of Grass* years, we discover another pattern. "Dear Brother Walt," he writes from Jamaica, New York, on April 3, 1860, signing the letter "Your affectionate Brother Jeff."[17] Though Jeff occasionally varies his own signature, Walt is invariably *Walt*. Thus it seems likely that Walt was called Walt by his siblings before 1855, but not invariably. And not by his parents. During his father's lifetime, Whitman was content to publish his work as Walter Whitman, though he occasionally used a pseudonym such as "Paumanok" or "J. R. S." (Later, he was to use such pseudonyms as Velsor Brush, Mose Velsor, and George Selwyn.) Whitman cannot, however, have been called Walt rather than Walter by his siblings to differentiate him from his father, since his siblings were not in the habit of referring to their father as Walter. On the eve of his father's death, as the outsetting American bard, he renamed himself in such a way as to perpetuate a personal past while signaling his newfound freedom from it. America, we recall,

> does not repel the past or what it has produced under its forms or amid other politics or the idea of castes or the old religions. . . . accepts the lesson with calmness. . . . is not so impatient as has been supposed that the slough still sticks to opinions and manners and literature while the life which served its requirements has passed into the new life of the new forms. . . . perceives that the corpse is slowly borne from the eating and sleeping rooms of the house . . . perceives that it waits a little while in the door . . . that it was fittest for its days . . . that its action has descended to the stalwart and wellshaped heir who approaches . . . and that he shall be fittest for his days. (*LG* 1855, p. 5)

The erotic experiences in Whitman's life between 1848 and 1854 that enabled him to conceive his visionary *Walt* persona remain obscure and warrant further investigation. Certainly, as Walt he writes like a man relieved of a tremendous burden, though there is always the sense that the depressions which were a paternal family legacy and by which he had previously been threatened might recur.[18] Hysteria looms on the horizon. To stabilize his newly acquired emotional poise and intellectual aplomb, Whitman creates a survivor's narrative within "Song of Myself" that potentially links him to his audience. He also remains uncer-

tain as to the affective strength of his story, asserting at the poem's conclusion, proudly, but also wistfully,

> You will hardly know who I am or what I mean,
> But I shall be good health to you nevertheless,
> And filter and fibre your blood.
>
> Failing to fetch me at first keep encouraged,
> Missing me one place search another,
> I stop some where waiting for you
> (LG 1855, p. 86)[19]

Scholars have debated whether the lack of terminal punctuation (the period reappears in 1856) was intentional.[20] But there is a certain poetic
justice in its absence within a poem that resists the full burden of traditional modes of closure—as Whitman himself, throughout the rest of
his life in poetry, was to do.

Whitman's letters during these years 1848–54 are both few in number (seven if the count is generous) and comparatively uninformative.
Consider, for example, a letter from New Orleans to his mother. Dated
"Tuesday morning, 28th March" [1848], it is concerned with money,
health, and silence. There is also a pastoral idyll of the sort that Whitman
and his mother entertained between themselves virtually to the end of
her life. He mentions a farm, but who would work this farm? Surely not
Whitman and surely not his father, who is already erased from the text.

> Dearest Mother;
>
> In one of my late letters, I told Hannah [his sister, then living at home]
> that if you did not receive money, by a letter from me, to pay the interest on
> the 1st of May, she must go down to the bank and draw $31 1/2, and pay it
> at the insurance office, and get a receipt for it. However, I may send money
> in a letter before that time—or part of it. O, mother, how glad I was to hear
> that you are quite well, again. Do try to keep so; you must not work—and
> they must all be kind to you. If you only keep well till I get home again, I
> think I shall be satisfied. I began to feel very uneasy, not hearing from you
> so long. My prospects in the money line are bright. O how I long for the
> day when we can have our quiet little farm, and be together again—and
> have Mary [his other sister] and her children come to pay us long visits.
> I wrote to Mary yesterday.
> W. W. (Corr 1:33)

If there was a New Orleans romance, Whitman's mother would not have
been one of the first to know. And if Jeff, the fourteen-year-old brother
who accompanied Walt, knew, he never told—either in these letters

home or subsequently.[21] We are all familiar with the genre: reassuring news to an anxious parent. The unusual features here are the mother's silence despite repeated entreaties from both sons, and Whitman's position as the absent manager of the family's financial and emotional well-being. As David Cavitch has suggested, the future poet terminated his New Orleans stay primarily because he felt urgently needed at home—though there were conflicts with his southern employers, almost inevitably. Sooner or later, Whitman quarreled with his bosses, whatever their politics. And the political circumstances here were challenging in the extreme.[22]

Turning to the next letter in Whitman's preserved correspondence, we discover a brief note of April 24, again to his mother. From New Orleans, *Jeff* was the expansive letter writer. "Dear mother," Walter Whitman wrote,

> I shall write to you myself in a few days. O how I long to see you. Hannah must get $31 1/2 from the Bank to pay the interest. If she just asks for Mr. Hegeman [a bookkeeper in the Atlantic Bank] and tells him she is my sister, he will show her every accommodation. (*Corr* 1:36)

The next letter is dated "Brooklyn, Jan. 15, '49," and addressed to Tunis G. Bergen, an official of the Brooklyn city treasury. Whitman, who was an editor-printer at the time, explained, "It would be a great obligation to me, if you would present the enclosed bill and start it on its passage, so that I could get my pay as quickly as possible. For, like most printers, I am horribly in need of cash. Do, my dear sir, oblige me, in this matter, if possible" (*Corr* 1:37).

Before 1855, there are four remaining letters, none of them dated after August 1852. The first, written in June 1850, offers to serialize and to condense a Danish historical novel, *The Childhood of King Erik Menved,* an offer that was not accepted (*Corr* 5:282–83).[23] The second, to Carlos D. Stuart, and dated October of about 1850, was, in effect, a job application (*Corr* 1:38). Stuart was the editor of a New York daily. So far as is known, nothing came of Whitman's request for work, though his ideas for salary were "*very* moderate." The third, to W. M. Muchmore, a dealer in coal and wood in Brooklyn, was a request that Muchmore, "if convenient," remind Tunis G. Bergen of Whitman's unpaid bill for advertising ($50) (*Corr* 1:38–39). The last of these pre–*Leaves of Grass* letters, dated August 14, 1852, was addressed to Senator John Parker Hale of New Hampshire, Free-Soil candidate for president.

With that extraordinary lack of tact he could exhibit when attempting to curry favor with powerful men (he was not a good flatterer), Whitman concluded,

> How little you at Washington—you Senatorial and Executive digni-
> taries—know of us, after all. How little you realize that the souls of the
> people ever leap and swell to any thing like a great liberal thought or prin-
> ciple, uttered by any well-known personage—and how deeply they love
> the man that promulges such principles with candor and power. It is won-
> derful in your keen search and rivalry for popular favor, that hardly any
> one discovers this direct and palpable road there. (*Corr* 1:40)

Here is the same movement one observes in Whitman's 1856 open letter to Emerson: from compliment ("You must not only not decline the nom-ination of the Democracy at Pittsburgh, but you must accept it grace-fully and cordially") to more or less veiled insult.[24] Speaking for "the young men of our land—the ardent, and generous hearts," Whitman wrote as though he were angling for a position in Hale's administration, perhaps as a reward for writing a campaign biography. Given the low probability that Hale would engage Whitman to write such a biography —as the successful Democratic candidate Franklin Pierce did with his longtime friend and Bowdoin College classmate Nathaniel Hawthorne— the letter is primarily altruistic along bossy, self-expressive lines:

> O, my dear sir, I only wish you could know the sentiments of respect and
> personal good will toward yourself, with which, upon seeing a telegraphic
> item in one of this morning's papers, that you would probably decline, I
> forthwith sat down, and have written my thoughts and advice. I shall make
> no apology; for if sentiments and opinions out of the great mass of the
> common people are of no use to the legislators, then our government is a
> sad blunder indeed. (*Corr* 1:40)

Yet altruism competes with arrogance, which in the end wins. Republi-can idealism is ousted by Whitman's need to scold.

Taken together, these letters do not provide much, if any, insight into Whitman's putative awakening to love—with the possible exception of the first letter written to his mother, which underscores his long-standing devotion to her and her continuing dependence on him. Nor are Whit-man's notebooks much help here. There are the "Young America" po-litical statements,[25] the religio-philosophical statements, the observa-tions on language. And there are the apparently random jottings that suggest Whitman's abiding interest in passing strangers, most of them men. But on the whole, there is less evidence of a transformative ro-mance than we have for a nominally reclusive writer such as Dickinson, whose impassioned letters to Susan Gilbert Dickinson and to "Master" are by now in the public domain.[26] Outside of the compass of his poems, Whitman obliterated the historical record more thoroughly.

To Horace Traubel, however, Whitman alluded guardedly and in passing to "one sparkling fellow in particular I fancied," whom he met at the Brooklyn studio of the sculptor Henry Kirke Brown, probably in 1850. "They were big, strong days—our young days—days of preparation: the gathering of the forces," he told Traubel. The memory of those times still excited him. "I fell in with Brown, the sculptor," Whitman remarked,

> was often in his studio, where he was always modelling something—always at work. There many bright fellows came . . . there we all met on the freest terms. I have been in contact with the Longfellow circles,[27] but they were literary, polite: I was not their kind—was not au fait—so preferred not to push myself in, or, if in, to stay in. The Brown habitues were more to my taste. There I would meet all sorts—young fellows from abroad stopped here in their swoopings: they would tell us of students, studios, the teachers, they had just left in Paris, Rome, Florence: one sparkling fellow in particular I fancied: he spoke of Beranger—I was greatly interested; he either knew Beranger or knew a heap about him. In this crowd I was myself called Beranger: my hair had already commenced to turn gray. (*WWWC* 2:502)

Surrounded by artists whom Whitman later identified, albeit indirectly, with "Greek" customs (he was to associate the celebrated sculptor John Quincy Adams Ward with John Addington Symonds, for example), Whitman became, for the first time, a member of a sophisticated cultural coterie.[28] As "Beranger," he was likened to "the French Poet of Freedom," the lyricist identified, as Whitman was to be, with radical social causes.[29] If in describing this scene to Traubel—and he recalled it with pleasure almost forty years later—Whitman was hinting at the vitality of New York's male-homoerotic subculture in the early 1850s, he was recreating a milieu about which remarkably little is known, even today. The "one sparkling fellow in particular" he fancied disappears into the crowd. Under these circumstances, the social complexity of their relationship is virtually irrecoverable. So not only is there no dark lady to explain Whitman's development during this period, but we cannot attend closely to the development of his particular romantic friendships. Meeting him after the Civil War, Edward Carpenter commented on the "tragic element in [Whitman's] nature" which "possibly prevented him ever being quite what is called 'happy in love affairs.'" Carpenter further noted, "He celebrates in his poems the fluid, all-solvent disposition, but often was himself less the river than the rock. In these moods, fixed, silent, and unquestionable, he was a thing you might try your strength upon, but which you were not likely to move!" Carpenter, who adored Whitman, who was himself homosexual, and who had the advantage of direct observation, could not account for Whitman's periods of physical and emotional inaccessibility, and did not advance homophobia as a reason.[30]

In any event, Whitman was writing a good deal of art criticism in the early 1850s, and the Brown circle invited him to address the first awards ceremony of the short-lived Brooklyn Art Union on March 31, 1851.[31] For a variety of reasons, the speech marks an important phase in Whitman's esthetic development. Describing the artist as a freedom fighter and arguing that "all men contain something of the artist in them," Whitman began by attacking the low repute in which the true artist is held, "among such a people as the Americans, viewing most things with an eye for pecuniary profit." Given the hostile cultural situation in which the American artist finds himself, the true artist must look to Eastern and especially to Greek sources for his inspiration.

> Nay, may not death itself, through the prevalence of a more artistic feeling among the people, be shorn of many of its frightful and ghastly features? In the temple of the Greeks, Death and his brother Sleep, were depicted as beautiful youths reposing in the arms of Night. At other times Death was represented as a graceful form, with calm but drooping eyes, his feet crossed and his arms leaning on an inverted torch. Such were the soothing and solemnly placed influences which true art, identical with a perception of the beauty that there is in all the ordinations as well as all the works of Nature, cast over the last fearful thrill of those olden days. Was it not better so? Or is it better to have before us the idea of our dissolution, typified by the spectral horror upon the pale horse, by a grinning skeleton or a mouldering skull? (*UPP* 1:243–44)

However impulsive and ideologically unmarked Whitman's erotic experiments had been heretofore, by 1851 he was moving intuitively toward an affirmation of "Greek" values as the basis of a redeemed community. "The beautiful artist principle sanctifies that community which is pervaded by it," he explained. "A halo surrounds forever that nation.—"

> There have been nations more warlike than the Greeks. Germany has been and is more intellectual. Inventions, physical comforts, wealth and enterprize are prodigiously greater in all civilized nations now than they were among the countrymen of Alcibiades and Plato. But never was there such an artistic race.

At some later time, perhaps in the 1860s, Whitman noted, after reading the Bohn edition of Plato,

> *Phae-drus* (Plato) purports to be a dialogue between Socrates & Phaedrus— the latter a young man, who, coming to Socrates, is full of a discourse by Lysias on *Love*—he reads it to S.—who finally proceeds to give a discourse on

the same theme—by love he evidently means the passion inspired in one man, by another man, more particularly a: beautiful youth. The talk seems to hinge on the question whether such a youth should bestow his "favors" more profitably on a declared "lover," or on one not specially so ... His whole treatment assumes the illustration of Love, by the attachment a man has for another man, (a beautiful youth as aforementioned, more especially)—(it is astounding to modern ideas). (*NUPM* 5:1882)

The carefully elaborated, officially sanctioned institutionalization of homosexuality which existed in classical Greece might well have astonished Whitman in the 1860s. But in 1851, the extent to which Whitman's references to Greek culture constitute deliberately coded references to male-homoerotic practices is difficult to determine.[32] As previously noted, he appears to have been moving somewhat haphazardly toward the creation of a homosexual discourse which would eventually be unerringly acknowledged by many others, whatever his own prudential blindness.[33]

Speaking in Brooklyn not necessarily as a member of a sexual subculture but unmistakably as a seeker after moral beauty in a money-driven culture, Whitman ironically likened himself and other unknown artists to "an ample palace of surpassingly graceful architecture, filled with luxuries and gorgeously embellished with fair pictures and sculpture," standing "cold and still and vacant." Artists, he asserted, often failed to appreciate their own worth. As an alternative to self-pity, he prescribed a sacred duty to "go forth into all the world and preach the gospel of beauty" (*UPP* 1:242–43). Yet Whitman remained troubled by this vision of himself as an empty palace, never to be known and enjoyed by its rightful owner. It proved to be a haunting fantasy of neglect, privatization, and feminization, inscribing an identity Whitman was consciously determined to suppress.

In an early notebook entry, which served as the basis of his long, unpublished free-verse poem "Pictures," Whitman further developed his expanding conception of himself as a man of the people. "Who is this," he asked himself theatrically, "with rapid feet, curious, gay—going up and down Mannahatta, through the streets, along the shores, working his way through the crowds, observant and singing?" (*NUPM* 4:1299). The "Pictures" notebook adumbrates "Song of Myself" in its presentation of an imagination unbounded by space and time, yet strangely literalized within the body of a single individual, himself. Whitman eventually dropped the cumbersome head-as-art-gallery metaphor that controls his notebook draft. But he was more persistent in furnishing himself with lovers who were alternative, cross-class personae:

> And there hang, side by side, certain close comrades of mine—a Broadway
> stage-driver, a lumberman of Maine, and a deck-hand of a Mississippi
> steamboat;
> And again the young man of Mannahatta, the celebrated rough,
> (The one I love well—let others sing whom they may—him I sing, for a
> thousand years!)
>
> <div align="right">(<i>NUPM</i> 4:1303–4)[34]</div>

Describing himself as "The phallic choice of America" who "leaves the finesse of cities" and all the "achievements of literature and art" to "enjoy the breeding of full-sized men, or one full-sized man or woman, unconquerable and simple," Whitman rounded out his portrait of "inimitable pictures." Materials that might have provided the basis for despair were in the process of being transmuted into a more hopeful narrative. Although Whitman's association of the "artist race" with his own feminization was to persist, he was all the more determined to slake "the unquenchable thirst of man for his rights" (*UPP* 1:246).

In 1852, the year of Whitman's last extant pre–*Leaves of Grass* letter, Walter Whitman Senior suffered a severe stroke from which he never recovered. His father's prolonged illness and "many bad spells" quickened the emerging poet's desire to live among a people "pervaded by love and appreciation of beauty," especially since "manly worth cannot be monopolized by any circle of society" (*UPP* 1:246, 244). When a brief obituary of his father appeared in a local newspaper, Whitman saved it, along with other family materials, and carefully corrected several errors in dating. Emended, the newspaper notice reads as follows:

> DIED. In Brooklyn, on the night of July 11th, 1855, WALTER WHITMAN, senior, after an exhausting illness of nearly 3 years, from paralysis. Born at West Hills, town of Huntington, L.I., July 14th, 1789; was mostly a resident of New York city and Brooklyn; a carpenter. His death was easy and unconscious. Buried in the Cemetery of the Evergreens. Present: His widow, and a large family of sons and daughters. (*NUPM* 1:17)

In a long letter to her daughter Hannah, who was by then married and living in Vermont, Louisa Whitman explained,

> i sent for jeffy . . . and walter came they felt very much to blame themselves for not being home but they had no idea of any change your father had been [ill] so long and so many bad spells . . . mary took it very hard that she could not see her father she was very sick coming from the evergreens where poor father was laid in a quiet spot . . .[35]

Though Whitman himself was apparently away from home when his father died, he had been very much present during the years immediately preceding. Real estate in Brooklyn was booming in 1852–53 and he managed the family business, saving enough from the profits to stave off his return to another full-time editorial position. One of his account notes indicates that his father was still doing days' work during the summer of 1852, having hired himself out to another carpenter, Minard S. Scofield, for twenty-three and a half days in July and August.[36] Perhaps hard work in the hot sun helped to precipitate his paralytic stroke. In any event, despite legends to the contrary, Whitman probably never worked as a carpenter himself. Acquiring property, supervising the building of houses and then selling them, earning the occasional dollar through freelance journalism, by May 1854 Walt had bought a house on Ryerson Street in his mother's name, for her to hold, according to the deed, "without concurrence of her husband at any time."[37] But by then, economic hard times had set in, the housing boom was over, and Whitman was hard at work on *Leaves of Grass*.

In speaking of the book that was to become his life's work, he subsequently explained that the first edition was "written under great pressure,—pressure from within. He felt that he *must* do it."[38] As if to confirm that statement, in March 1854 he linked the beauty and heroism of the typical American carpenter to the classical Greek tradition of male divinity. "I claim for one of those framers over the way framing a house," he wrote, "The young man there with rolled-up sleeves and sweat on his superb face, / More than your craft three thousand years ago, Kronos, or Zeus his son, or Hercules his grandson."[39] And then, on the other side of this manuscript draft for lines from Section 41 of "Song of Myself," he described some of the young men who were crucial to his burgeoning conception of himself as America's phallic choice.

March 20th '54

Bill Guess, died aged 22.
    A thoughtless, strong, generous animal nature, fond of direct pleasures, eating, drinking, women, fun &c.—Taken sick with the small-pox, had the bad disorder and was furious with the delirium tremens.—Was with me in the Crystal Palace,—a large broad fellow, weighed over 200.—Was a thoughtless good fellow.—
    Peter——large, strong-boned youn[g] fellow, driver.—Should weigh 180. —Free and candid to me the very first time he saw me.—Man of strong self-will, powerful coarse feelings and appetites—had a quarrel,—borrowed $300—left his father's, somewhere in the interior of the state—fell in with a couple of gamblers—hadn't been home or written there in seven years.—I liked his refreshing wickedness, as it would be called by the orthodox.—He seemed to feel a perfect independence, dashed with a little resentment, toward

the world in general.—I never met a man that seemed to me, as far as I could tell in 40 minutes, more open, coarse, self-willed, strong, and free from the sickly desire to be on society's lines and points.—

George Fitch.—Yankee boy—Driver.—Fine nature, amiable, of sensitive feelings, a natural gentleman—of quite a reflective turn. Left his home because his father was perpetually "down on him".—When he told me of his mother, his eyes watered.—Good looking, tall, curly haired, black-eyed fellow, age about 23 or 4—slender, face with a smile—trowsers tucked in his boots—cap with the front-piece turned behind.— (*NUPM* 1:199–200)

Gay Wilson Allen has suggested that these observations were based on visits to Dr. Roosa's New York Hospital where sick stage drivers, among others, were treated.[40] If so, Whitman is describing, or fantasizing, casual sexual contacts: generous, 40 minutes, turned behind. But whatever the immediate occasion of these notations, Whitman's long-standing desire to make something permanent of himself, to find "form and union and plan" and an "eternal life" of "happiness" (*LG* 1855, p. 85) by gratifying the physical and spiritual needs of other men, had by 1854 taken on terrible urgency.

Whitman's "rough" persona emerged out of a history of social and psychic vulnerability that, in the 1855 *Leaves of Grass,* is only partially (though at times giddily) transcended. "I cannot understand the mystery," he explained in an often quoted, early notebook entry, "but I am always conscious of myself as two—as my soul and I; and I reckon it is the same with all men and women" (*NUPM* 1:63). The last part of this statement is pure wish fulfillment, though it has one characteristic Whitmanian ring: the move outward, the urge to connect. Social alienation is experienced as self-alienation, which is then normalized as a universal estrangement. Surely Whitman was wrong in thinking that "all men and women" are conscious of themselves as two. But he was right in understanding self-division as the basis of his defiant language experiment. To the extent that he could transform the Walter who feared erotic intimacy into the roughened, devil-may-care Walt, he hoped to defeat the deeply inhibiting forces which impeded his ability to feel pleasantly at home in the world. In the next two chapters, I will continue to trace the development of the more tender persona of the *Calamus* poems, a figure who in many ways rescued Whitman from too much roughness by providing him, at last, with meat and drink for natural hunger.[41]

Figure 1.   The farmhouse at West Hills,
near Huntington, Long Island, New York,
where Whitman was born on May 31,
1819. It was built by his father, a skilled
carpenter. Library of Congress.

Figure 2.   Walter Whitman, the
poet's father. He died in July 1855,
the month in which the first edition
of *Leaves of Grass* was published.
The photograph probably antedates
1852, when Walter Senior was
stricken with a wasting illness.
Library of Congress.

Figure 3.   Louisa Van Velsor
Whitman, the poet's mother, in 1855.
Walt idealized her and persuaded
his friends to do the same. Library
of Congress.

Figure 4. The earliest known photograph shows Whitman the dandyish man about town. Early 1840s. He created a vivid impression, and William Cauldwell, a printer who worked in the building at 142 Nassau Street that housed the *New York Aurora*, a newspaper Whitman was editing, had no trouble recalling sixty years later that "he usually wore a frock coat and a high hat, carried a small cane, and the lapel on his coat was almost invariably ornamented with a boutonniere." Ed Folsom Collection.

Figure 5. Whitman the journalist in New Orleans, in 1848. He and his younger brother Jeff stayed only four months and were homesick, but Whitman used this experience to link erotic and racial themes in his emerging free-verse poems. Ed Folsom Collection.

Figure 6.   Whitman in
1854, when he was writing
the first edition of *Leaves
of Grass*. His Canadian
psychiatrist friend,
Dr. Richard Maurice
Bucke, later called this
photograph "the Christ
likeness." Ed Folsom
Collection.

Figure 7. The studiously insolent frontispiece for the 1855 *Leaves of Grass,* engraved by Samuel Hollyer after a daguerreotype made by Gabriel Harrison. In the eyes of many, there is a red flannel undershirt showing, and the hand-on-hip, hand-in-pocket pose contributes to the unconventional author's seductive allure. Charles E. Feinberg Collection.

Figure 8. The formal frontispiece for the 1860 *Leaves of Grass.* Steel engraving from an 1859 painting by Charles Hine. Dressed up and looking thoughtful but con-strained, Whitman was seeking to dispel the "rough," "queer person" image he had begun to inspire. Charles E. Fein-berg Collection.

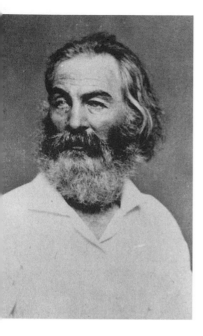

Figure 9.   The compassionate
Whitman during the Civil War,
in about 1862. A friend thought
he looked sorry for the world.
Photographed by Mathew
Brady in New York. Ed Folsom
Collection.

Figure 10.   Whitman and his
loving comrade Peter Doyle,
an Irish immigrant and former
Confederate soldier, in Washington, D.C., about 1869. They
met on a streetcar Pete was
driving, probably in the winter
of 1865–66. The charming but
uneducated workingman was
uncomfortable with Whitman's
intellectual friends and vice
versa. Charles E. Feinberg
Collection.

Figure 11. Whitman and his tempestuous "darling," Harry Stafford, a New Jersey farm boy, in the late 1870s. Whitman helped him to find employment, as he had apparently done for Fred Vaughan in the 1850s. There is no known photograph of Fred, a Broadway stagecoach driver who probably inspired some of the *Calamus* poems. During the flourish-years of his romance with Harry, to whom he gave a ring, Whitman was recovering from the depression that had been plaguing him since January 1873, when he suffered a paralytic stroke from which he never fully recovered. In the photograph, the cane in his hand is no longer decorative. A boarder at the Stafford farm, the poet enjoyed nude bathing in Timber Creek, and Harry's mother, Susan Stafford, pleasantly reminded him of his own. Edward Carpenter Collection, Sheffield (England) Archives.

Figure 12. Whitman in May 1891, the last year of his life, photographed by Samuel Murray. Library of Congress.

Figure 13. Whitman's two-story house on Mickle Street, Camden, New Jersey, the shortest on the block. He bought it in March 1884, called it his "shanty," and died there on March 26, 1892, at the age of seventy-two, surrounded by a group that included Horace Traubel, his biographer and friend. By permission New Jersey Division of Parks and Forestry, Walt Whitman House, Camden, New Jersey.

Faith in Sex

Leaves of Grass *in 1855–56*

Whitman's anxiety about "neuters and geldings" (*LG* 1855, p. 47) re-surfaces in the open letter he addressed to his patron Emerson in August 1856.[1] While calling for "that new moral American continent without which . . . the physical continent remain[s] incomplete, may-be a car-cass, a bloat," the poet advanced revolutionary claims for the "empow-ered, unabashed development of sex." "The courageous soul, for a year or two to come, may be proved by faith in sex," he wrote to Emerson, "and by disdaining concessions" (*LG*, p. 740). "Of course, we shall have a national character, an identity," he stated, and since he was consider-ing a lecture tour modeled after Emerson's lyceum lectures,[2] he prom-ised "to meet people and The States face to face, to confront them with an American rude tongue" (*LG*, pp. 732–33). Yet as he began to spec-ify his intentions, he expressed contempt for the "non-personality and indistinctness of modern productions," claimed that the present age was an anomaly, and reaffirmed what he called "common human attrib-utes." The recovery of sexual "facts" rather than the perpetuation of sexual fictions seemed to be his goal. But what were the facts and what were the fictions? For whom did he claim to be speaking? Was "sex" ex-clusively heterosexual? So it appeared, for he complained vehemently, "In the scanned lives of men and women most of them appear to have been for some time past of the neuter gender . . . In orthodox society to-day, if the dresses were changed, the men might easily pass for women and the women for men" (*LG*, pp. 739).

The lecture tour never happened, and it is not clear what Whitman would have said had he had the opportunity to confront the American people with a rude tongue. As we saw previously, rudeness was only one of his guises, and in this chapter I would like to look further at his use of the defamiliarized body as a symbol of democratic community. As described by Whitman in 1855–56, democratic sexual desire is only loosely bound to individuated personal relationships. I will therefore proceed to examine both "democratic" and "undemocratic" elements in the poems, which attempt to renegotiate traditions of literary authority for modern times.[3]

TWENTY-EIGHT YOUNG MEN

In an extended self-introduction in the 1855 poem "Song of Myself," Whitman issued a challenging invitation, in which he tried to use literature to demonize the category of the literary. That is, he set himself an impossible task.

> Have you reckoned a thousand acres much? Have you reckoned the earth
>   much?
> Have you practiced so long to learn to read?
> Have you felt so proud to get at the meaning of poems?
>
> Stop this day and night with me and you shall possess the origin of all
>   poems,
> You shall possess the good of the earth and sun. . . . there are millions of
>   suns left,
> You shall no longer take things at second or third hand. . . . nor look
>   through the eyes of the dead. . . . nor feed on the spectres in books,
> You shall not look through my eyes either, nor take things from me,
> You shall listen to all sides and filter them from yourself.
>
> I have heard what the talkers were talking. . . . the talk of the beginning
>   and the end,
> But I do not talk of the beginning or the end.
>
> There was never any more inception than there is now,
> Nor any more youth or age than there is now;
> And will never be any more perfection than there is now,
> Nor any more heaven or hell than there is now.
>
> Urge and urge and urge,
> Always the procreant urge of the world.
>
>   (LG 1855, p. 26)

In this exemplary passage, Whitman evidently rejects poetry as it had previously been written, othering it as insubstantial and elitist. *His* poetry was to affirm common human attributes, and to do so he would need to keep himself as a distinct individual out of the big picture. He thus continues,

> Out of the dimness opposite equals advance. . . . Always substance and
>   increase,
> Always a knit of identity. . . . always distinction. . . . always a breed of life.
>   (*LG* 1855, pp. 26–27)

The life of poetry emerges not just from identity and not just from distinction but from their mutual relationship to some as yet unnamed third figure. That third figure is the democratic poet as autobiographical presence. Neither identity nor distinction has priority in Whitman's sequence; neither identity nor distinction is real without the other. Ideally, the relationship of poet to reader defamiliarizes reading conventions based on authoritarian models of unity. Grounding his literary authority in gender archetypes that include masculine and feminine elements, Whitman wrote to Emerson, and to his own readers, "The mothers and fathers of whom modern centuries have come, have not existed for nothing; they too had brains and hearts." "Of course all literature, in all nations and years, will share marked attributes in common," he asserted, "as we all, of all ages, share the common human attributes." He added, confidently, "What is to be done is to withdraw from precedents" (*LG*, p. 735).

Romancing Emerson as "dear Friend and Master," Whitman did not resolve the tension between "distinction" and "the knit of identity" to which his poetry alludes. The project becomes clearer, however, once we take Whitman's family archetypes seriously as models for reading. "Have you ever loved a woman?" he asks provokingly in "I Sing the Body Electric." "Your mother. . . . is she living?. . . . Have you been much with her? and has she been much with you? / Do you not see that these are exactly the same to all in all nations and times all over the earth?" (*LG* 1855, p. 122). The last question in this loaded series is the giveaway. It is too extreme, and the "knit of identity" is less interesting than the "distinction."

"Wording the future" by showing "the true use of precedents" (*LG*, p. 740), Whitman angrily sought to *withdraw* from precedents. Though in Benedict Anderson's terms he was seeking to establish an "eroticized nationalism,"[4] and though in his own terms he was seeking to create a "new [sexual] Bible" (*NUPM* 1:353), as a poet who believed that he lacked intellectual authority (compared, say, to Homer or Shakespeare or Tennyson) he felt that the emotional power of his own distinct experi-

ence had to be important. We have seen that Whitman lived closer to la-
boring men than most other poets of his time. We have also seen that
Whitman distrusted his own body because it housed an emotionally vulnerable self. If "an American rude tongue" was to express his faith in
sex and the people, his poetry would suggest that the various kinds of
love and friendship he had experienced—including familial love—were
both sociable and socially isolating.

In the 1855 and 1856 *Leaves of Grass,* Whitman's populist "faith
in sex" revealed both the confidence and the confusion of a self seeking to redeem an ambivalent personal past. For despite the constancy
of his desire to sight that new moral American continent without which
the physical continent remained incomplete, may-be a carcass, a bloat,
in proliferating masculinities Whitman was unsure what precedents that
new moral American continent might sustain. And so, at his most anxious, he seemed to cram his notebooks and his poems with all words, to
be afraid of leaving any thing or person out. "Literature is full of perfumes," he noted, reminding himself that "I follow animals and birds"
(*NUPM* 1:79). And always the lists, looking for a new, purer, and more
unbroken language of love: "Breathjuice—Airscents—Airsmells—Air-
odor—Loveodor—Airdrifts—Breathsmoke—Airjuice for you—Air-
sough" (*NUPM* 1:195).

In earlier chapters, we observed that Whitman's critique of nervous-
ness about the body, sex, and gender emerged not only out of shrewd
readings of popular, mid-nineteenth-century American texts (as David S. Reynolds has described them), but also out of his specific experience of family, work, and friendship.[5] For example, though Whitman
never directly acknowledged that his early experience, including his
reading, inhibited his ability to feel unselfconsciously valued as a person
and for himself, he approaches such a confession through figural indirection in "There Was a Child Went Forth."[6] Moreover, as we have seen,
his early fiction provides a more detailed (though also screened) account
of his role in absorbing his original family's emotional burdens, specifically their inability to meet and fuse. His early fiction indicates that in
childhood and adolescence he felt called upon to assuage his mother's
loneliness, as he was to do quite consistently in later life: not only after
his father's death in 1855 and the marriage of his younger brother Jeff
in 1859, but much earlier on. Yet this fiction screens other emotional realities as well. During adolescence especially, Whitman felt that his own
inner realities had been insufficiently responded to by both of his parents. They had not, in his terms, "really absorb'd each other and under-

st[oo]d each other"; the "dividing line" was too deep; they had not "met and fused" (*SD* 797). Thus his revisionary poetics of the democratic and sexual body emerged first out of his own need for a new language of love, a need shaped by the various impediments he had encountered during his "long foreground," as son and brother, friend, worker and lover. These distinct experiences influenced his imagination of himself as public intellectual, rebounding from the political and economic uncertainties of the Jacksonian era to preach a new gospel of the body without fear, the expanding body politic and poetic, secure in its various "natural" appetites, whatever they might happen to be.[7]

As an autobiographical poet with an ambitious social mission, Whitman sought to describe a procreative community to which, in theory, anyone might belong. In 1855 and 1856, this community included men and women working together, as well as men working with and loving men, as well as self-loving men and self-loving women. That the health reformer and poet stigmatized "onanists" (*LG* 1855, p. 105), venerealees (*LG* 1855, p. 113), "roues" (*LG* 1855, p. 120), drunkards, and prurient romances is not necessarily inconsistent with my argument. Partly Whitman favored chastity in the sense of self-regulation, partly he tolerated prostitution. Partly he believed that not all could or would marry and that unmarried people such as himself were entitled to a sex life. Partly he understood that the familiar material body was always subject to silencing, not least by death; partly he believed that the more ghostly spiritual body might realize itself in unknown future spheres. Thus Whitman's attitude toward the defamiliarized body was inconsistent. He was fascinated by the "procreative" potential of the female womb, by the promiscuous power of the hot and sweaty male lover, the "truant" who could not be counted on for very long, and by the darkness he identified with a gentler third term, possibly someone of the neuter gender (*LG* 1855, p. 107). This mysterious figure was responding to a psychological emergency of ambiguous origin. He was "double," as was the Whitman who wrote of "my soul and I," who felt that he was leading both a familiar and an unfamiliar life, and who wanted the one to accommodate the other (*NUPM* 1:63). Both were necessary to his poetry, with its knit of identity, its distinctions, and its unprecedented "breed of life."

Both in and out of the game of love and watching and wondering at it, Whitman was influenced by his observations of family life, of the communities of work and friendship to which he had belonged, and of available languages of power. As I have been suggesting, he often translated these languages into family archetypes, which fail to accommodate his interest in the androgynous gender. For example, in the 1856 letter to Emerson, Whitman regroups the disparate (United) States for an imagined family portrait. "Up to the present," he explained,

> the people, like a lot of large boys, have no determined tastes, are quite unaware of the grandeur of themselves, of their destiny, and of their immense strides—accept with voracity whatever is presented them in novels, histories, newspapers, poems, schools, lectures, every thing. Pretty soon, through these and other means, their development makes the fibre that is capable of itself, and will assume determined tastes. The young men will be clear what they want, and will have it. They will follow none except him whose spirit leads them in the like spirit with themselves. Any such man will be welcome as the flowers of May. Others will be put out without ceremony. How much is there anyhow, to the young men of These States, in a parcel of helpless dandies, who can neither fight, work, shoot, ride, run, command—some of them devout, some quite insane, some castrated—all second-hand, or third, fourth, or fifth hand—waited upon by waiters, putting not this land first, but always other lands first, talking of art, doing the most ridiculous things for fear of being called ridiculous, smirking and skipping along, continually taking off their hats—no one behaving, dressing, writing, talking, loving, out of any natural and manly tastes of their own, but each one looking cautiously to see how the rest behave, dress, write, talk, love—pressing the noses of dead books upon themselves and upon their country—favoring no poets, philosophs, literats, here, but dog-like danglers at the heels of the poets, philosophs, literats, of enemies' lands. (*LG,* p. 737)

"Submit to the most robust bard till he remedy your barrenness," he counselled. "Then you will not need to adopt the heirs of others; you will have true heirs, begotten of yourself, blooded with your own blood" (*LG,* p. 734).

Ironically, as Whitman sought to democratize models of reading based on the hierarchical relationship of father to child, he found himself mimicking aggressions which in their threatening intensity he associated with the quick loud word of the authoritarian father ("strong, selfsufficient, manly, mean, angered, unjust" [*LG* 1855, p. 139]). He saw this irritable, obtuse, uncaring father everywhere: in the Congress, in the President's house, in the schools and churches, and in the phallogocentric traditions of an elitist Eurocentric literature which did not understand the first word of the true meaning of love. Turning to the American nation that, in his more pessimistic moods, he experienced as an unreal aggregation of immature individuals with whom he had nothing in common, Whitman emphasized the sacramental status of the human body: anyone's body, but most especially his own. Radically leveling distinctions between socially constructed types, his imagination carried him back to an aboriginal state in which the liquid might marry the solid, and he himself might be singled out for exceptional good fortune. In linking physical robustness and poetic authority, Whitman was determined to free himself from the disempowerments he associated with a morbid culture, with the shallowness of his friendships, and with his own uncertain (even to him) erotic history. Thus in the 1856 "Poem of The Sayers of The Words of The Earth," he commanded, exhorted, and complained,

> Accouche! Accouchez!
> Will you rot your own fruit in yourself there?
> Will you squat and stifle there?
>
> The earth does not argue,
> Is not pathetic, has no arrangements,
> Does not scream, haste, persuade, threaten, promise,
> Makes no discriminations, has no conceivable failures,
> Closes nothing, refuses nothing, shuts none out,
> Of all the powers, objects, states, it notifies, shuts none out.
>   (*LG* 1856, pp. 324–25)

Like the sudden eruption of the "strong, selfsufficient, manly, mean, angered, unjust" father who isolates the poet-hero in "There Was a Child Went Forth," this unexpected attack on the ambiguously sexed reader/ writer is the poem's emotional center. It resumes the personal and national family usages that have estranged Whitman from the model of serenity he seeks to emulate, as exemplified by the mythologized "eloquent dumb great mother" who "never fails" (*LG* 1856, p. 325). As a child, Whitman longed to be transported into another environment, in which the harsh line dividing person from person might suggest "contact, junction, the solid marrying the liquid—that curious, lurking something" (*SD* 796). As an adult, he wished to be shielded from the emotional stillbirths and psychological abortions produced by the disorder of his many and shortlived homes.

The outraged but also heartsore rhetoric quoted above is taken from the poem later called "Song of the Rolling Earth," which states flat out that "Human bodies are words" and that "I myself am a word" (*LG* 1856, pp. 322, 323). In textualizing the body, the poet seeks to reaffirm common human attributes. He also seeks to rob the specifically male body of its masterful social sting. "Were you thinking that those were the words—those delicious sounds out of your friends' mouths?" he taunts us. "No, the real words are more delicious than they" (p. 322). The drive

is evidently to reconfigure inner and outer realities so that the dangerous psychological elements may be expelled, or translated into a new
tongue. The poetry of 1855–56 enacts an incomplete drama of trans-
ference from one family to all families, from fathers (and brothers and
sisters) who are loved only by allowance to fathers (and brothers and sisters) who are loved by "personal love" (LG 1855, p. 118). Intermittently but powerfully, this poetry uses family relationships as the model
for nonfamilial male-homoerotic love.

Both as an antebellum American dissatisfied with his country, and as
an erotically curious man adrift with his globalized "Urge and urge and
urge, / Always the procreant urge of the world," in the first two editions
of Leaves of Grass the poet famously celebrated his own "live body"
(LG 1855, pp. 25, 123) rather than the historical, philosophical, or psychological consistency of his project. Dismissing sexual, familial, national, and literary precedents, he hoped "to cease not till death" but also
hoped not to cease as his bitterly disappointed and disappointing father
did in the very month in which the first Leaves of Grass was published.
Although America could be rhetorically reconfigured as an earth mother
who "does not withhold" and is "generous enough," the first two editions of Leaves of Grass mandate the death of the harshly critical father
who could not or would not quell the competing lusts by which his children were driven. In part, then, "faith in sex" is intended to displace a
more traditional fear of the avenging Father.

Powerfully repressing personal and national narratives of "[im]per-
fect health," in the 1855 Leaves of Grass Whitman sought to meld various discrete audiences into an emotionally unified, organically connected
interpretive community: a nation of nations. Living in what Benedict
Anderson reminds us was "a society fractured by the most violent racial,
class and regional antagonisms," [8] Whitman further repressed narratives
that perpetuated the association between manliness, individuation, and
aggression. Indeed, the Whitmanic speaker finds psychic wholeness
by surrendering to the "feminine" need to regress. These unifying, un-
aggressive regressions take many different forms, including the use of
the sexually transgressive body as "the origin of all poems" (LG 1855,
p. 26). For example, a potentially feminizing body-logic dominates the
opening of "Song of Myself." "Houses and rooms are full of perfumes,"
Whitman writes, "the shelves are crowded with perfumes, / I breathe the
fragrance myself, and know it and like it, / The distillation would intox-
icate me also, but I shall not let it" (LG 1855, p. 25). Poised here at the
start of his great career, the poet/speaker presents us with a multivalent

image which accrues meaning only in relation to what follows. These perfumes probably represent books or culture, in association with woman's sphere, the home, but this association is not subjected to close scrutiny, since Whitman's style, with its nervous profusion of images, tends to move us away from any particular scene or gender or erotic desire before we have had a chance to examine it fully.

In fact it might appear that these excessively crowded houses or rooms have no particular owner, and that in belonging to everyone, they belong to no one. Clearly, these spaces are not identified with a particular city or nation, and they would seem oppressively isolated from each other, were they not organized by a common symbolic language whose endpoint, absorption by the maternal night, is death. Though he claims to like this all-pervading, common language as much as the next person, the more highly individuated persona quickly escapes into the out of doors, where he finds a reason for being. That the persona is looking for some kind of authenticating love becomes clearer as we read on into the poem. "The atmosphere is not a perfume," he writes, "it has no taste of the distillation. . . . it is odorless, / It is for my mouth forever. . . . I am in love with it, / I will go to the bank by the wood and become undisguised and naked, / I am mad for it to be in contact with me" (*LG* 1855, p. 25).

In a number of important ways, this opening departure scene in "Song of Myself" anticipates the subsequent voyage and vision of the erotically deprived twenty-ninth bather who owns the "fine house by the rise of the bank" but who does not own herself. In each instance, lovemaking occurs in a pastoral setting which liberates both the Whitman persona and the twenty-ninth bather from a home-bound life. Both personae select fantasy lovers who are unaware of their presence, a point to which I will shortly return. In the opening scene, Whitman claims to be in love with the atmosphere; analogically, he implies the boundlessness of his love for human beings undifferentiated by gender. This claim is not fully persuasive; that is, he himself is not fully persuaded by it. Yet his unconventional lovemaking prepares him to violate other erotic taboos, for example the prohibition against anonymous, male-homoerotic sex. Thus in Section 11, the speaker/poet identifies with a woman who wants to make love with twenty-eight undifferentiated young men whom she has never met, whom she knows only through observation, and who are unaware of her presence. The speaker/poet authorizes her anonymous, indiscriminate lovemaking, while inviting readers to eavesdrop on her frustrations. "Which of the young men does she like the best?"

he inquires, "Ah the homeliest of them is beautiful to her." Because her desire is also his, has no independent life of its own, and serves as a screen for homoerotic pleasure, in fantasy he fuses his body with hers when he remarks on the multiply desirous "unseen hand" which passes over the bodies of the young men, descending "tremblingly from their temples and ribs" toward their genitals (*LG* 1855, p. 34). This hand may be hers, or his, or both. The nervous but also devotional caress he shares with this figure of his re-forming imagination suggests that Whitman does not intend to cast himself as either a man or a woman. Rather, he indicates that gender is a cultural imposition that art is bound to shrug off, sooner or later. In violating the bourgeois convention that love-making take place in the home among people who know each other—heterosexual marriage being the legitimating social structure—Whitman moves away from the norms of middle-class propriety into a more thoroughly anonymous and fantasy-ridden mode.

When the persona projects his desire onto such figures as the atmosphere, the magnetic nourishing night, and the coolbreathed earth, he successfully re-forms erotic encounters he may have had with particular men and women. The caressable young men of Section 11, for example, are shockingly unaware of the poet/lover's presence. Each unthinking individual is taken unawares, and each is part of a homogeneous group that is equally and unknowingly taken. The fantasy figures are all so friendly. Contrary to what we might expect, there is no enmity between them. Nor is conflict introduced by the speaker and his womanly persona, the twenty-ninth bather.[9] Here fantasy authorizes erotic cross-dressing and the speaker remains "the caresser of life wherever moving" (*LG* 1855, p. 35), a self-conception consistent with his belief that the American bard has nothing to do with special interests, including special sexual interests. As the caresser of life wherever moving, Whitman exposes what Michel Foucault has mockingly called Puritanism's "triple edict of taboo, nonexistence, and silence."[10] But his bathing scene also dramatizes the homoerotic poet's imposition of a further taboo, since male-male desire can be expressed only if depersonalized and negotiated through a female participant-observer. The twenty-eight young men "do not know . . . [and] they do not think." Were they to know and think, this scene would have a different outcome.

In the 1856 letter to Emerson and in the first two editions of *Leaves of Grass*, Whitman begins to claim same-sex desire only to disown it. Consider, for example, the curious dynamic in Section 32, where the speaker moves into his notable French mode, the English language being associated with the Puritanism of Foucault's tricky repressive hypothesis.[11] In this empowering homoerotic episode, the speaker and his "amie," a "gigantic beauty of a stallion," cavort briefly. Then the speaker abandons this exciting companion who is "fresh and responsive to [his] caresses," and we are perhaps not likely to ask why, since we can always assume that a horse is just a horse. But as symbol-readers, we see something else. At first choosing to go with the stallion "on brotherly terms," the speaker ends up feeling that he has exploited this potentially perfect mate, whose "well built limbs," "trembl[ing] with pleasure," recall the trembling unseen hand of Section 11. In the later episode, Whitman converts his fear of exploitation into an assertion of autonomy, but does not purge competition from his model of erotic exchange. "I but use you a moment and then I resign you stallion," he writes, "and do not need your paces, and outgallop them, / And myself as I stand or sit pass faster than you" (*LG* 1855, p. 56).

Though he has previously been tempted to turn and live with the animals because they are so placid and self-contained, the Whitman persona is unable to let go of civilization and its discontents. The animals whom he has observed, "sometimes half the day long," have always brought him magical tokens of himself, unlike the people he knows all too well, who lie awake in the dark, weeping not only for their sins but also for their worldly failures, including their failures to gratify the deeply inculcated mania for owning *things*. Escaping from the city into the country temporarily enables him to move out of this overly demanding, competitive mode, but return visits constitute an aberration. The restless "Song of Myself" persona rarely finds any scene worth lingering over, since he prefers erotic anonymity, for the reasons we have been considering. Adventures into which he enters avidly quickly reinscribe the speaker's need to be in control, as fears of exploitation coincide with fears of being exploited—even in male-homoerotic relationships that are later praised, in 1860, for their democratic potential.

Its wit notwithstanding—the horse-loving speaker describes himself as "not too exclusive"—Section 32 is an overdetermined example of the Whitman persona's inability to shrug off the intrusive, exploitative social structure by which his passional life has previously been marked. The speaker who earlier fancied himself "Stout as a horse, affectionate, haughty, electrical" (*LG* 1855, p. 27) prefers muscular men, but in 1855–56, all of his erotic relationships are represented as transitory. In "Song of Myself," for example, changes of scene express Whitman's need to abandon thoughts and feelings he cannot endure. He takes his leave of others, including his feminized "amie," before they can take their leave of him. *Leaves of Grass:* the title itself suggests departure. Or a backward glance o'er traveled roads. Or, as he called some of his poems later on, "Songs of Parting."

In Section 3 of "Song of Myself," the departure dynamic is temporarily reversed, when "a loving bedfellow sleeps at [his] side all night and close on the peep of the day, / And leaves for [him] baskets covered with white towels bulging the house with their plenty" (*LG* 1855, p. 27). Whitman compares this loving bedfellow to God, who symbolically impregnates him and leaves behind an exquisitely clean food-relic (something like a perfect baby, a perfect homoerotic memory, a perfect book). The speaker, however, is not unambivalently willing to accept this gift because of the psychological vulnerability with which it is associated. Gazing after his departing lover, the speaker's voice turns shrill and he accuses his hungering eyes of prolonging a desire his mind cannot understand. The rational alternative is to "forthwith cipher and show me to a cent, / Exactly the contents of one, and exactly the contents of two, and which is ahead?" Such impersonal exactitude reduces him to despair. This episode, then, defines the sleeping Whitman as an erotic victim and justifies the defensive structure that governs the poem. Abandoned by his beloved male muse, Whitman can only describe himself as "Both in and out of the game [of love], and watching and wondering at it" (*LG* 1855, p. 28).[12]

There's no point in loving an unreliable god, and I am suggesting that the traumatized speaker takes himself out of the game of love even when it appears that there are particular versions of this game he might win. However, the reality-testing in which he engages is limited, and he collapses "the real or fancied indifference of some man or woman I love." Probably Whitman means to suggest that when gender does not signify, neither does reality, by which he means history. But when the real determines which differences matter, he himself is not in love. Consequently, he concludes Section 24 with the lines, "Winds whose soft-tickling genitals rub against me it shall be you, / Broad muscular fields, branches of liveoak, loving lounger in my winding paths, it shall be you, / Hands I have taken, face I have kissed, mortal I have ever touched, it shall be you." Evidently none of these fantasy figures responds to him as a coherent person, and this imagination of a psychologically scattered self leads him to say, "I dote on myself. . . . there is that lot of me, and all so luscious," and then, "Each moment and whatever happens thrills me with joy" (*LG* 1855, p. 49).

Many of these imaginary interactions have a vaguely or explicitly sacramental quality, especially when the speaker is most thoroughly impregnated, as in the brief encounter in Section 3 with a lover who comes "As God," and in the longer lasting, soul-ful encounter in Section 5, which is introduced with the plea, "the other I am must not abase itself to you, / And you must not be abased to the other" (*LG* 1855, p. 28). These lines thematize Whitman's concern with exploitation and humiliation, even when he is alone. In general terms, the speaker is unable to realize himself; in more specific terms, he is unable to trust himself to other men.

In Section 3, for example, the rounded baskets that cause his "house" to bulge prefigure the abnormally swollen white bellies of the twenty-eight caressable young men in Section 11, a passage in which, as we have seen, male-male desire is subordinated to and constructed by the female gaze. In Section 5, as the persona finds himself seized by both the "hand" and the "spirit" of God, he represents this spirit as his own soul, which extorts nothing from him except the willingness to submit. As a consequence of this devotional compromise,

> Swiftly arose and spread around me the peace and joy and knowledge that
>   pass all the art and argument of the earth;
> And I know that the hand of God is the elderhand of my own,
> And I know that the spirit of God is the eldest brother of my own,
> And that all the men ever born are also my brothers. . . . and the women
>   my sisters and lovers,
> And that a kelson of the creation is love;
> And limitless are leaves stiff or drooping in the fields,
> And brown ants in the little wells beneath them,
> And mossy scabs of the wormfence, and heaped stones, and elder and
>   mullen and pokeweed.
>
> (LG 1855, p. 29)

But this feeling does not last. Feminization cannot be a permanent mode. The "neuter gender" is too threatening.

In "Song of Myself," physical intimacy does not often produce spiritual intimacy. This point is further emphasized by the triangulation of Section 11, in which the poet/speaker watches a desiring woman who watches the floating, bulging men; the mutuality of the gaze is frustrated, doubly frustrated. Just as the twenty-eight young men are completely unaware of being observed, let alone "seize[d] fast" by the woman's longing, so too the love-starved woman whom they "souse with spray" is completely unaware of the speaker who voyeuristically watches her. The anonymous mode prevails, as does unrealization.

Whitman locates the most fully visionary scene of sexual instruction early in the poem; the marriage of body and soul in Section 5 is never again so fully rendered. From a biographical perspective, one of the interesting features of this passage is its recuperation of the figure of the violent elder brother who rarely, if ever, enters into Whitman's descriptions of his youth but who uncannily reemerges at crucial moments in the poetry: both here and at the conclusion of "Passage to India," in which Whitman's image of a successful spiritual quest terminates as follows.

> Reckoning ahead O soul, when thou, the time achiev'd,
> The seas all cross'd, weather'd the capes, the voyage done,
> Surrounded, copest, frontest God, yieldest, the aim attain'd,
> As fill'd with friendship, love complete, the Elder Brother found,
> The Younger melts in fondness in his arms.
>
> (LG, pp. 419–20)

In writing these lines, which were much noticed by Hart Crane,[13] Whitman was probably not thinking specifically of his brother Jesse, who ran away to sea when Whitman was about the age of the confused adolescent in "The Sleepers." The "Sleepers" protagonist searches for his sexual identity on what he calls the "Pier out from the main" (LG 1855, p. 108), strangely imploring, "let me catch myself with you and stay. . . . I will not chafe you; / I feel ashamed to go naked about the world, / And am curious to know where my feet stand. . . . and what is this flooding me, childhood or manhood. . . . and the hunger that crosses the bridge between" (LG 1855, p. 108). These lines have never been effectively glossed, but we would do well to recall Whitman's curious suggestion in "Song of the Rolling Earth" that "Human bodies are words, myriads of words" and that "In the best poems re-appears the body, man's or woman's, well-shaped, natural, gay, / Every part able, active, receptive, without shame or the need of shame" (LG, p. 219). Looking to his shameful older brother Jesse as if to a missing pier/peer, Whitman needed to fold this overly passionate missing person back into his songs of the growth of his own emotional and other nature. That he should choose to do so directly in "Passage to India" and indirectly in Section 5 of "Song of Myself" suggests something of the power of the Elder Brother's hold on his imagination, early and late. Suffused with the songs of the second son, Jesse is re-presented as a composite psychological possibility rather than as a unique historical being. This troublesome brother's ghostly presence continues to inform the text, however, as Whitman piles up "mossy scabs of the wormfence, and heaped stones, and elder and mullen and pokeweed" in a brilliantly improvised ceremony which soothes and displaces the anger he continued to feel toward Jesse and which anticipates some of the underground torment of Robert Frost's "Home Burial," a homely pastoral Whitman would have admired.[14] "Elder." The elder brother. "Mullen." Rhymes with sullen. "Pokeweed."[15] The name is phallic, but is it playful or hostile or both? Though my dictionary tells me unequivocally that a worm fence is "a zigzag fence with each section consisting of usu. six to eight rails that interlock with the rails of adjacent sections and are supported by crossed poles—called also *snake fence, Virginia fence,*" the wormfence in this passage also signifies Whitman's interest in the death or decay of ego boundaries.[16] Do good fences make good neighbors? It's hard to tell. In the case of Jesse, whom Whitman subsequently committed to an insane asylum, without any obvious remorse, probably yes.

Following this astonishing but short-lived integration of body and soul, the speaker moves immediately into the extended meditation beginning, "A child said, What is the grass? fetching it to me with full hands" (*LG* 1855, p. 29), a meditation which circles around the themes of procreation and death. The child's apparently casual question unrepresses an attitude toward "nature" the speaker wants to investigate, and the ontological crisis subtly suggested by Section 5 becomes the main theme of Section 6. In dialogue with each other, Sections 5 and 6 underscore the persona's need to be reconciled to the hurtful father we encountered in "There Was a Child Went Forth," who propels the "fatherstuff at night" before inflicting other blows on his unsuspecting household intimates. The residual language of the soul stabilizes Whitman's faith in sex. Without access to this traditionally authoritative vocabulary, men may propel the fatherstuff at night, but they can never earn the trust of the child who asks, "What is the grass? fetching it to me with full hands." Though Whitman says that he cannot answer the child, he hopes to counteract the excesses of individualism by reanimating the "soul" of a democratic culture.

As a sexually and psychologically transformative figure not yet translated into anyone else's language, Whitman's "soul" is associated with traditional understandings of the Muse and with what we would now call the preconscious mind. This totemistic figure has the power to reconcile him to his experience of "the other I am," the self-in-society defined by its phantasmal, rather than its real and consequential existence. Sections 5 and 6 of "Song of Myself" thus reflect the visionary poet's uncanny ability to re-form himself as part of a crowd, whether that crowd be understood as an eternal religion, an eternal family, an eternal nation,

or an eternal profession. This, too, emerged out of his unhappy and restless youth. He learned that no one person could ever permanently define
or dominate any significant social undertaking: not his father, not his
brother Jesse, surely not his smiling sister Mary (only eighteen months
younger than he), and not even his hard-pressed mother, though if any
one might prevail, it was she. Still, the erotic vulnerabilities which were
his by temperament and by experience mandated the subsequent anonymity of his passional life. Just as in "There Was a Child Went Forth"
the Whitman persona suggests that he cares for and understands the
people he loves much more deeply than they care for or understand him,
so Whitman felt. He said as much to Horace Traubel late in life and he
indicates as much in the passages we have been reading. Early on, he experienced a loss of passional identity at home, which continued to plague
him during his youth and early manhood. *Leaves of Grass,* which he often described as his child, was an inspired attempt to recuperate this
loss. Its birth was accelerated, as Paul Zweig has suggested, first by his
father's social eclipse, which was empowering for Whitman, and then by
his father's lengthy dying.[17] Small wonder that Whitman always exaggerated the degree to which he was ignored by the critics and that he
tried to block comparisons with other writers by exaggerating his ignorance of literary conventions. Given that the project originated in the
traumas and rivalries of his youth, family-obsessed traumas and rivalries not assuaged, and in some instances intensified, by his subsequent
"quickbroken" relationships (*LG* 1855, p. 139), Whitman turned to his
readers for continuing affirmation of his identity. If readers could understand and accept him, they could undo the blindness of the patriarchal gaze.

This was Whitman's erotic double bind: he wanted to be understood
but he was afraid of being understood. He had been conditioned to relative anonymity at home during his childhood and youth and he perpetuated this relative anonymity as an adult lover.[18] Inconstant in his affections, quick to anger and despair, for Whitman the important issues
were connection and control. Cultural prohibitions against male-male
physical intimacy may explain some of his anxiety, but Whitman makes
the more general point, even in his 1860 *Calamus* poems, that men and
women living in a generationally fragmented culture will need to fight
against their depersonalization as lovers. Thus at that moment in "Song
of Myself" when a child turns to the speaker, inquiring "What is the
grass?" the fullness of the poet's response is therapeutically telling. His
willingness to admit what he doesn't know makes him the perfect con-

fidant; the child who asks this question is affirmed by a nurturing textual environment in which skepticism is tolerated, vulnerability shared. Unfortunately, the Whitman family never developed a narrative to explain itself to itself; the experience of the family remained to a significant degree unspoken and beyond comprehension except that, in Christopher Bollas's terms, Whitman made it his life work to remember for others.[19] In his struggle to celebrate vulnerability as well as strength, the poet provides a powerful critique of the feeling "the body gives the mind / of having missed something."[20] Ambivalently positioned in relation to the multiple narratives, spoken and unspoken, which had informed his early life, he remained unsure of what that unifying something was. In attempting to reintegrate a social self always threatening to break down into its acutely autonomous parts, Whitman turned toward his own body as an object of desire, listening to its rippling echoes and buzzed whispers, exploring the multiple uses of its loveroot, silkthread, crotch and vine. Disappointed in his early quest for loving comprehension, he rewrote the story of those disappointments as a song of his faith in sex, and in so doing resisted the melancholy tide that had submerged his father and driven his elder brother from home. Throughout the first two editions of *Leaves of Grass,* Whitman is searching for those profoundly re-membering feelings the body gives the mind and the mind gives the body of having *found* something. That something, he insisted, was himself, loving himself body and soul and waiting for "you" to do the same.

THE FLESH AND THE APPETITES

Through poetry, Whitman entered into a psychologically restorative lyric world in which scenes of erotic initiation could be reconfigured. In this lyric utopia, "the smoke of my own breath" is a sufficient origin, whereas in the tobacco-stained, working world of taverns and farms and houses with which Walter Senior had actually been associated, any workingman's control of his body (and by extension of his social role) had been very limited indeed. Although estrangement between fathers and sons was a common fate in Jacksonian and post-Jacksonian America, Whitman felt it more than most. Ideally, his faith in sex linked him to the past, as well as the future, and he hoped that his poetry of the flesh and the appetites would not betray its domestic, working-class roots.

As the antebellum Whitman resisted the power of the genteel literary classes to shape his professional life, he tirelessly promoted his books, carefully controlling the circumstances of their production and publishing the first two editions of *Leaves of Grass* himself. During this time he frequented Pfaff's, the artsy beer cellar he visited with physicians from the New York Hospital and where he met such friends as Henry Clapp, who as editor of the *Saturday Press* was to help Whitman secure a publisher for his 1860 volume. Pfaff's was one of the places Whitman took his musical brother Jeff, as well as such young, working-class friends as Fred Vaughan, the stage driver to whom he was much attached. So far as we know, however, Whitman's personal and professional correspondence in 1855–57 was extremely limited. Whereas Emily Dickinson, for example, is known to have shared poems-in-progress with her sister-in-law Susan Gilbert Dickinson and to have rewritten at least one of them in response to Sue's criticism,[21] Whitman did not usually share unpublished poems with his intimates, either through the mails or in person. The "passionate friendliness" he described in the 1856 open letter to Emerson did not extend that far (*LG*, p. 741).

The following atypical episode, then, is worth pausing over. It sheds further light on Whitman's sense of "democratic" audience. In 1858, Whitman brought the manuscript of "Out of the Cradle Endlessly Rocking" to an admiring and unconventional domestic circle dominated by Abby Hills Price, a radical feminist reformer whom he had met through a mutual friend in 1856. Abby shared many of Walt's political values, as Ellen O'Connor and Anne Gilchrist were later to do, and her Brooklyn home provided a restful and stimulating alternative to his own. Although he was not eager to be lionized and resisted Abby's attempts to show him off to her guests, he made an exception for George B. Arnold, a former Unitarian minister who dabbled in spiritualism and who lived in the other part of the house. Thus, on the day when Whitman shared the new poem Abby had coaxed him into bringing along, no outsiders were present. (Abby's husband was a self-effacing businessman who seems to have played no part in their teas.) Diffidently, Whitman insisted that Abby and Arnold each read the poem aloud before he agreed to do so himself. When the three readings were over, the poet turned to Abby Price, then to Arnold, then to Abby's astonished teenage daughter Helen, asking each one of them what they would suggest "in any way." Whitman, who preferred Abby's reading, had already mentioned that the poem was based on a "real incident," but he did not tell them what it was.[22] Even with an intelligent and admiring private audience he trusted, Whitman felt the need to conceal the poem's occasion.

Those assembled probably sensed that his verse, which was "all about a mocking bird," was also, at several removes, all about romantic frustration. And in the early days of their acquaintance, Abby Price dared to ask Walt directly whether he had ever been in love. According to her observant daughter Helen,

> After a long pause he answered somewhat reluctantly, I thought, "Your question, Abby, *stirs a fellow up.*" Although he would not admit that he had ever been "really in love," he took from his pocket a photograph of a very beautiful girl (remember, he was still in his thirties) and showed it to us. That is all we ever knew about the original of the picture either then or afterwards, but I well remember the girl's exceptional beauty.[23]

On yet another occasion, when, as Helen Price recalled, the assembled group was talking about friendship,

> [he] said that there was a wonderful depth of meaning ("at second or third removes," as he called it) in the old tales of mythology. In that of Cupid and Psyche, for instance; it meant to him that the ardent expression in words of affection often tended to destroy affection. It was like the golden fruit which turned to ashes upon being grasped, or even touched. As an illustration, he mentioned the case of a young man he was in the habit of meeting every morning where he went to work. He said there had grown up between them a delightful, silent friendship and sympathy. But one morning when he went as usual to the office, the young man came forward, shook him violently by the hand, and expressed in heated language the affection he felt for him. Mr. Whitman said that all the subtle charm of their unspoken friendship was from that time gone.[24]

Despite the poet's personal reticence with George B. Arnold and the Prices, there is a correspondence that takes us further into the talk about friendship in which Whitman was participating during these extraordinary times. For in March 1860, while he was in Boston seeing the third edition of *Leaves of Grass* through the press, the poet offered to send his young stage-driver friend Fred Vaughan some proof sheets in advance of publication. More than any other single gesture, this "kind offer," as Vaughan called it, indicates the seriousness of Whitman's attachment to him. While Whitman was in Boston, Vaughan heard Emerson lecture on manners and touch on the theme of friendship. According to Vaughan, Emerson said that "a man whose heart was filled with a warm, ever enduring *not to be shaken by anything* Friendship was one to be set on one side apart from other men, and almost to be worshipped as a saint."[25] "There Walt," he wrote,

> how do you like that? What do you think of them setting you & myself, and one or two others we know up in some public place, with an immense plac-

ard on our breast, reading *Sincere Freinds! ! !* Good doctrine that but I think
the theory preferable to the practice.

The friendship between Whitman and Vaughan did not survive the various pressures—Vaughan's marriage, Whitman's move to Washington—
to which it was subjected, but Vaughan's distinction between the theory
and practice of friendship seems crucial. Apparently Whitman later felt
that he had crossed some boundary with Fred or that Fred had crossed
some boundary with him, for when he was at a crisis point in his relationship with Peter Doyle in 1870, he cautioned himself to remember
Fred (*NUPM* 2:890). All we can know for certain is that in *Leaves of
Grass* in 1855 and 1856, Whitman was still working to divest himself of
loyalties to any personal audience that might narrow his poetic range,
impede his well-publicized love affair with himself, or constrain his aggressive courtship of his country. Most consistently, he wanted to present himself as an American original who was not *too* original. How this
desire played out in terms of his evolving and re-forming faith in sexualities rather than in "sex" remains to be considered.

If Whitman's body defines him in the 1855 and 1856 *Leaves of Grass,*
his body, like the American landscape with which it is associated, is not
a constant signifier on whose continuity of meaning either he or we can
count. For example, he cannot depend on its gendered stability. Whereas
male gender is usually defined in terms of erotic choice, there are numer-
ous scenes in the 1855 *Leaves* that undo that choice: to name but one,
the ride with the sexy stallion. In the 1856 volume, as Whitman introduced a more direct vocabulary of male-homoerotic desire, he also gendered himself more emphatically, and it was this latter project that provoked the most contemporary indignation. When he wrote "A woman
waits for me—she contains all, nothing is lacking, / Yet all were lacking,
if sex were lacking, or if the moisture of the right man were lacking"
(*LG* 1856, p. 240), his contemporary audience was not pleased. Even if
some of Whitman's avant-garde allies enjoyed his scandalousness, ordinary American readers were intent on maintaining a sex/gender system
which was emotionally familiar. We may wonder whether Whitman intended to satirize misogynist sexual norms, but he paid a high price for
his uncensored speech.

Even before the 1855 *Leaves* had been published and reviewed, Whitman was well aware that he was asking readers to reexamine their own
sexual values and that this challenge was likely to provoke a literary scan-
dal. After all, when he described his robustly masculine poet in the 1855

"Preface," Whitman placed him "where the future becomes present," glowing a moment "on the extremest verge." But this same virile poet is "most wonderful in his last half-hidden smile or frown." "By that flash of the moment of parting," Whitman contended aggressively, "the one that sees it shall be encouraged or terrified afterwards for many years" (*LG* 1855, p. 12). Should the poet transgress the gender boundary that links him to his equally bounded audience in the present? Whitman was inconsistent on this point, but he knew full well that to challenge an audience *was* thrilling and frightening. He himself had found it so.

During the 1850s, Whitman's attempts to dismantle a binary sex/gender system and to embody male-homoerotic theories and practices were empowered and constrained by the response of his friends to the risks he was taking. For example, his project was defined by an idealizing discourse of the soul about which he professed not to be curious but which he was reluctant to abandon. The relationship between body and soul was one of the topics he discussed in 1856–57 with George B. Arnold, Abby Price's spiritualist friend, and in 1857 he told a Dutch Reformed minister who admired his poetry that he had "perfect faith in all sects, and was not inclined to reject one single one" (*Corr* 1:43). This rejection of religious orthodoxy was compatible with Whitman's vision of an inclusive rather than an exclusive audience for his poetry and with his purported indifference to conventional forms. Be that as it may, friends such as Fred Vaughan, whom Whitman romanticized in the poetry as "roughs," were in fact deeply concerned with keeping up appearances. Because of Fred's importance as a representative of Whitman's personal audience during the 1850s, I would like to return to his 1860 letters to Whitman, which include allusions to religion and to money.

Laughingly, Fred described himself and Walt as freethinkers, but when angered by Walt's sluggard manners as a correspondent, he wrote impulsively, "What the devil is the matter," a phrase that echoes Whitman's language to Abraham Paul Leech some twenty years earlier. When filled with the sentiments of a sincere friend, Fred exclaimed, "I hope to God it [the 1860 *Leaves*] may be not only a success as regards its typography, appearance and real worth, but also pecuniarily a success." When Vaughan criticized Emerson's delivery of the "Manners" lecture as strained, hesitating, and repetitious, he noted that Emerson had spoken in Father Chapin's church, a statement suggesting that Fred already knew the minister and that Walt would recognize his name.[26] When Vaughan humorously described himself as "under the *painful* necessity of telling a lie to keep up [Whitman's] reputation," he demonstrated his ability to manipulate the moralistic vocabulary in which he had been instructed. And when Vaughan quoted poetry to Whitman, this is what he wrote: "A well filled pocket, now & then, is relished by the best of men." Vaughan was apparently Whitman's romantic obsession of the mid-1850s. If he believed in the flesh and the appetites, he also believed in hard work and its ability to produce results. Fred hoped to prove his father wrong. (His father had accused him of being lazy, but his mother denied it.) Although Fred felt that he had disappointed both his father and mother, to say nothing of himself, he was identified with the poet who had justified Louisa's faith in his work. "I used to tell your Mother you was lazy and she denied it," Fred wrote. He subsequently remembered that Emerson had refused to lend Whitman money, pleading *"impecuniosity."* [27] This solicitation probably occurred in 1857, when Walt was in debt and before he returned to a full-time editorial position. In short, Fred could not afford to ignore the moral boundaries maintained by the people who employed him, and it is possible that Walt himself employed Fred when he was editor of the *Brooklyn Daily Times* in 1857–59. [28]

Small wonder, then, that the Whitman who wanted poetry to express the flesh and the appetites also wanted *his* poetry to exhibit caution. Fred and people like him were an important part of the audience Whitman cared about, the audience that influenced his sense of social mission. In "Crossing Brooklyn Ferry," the major new poem of the 1856 volume, Whitman asks whether it is possible to live fully in one's time and body while maintaining a purchase on the future. Together, Vaughan and Whitman traveled the ferry route many times. When Whitman accuses himself of erotic cowardice in the poem's most memorable passage, he suggests that his ability to sublimate desire links him to readers yet unborn: to you and me. Although Whitman also subverts this line of argument, as we might expect, the Vaughan who later described himself as "now cursing now praying" was more impulsive than the Whitman who expressed male-homoerotic desire at several removes in verse. Vaughan's later life was filled with tragedy. [29] In the 1850s, however, he was hoping to rise in the world and he was hoping that Whitman would help him do it. Fred genuinely *wanted* the 1860 *Leaves of Grass* to be a financial success. Here, then, is a nice irony. Vaughan, whom Whitman could romanticize as a "rough," was deeply conflicted about the "seize the day" undercurrent in "Crossing Brooklyn Ferry," the poem he or someone like him helped to inspire. By 1862, when he was desperate to have Whitman attend his wedding, Whitman would have been the only guest. Did Whitman support him in yet another hour of chronic need? Was this why Whitman cautioned himself in 1870 to remember Fred Vaughan? Was Fred Vaughan his prime example of someone he had already helped too much and who had become an overly demanding friend and lover?

During the 1850s, Whitman's immediate personal audience included Fred Vaughan and people like him, whose imagination of the future was sharply bounded by the material limitations of the present. The Whitman persona, however, has a more fluid relationship to the present and to his own body, which is seemingly as variable as the words he uses to describe it. Depending on relational context, Whitman seeks to become more or less embodied, to have a more or less historically situated social identity, and to have a more or less individuated sense of himself as a person not inscribed by language within the post-oedipal symbolic order. For example, at the conclusion of "Song of Myself" the speaker tries out the idea that he can outwit death by escaping from his body. Identifying himself with his poem, he imagines that his poem's ending signals his death, voice and life being coequal and coterminous. Working his way around this unfortunate coincidence—for poems *do* need to end, whereas desire is fantasized as immortal—Whitman claims to shed his body, to effuse his flesh "in eddies and drift it in lacy jags." "If you want me again look for me under your bootsoles," the materially decomposing persona explains, anticipating that moment in Dickinson's "I felt a Funeral, in my Brain" when mourners "creak across [her] Soul / With those same Boots of Lead, again." [30] The effect in Whitman, however, is very different; he feels affirmed, rather than imposed upon, by the loss of corporeal, emotional, and intellectual identity, since he imagines a rebirth into some larger All. Once the speaker sheds his body, which is conceived as a social limit, his problems of longing and belonging disappear. Whitman hints, however, that these problems will recur, for "I stop some where, waiting for you." [31]

Dying authenticates Whitman's claim, announced at the poem's inception, that "Every atom belonging to me as good belongs to you" (*LG* 1855, p. 25). Atomized into his component parts, he shares in a universalized, ungendered identity to which everyone and everything potentially belongs. In seeking to divest himself of the ideologically marked male body, Whitman aimed to liberate himself from the culturally produced, discursively constructed masculinity that it symbolized. Thus if Dickinson was afraid to own a female body because femininity could be read as a grotesque divergence from a masculinized norm, Whitman could represent freedom from the fate of gendered identity as an escape from time and history. To escape from a unique body might be to step out from behind a screen, to enter a more authentically human sphere. As he announced in the poem "So Long!" which concluded the 1860 volume,

> Camerado, this is no book,
> Who touches this touches a man,
> (Is it night? are we here together alone?)
> It is I you hold and who holds you,
> I spring from the pages into your arms—decease calls me forth.
>
> $\qquad\qquad\qquad\qquad\qquad$ (*LG*, p. 505)[32]

Just as a "camerado" does not correspond to a word found in any dictionary, a man who is a book is no longer defined by the corporeal limitations of his sex. Equally, a living book or a living imagination is no longer confined by literary convention. In *Leaves of Grass*, collapsing the distinction between life and death can encourage other minglings. That is why "To die is different from what any one supposed, and luckier" (*LG* 1855, p. 30).

The pattern of symbolic death and rebirth I have been tracing in Whitman as in Dickinson indicates the need urgently felt by both poets to forge new ways of being in the world. To the extent, however, that Whitman's project depended on his desire to actualize himself in an immediate human community, there was little future for him in disembodiment. More often than not, he suggests that "the supernatural [is] of no account" and that the imagined loss of corporeal presence does not facilitate "perpetual transfers and promotions" (*LG* 1855, pp. 72, 84). Here we move further into one of the more curious features of Whitman's project: his protestations against technologies of the book that supposedly prevented him from fulfilling his promise of unmediated presence. Let us recall that Whitman served as his own publisher for the 1855 volume, setting some ten pages of the book's type himself. On the first page of the first untitled poem, addressing readers and his ungendered "soul" as one, he moved somewhat abruptly to dissolve the cultural identity that he associated with strangely anxious mappings of the male body. Heartbeat, breath, music, speech, and nonhuman sounds originating in nature provided him with models of erotic and authorial authenticity. These models, like the belched words of his own voice loosed to the eddies of the wind, could not be constrained within existing literary convention. Seeking to undo the constitutive oppositions embedded in the undemocratic language of his culture, at the personal level Whitman was looking for the kind of unoppositional relationship that, as he said, was not in any previously published book. The problem was how to include it in *his* book. Allusions to sexual intercourse were one solution.

Thus at the start of the second poem in his 1855 sequence of twelve, the poet of "Song of Myself" issued a curious invitation to readers whose own need for democratizing "contact" might be almost as great as his own:

> Come closer to me,
> Push close my lovers and take the best I possess,
> Yield closer and closer and give me the best you possess.
>
> This is unfinished business with me. . . . how is it with you?
> I was chilled with the cold types and cylinder and wet paper between us.
>
> I pass so poorly with paper and types. . . . I must pass with the contact of
>   bodies and souls.
>
> I do not thank you for liking me as I am, and liking the touch of me
>   . . . . I know that it is good for you to do so.
>
> (*LG* 1855, p. 87)

As Ezra Greenspan points out in *Walt Whitman and the American Reader,* "A more cautious Whitman would later remove these lines from the poem, but in 1855, his fervor far outpaced his common sense."[33] This is a shrewd observation, and as Greenspan further notes, Whitman was pursuing more than one kind of "unfinished business" in protesting against paper and types. Seeking to alert us to the relationship between typecasting, in the modern sense of stereotyping, and the institutions of authorship, Whitman attacked idealized traditions of reading, hoping to clear the deck of impossible types, who falsely model what we, as a society, are and can be. "Because you are greasy or pimpled—or that you was once drunk, or a thief, or diseased, or rheumatic, or a prostitute—or are so now—or from frivolity or impotence—or that you are no scholar, and never saw your name in print. . . . do you give in that you are any less immortal?" (*LG* 1855, p. 88). These are the perfectible people Whitman includes in his democratic community of readers, whereas other authors leave them out.[34]

We are nevertheless dealing with "a large poet's large inconsistencies."[35] In "A Song for Occupations," Whitman offers to restore other people's false and fractured lives to an originary wholeness, as he did in "Song of Myself." But in this later, more pressured narrative, Whitman's anxiety about his ability to re-form literary and social convention is more apparent, and he is not content with suggesting that he would like

to have sexual contact with readers, whoever they are. "If you have become degraded or ill," he writes, "then I will become so for your sake."
In relieving others of their personal burdens, he also offers to substitute
himself for the reader's "lover or husband or wife." "If your lover or
husband or wife is welcome by day or night," he suggests, "I must be
personally as welcome." The trope of turning husbands out of bed was
part of the nineteenth-century women's friendship tradition, but the coerciveness of Whitman's "must" is jarring. Erotic coerciveness, however,
emerges out of a sociohistoric context in which the male friendship tradition as Whitman understands it is underdeveloped. "If you meet some
stranger in the street and love him or her, do I not often meet strangers
in the street and love them?" he asks (*LG* 1855, p. 88). In "Occupations,"
these street meetings do not lead anywhere; they are the product of a society in which art has no social function and the poet's imagination of
social intimacy is correspondingly impoverished.

M. Wynn Thomas has argued that "the loss of the conception of the
complete human being is what Whitman vehemently charges his society
with," and that "what Whitman encourages, therefore, is the carrying
of preoccupations that characterize private life into the wider public domain." [36] Carrying over those preoccupations involves perpetuating pains
as well as pleasures, and we have seen that there was no unwounded private life to which Whitman could unambivalently appeal.[37] Emerging
from the poem, he felt that his was a thankless task. He had been unable
to find his true occupation in fantasies of sexual closeness with other
people's lovers or husbands and wives. He needed someone of his own
and feared that he was prostituting his talent. As he explained harshly
in another self-review, "If health were not his distinguishing attribute,
this poet would be the very harlot of persons" (*CH* 39–40).

Protesting any barrier to intimacy with readers whom he was trying
to imagine as perfectly responsive to his desires, Whitman took on the
transparent identity of "the largest lover and sympathizer that has appeared in literature" (*CH* 39). But this was a phantasmal existence, in
which the poet experienced himself as a "gigantic embryo or skeleton of
Personality" (*Corr* 1:246). Singing the flesh and its appetites, he warily
underscored his physical and emotional remoteness from the very readers on whom he was depending for identity. "My final merit I refuse
you," he announced firmly, "I refuse putting from me the best I am. / Encompass worlds but never try to encompass me, / I crowd your noisiest
talk by looking toward you. / Writing and talk do not prove me, / I carry

the plenum of proof and every thing else in my face, / With the hush of my lips I confound the topmost skeptic" (*LG* 1855, p. 51).

As Tenney Nathanson has suggested, "It would clearly be illegitimate to treat biographical material, in the particular form of Whitman's personal anxieties, as the exclusive determinants of the poet's presence. But we can point to such material as one crucial source of *Leaves of Grass*."[38] We can never understand all of those personal relationships that produced either Whitman's "faith in sex" or the anger he expresses toward the audience addressed within the 1855 and 1856 poems. It is nevertheless worth remarking (as Paul Zweig has beautifully done) that even before Walter Whitman Senior's death in July 1855, Walter Whitman, Junior, was functioning in all but name as the head of his family— together, of course, with his mother. In some ways, Whitman's role as surrogate father and, by extension, surrogate husband was inconsistent with his role as emerging poet; in other ways, the psychological pressures attendant on this role intensified his quest for an ampler life of his own. As Whitman began to impersonate his working-class father in his persona as working-class poet, the impersonation re-created not the father he had known, but the father he wished he had known, who could authorize

> Words of approval, admiration, friendship. This is to be said among the young men of These States, that with a wonderful tenacity of friendship, and passionate fondness for their friends, and always a manly readiness to make friends, they yet have remarkably few words of names for the friendly sentiments.—They seem to be words that do not thrive here among the muscular classes, where the real quality of friendship is always freely to be found.— Also, they are words which the muscular classes, the young men of these states, rarely use, and have an aversion for;—they never give words to their most ardent friendships.[39]

It is also worth remarking that Whitman's younger brother Jeff, whom he took to New Orleans, and whom he described to Traubel as his only "real brother" and "understander" (*WWWC* 3:541), had begun to seek an ampler life of his own.[40] Jeff turned twenty-three in July 1855, and while still sharing many of Walt's enthusiasms, including the Italian opera, he too associated music, vocalism, and love.[41] We do not know when Jeff began to court Martha Mitchell (Mattie), whom he married in February 1859 and whom he then brought to live in the Whitman home on Classon Avenue, but Jeff and Mattie were engaged for several years before their marriage.[42] Afterwards, Jeff continued to interest himself in Walt's career and, inspired by Walt, the young couple named their first child "Manahatta." Walt, however, was no longer as important to this only "real brother" as he once had been.[43]

Whether or not Whitman's sense of social isolation was intensified by Jeff's marriage, his hunger for words of "approval, admiration, friendship" had certainly preceded it. An exclusively domestic audience could never satisfy him; his ambitions had always been larger. "The pay on Saturday night," he wrote in the 1855 "Song for Occupations," "the going home, and the purchases; / In them the heft of the heaviest. . . . in them far more than you estimated, and far less also, / In them, not yourself" (LG 1855, p. 96). Whitman's nighttime excursions to New York provided one avenue of escape from the "not yourself," from the potentially depressing domestic pressures to contribute and conform. So too did visiting hospitals, walking in the city, opera-going, reading, and writing poetry, praised by Emerson for its originality, in which he promised to offer "no representative of value—but [to] offer the value itself" (LG 1855, p. 89).[44]

As he successfully defended himself against the merger of his personality into the limiting occupations of the Whitman family, the "friendly" poet hoped to see infinite possibilities in ordinary men and women and in himself. "This is what you shall do," he wrote in the 1855 "Preface" to Leaves of Grass, "Love the earth and sun and the animals, despise riches, give alms to every one that asks, stand up for the stupid and crazy, devote your income and labor to others, hate tyrants, argue not concerning God, have patience and indulgence toward the people, take off your hat to nothing known or unknown or to any man or number of men, go freely with powerful uneducated persons and with the young and with the mothers of families" (LG 1855, pp. 10–11). The pressure is palpable, the solution absurd. In the following year, Whitman continued to renegotiate his strained relations with "the muscular classes," and with the well-to-do. Thus in The Eighteenth Presidency! he addressed himself "To Editors of the Independent Press, and To Rich Persons":

> Circulate and reprint this Voice of mine for the workingmen's sake. I hereby permit and invite any rich person, anywhere, to stereotype it, or re-produce it in any form, to deluge the cities of The States with it, North, South, East and West. It is those millions of mechanics you want; the writers, thinkers, learned and benevolent persons, merchants, are already secured almost to a man. But the great masses of the mechanics, and a large portion of the farmers, are unsettled, hardly know whom to vote for, or whom to believe. I am not afraid to say that among them I seek to initiate my name, Walt Whitman, and that I shall in future have much to say to them. I perceive that the best thoughts they have wait unspoken, impatient to be put in shape; also that

the character, power, pride, friendship, conscience of America have yet to be proved to the remainder of the world.[45]

The pamphlet was never published, James Buchanan was elected, and the "government sublime" Whitman hoped to inaugurate remained a distant dream.

Seeking to free himself and his country from economic tyranny and political confusion, Whitman insisted that good feelings could be inspired by "A few light kisses. . . . a few embraces. . . . a reaching around of arms, / The play of shine and shade on the trees as the supple boughs wag, / The delight alone or in the rush of the streets, or along the fields and hillsides, / The feeling of health. . . . the full-noon trill. . . . the song of me rising from bed and meeting the sun" (*LG* 1855, p. 26). Such feelings could not be purchased. Nor could even more powerful sexual feelings be predetermined, disciplined, or contained. "The words of *the Body!*" he wrote, "The words of Parentage! The words of Husband and Wife. The words of Offspring! The word Mother! The word Father!" (*Primer* 4). Then, further on, "The blank left by words wanted, but unsupplied, has sometimes an unnamably putrid cadaverous meaning. It talks louder than tongues. What a stinging taste is left in that literature and conversation where have not yet been served up by resistless consent, words to be freely used in books, rooms, at table, any where, to specifically mean the act male and female" (*Primer* 20).

> Likely there are other words wanted.— Of words wanted, the matter is summed up in this: When the time comes for them to represent any thing or any state of things, the words will surely follow. The lack of any words, I say again, is as historical as the existence of words. As for me, I feel a hundred realities, clearly determined in me, that words are not yet formed to represent. Men like me—also women, our counterparts, perfectly equal—will gradually get to be more and more numerous—perhaps swiftly, in shoals; then the words will also follow, in shoals.—It is the glory and superb rose-hue of the English language, any where, that it favors growth as the skin does—that it can soon become, wherever that is needed, the tough skin of a superior man or woman. (*Primer* 21)

Toughened by words, whose therapeutic force he freely acknowledges, Whitman traced the origin of sexual feelings back to childhood; linking sexual frankness and moral courage, he sought to attribute his book's self-declared healthy-mindedness to his physical and spiritual intimacy with his mother, with mothers in general, with children, and with everything humble, inarticulate, and unformed. "The little one sleeps in its cradle," he wrote perfectly unobtrusively, "I lift the gauze

and look a long time, and silently brush away flies with my hand" (*LG*
1855, p. 31). "On women fit for conception I start bigger and nimbler
babes," he wrote jocularly, "This day I am jetting the stuff of far more
arrogant republics" (*LG* 1855, p. 71). And, magically, this:

> Tenderly will I use you curling grass,
> It may be you transpire from the breasts of young men,
> It may be if I had known them I would have loved them;
> It may be you are from old people and from women, and from offspring
>   taken soon out of their mothers' laps,
> And here you are the mothers' laps.
>
> This grass is very dark to be from the white heads of old mothers,
> Darker than the colorless beards of old men,
> Dark to come from under the faint red roofs of mouths.
>
> O I perceive after all so many uttering tongues!
> And I perceive they do not come from the roofs of mouths for nothing.
>   (*LG* 1855, p. 30)

As Whitman tracked the career of a blade of grass from the hands of
a child into the realm of pure symbol, he thought of the grass as itself a
child, "the produced babe of the vegetation," and as "the flag of [his]
disposition, out of hopeful green stuff woven." Yet this "uniform hiero-
glyphic" also resembled "the beautiful uncut hair of graves" (*LG* 1855,
p. 29). As hope and despair interpenetrate in the lines quoted above,
even the little one sleeping in its cradle needs a fuller defense against social aggression than the poet alone can provide. Lifting the gauze to take
a closer look and becoming the child's protector—or, in the words of
his early story, the child's "champion"—the poet is nevertheless responsible for introducing the danger he makes it his mission to deflect. Paradoxically, those silent brushes with social aggression and death (as exemplified by the flies) speak to us of feelings we can only guess at. For
example, would Whitman like to *be* the sleeping babe? Is that why he
lifts the gauze? Does he secretly resent the little one's access to the mother,
or his lack of a consciousness of danger, especially those dangers associated with the adult eye and hand?[46] What happens to the sleeping
babe once the silenced speaker departs? In Whitman's imagination, is
the emerging child permitted to have a life independent of *him*?

These emotional issues are similarly vexed in the longer passage
quoted above. As the speaker directs our attention to his tenderness, he
hints at darker feelings attached to those whom he cannot both know
and protect. The "offspring taken [too] soon out of their mothers' laps"
are like the young men whom he has inexplicably lost. Will others fol-

low? Was Whitman imagining a postsexual life or a more vigorous life of the body to come? If the poet cannot protect, it seems that he cannot know. But knowing is a form of intrusion; the poet's loving and thirsting gaze is not neutral. Whatever the emotional realities, Whitman indicates that brushes with death have inspired his central symbol. The knowledge of what he calls death has forced him to try to make language and love coincide.

Despite the urgency of his "language experiment" (*DBN* 3:729 n), which tries to brush away death—to disperse its emotional power—without perpetuating Christian conventions of a God-centered afterlife, in the passage quoted above the poet emphasizes that he has no effective guides in his struggle. The fathers and mothers are victims, too, and their surreal language has no meaning. Enormously enlarged details aside, all that resonates is a shared, domesticated helplessness. Under these circumstances, small wonder that many of Whitman's critics were unwilling to credit either the intelligence or the morality of his project. Whitman's struggle against death was dependent on a secular life force he associated with "Echoes, ripples, and buzzed whispers. . . . loveroot, silkthread, crotch and vine" (*LG* 1855, p. 25). His critics, believing in their own superior solidity and soundness, needed, as Whitman too sometimes did, more literally to "get what the writing means" (*LG* 1855, p. 43).

"His language is too frequently reckless and indecent," noted the first official reviewer, Charles A. Dana, in the *New York Daily Tribune,* "though this appears to arise from a naive unconsciousness rather than from an impure mind. His words might have passed between Adam and Eve in Paradise, before the want of fig-leaves brought no shame; but they are quite out of place amid the decorum of modern society, and will justly prevent his volume from free circulation in scrupulous circles." Dana granted that there was "much of the essential spirit of poetry beneath an uncouth and grotesque embodiment" (*CH* 23). "Politeness this man has none, and regulation he has none. A rude child of the people!" protested an anonymous reviewer in 1855 (*CH* 46). (The reviewer turned out to be Whitman himself.) "For the purpose of showing that he is above every conventionalism," Edward Everett Hale explained in the *North American Review,* "Mr. Whitman puts into the book one or two lines which he would not address to a woman nor to a company of men" (*CH* 51). Writing to James Russell Lowell in an 1855 letter, Charles Eliot Norton observed decisively, "There are some passages of most vigorous and vivid writing, some superbly graphic descriptions, great stretches of imagination,—and then, passages of intolerable coarseness, —not gross and licentious but simply disgustingly coarse. The book is such indeed that one cannot leave it alone for chance readers, and would be sorry to know that any woman had looked into it past the title page" (*CH* 30). Comparing Whitman unfavorably to a female prostitute, the scurrilous Rufus N. Griswold ranted hysterically against *Leaves of Grass* as "a mass of stupid filth" (*CH* 32–33). A British reviewer asked brutally, "Is it possible that the most prudish nation in the world will adopt a poet whose indecencies stink in the nostrils? . . . The depth of his indecencies will be the grave of his fame, or ought to be, if all proper feeling is not extinct. The very nature of this man's compositions excludes us from proving by extracts the truth of our remarks; but we, who are not prudish, emphatically declare that the man who wrote page 79 of the *Leaves of Grass* deserves nothing so richly as the public executioner's whip" (*CH* 57).[47] "Impious and obscene," written with "an ithyphallic audacity that insults what is most sacred and decent among men" (*CH* 62–63), *Leaves of Grass* was roundly condemned as unreadable, and especially unreadable by women, though Henry David Thoreau scoffed, "As if a man could read what a woman could not. Of course Walt Whitman can communicate to us no experience, and if we are shocked, whose experience is it that we are reminded of?" (*CH* 67–68).

Unlike Thoreau, most early readers had no doubt whose experience they were being reminded of. An anonymous reviewer (Whitman again) announced that "To give judgment on real poems, one needs an account of the poet himself":

> Very devilish to some, and very divine to some, will appear the poet of these new poems, the *Leaves of Grass,* an attempt, as they are, of a naive, masculine, affectionate, contemplative, sensual, imperious person, to cast into literature not only his own grit and arrogance, but his own flesh and form, undraped, regardless of models, regardless of modesty or law, and ignorant or silently scornful, as at first appears, of all except his own presence and experience, and all outside the fiercely loved land of his birth and the birth of his parents, and their parents for several generations before him. (*CH* 45–46)

It was characteristic of Whitman to introduce his parents, grandparents, and great-grandparents into an anonymous self-review to authorize his offenses against "politeness and good breeding."[48] "A Bachelor, he professes great respect for women," Bronson Alcott noted with some wonderment after meeting Whitman in the fall of 1856. "Of Scotch descent by his father; by his mother, German. Age 38, and Long Island born" (*CH* 65). Alcott got some of his facts wrong: the Scotch, the German, the age. But in other respects, his account of visiting the Whitmans on Classon Avenue, where they were then living, is more interesting. Alcott went on to describe an unmade bed shared by Whitman and his brother Eddy, a barely concealed chamber pot, and startling unframed prints— a Hercules, a Bacchus, and a satyr—"pasted . . . upon the rude walls":

> He had told me on my former visit of his being a house-builder, but I learned from his mother that his brother was the house-builder, and not Walt, who, she said, had no business but going out and coming in to eat, drink, write, and sleep. And she told me how all the common folks loved him. He had his faults, she knew, and was not a perfect man, but meant us to understand that she thought him an extraordinary son of a fond mother. (CH 65–66)

This account eerily juxtaposes the "naive" domestic values represented by Louisa Whitman with the aggressive "masculine" values represented by Whitman's lusty Greek prints. Taking us into forbidden territory, Alcott depicts a talkative mother who turns aside her son's most provocative statements, who nevertheless hints that she knows more than she lets on, and who, if Alcott's language is to be believed, is a secret snob. Airily excusing Walt's faults, whatever they may be, Louisa insists on her own zone of privacy, while correcting his misrepresentations of his contributions to the family. So what *were* Walt's faults? His failure to make the kind of money the family needed to escape from being "common folks," as he pursued the poorly paid business of poetry rather than the potentially lucrative business of house-building? Or his failure to share the rich inner life that informed those poems with her? For Louisa, with her intuitive worldliness, surely knew that a poet's life consisted of more than eating, drinking, writing, and sleeping. Yet if she had any thoughts of her own about the provocative prints on the rude walls of the male dormitory with the unmade bed, Walt's mother certainly never hinted to Alcott or to anyone else that she had any interest in the sexual thematics of her son's life or work. Later, though, in a letter written from Burlington, Vermont, where she was visiting her daughter Hannah and still following her own inner light (a house in the country), Louisa raised the unlikely but to her threatening idea that Whitman might marry.[49] This letter illuminates Whitman's interactions not only with his mother but with other members of his personal audience, the audience of unidentified family members, friends, and lovers transfigured and rewritten into the imaginary planes of the poems we have been examining. In particular, this letter brings Whitman's sister Hannah, with whom he was closely identified, back into the family picture from which she is usually erased. As he explained in "A Backward Glance O'er

Travel'd Roads" (*LG*, pp. 573–74), "It must be carefully remember'd that first-class literature does not shine by any luminosity of its own; nor do its poems. They grow of circumstances, and are evolutionary. The actual living light is always curiously from elsewhere—follows unaccountable sources, and is lunar and relative at the best."

THE TWENTY-NINTH BATHER

As Whitman struggled to place his faith in sex as a source of pleasure rather than pain, and to free himself from the role of erotic victim, the example of his sister Hannah's tormented marriage was much in his mind. Hannah Whitman Heyde, the younger sister to whom Whitman was deeply devoted, was married in March 1852 when she was twenty-eight years old. Born on November 28, 1823, she is a possible model for the reclusive, fantasy-ridden "twenty-ninth bather" in "Song of Myself" we visited earlier in this chapter. For no apparent reason, Whitman surrounds this figure with iterations of the number twenty-eight, which he described as the age at which he began to write *Leaves of Grass,* and critics have exercised their ingenuity in explaining its allegorical significance. Many of these explanations link the number twenty-eight to the female menstrual cycle or to the lunar calendar. I would like to propose that the number twenty-eight was further determined because of its association with Hannah's birth date and age at the time of her marriage, and to see where this speculation takes us. I intend to suggest that Whitman's empathic identification with Hannah as an erotic victim influenced his understanding of the democratic poet's social mission, and that the healing touch he attributed to his "unseen hand" in Section 11 of "Song of Myself" was partly inspired by his desire to free his sister from the false body of her married life.

Shortly before he resigned from the *Brooklyn Daily Times* in late June 1859, and at the very moment when (it appears) he was returning to intensive work on the *Calamus* sequence, Whitman published an editorial on the theme of sexual repression, which examined the frustrations of single women. Attributing to them "a shameful sense of ignorance—a vague, eager desire for knowledge," he suggested that "It is hard to fast when so many are feasting," and he inquired whether we can really expect unmarried women "to drown forever the reproaches of Nature, that will make herself heard." "If not," he continued, "surely the most phlegmatically proper of her sex does sometimes feel sad and dissatisfied when she thinks that she has never been able to care for any one more than for her own brother." [50] In this editorial, familial rhetoric provides an important vocabulary of erotic desire, as it does throughout *Leaves of Grass,* but Whitman's sexualization of the sister-brother relationship is unusual. Moreover, because Hannah married late, he had ample opportunity to consider the erotic longings of the single woman with whom he had grown up and whom he knew better, so far as we can tell, than any other single woman then or later.

In asking "Can All Marry?" Whitman asserted that unmarried men have a "thousand and one safety-valves to superfluous [erotic] excitement," such as "the counteracting resources of bodily and mental exertion," but in Section 11 of "Song of Myself" these masculine resources seem far from sufficient. In fact the emotional power of the story depends on our awareness of the narrator's dilemma, which links him to his richly dressed heroine and triangulates the scene. Like her, Whitman as narrator wears a mask, the mask of the detached observer who seems to accept heterosexual norms for young, friendly, and unthinking men. In his "lonesome" lyric, Whitman's designated audience expands to include a woman who is structurally unable to hear him when he addresses her. As a literary character, she is unable to respond to the poet who "see[s]" her, and in seeing her, tries to imagine a way to make her desire visible to others.

> Twenty-eight young men bathe by the shore,
> Twenty-eight young men and all so friendly;
> Twenty-eight years of womanly life, and all so lonesome.
>
> She owns the fine house by the rise of the bank,
> She hides handsome and richly drest aft the blinds of the window.
>
> Which of the young men does she like the best?
> Ah the homeliest of them is beautiful to her.
>
> Where are you off to, lady? for I see you,
> You splash in the water there, yet stay stock still in your room.
>
> Dancing and laughing along the beach came the twenty-ninth bather,
> The rest did not see her, but she saw them and loved them.
>
> The beards of the young men glistened with wet, it ran from their long hair,
> Little streams passed all over their bodies.
>
> An unseen hand also passed over their bodies,
> It descended tremblingly from their temples and ribs.
>
> The young men float on their backs, their white bellies swell to the sun. . . .
>   they do not ask who seizes fast to them,

They do not know who puffs and declines with pendant and bending arch,
They do not think whom they souse with spray.

                                                    (*LG* 1855, p. 34)

Splashing in her room while bathing as Hannah Whitman might have
done and as Whitman might have seen her do, the twenty-ninth bather
becomes the poet who becomes her in the line, "An unseen hand also
passed over their bodies." This hand(writing) reconfigures erotic identities that are both culturally and personally specific. Identities fuse as
they disintegrate, turning on a word, "hand," which includes the first
syllable of her first name, Hannah, and which forms an off rhyme with
her last, Heyde. So far no one has considered Hannah (Heyde) as a possible source for this (hiding) vignette, perhaps because Hannah owned
no fine house at the time of her marriage, did not live on a river, was not
known to engage in group sex, did not literally share a hand with Whitman, and so forth. More generally, biographical critics have not found
Hannah a compelling figure and have been content to write her off as
neurotic and hysterical.

As Whitman tried to rewrite traditions of the body that separated
men from men, women from women, and women and men from each
other, Hannah's actual experience provided a formidable challenge. For
by the time the 1855 *Leaves of Grass* was published, she was beginning
to settle into a life of mutual torment with her husband Charles, a French-
born landscape artist to whom she had been introduced by Walt, her
adored older brother. At one time Walt thought well enough of Charlie
Heyde to bring William Cullen Bryant to his Brooklyn studio, but eventually he came to see Heyde as "a serpent," "a viper," "a damned lazy
scoundrel," a "constant spear in his side," a "skunk," a "bug," a "leech,"
and "the bed-buggiest man on the earth" (*WWWC* 3:500, 2:493,
7:369, 7:23, 3:498). Little is known about Hannah's life before this disastrous marriage, except that she liked flowers, had an interest in fashion, was probably good-looking, and was more of a reader than the
other Whitmans except for Jeff. We also know that while he was in New
Orleans, Whitman trusted her with money (*Corr* 1:33, 36). Hannah
was eager for an education, but her subsequent claim to have attended
a "select school in Brooklyn" and a girls' boarding school in Hempstead, Long Island, was probably a reverie rather than a reality.[51] Like
her mother, she was very conscious of what might have been, and she remembered all those rich acres the ancestral Whitmans had, over the
years, lost.[52] Ironically, Hannah, who survived her husband and who

inherited money from both Walt and George, did end up owning a "fine house" near the water—ironically, that is, if we credit the "twenty-ninth bather" model—but her life was emotionally impoverished. In the 1860s, for example, she was often too depressed to write home, and was ashamed of her failure to accomplish even simple tasks, such as crocheting the scarf she had intended to present to Walt, who was always sending her gifts: books to read, letters from their mother he had received and then passed along to her, magazines, money, encouragement. But Hannah, described in her obituary as "a woman of keen intellect, of broad culture, of great independence of mind . . . a delightful conversationalist," had qualities of heart and mind that could cause her to seem glamorous in her need.[53]

As early as 1844, Whitman seems to have been predicting trouble for Hannah. In the sketch "My Boys and Girls," which he published in the aptly titled *Rover*, the narrator mentions an untrustworthy "child of light and loveliness" who makes him uneasy because he finds her blooming before her time and sexually provocative. This fantasy child is described as "a very beautiful girl, in her fourteenth year." "Flattery," we are told, "comes too often to her ears." Working within the sentimental convention that associates sexual experience, childhood, and death, Whitman notes, "From the depths of her soul I now and then see misty revealings of thought and wish, that are not well. I see them through her eyes and in the expression of her face." Here he prefigures his later knowledge of sexual fantasy in the 1855 *Leaves of Grass,* in which he comments on his ability to see through other people's masks and disguises, whether they want him to or not. But in this early sketch, the narrator is afraid to merge his point of view with Hannah's or to express his sexuality through hers. He remarks paternally and fraternally,

> It is a dreary thought to imagine what may happen, in the future years, to a handsome, merry child—to gaze far down the vista, and see the dim phantoms of Evil standing about with nets and temptations—to witness, in the perspective, purity gone, and the freshness of youthful innocence rubbed off, like the wasted bloom of flowers. Who, at twenty-five or thirty years of age, is without many memories of wrongs done, and mean or wicked deeds performed? (*EPF* 248)

There is some question as to when this sketch was written, but Hannah's subsequent fate, coupled with her tales of a romantic elopement at sixteen, as well as her other self-representations and misrepresentations, would seem to justify Whitman's concern. Interviewed by Horace Traubel after the poet's death, George Whitman was asked to comment on Walt's relations with his siblings and ventured the opinion, "He was fondest of Han if he had any preference." [54] Building on George's remark, Clarence Gohdes and Rollo G. Silver describe Hannah as the favorite sister of all the brothers. [55] And viewing family relations through his careful study of George's Civil War letters and diary, Jerome Loving further suggests, "The fourth child, Hannah was—for no obvious reason—the favorite of all the family members, including Walt. Perhaps she shared, to some extent, Walt's aesthetic bent." [56]

In fact Hannah prided herself on having participated in the artistic circles frequented by both Walt and her future husband, who had already met William Cullen Bryant even before Walt brought Bryant to Heyde's studio. Eventually Heyde became an artist of some modest distinction, and according to Katherine Molinoff had written "a small volume of very bad verse" by the time Whitman brought him home to meet Hannah. [57] But Heyde's personality deteriorated during his marriage, a deterioration abetted not only by his problems with Hannah but also by his problems with alcohol and his career. The change in Heyde's personality can be seen in his correspondence with Whitman. For example, just after Whitman had been in Boston in 1860 seeing the third edition of *Leaves of Grass* through the press, Heyde wrote to him pompously but encouragingly,

Dear Walt.

Recieved your book, also a letter for Han.—Feel proud myself—the copy I now have is just the thing to handle frequently—I like the poems better than those issued first. I like the portrait, it looks very much as you do at the present time. It has a little air of a foreign savan—however—but it is a good likeness.

I think that some of the poems open splendid—grandly—there is a fault or eccentricity however, in some, that is, they diverge too abruptly from a lofty theme or elevating imagery into common place—ordinary—and repulsive object, or subject matter—But they are poems of the thouroughfare of life passions and emotions of the universe and humanity—on all sides taken—as they approach and appear—without selection—sympathies utterd and communion held with all in turn and none rejected—Poems of glorious, liberal, soul filld emotion. They will be read—they must have a place—But you'l write a perfect poem one of these days, filld with nature sublimely—Your thoughts are true thoughts—Common sense is the best philosophy—Cant has too long ruled the world and judged the case of erring humanity—Your Poems are sustaining—I hope that there will be a jolly

good fight over them—The public are lazy—and need some disturbance
to arouse them [. . . .]

Give us more poems Walt—I hope there'l be a genearl big row—in the
papers—Stir em up well—I look for it.

Charlie (*Clews* 215–16)

As his own troubles intensified, Heyde began to bombard the Whitmans with abusive letters. He was also excruciatingly jealous of Walt's
growing reputation, and by 1866 "that fool Heyde," as Walt told his
mother, had written a "long letter to [Henry Jarvis] Raymond, editor
of the N. Y. Times," identifying himself as Whitman's brother-in-law
and disparaging *Leaves of Grass*. "In it he said 'Walt was a good fellow
enough-but'—& then he went on to run down Leaves of Grass, like the
rest of 'em. . . . Raymond seemed to think the man was either crazy or
a fool, & he treated the letter with contempt. . . . The puppy thought I
suppose that he could get his letter printed, & injure me & my book"
(*Corr* 1:303). (Heyde had apparently been provoked by William Douglas O'Connor's spirited public defenses of Whitman [*Clews* 224].)
Months before writing to the *Times,* however, he had intemperately
written to Whitman, complaining bitterly about his wife,

> Perhaps I would not look upon "Leaves of Grass" with so much melan-
> choly regard, if I was not experiencing a practical version of it: Irregular—
> disorderly: indifferent, or defiant—the lower animal instincts—no account-
> ability, no moral sense or principle—No true, inherent, practical sympathy
> for anything; myself; disappointments, or endeavours. Nothing of me, or
> of the future to arise for me, out of my labour, and progressions.
>
> Han has no more moral sense of marriage than an Ethiopian, of the
> field—Gives herself to a man and nothing more. (*Clews* 222–23)

Hannah never learned to cook and she was an erratic housekeeper at
best, but Heyde's self-pitying invective left the Whitmans in no doubt
about his character. "Walter i have had a letter from heyde the most awful onc yct," Louisa reported in March 1868. Then, three weeks later,
"Walter. . . . i had a letter or package from charley . . . three sheets of
foolscap and a fool wrote on them." That little conceited fool, she called
him. The same old Charley.

Though partly silenced, Hannah left enough of a written record to
suggest that she had a lively mind, a sympathetic heart, and a fatal fascination with self-recrimination. Abject and depressed, she unburdened
herself to the Whitmans through the mail, and during the recurrent crises which surrounded her, she longed to leave her controlling, irritable,

and withholding husband and to return to her loving "Mammy" and "the boys." In response to her vivid descriptions of Heyde's "violent angry fits," the Whitmans often thought of rescuing her, but those plans never came to anything. At the last minute, Hannah's fears of being even *more* socially dislocated as a woman separated from her husband always got the better of her, and she turned back to Heyde. Heyde, in turn, threatened to leave Hannah many times, reporting to Louisa that she had unjustly accused him of having sexual intercourse with his female students, that Hannah was a "she devil, to men," and that "all the pleasure he has is with his fellow artists." [58]

As a childless, unhappily married woman with, in her own view, "no talents [and] very little education," Hannah depended on her family for emotional support. [59] Visits were few and far between, but her brother's career was crucial to her self-esteem. [60] Just as Whitman's narrative of personal and national identity was informed by an audience that included *her,* so Walt as the author of *Leaves of Grass* wanted Hannah Whitman Heyde to believe in the coming day of the "organic equality" of the sexes, without which, as he noted in his open letter to Emerson, "men cannot have organic equality among themselves" (*LG,* p. 739). [61] In the 1855 "Song for Occupations," the poet characteristically insists that "The wife—and she is not one jot less than the husband" (*LG* 1855, p. 89). Heyde thought differently and told Hannah as much, though not so much at the level of abstraction as at the level of personal attack. Hannah vividly described their quarrels in her letters home, and despite her self-distrust, she tried to believe that a husband and wife were, in her words, "one as good as another." [62] As she struggled to accept the "ups and downs" of a marriage that all too often brought out the worst in both partners, Hannah Whitman Heyde lamented the fact that she had placed her whole dependence on a single volatile individual who seemed unaccountably intent on humiliating her. In the early years of her marriage, she told the story of a romantic escapist who loved a certain person ardently and whose love was not returned. The 1855 and 1856 editions of *Leaves of Grass* do not linger long over the plight of a vulnerable individual, ill at ease with the "uppertendom," who suffers from jealous despair. [63] Appropriately reconfigured, that story would unfold in the next book as Whitman's own.

While the twenty-ninth bather in "Song of Myself" emerges out of Whitman's imagination, as do the twenty-eight young men who are to some extent based on his brothers, I have tried to show that the poet identified with his sister Hannah, that he did see her, as he claimed to see the reclusive bather, and that he saw some of her problems as mirroring his. Whitman's faith in sex took many forms, but it was always a competition with social dis-ease, a fate exemplified by Hannah. In one of her most poignant letters, written some time after her father's death in 1855 and before Jeff's marriage in 1859, she remarked, "How much I used to think of home, long ago, when I lived home, I mean. I used to think I was entirely killed if one of the boys talked of going away." And "dont see any body here as good looking as Jeffy," and "Mammy . . . I often immagine I see you going about," and "I think I shall come home this fall," and "I am alone much of the time," and "I stay in my room much of the time," and "tell Walt to write to me," and "give my best love to all my brothers." In this emotionally gripping letter, Hannah's desire to "seize fast" shines through, even though, as she explains, after breaking out of her fear of Charley by attending a concert with a "good clever woman," a Miss Smith, where she had a "conspicuous" seat and felt underdressed amid "the uppertendom" of Burlington, "I was *down down* considerable, for going out with one that used to be a pastry cook, I dont suppose I shall ever rise again, I hope I shall have your sympathy," and "I expect you say enough of art and Artists." [64]

As an artist in words, Whitman tried to give his readers something other than a sentimental token of home to which they could "seize fast." In his 1856 open letter to Emerson, he suggested, as we have seen, that "the courageous soul, for a year or two to come, may be proved by faith in sex, and by disdaining concessions." The conditional tense of this statement is interesting, for a year or two to come is not so very long, and the idea that as a faith healer he could move easily between the body politic and the body personal was going to be difficult to sustain. Whitman concluded his blustery apologia with an allusion to "passionate friendliness," and with obsequious flattery of his "dear Master." In the 1855 and 1856 *Leaves of Grass,* Whitman had not decided on the meaning of sex in his own life, but his faith in himself as an experimental poet with an ambitious social mission had been firmly established. And so he signed off boldly, as "WALT WHITMAN," and as one still curious about why "manly friendship, everywhere observed in The States," remained so "unseen" in language (*LG,* p. 739).

FIVE

The Politics of Love in the 1860 *Leaves of Grass*

In May 1860, the firm of Thayer and Eldridge produced a new edition of *Leaves of Grass,* which Whitman himself pronounced typographically "'odd'" and odd in other ways as well (*Corr* 1:52). As he explained in a letter to his brother Jeff, this new and enlarged book was the first edition of *Leaves of Grass* to be "really *published,*" and for the moment he took an author's justifiable pride in having unambiguously entered the marketplace. "The book will be a very handsome specimen of typography, paper, binding, etc," he wrote from Boston, where he was seeing his delayed manuscript through the press, "and will be, it seems to me, like relieving me of a great weight—or removing a great obstacle that has been in my way for the last three years. The young men that are publishing it treat me in a way I could not wish to have better. They are go-ahead fellows, and don't seem to have the least doubt they are bound to make a good spec. out of my book. It is quite curious, all this should spring up so suddenly, aint it" (*Corr* 1:51).

Curious indeed, but also produced by much toil. Thayer and Eldridge, the eager young men, had written to Whitman in February, a month after he published an anonymous self-review called "All About a Mocking-Bird" announcing the birth of "the true 'Leaves of Grass,'" which he pronounced an advance over its predecessors in "quantity, quality, and in supple lyrical exuberance." [1] The book was undeniably larger than either the 1855 or 1856 *Leaves of Grass,* many of the old poems had been revised, and some of the new ones were indeed surpassingly supple and lyrical. Exuberance, however, is a curious word to describe the overall effect of the volume, which interrogates poetic power in complicated ways, as does the lushly evocative literary performance Whitman had featured in his self-review, and which we now know as "Out of the Cradle Endlessly Rocking." (The poem was called "A Child's Reminiscence" when it was published in the Christmas issue of the *Saturday Press* on December 24, 1859, and then "A Word Out of the Sea" in the 1860 *Leaves of Grass*.) Figuratively, this emblematic autobiography describes the collapse of a seemingly perfect two-parent family and the end of a seemingly idyllic boyhood. As the poet identifies with both he-bird and she-bird—the one abandoned, the other abandoning—he finds his mature self in reclaiming "the fire, the sweet hell within, / The unknown want, the destiny of me" (*LG* 1860, p. 276).

Despite the fact that poetic power emerges from this history of erotic bereavement—for love (in the past tense) and death *are* the words out of the sea—Whitman was exquisitely sensitive to charges of *ennui* or morbidity, especially insofar as those charges were aimed at his literary and sexual project. He deeply distrusted that "individualism, which isolates," and already believed, as he later announced in *Democratic Vistas,* that "the master sees greatness and health in being part of the mass" (*DV* 948–49). Thus in advertising his new book as supple and exuberant, he was hoping to defend himself against uncomprehending or bizarrely motivated attacks on his intelligence and character, of which there were plenty.[2] He was also prepared to publish the book himself, as he had his earlier works, and his friends the Rome brothers set proof for him before Thayer and Eldridge entered the picture. "Those former issues," he explained vehemently in "All About a Mocking-Bird," "published by the author himself in little pittance editions, on trial, have just dropped the book enough to ripple the inner first-circles of literary agitation. The outer, vast, extending, and ever-widening circles, of the general supply, perusal, and discussion of such a work, have still to come."[3]

In this revealingly defensive self-review, Whitman's grandiose language expanded to fill the gulf between himself and the general reader, with whom he feared (and somewhat hoped) that he had little in common. For if the mature poet of "Out of the Cradle Endlessly Rocking" justifies his vocation as a response to erotic bereavement, he translates this loss into a "new style ... removed from previous models" (*Corr* 1:44), whose meaning eludes definition in the as yet incomplete present. This new style unsettles the traditional family romance later described by Freud.[4] Freud's account of individual maturation imagines discrete phases of development and produces gender-specific behavior; Whitman hoped that the new style forced upon him for "American purposes" might authorize more fluid forms of attachment. As he explained in a letter to the editors of *Harper's Magazine,* "Every really new person, (poet or other,) *makes* his style—sometimes a little way removed from the previous models—sometimes very far removed" (*Corr* 1:460). For our purposes and for Whitman's, the word "sometimes" is key. Any author needs to differentiate himself or herself from previous models. But whether Whitman was willing to set himself continuously apart from middle-class models of sexual identification and desire remained an urgent and open question. Could he persuade the American public to accept "adhesiveness or love" as that which "fuses, ties, and aggregates, making the races comrades, and fraternizing all" (*DV* 948–49)? Like women, African Americans were identified with the body; might an expanded discourse of sexual feeling eventually amplify their power in the public sphere as well?

"Out of the Cradle Endlessly Rocking" beautifully associates poetic power and personal suffering, as Whitman claims that his own frustrations have sensitized him to the needs of others. But how consistently did the Mocking-Bird poet intend to sacrifice his own interests to advance the cause of others, for example the cause of his dusky demon and brother? In minstrel shows, mockingbirds were associated with African Americans, yet despite the poem's black/white imagery and regional emphases, it is still possible to read "Out of the Cradle" without noticing its specifically racial dimension. None of the contemporary reviews commented on this theme, and Whitman wondered whether a formally sophisticated, psychologically inclusive art of indirection could speak both in its own time and to poet-readers of the future.

Consider the *Calamus* narrative, which translates Whitman's personal history of homoerotic love into a new "tongue." Here race as a category of social analysis is subsumed by gender and perverse sexual desire. Implicitly, we read *Calamus* as the story of unconventional *white men.* Emerging *out* of personal and social experience but still tied *to* it, the *Calamus* poems underscore competing conceptions of the culturally functional self—as does the 1860 *Leaves of Grass* more generally. These competing conceptions are responsible for the oddities Whitman described in the letter written from Boston to his brother Jeff. What, for example, are we to make of Whitman's cartoonlike visual symbols: his rising and setting suns, butterflies and pointing fingers, globes and weighted-down clouds—to say nothing of his various typefaces, filigree decorations, and idiosyncratic capitalization: "I saw in Louisiana a live-oak growing" (*LG* 1860, p. 364). Probably Whitman wished to reveal the arbitrary nature of any single stylistic choice or medium, and, as the Mocking-Bird poet, he ironized style as performance. To the extent, then, that Whitman might be understood as mocking a hegemonic sexual style through his arbitrary-seeming visual devices, he was further opening up a space for what he called a "new friendship" between men.

By the same stylistic logic and as if to compensate white *women* for their potential loss of power within his emerging homoerotic-friendly republic, at the level of metaphor he suggested that his intervention would provide Woman—traditionally the bearer of emotion in culture—with an enhanced public role. Homoerotic culture need not exclude women, but it *did* need to redefine both their public and private function. Whitman in 1860 continued to believe that the literary artist could intervene most powerfully in social reorganization by waging a parodic war of words rather than an actual war of arms. Although he described his words as weapons, he mainly knew that to be an artist was to participate in some fights and to ignore others. There were times when he lost his balance, but on the whole he wanted to substantiate multiple erotic freedoms rather than to reinscribe a single sexual style. And so racial justice mattered to him, but it was far from his most important issue. Addressing himself to present and future readers, the speaker, "FULL of life, sweet-blooded, compact, visible" (*LG* 1860, p. 378), looks back to the house of maternity as he has never known it. In so doing, the Mocking-Bird poet affirms his own struggle; the fight for sexual freedom and for a liberating rather than a confining domesticity matter most.

"States!" the poet declaimed without any apparent irony, in *Calamus* 5,

> Were you looking to be held together by the lawyers?
> By an agreement on a paper? Or by arms?
>
> Away!
> I arrive, bringing these, beyond all the forces of courts and arms,
> These! to hold you together as firmly as the earth itself is held together.
>
> The old breath of life, ever new,
> Here! I pass it by contact to you, America.
>
> O mother! have you done much for me?
> Behold, there shall from me be much done for you.
>
> (*LG* 1860, p. 349)

"Affection" did not of course succeed in solving what Whitman optimistically called "the problems of freedom," however determined he was to

identify love, social justice, America, motherhood, and the tally of his
own ambiguously sexed white male voice. Nevertheless, with the 1860
Leaves of Grass, Whitman issued a powerful challenge to contemporary
understandings of the proper and even possible relationship between
that "individualism, which isolates," and "adhesiveness or love," which
"fuses, ties, and aggregates, making the races comrades, and fraternizing all." For in this new book, he attempted to convert an American attitude of social distrust between men into a national and international
aesthetic of affection, loyalty, and love. As exemplified by "Out of the
Cradle Endlessly Rocking," the poet drew on the fabled resources of his
own personal past to escape not only from "the cries of unsatisfied love"
but also from the hate-filled cries of the present.[5] One might think that
the novels, poems, plays, personal letters, diaries, sermons, and political
speeches that after several hundred years had so effectively generated
metaphors of American society as a unified, intact family might have
been exhausted. Yet Whitman was deeply reluctant to let those unifying
metaphors go. His self-review, for example, while chanting the multi-
vocality of American culture—as exemplified in his own "songs" by such
diverse influences as the Italian opera, piano tunes, negro bands, Homer,
Shakespeare, Milton, the Hebrew canticles, Pope, Byron, Wordsworth,
German and French singers, and by extension all foreigners—nevertheless equated foreign influence with the wrong kind of national childhood, that is, with social, political, and economic dependency. Furthermore, as Whitman's allusion to the performance of negro bands attests,
he was also concerned with racialized foreignness: with the conversion
of race into otherness. Despite the breadth of his embrace, an enduring
part of Whitman equated cultural pluralism with an infantile ensemble
in which "all the sounds of earth and hell were tumbled promiscuously
together." Bumping up against the slavery crisis, which haunted even the
seemingly timeless, stately progressions of "Cradle," Whitman effectively
translated the problems of "America" and of "democracy" into a more
soothing and politically evasive language of feeling. Escaping into what
he hoped would be a more tractable future, the Mocking-Bird poet thus
represented himself as the founder of a bold race of giants, located in
"the great West," where the eager "children of the prairies" were waiting to be supplied with "copious thousands of copies" of his new book.

I do not mean to suggest, however, that Whitman's reconfiguration of
relations among men was motivated primarily by his desire to solve the
problems of "America" and of "democracy," which, as he explained in
Democratic Vistas, he proposed to treat as "convertible terms" (*DV*

930). The ideal American democracy of the future, whatever else it might be, would have to accommodate *him,* in his emerging but still "furtive" (homo)sexual role. As I have been suggesting, the convergence of personal and political motives enabled Whitman to extend his imagination of national "ensemble" to thematize eroticized relations between men. I shall argue that in so doing Whitman came close to freeing himself from the prolonged ambivalence toward intimate male bonding described in previous chapters.

Whitman's eroticization of the homosocial friendship tradition as it had been written up to his time is especially pronounced in the sequence of forty-five lyrics grouped together under the title *Calamus-Leaves,* and then simply *Calamus,* a Greek-derived word the poet intended to signify both botanically and phallically. "The recherché or ethereal sense of the term, as used in my book," he later explained, "arises probably from the actual Calamus presenting the biggest & hardiest kind of spears of grass." He further suggested that "'Calamus' is a common word here," meaning in the United States, and that this large aromatic grass, often called "sweet flag," was in abundance "all over the Northern and Middle States" (*Corr* 1:347). Whitman identified this native-grown yet recherché "root of washed sweet flag" with the "occult convolutions of his brain" (*LG* 1855, p. 49), with his spiritualized body's "rich blood" and seminal "milky stream," and with his "adhesive" heart's desire.[6] Because he was concerned not only about the apparent failure of political parties and "kept editors" to establish an enduring social and political union, but also about the undemocratic and possibly morbid connotations of manly love, he constructed a sequence of fifteen poems titled *Enfans d'Adam* (later renamed *Children of Adam*), in which the female presence was central. "Theory of a Cluster of Poems," Whitman recorded in one of his preliminary notebook entries: "The same *to the Passion of Woman-Love* as the 'Calamus-Leaves' are to adhesiveness, manly love" (*NUPM* 1:413). Using several poems previously published and writing some new ones, Whitman grouped these Adamic poems together after organizing the more subtle if heartwrenching *Calamus* sequence. It is ironic, then, that in the United States as well as in England, the "Woman-Love" poems were attacked for their supposed indecencies.[7] In England, however, the "Man-Love" *Calamus* poems were more readily received as an important passage in the history of intensely charged male-male desire, as "this beginning" not of "me" but "of us" (*LG* 1860, p. 450; *LG,* p. 488).[8] These occult and daring representations of love between men have in some measure justified Whitman's hope that his third book might be a "divine volume" (*LG*, p. 657) or, as he also called it, a "New Bible" (*NUPM* 1:353). But while reminding himself that "The greatest poems may not immediately be fully understood by outsiders any more than astronomy or engineering may.—The work of the poet is as deep as the astronomer's or engineer's, and his art is also as farfetched" (*NUPM* 1:371), Whitman was not conceding to those who sought to marginalize him as a "queer person" (*Corr* 1:4). On the contrary. Whitman ardently hoped that the 1860 *Leaves* would confirm his reputation as a distinguished artist, rather than as "the 'rough,' the 'eccentric,' 'vagabond' or queer person, that the commentators, (always bound for the intensest possible sensational statement,) persist in making him"[9]—however much he himself had fostered the rough, eccentric, vagabond, and queer person myths. And so he dressed up for his frontispiece portrait, looking thoughtful and corpulent, curly-haired and constrained. Gone is the studied insolence of his younger, brasher self.

Let us return for the moment to Whitman's self-review, in which he suggested that his literary apprenticeship was over. Here his voice remained uncertainly pitched, in part because the genre of the anonymous self-review was too strange even for him.

> LEAVES OF GRASS has not yet been really published at all. Walt Whitman, for his own purposes, slowly trying his hand at the edifice, the structure he has undertaken, has lazily loafed on, letting each part have time to set—evidently building not so much with reference to any part itself, considered alone, but more with reference to the ensemble—always bearing in mind the combination of the whole, to fully justify the parts when finished.

Perhaps Whitman was recalling the language supplied several years earlier by his friend Hector Tyndale, a traveled and cultivated Philadelphia merchant, who had suggested that Whitman's poems were lacking "'in massiveness, breadth, large, sweeping effects, without regard to detail.'" He urged Whitman to strive for "'largeness, solidity and spaciousness,'" without troubling himself with parts (*NUPM* 1:351). This was bad advice, and Whitman troubled himself a great deal about justifying both the broad effects and the parts of his sexual project.[10] As did Ralph Waldo Emerson, who even as type was being set tried to get him to eliminate or tone down the fifteen "Amorous, mature" poems Whitman felt were needed to counterbalance the more unusual or "recherché" male-male intensities of the *Calamus* grouping.[11]

With several interesting exceptions, in these more theoretical woman-centered poems the speaker does not risk disappointment, defeat, and death as he does within the more lyrical and elegiac *Calamus* grouping.

Yet this supposedly more conventional sequence is full of quirky detail, beginning with the apparent misspelling or deliberate creolization of the title *Enfans d'Adam*, which Whitman subsequently regularized to *Children of Adam*. A consideration of the apparently illogical thought and feeling of this still deservedly controversial section may serve to introduce Whitman's ambivalent quest for lovers and perfect equals in the 1860 *Leaves of Grass*. As an artist who claimed to speak for the ordinary man and woman rather than for the "literary classes," Whitman was not above privileging his superior insight into the supposed laws of human nature and of human relationships, including the egotism to which he was no stranger. I mention this egotism now because the *Children of Adam* poems demonstrate Whitman's concern with power inequalities in heterosexual relations in and out of marriage. He himself is implicated in these inequalities: the poems critique power in its various sexual guises; in their "farfetched" way, they also covet it.

ENFANS D'ADAM

Of course, the *Enfans d'Adam* sequence has no exclusive purchase on apparent illogicality, for the volume as a whole has little in common with the hierarchically organized "cathedral" structure recommended by Tyndale as a model. But considered as an inquiry into the relationship between desire and social forms, the *Enfans d'Adam* sequence is unusually subject to multiple interruptions, or silencings, even for Whitman. For example, in the second poem of the sequence, the speaker moves from "singing the phallus, / Singing the song of procreation, / Singing the need of superb children, and therein superb grown people" to "Singing what, to the Soul, entirely redeemed her, the faithful one, the prostitute, who detained me when I went to the city, / Singing the song of prostitutes." The first poem had concluded with a seemingly lovely image of democratic sexual politics: "By my side, or back of me, Eve following, / Or in front, and I following her just the same." [12] In the mental and physical space between poems one and two, Eve disappears, as do all women, along with the image of Whitman as a follower. After a brief excursion into phallic preening, praise of procreation, veiled homoerotic tenderness, and veiled autoerotic shame, the speaker's diffuse "muscular urges" are now located within a desiring but degendered body. From this mythic location Whitman produces the "true song of the Soul, fitful, at random" (*LG* 1860, p. 288).

This dehistoricized, disembodied speaker searches for some essential

value "yet unfound," having "diligently sought it, ten thousand years."
But in lines Whitman eliminated in 1881, a new historical identity is
constituted around the idea of female prostitution. Since "The Soul" is
associated with "her," "the faithful one," "the prostitute," "me" and
"I," these figures all seem like parts of the same person. That is, the idea
of prostitution has the effect of regendering the speaker. There is no attempt to describe the prostitute as an individual and in that sense the
speaker has not found a lover and perfect equal. But by insisting on her
fidelity to him, he has begun to collapse the distinction between leader
and follower that made it impossible for him to pursue his idyll with
Eve. Collapsing this distinction is crucial to his sexual and political project and, as I will suggest, works best in the poems on male-male love,
where gender inequalities can seemingly be banished to the margins of
his discourse.

Whatever his conscious ideological intent, Whitman recounts a turning *away from* rather than *toward* emotional and sexual intimacy, even
as he seeks ontological clues that will focus homoerotic longings he
is not yet willing to claim as his own. Appropriating biblical myth,
and comparing himself both to Adam and Adam's descendants, he calls
for "Potent mates, daughters, sons" (*LG* 1860, p. 287) without quite
calling for potent wives. Because women cannot really be trusted, he
addresses himself to "the perfect girl who understands me—the girl of
The States" (*LG* 1860, p. 290). Yet throughout the *Enfans d'Adam* sequence, which emerged out of a dense and densely sexist historical context, Woman functions mainly as an inferior power position; the title itself diminishes Eve's importance. Whitman had first introduced Adam
and Eve, those traditional exemplars of patriarchal marriage, in the last
(and worst) poem of the 1855 *Leaves*, now called "Great Are the Myths,"
which he dropped from the much revised and expanded volume in 1881.
"Great are Adam and Eve. . . . I too look back and accept them" (*LG*
1855, p. 142), he wrote, without being able to do so. Several pages later,
after praising the cultural supremacy of English speech ("the mother of
the brood that must rule the earth with the new rule"), he introduced
a list comprised of such lawful pleasures as "commerce, newspapers,
books, freetrade, railroads, steamers, international mails and telegraphs
and exchanges," including "marriage" as one of "the old few landmarks
of the law," an antipassional positioning if ever there was one (*LG* 1855,
p. 144). Evidently Whitman's list of social institutions that are not to be
"disturbed," however disturbing they may be, begs the following question. How can commerce, newspapers, marriage, and other competing

social institutions be integrated? Having written himself into an ideological impasse in which he supports legal tradition *and* proclaims its
meaninglessness to the upstart eternal or universal soul that judges paradoxically and perfectly, Whitman concludes,

> Great is life . . and real and mystical . . wherever and whoever,
> Great is death. . . . Sure as life holds all parts together, death holds all
>   parts together;
> Sure as the stars return again after they merge in the light, death is great
>   as life.
>
> (LG 1855, p. 145)

With this 1855 poem, Whitman dismantles marriage, reducing it to
a mere legality. Yet he proves himself an unreliable revolutionary. First,
he insists that throughout human history the same ideals have governed
interpersonal relationships, and he seemingly approves of these traditional norms of social organization. But second, he suggests that to
question a single part of this habitually organized project is to precipitate the collapse of the whole. He himself is unwilling to risk this total
reconfiguration of the moral imagination, yet as a "perfect judge" he
hopes that we won't believe him when he declares that he has "absolute
faith." He both wants and does not want to perpetuate his "odd" self-
revisions, which reflect competing loyalties. Whether intentionally or
unintentionally, Whitman encourages a resisting reading. His declara-
tions of faith are assaultive, and the poem appears not to have an immediate occasion. Perhaps Whitman was reading something (a letter?)
or had just heard something that sent him over the edge. Representing
himself as a naive believer in all the myths that have governed human
history, including the immortality of the soul, the poet circumvents such
conventional genres as the love lyric, the political or social satire, and
the religious or philosophical meditation, to inscribe something significantly more abstract: an appeal to death itself as the joiner, destined to
hold all the social parts together, even when—especially when—the
poet himself cannot imagine their integration. If the speaker cannot or
will not distinguish between just and unjust laws, and between "marriage, commerce, newspapers, books, freetrade, railroads, steamers, international mails and telegraphs and exchanges," how much more cynical about the structures that govern intimate human relations can we
expect him to become? And so the 1855 *Leaves of Grass* ends with the
words, "Death is as great as life." [13]

Five or so years later, dreaming of himself as a supremely potent lover
of his medium, language, which even in his despair he had called "the

mightiest of the sciences" (LG 1855, p. 144), Whitman continued to
rewrite the regulatory heterosexual myths that have determined and, he
believed, deformed human history.[14] In the *Enfans d'Adam* sequence,
directing our attention to his "resurrection, after slumber," he appears
eager to seduce us into accompanying him on his journey toward a better place, a lusher, more androgynous garden. "(Hark, close and still,
what I now whisper to you," he writes, "I love you—O you entirely
possess me, / O I wish that you and I escape from the rest, and go utterly
off—O free and lawless, / Two hawks in the air—two fishes swimming
in the sea not more lawless than we)" (LG 1860, p. 289). This revital-
ized place is intermittently represented as less emphatically gendered.
For example, the speaker, having welcomed "the sight of the perfect
body, / The swimmer swimming naked in the bath, or motionless on
his back lying and floating," seems to identify with "The female form
approaching—I, pensive, love-flesh tremulous, aching." This language
occludes the difference between Whitman as woman and Whitman as
observer of woman. But the speaker then breaks into this intensifying,
sexually indeterminate moment by announcing, "The slave's body for
sale—I, sternly, with harsh voice, auctioneering,"

> The divine list, for myself or you, or for any one, making,
> The face—the limbs—the index from head to foot, and what it arouses,
> The mystic deliria—the madness amorous—the utter abandonment[.]
> (LG 1860, p. 289)

This particular interruption hearkens back to his interaction with the
faithful prostitute, and it appears that the speaker feels enslaved by his
dalliance with the female form. The slave's body is unmarked by gender,
but I have always assumed that Whitman had a male slave body in mind,
since the function of the figure is to divert us from his imaginary fusion
with the feminine. Other readings are of course possible, and the self-
abandonment motif may go in a number of different directions, especially in the direction of the love-slave.[15] But to my ear there is nothing
erotic about this passage, although Whitman, in dissolving the slave's
body into its component parts, may also be trying to redeem it for his
"divine list," his democratic catalogue of unfallen children of God.

   After seeking to extricate himself from a racial and sexual trap, which
in its attempt to collapse binaries also reinscribes them, Whitman turns
to the reader for help, and then returns to his attempt to write persua-
sively about the love of real men for real women by swearing fidelity to

"the woman that loves me, and whom I love more than my life." As we may now have come to expect, this pledge is rapidly exhausted. Throughout the *Children of Adam* sequence (to call the poems by their revised name), Whitman seeks to rewrite the myth of patriarchal marriage without being able to come to terms with his own fear of feminization, which he associates with lawlessness in the form of erotic self-abandonment. Following Eve, he becomes Eve, which is both a frightening and a thrilling experience. The emotional logic of the sequence depends on this paradox, which I wish to consider now in greater detail.

The most moving (in the sense of emotionally compelling) poem in the sequence famously exists in two radically different versions. Its emotional appeal is partly dependent on this liberating doubleness.[16] As published in 1860, "Once I passed through a populous city" presents the speaker as a man with a memory he cannot or will not shake off. For whatever reason, he has separated from "that woman who passionately clung to me," who held him "by the hand," mutely imploring him not to go, "with silent lips, sad and tremulous" (*LG* 1860, p. 311). Though his destiny takes him elsewhere, stereotypically all he remembers is her. A romantic ballad of hopeless love, the poem links idealized love and guilt, as Whitman identifies with the woman whom he has abandoned and who still faithfully keeps his shrine. In its manuscript form, however, Whitman's woman is a man and the poem reads as follows.

> Once I passed through a populous city, imprinting on my brain, for future use, its shows, architecture, customs and traditions
> But now of all that city I remember only the man who wandered with me there, for love of me,
> Day by day, and night by night, we were together.
> All else has long been forgotten by me—I remember, I say, only one rude and ignorant man who, when I departed, long and long held me by the hand, with silent lip, sad and tremulous.
>
> (*UPP* 2:102)[17]

There are minor differences between the version Whitman published in 1860 and the manuscript version first published by Emory Holloway in 1920: for example Whitman's male lover has a silent lip, whereas his female lover has silent lips, a difference that now signifies in relation to Luce Irigaray's classic essay, "Ce sexe qui n'en est pas un" ["This Sex Which Is Not One"].[18] There are also minor differences between both versions and the text Whitman eventually settled on as definitive in 1881. But the tonal difference is most marked in two directions. Whitman clearly knows "the man" better than the figure he first identifies vaguely as "a woman," and she is portrayed as Whitman's social equal, whereas the man is "rude and ignorant." Although one of the first biographers suggested that she was "of a higher social rank than his own," there is nothing in the 1860 poem to support this idea. The manuscript, however, is emphatic. The "youth" who wanders with Whitman is not his social equal.[19]

Although we have already seen Whitman romanticizing both rudeness and ignorance, as Wordsworth (among others) had taught him to do, here this aggressive judgment unsettles the poem. In condescending to his beloved, the speaker flirtatiously exploits him. So this description is uncomfortable on two counts. It indicates Whitman's lack of erotic self-confidence—we hear him wondering: Would a youth full of manners and learning want *him?*—and it belittles the beloved's intelligence, while seemingly praising his style. Rudeness was one of Whitman's major erotic tropes, and it functions brilliantly in such poems as "I Saw in Louisiana a Live-Oak Growing," from the *Calamus* sequence, where the idealized tree's look, "rude, unbending, lusty," makes the speaker think of himself (*LG* 1860, p. 364), or at least of his hopes for himself, if he could only learn to relax and enjoy life without subjecting it to too much analysis. Along related lines, in "I Sing the Body Electric," the third poem in the *Enfans d'Adam* sequence, Whitman had taunted the reader, "Do you know so much yourself, that you call the slave or the dull-face ignorant?" (*LG* 1860, p. 297), a question marking the difference between book-learning and heart-learning, identifying racial and ethnic prejudice with the wrong kind of egotism, and pointing sentimentally toward a democracy of feeling which might rescue the body politic from its various diseases. While ignorance was not always attractive to Whitman, the homoerotic fantasy of a rudely unconventional and lawless friend, censored in the published version of "Once I passed through a populous city," powerfully reemerges in the preceding poem, *Enfans d'Adam* number 8, in which Whitman writes,

> Native moments! when you come upon me—Ah you are here now!
> Give me now libidinous joys only!
> Give me the drench of my passions! Give me life coarse and rank!
> To-day, I go consort with nature's darlings—to-night too,
> I am for those who believe in loose delights—I share the midnight orgies of
>   young men,
> I dance with the dancers, and drink with the drinkers,
> The echoes ring with our indecent calls,

I take for my love some prostitute—I pick out some low person for my
  dearest friend,
He shall be lawless, rude, illiterate—he shall be one condemned by others
  for deeds done;
I will play a part no longer—Why should I exile myself from my
  companions?
O you shunned persons! I at least do not shun you,
I come forthwith in your midst—I will be your poet,
I will be more to you than to any of the rest.

(LG 1860, pp. 310–11)

Perhaps the (male) prostitute, the low person, and the dearest friend
are one and the same. Perhaps the speaker's encounter with the (female)
prostitute prepares him for other sexual adventures. But whether or not
the prostitute is a man, the male lover clearly is. And in this poem, Whitman's beloved friend is outside the law because, it seems, he has nothing
to lose and doesn't know any better, unlike the speaker whose self-
esteem and reputation are at stake. Whitman says that he will play a part
no longer, but lawlessness, rudeness, and illiteracy don't come easily to
him. As an intellectual, he hopes to learn how to consort with nature's
darlings, dance with the dancers, drink with the drinkers, and so forth.
Here is the journalistic Whitman looking for new material, broadening
his horizons. But the journalist-poet who is in the wrong (now right)
part of town is unwilling to give up his morally privileged point of view.
He knows what's indecent and what isn't; though he would like to have
the power to redefine obscenity, he would be a fool to believe that such
power actually inheres in him—a fool, a madman, or an ego-obsessed
poet. Versions of this story and these feelings remain in the manuscript
draft of "Once I passed through a populous city," in which Whitman
similarly counts on a lower-class other to initiate him into a world of
loose delights. Though he chose not to publish the male-gendered version of his narrative of "passing," a new psychological and literary style
about which he was deeply ambivalent had been forced upon him. In the
Calamus sequence, as Robert K. Martin observes, Whitman continued
to "search for a form for the expression of love between men."[20] The
elegiac tone persists, for in Whitman's experience male-male love both
banished melancholy and induced it. Looking to the future, however,
the poet hoped that his partial confessions would spare others the pain
and reinforce the pleasure that had inspired his art. And so he forged on,
for American purposes and for his own, redefining his relation to literary tradition, to his audience, and to a conflicted self.

CALAMUS

There have been suggestions that "I Saw in Louisiana a Live-Oak Growing" was drawn directly from Whitman's experience in New Orleans,
and it seems likely that this poem was based in part on the love affair
Whitman had in that Southern city with a vulnerable youth whom he seduced and abandoned. This youth reminds him of himself. The poem's
landscape is pastoral and dreamlike; the isolation of the setting mimics
the frightening, unbounded solitude Whitman tends to associate with urban rather than with rural life. The tree signifies primarily as a solitary
singer, and Whitman feels some understandable resentment about his
tree-rival's capacity for self-reliant utterance out of a seeming void. Despite the poet's identification with his symbol, this tree can't really be
humanized, for to be human is not merely to take up space, to talk, and
to feel happy, but to need a society of like-minded friends. Resenting and
coveting the tree's self-sufficiency, Whitman maims and appropriates
what he can, and, carrying it back to his room, drapes the now-broken
twig with moss. As a curious token of manly love, Whitman's incomplete art work reminds him of his absent "friends," while underscoring
the rivalry that troubles male-male affection.[21]

In this brilliantly lit yet shadowy poem about what it means to be human, to be a poet, and to be a public figure, Whitman distinguishes himself from his leafy precursor through his need for intelligent affection.
For this is a poem in which Whitman, with his self-divisions, despairs of
ever finding the beloved, intuitive, and knowledgeable life companion
for whom his heart aches. Rudeness and lustiness are not all. Moreover,
to the extent that Whitman romanticizes the tree's freedom from the
conventional rivalries of male gendering, he introduces a covertly racialized other, tropically dark and glistening, whose power he wishes to appropriate.[22] Whitman's fashionable melancholy functions to conceal his
imperial designs. Although he "naturally" suffers from the sentimental
heartsoreness that seems neverending, he returns to his room with his
spoils. Taming the public rival, Whitman replicates the symbolic logic of
the humiliation-driven male economy from which he seeks to escape and
against which he needs his dream-friends to defend him.

As we might expect, the rivalry that emerges as a key component of
male bonding for the Whitmanian subject remains an obstacle to love in
other poems of the *Calamus* sequence. Sentimental revery provides a buf-
fer against such rivalry but ultimately proves insufficient. Throughout

the sequence, Whitman engages in a number of experiments which seek to carry over the episodic good feeling generated by his private associations into the public sphere. To the extent that he can reconfigure these episodes as culturally significant, he hopes to heal the division between the me and the not-me, produced in part by the dissociation of young men from the work, the vision, and the affections of their fathers. And mothers too, for the ideals Whitman associated with societal perfection were often figured through the republican mother.[23] "When fathers firm, unconstrained, open-eyed—When breeds of the most perfect mothers denote America, / Then to me ripeness and conclusion," Whitman writes in "So Long," the concluding text of the 1860 *Leaves of Grass* (p. 452). But until that time, other solutions would have to do.

In *Enfans d'Adam,* for example, the poet had proposed "sex"—actual and figurative—as a solution to the problem of defining a significant, culturally mature literary vocation in America. Sex functions more obliquely in *Calamus,* but as I suggested a moment ago, there is plenty of revery designed to reconfigure the anxiety-producing, competitive, or even punitive structures of desire that impede or preclude male intimacy. For example, in *Calamus* 19, which immediately precedes "Live-Oak," the speaker redefines bravery to include heart-courage, and begins by asking the implied listener or reader, "Mind you the timid models of the rest, the majority? / Long I minded them, but hence I will not—for I have adopted models for myself, and now offer them to The Lands." As America's new male model, Whitman emphasizes his unglamorous white working-class affiliations when he directs our attention to his "swarthy and unrefined face," unkempt beard, "brown hands, and . . . silent manner . . . without charm." However unprepossessing these attributes— I take it that his tired "gray eyes" are not particularly alluring—this speaker poses no threat to the superior class status of the fantasized listener.[24] His beard is unclipped on his neck, but woolly and benign. Far from exemplifying the lawless energies described and mocked in "We Two Boys" (*Calamus* 26), this less commanding speaker is intent on pleasing and being pleased. "Yet comes one, a Manhattanese," he writes, "and ever at parting, kisses me lightly on the lips with robust love, / And I, in the public room, or on the crossing of the street, or on the ship's deck, kiss him in return; / We observe that salute of American comrades, land and sea, / We are those two natural and nonchalant persons" (*LG* 1860, p. 364).

Whitman's erotic reveries are not confined to the United States alone.

At a number of immensely pressured points in the *Calamus* sequence, he transgresses national boundaries to achieve a desired sentimental end. Following shortly after the live-oak meditation, for example, in *Calamus* 23, he explains,

> This moment as I sit alone, yearning and thoughtful, it seems to me there are other men in other lands, yearning and thoughtful;
> It seems to me I can look over and behold them, in Germany, Italy, France, Spain—Or far, far away, in China, or in Russia or India—talking other dialects;
> And it seems to me if I could know those men better, I should become attached to them, as I do to men in my own lands,
> It seems to me they are as wise, beautiful, benevolent, as any in my own lands;
> O I know we should be brethren and lovers,
> I know I should be happy with them.
>
> (LG 1860, p. 367)

Similarly, in "Long I thought that knowledge alone would suffice me" (*Calamus* 8, which Whitman never reprinted), the speaker overflows national boundaries ("Take notice, you Kanuck woods"), but the effect is very different. Renouncing his mission as America's imperialist bard to romp with the "One who loves me [and] is jealous of me, and withdraws me from all but love" (*LG* 1860, p. 354), he explores a more privatized, dependent, and feminized mode. In this subsequently suppressed poem, the speaker begins by recounting the history of his career, which he distorts in order to emphasize the drama of his self-transformation. The claim is that he had previously been uninterested in erotic relationships and motivated solely by a patriotic creed. (That the democratic poet had been frustrated by an unresponsive national and international audience remains implied rather than directly stated, like so much else in this superbly elliptical and tonally ambiguous self-portrait.) As he searches impatiently for a new kind of knowledge, the emerging homoerotic poet is frankly flattered by his lover's jealous need to withdraw him from, as he puts it, "all but love." Lover X is "jealous of" Whitman in several senses. Most obviously, he wants Whitman for himself and demands all of his sexual energy, attention, and affection. Less obviously, as a representative of the homoerotic private sphere, he feminizes Whitman, and this influx of femininity at first proves authenticating for the speaker, who is now out from behind a mask.[25]

That Whitman could not drop this mask for any length of time is part of a larger and by now well-known story. The British man of letters John

Addington Symonds, for example, first encountered Whitman through this poem in 1865, when his close friend F. W. H. Myers read it to him at Cambridge.[26] (Myers was a founder of the Society for Psychical Research.) Yet when Symonds persisted in his decades-long campaign to enlist Whitman as a homosexual rights advocate, the poet responded by condemning "morbid inferences" and boasting of six illegitimate children. In an infamous letter of August 1890, Whitman explained, "Tho' always unmarried I have had six children, two are dead—One living southern grandchild, fine boy, who writes to me occasionally. Circumstances connected with their benefit and fortune have separated me from intimate relations" (*Corr* 5:73). Biographers agree that these are the children of fancy.[27]

Perhaps late in 1871, Symonds initiated the correspondence by sending Whitman a copy of his *Love and Death,* inscribed on the title page, "To the Prophet Poet / Of Democracy Religion Love / This Verse / A Feeble Echo of His Song / Is Dedicated" (*Corr* 2:158). A cover letter noted that the poem "is of course implicit already in your Calamus, especially in 'Scented herbage of my breast.'" Whitman responded warmly in late January 1872, calling the poem "beautiful & elevated," saying he had "read & re-read" it, that he considered it "of the loftiest, strongest & tenderest," and that "I should like to know you better." The letter concluded, "Pray dont think hard of me for not writing more promptly. I have thought of you more than once, & am deeply touched with your poem." Despite this auspicious beginning, the correspondence culminated, as I have suggested, in one of the sorriest episodes in Whitman's life. In August 1890, Symonds wrote,

> In your conception of Comradeship, do you contemplate the possible intrusion of those semi-sexual emotions & actions which no doubt do occur between men? I do not ask, whether you approve of them, or regard them as a necessary part of the relation? But I should much like to know whether *you are prepared to leave them to the inclinations & the conscience of the individuals concerned?*

A mild enough question, but Whitman responded emphatically,

> Ab't the questions on Calamus pieces &c: they quite daze me. . . . that the calamus part has even allow'd the possibility of such construction as mention'd is terrible—I am fain to hope the pages themselves are not to be even mention'd for such gratuitous and quite at the same time entirely undream'd & unreck'd possibility of morbid inferences—wh' are disavow'd by me & seem damnable. (*Corr* 5:72–73)

Though a number of critics have amplified Whitman's response to suggest that he had his reasons (as undoubtedly he did), the fact remains that Whitman's fears got the better of him. In his letter of August 3, Symonds specifically asked Whitman to endorse the decriminalization of consenting homosexuality between adults in England and the United States, which he refused to do.

That Whitman could not publicly abandon his heterosexual persona for any length of time is very much part of the history of "Long I Thought" (*Calamus* 8), which in setting forth the antagonism of public and private spheres seems to choose the latter as having definitely the better claim. Yet the speaker who turns from the politics of poetry to the politics of male-male marriage will find that more intimate politics equally demanding. As Symonds noted in his 1890 essay "Democratic Art," "No individual man can be wholly original," and the bard who celebrates male homoeroticism as the bonding emotion of nations cannot wholly exclude women from his project.[28] Nor does he unambiguously want to. In representing the intimate and physical love of male comrades and lovers, Whitman eases the tension between public performance and private perversity by a legitimating refeminization of male-male love. This tension is further eased by tropes of marital fidelity, comradeship, and brotherhood which mystify the politicized gender anxieties aroused by homoerotic relationships and which further defend Whitman against the unresponsive audience he leaves behind.[29] We may be forgiven for suspecting that the quasi-marriage into which Whitman enters in "Long I Thought" will quickly reproduce the undemocratic gendered anxieties of the public sphere. But this is knowledge from which the poem seeks to defend us.

Surely the speaker's world elsewhere cannot last long. Nor do we steadfastly want it to. The community he forms with his lover is founded on jealousy; we are right to suspect that jealousy will undo it.[30] For the moment, however, the poet who had turned to literature for his knowledge of male heroism—"the examples of old and new heroes . . . of warriors, sailors, and all dauntless persons" and who was further inspired by the idea that "it seemed to me that I too had it in me to be as dauntless as any—and would be so"—happily finds himself put to the test of a real attachment (*LG* 1860, p. 354). There is a sense, then, in which his lover's jealousy is reassuring, as it was to Symonds, who described the poem as a trumpet call and was puzzled to discover in 1867 and subsequently that the poem which first "thrilled" him had disappeared from view. Why, he inquired of the aging poet in 1889, "have you so consistently omitted this in the canon of your works?"[31]

Whitman never answered, but critics have often suggested that because the *Calamus* poems seek to lend public significance to homoerotic and homosexual attachments, Whitman excluded from *Leaves of Grass* the "all but love" poem we have been considering, along with several others that subvert the patriotic mystifications of his homoerotic project.[32] These mystifications include a brilliantly heterogeneous vocabulary whose daring confrontations are already pronounced in "Starting from Paumanok," the "Proto-Leaf" or long new opening poem of the 1860 volume, on which, his notebooks show, he had been working for many years. Phrenology, religion, the Anglo-American male friendship tradition, fancy French imports, garden variety romanticism—the offshoots of such radically disparate material cultures wind and twist around one another in "Paumanok," recreating identities, part historical, part fanciful, that might authentically populate those curiously empty lands seized by the white man and poet from his displaced Indian brothers. Whereas the Indian father who sits dumbly smoking with his friends in "Song of Myself" seems narcotized by the illusion of male power, the poet trapped by love but conscious of his own entrapment reclaims the center from his literary rivals. "Not he, adhesive, kissing me so long with his daily kiss," Whitman writes,

> Has winded and twisted around me that which holds me to him,
> Any more than I am held to the heavens, to the spiritual world,
> And to the identities of the Gods, my unknown lovers,
> After what they have done to me, suggesting such themes.
>
> (*LG* 1860, p. 13)

"After what they have done to me, suggesting such themes." Here the note of outrage is unmistakable, yet the greedily neologizing 1860 poet continues to hope that "Affection shall solve every one of the problems of freedom," that "Those who love each other shall be invincible," and that "They shall finally make America completely victorious, in my name" (*LG* 1860, p. 349). The fear already announced in this opening poem is that manly affection might rob him of his manhood and that the experience of loving another man might confine him to the margins of American life. Yet just as Whitman looks beyond Manhattan and the already aging cities of the Eastern seaboard to a romanticized "inland America" dreamily inhabited by the "tan-faced prairie-boy" whose youthful docility he fancies, so Whitman looks beyond the historical

jealousies of the world he has known to pronounce, at the extreme verge
of utterance,

> Americanos! Masters!
> Marches humanitarian! Foremost!
> Century marches! Libertad! Masses!
> For you a programme of chants.
>   (*LG* 1860, p. 7)

Let us return to the multiple ambivalences of the *Calamus* sequence.
The lyricist who renounces the public sphere is not sure that he can trust
the muse who ties him to a more spiritual, politically marginalized, and
homoerotic world. Thus whereas "Long I Thought" counterpoints the
loss of political agency and the access of erotic power, the next poem
takes a closer look at the unofficial marriage into which the speaker has
entered, while emboldened by the touching belief that "It is to be enough
for us that we are together—We never separate again" (*LG* 1860, p. 355).
"Hours continuing long, sore and heavy-hearted" (*Calamus* 9, later excluded from *Leaves of Grass*) explodes this privatized trope of eternal fidelity and suggests that Whitman was right to be wary of the lover who
demanded the sacrifice of his ambition. Now it is Whitman's turn to be
jealous, sleepless, physically agitated, and all the rest of it. "Pacing miles
and miles, stifling plaintive cries," he finds that his erotic value has diminished in giving up "all for love." During these "sullen and suffering
hours" while he contends with shame, he asks poignantly,

> I wonder if other men ever have the like, out of the like feelings?
> Is there even one other like me—distracted—his friend, his lover, lost
>   to him?
> Is he too as I am now? Does he still rise in the morning, dejected, thinking
>   who is lost to him? and at night, awaking, think who is lost?
> Does he too harbor his friendship silent and endless? harbor his anguish
>   and passion?
> Does some stray reminder, or the casual mention of a name, bring the fit
>   back upon him, taciturn and deprest?
> Does he see himself reflected in me? In these hours, does he see the face
>   of his hours reflected?
>   (*LG* 1860, pp. 355–56)

I can testify to the fact that not everyone sees himself or herself reflected in this poem, which evoked a laugh and the response "poor guy"
from an unsympathetic seminar I once taught. Yet for the humiliated
Whitman, this question—has any other man ever felt the same not only
out of like feelings but out of a like occasion—holds the key to oth-

ers. Such as: can an illicit love affair that ends unhappily be publicly acknowledged? Such as: what will be the effect of his loneliness on his writing? Such as: might his loss of face, sorrow, or degradation—he's not sure what to call it—make him more accessible to ordinary readers who have previously been offended by his bluff? Though his lover is lost to *him* (and the implication is clear that the lover who forgets him has found someone else), he can't imagine falling in love again; the emotional resilience on which he formerly prided himself is a thing of the past. Then, too, just when he thinks he is getting to be his more or less tolerable self again, "some stray reminder, or the casual mention of a name, bring the fit back upon him, taciturn and deprest."

During these unnaturally prolonged hours of his torment, he sees no way out of his romantic obsession except, as Elizabeth Bishop later suggested with some irony, to "*Write* it!"[33] Thus the next poem in the sequence (*Calamus* 10), which is addressed to "You bards of ages hence!" seeks to discriminate more finely between various types of poems and poetic identities.[34] But he no longer *feels* like a leader of his nation's moral imagination, and his prophetic "American" poems seem to bear no relationship to those motivated by erotic possessiveness. Nor does he care to be remembered by them. Unfortunately, the "tenderest lover" is also the sorest and most vulnerable. This erotic victim (unlike the poetic strong man) is filled with "the sick, sick dread lest the one he loved might secretly be indifferent to him" (*LG* 1860, p. 356). Indifferent to place, his happiest hours are spent in privatized rural settings, "through fields, in woods, on hills, he and another, wandering hand in hand, they twain, apart from other men." Or sauntering the city streets, with his arm over his friend's shoulder, his friend's arm over his.

In his identity as private lyric poet, Whitman offers to take us down "underneath this impassive exterior," but since he doesn't really trust succeeding generations to draw their own conclusions about his turbulent inner life, he composes an epitaph for himself. And it is a flattering one, if somewhat dictatorial.

> I will tell you what to say of me:
> Publish my name and hang up my picture as that of the tenderest lover,
> The friend, the lover's portrait, of whom his friend, his lover, was fondest,
> Who was not proud of his songs, but of the measureless ocean of love
>   within him—and freely poured it forth,
> Who often walked lonesome walks, thinking of his dear friends, his lovers,
> Who pensive, away from one he loved, often lay sleepless and dissatisfied at
>   night,

> Who knew too well the sick, sick dread lest the one he loved might secretly
>   be indifferent to him,
> Whose happiest days were far away, through fields, in woods, on hills, he
>   and another, wandering hand in hand, they twain, apart from other men,
> Who oft as he sauntered the streets, curved with his arm the shoulder of his
>   friend—while the arm of his friend rested upon him also.
>
> (*LG* 1860, pp. 356–57)

Despite his representation of himself as a blameless victim, the problem of social trust persists. What if the future bard (or "recorder," in the more neutral language that prevailed) sees something other than tenderness beneath the speaker's impassive exterior? What if in addition to seeing prohibited male-male desire he or she sees an emotional volatility that may not be wholly ascribed to a homophobic culture? Previously Whitman has described himself as arrogant and deceitful. Will the unknown recorder remember these weaknesses and suspect that Whitman's sexual attentions are short-lived? If so, how will he or she respond? Who *is* the empowered reader/recorder to whom Whitman makes his incomplete confessions?

The third of the problematic poems subsequently excluded from *Leaves of Grass* raises precisely this question.

> Who is now reading this?
>
> May-be one is now reading this who knows some wrong-doing of my
>   past life,
> Or may-be a stranger is reading this who has secretly loved me,
> Or may-be one who meets all my grand assumptions and egotisms with
>   derision,
> Or may-be one who is puzzled at me.
>
> As if I were not puzzled at myself!
> Or as if I never deride myself! (O conscience-struck! O self-convicted!)
> Or as if I do not secretly love strangers! (O tenderly, a long time, and never
>   avow it;)
> Or as if I did not see, perfectly well, interior in myself, the stuff of wrong-
>   doing,
> Or as if it could cease transpiring from me until it must cease.
>
> (*LG* 1860, pp. 361–62)

At first glance, the act of loving strangers seems to be a highly forgivable crime of which to accuse himself, if all he does is love them from afar. Yet sudden sexual temptations had interested Whitman at least as early as *Franklin Evans*, and in the first edition of *Leaves of Grass* the poet had asked, "If you meet some stranger in the street and love him or her, do I not often meet strangers in the street and love them?" (*LG* 1855,

p. 88). Sudden sexual temptations, and the strange meetings with which they are associated, can emblematize both the problems and the promise of democracy.[35] They generate, for example, the unexpected and classless intersections of the 1856 masterwork "Crossing Brooklyn Ferry," in which Whitman projects himself ecstatically into an unlimited future. His curious attachment to other people, to "Crowds of men and women attired in the usual costumes," to "the sailors at work in the rigging, or out astride the spars," and to "the pilots in their pilot-houses," ties him to the strangely observant reader of the future: to you and me. "Closer yet I approach you," he writes, "What thought you have of me, I had as much of you—I laid in my stores in advance, / I considered long and seriously of you before you were born" (*LG* 1860, p. 384).

We may read "Crossing Brooklyn Ferry" as suggesting that a broadly humanist mission precludes particular male-male homoerotic attachments. The poem both affirms and denies the value of individual sexual experience. The masculine poet-persona who places his faith in the masculine or feminine reader of the future is troubled by his own erotic cowardice in the present. He is a "solitary committer," a masturbator (*NUPM* 1:231; *LG* 1856, p. 217). Despite this fault, which was vividly demonized by antebellum medical and moral discourse, the great renunciation of homosexual love Whitman makes in secret is empowering. Because of his self-discipline and his suffering, he is able to imagine himself fusing men, genders, nations, and races together. Within the less heroic compass of "Who is now reading this?" a secret love is a deforming love.

In "Crossing Brooklyn Ferry," the temptation renounced by the Whitman persona is brilliantly rendered. When he hears the young men who call him clearly and loudly by his nighest name as they see him "approaching or passing," and when he feels their arms on his neck as he stands, "or the negligent leaning of their flesh" against him as he sits, or sees "many I loved in the street, or ferry-boat, or public assembly, yet never [tells] them a word," he emerges to testify that, whatever his particular fleshly temptations, he "lived the same life with the rest," and that every social being performs a part, "The same old role, the role that is what we make it, as great as we like, / Or as small as we like, or both great and small" (*LG* 1860, p. 384). Moreover, at this potentially alienated moment, when the poet looks back on "the actor or actress," he suggests that something escapes from the web of socially constructed or performative identity, that there is a real me capable of resisting its painfully compromised moment. In most poems of the *Calamus* sequence, however, this real me no longer exists as a separate and mocking entity because the speaker's social self is more substantial. That is, once the social self is experienced as real, the real me has no autonomous psychological function.

Calamus 40 makes this point by contrasting "That shadow, my likeness, that goes to and fro, seeking a livelihood, chattering, chaffering," with the writing self never doubting "whether that is really me." The writing self continues to thrive "among my lovers" at the end of the *Calamus* project, whereas in "As I Ebb'd with the Ocean of Life," both the "real ME" and an equally hostile eternal self block Whitman's access to substantiating types of "athletic love" (*LG* 1860, p. 341). Consequently, his confidence in the coincidence of writing self and erotic self collapses; antagonists multiply, and the real me is "real ME." This excessive typography underscores Whitman's conviction that there will never be any permanent community in which he can recognize himself as a familiar and acceptable (loving) person. He knows nothing and believes that "no man ever can" (*LG* 1860, p. 197). There are no young men to whom he may speak, no young men on whom he may lean. In the absence of this youthful community of men, Whitman experiences himself as a posthumous writer, his dead lips oozing forth words that may have a certain superficial charm—they glisten and roll—but that lead nowhere. Whereas progress usually depends not only on distance from the past but on movement toward a goal, in "As I Ebb'd with the Ocean of Life" the speaker is trapped in an unreal crossing. Isolated from the young men who call him "Walt," he is haunted by the "sobbing dirge of Nature" (*LG* 1860, p. 199). This female-identified voice of lamentation cannot feed his soul.

As Michael Moon has suggested, Whitman's *Leaves of Grass* project was designed to merge social and erotic experience.[36] While this merger is not fully achieved in the *Calamus* sequence, the events recounted, even when bitter and painful, are rarely described as unreal. Whitman recognizes the self that has been thwarted in love because he remembers the self that has succeeded. Memorably, in *Calamus* 11,

> And that night, while all was still, I heard the waters roll slowly continually up the shores,
> I heard the hissing rustle of the liquid and sands, as directed to me, whispering, to congratulate me,
> For the one I love most lay sleeping by me under the same cover in the cool night,
> In the stillness, in the autumn moonbeams, his face was inclined toward me,
> And his arm lay lightly around my breast—And that night I was happy.
> (*LG* 1860, p. 358)

These memories fortify him for the future. And so the cycle ends:

> When you read these, I, that was visible, am become invisible;
> Now it is you, compact, visible, realizing my poems, seeking me,
> Fancying how happy you were, if I could be with you, and become your
>   lover;
> Be it as if I were with you. Be not too certain but I am now with you.
>   (*LG* 1860, p. 378)

The project of realizing a self is ongoing, and it is possible. Even death does not thwart it, because the language of real (that is, commonly agreed upon) hope is conceived as more powerful.

Nevertheless, the *Calamus* poems reinscribe differences the visionary Whitman was determined to deny. As previously noted, Whitman distrusted that "individualism, which isolates," unless it could be made to speak to "adhesiveness or love, that fuses, ties and aggregates, making the races comrades, and fraternizing all" (*DV* 949). His theory of democracy rejected the claims of "destructive iconoclasms," and he insisted in *Democratic Vistas,* his postwar sexual manifesto, that "democracy alone can bind all nations, all men, of however various and distant lands, into a brotherhood, a family" (*DV* 948). Whitman's class-binding democracy always depended on his faith in the People, whereas many of the most interesting *Calamus* poems reflect his distrust of ordinary readers, not just of "the literary classes." This distrust is especially marked in poems that explore the paradoxical social fate of two together. These autobiographical-sounding poems critique the negative consequences of male-male romantic obsession, as well as the intolerance of a homophobic culture. Such intense relationships reinscribe the isolating individualism Whitman's *Leaves of Grass* project was intent on revising.

We would therefore do well not to exaggerate the strategic differences among the first three editions of *Leaves of Grass.* I have been describing Whitman's progress toward speaking the love that dare not speak its name, but in making heterosexuality public in 1855, 1856, and 1860, he was not simply leading us toward the promised land of male-male love. As Richard Rorty contends, Whitman was deeply critical of the negative consequences of sexual repression, but Rorty fails to remark that Whitman was also intent on telling a life story that was full of contradiction.[37] Consequently, Whitman never lets us linger for long in a pure sexual utopia, especially since he sees sexuality as partly constituted by sadism. Even after the physically attractive butcher-boy of "Song of Myself" puts off his killing-clothes, he "sharpens his knife at the stall in the market." The narrator enjoys his "repartee and his shuffle and breakdown"—the breakdown of what?—but the subordination of animal to human merely underscores the visual subordination of younger to older man and of worker to writer (*LG* 1855, p. 34). Whitman does his best to minimize these differences of class and occupation and language, but they persist. His career depends on them; had "these States" already "achieved our [true] country," there would have been no call for *Leaves of Grass*. In short, Whitman has no way of telling the story of a continuously unrepressed sexual life; he lives in the world as we still know it in this regard, a world whose successes are partly constituted by acceptable social sadism. The people Whitman knew and the character he inhabited were powerfully resistant to anything like the paradigm-shift he claimed to be, and in part was, seeking. Consequently, when Rorty suggests that "Whitman would have been delighted by rock and roll, drugs, and the kind of casual, friendly copulation which is insouciant about the homosexual-heterosexual distinction," he oversimplifies.[38] The loving and thirsting-eyed poet of "Crossing Brooklyn Ferry" was both seduced and threatened by the beauty of the male body. He was disintegrated, yet part of the scheme, sustained in the present by his faith in a community of the future. Had that perfect community already been achieved, there would be no projected intersection of time and timelessness in "Crossing Brooklyn Ferry." A draft notebook entry for the poem records that "Where the great renunciation is made in secret, that will allure me" (*NUPM* 1:232), and Whitman's refusal to concentrate on one particular lover ("English Johny," for example, who is mentioned on the recto of one of his loose compositional fragments [*NUPM* 1:228]), could, under some circumstances, reinforce his sense of connection to the whole human race. But if sexual secrecy was necessary to his project, it was also his project's undoing. Sexual secrecy as experienced by Whitman was profoundly self-isolating and one night with one sleeping lover was not enough.

As I have been suggesting, in the second (1856) edition of *Leaves of Grass* Whitman tends to emphasize the relationship between sexual love and social cohesion rather than the "destructive iconoclasms" of individual romantic obsession. This is true even of "Song of the Open Road," a companion piece to "Crossing Brooklyn Ferry," and more idiosyncratically expressed. In "Song of the Open Road," Whitman suddenly explains,

> Here is adhesiveness—it is not previously fashioned, it is apropos;
> Do you know what it is as you pass to be loved by strangers?
> Do you know the talk of those turning eye-balls?
>
> (*LG* 1856, p. 229)

"Here is the efflux of the soul," he continues,

> The efflux of the soul comes through beautiful gates of laws, provoking
>   questions,
> These yearnings, why are they? these thoughts in the darkness, why are they?

And then this passage, adapted from a notebook draft,

> Why are there men and women that while they are nigh me the sun-light
>   expands my blood?
> Why when they leave me do my pennants of joy sink flat and lank?
> Why are there trees I never walk under but large and melodious thoughts
>   descend upon me?
> (I think they hang there winter and summer on those trees, and always
>   drop fruit as I pass;)
> What is it I interchange so suddenly with strangers?
> What with some driver as I ride on the seat by his side?
> What with some fisherman, drawing his seine by the shore, as I walk by
>   and pause?
> What gives me to be free to a woman's or man's good-will? What gives
>   them to be free to mine?
>
>   (LG 1856, pp. 229–230)

As we might expect, the notebook passage is concerned with men alone.
(The brackets indicate Whitman's deletions.)

> Why [are] be there men I meet, and [many] others I know, that [when] while
> they are with me, the sunlight of Paradise [warms] expands my blood—that
> [if] when I walk with an arm of theirs around my neck, my soul [leaps and
> laughs like a new waked child] scoots and courses like [a caressed] an un-
> leashed dog [caressed]—that when they leave me the pennants of my joy sink
> flat [from the] and lank in the deadest calm?

After an interval, and noting that he is writing at home while his brother
Jeff is practicing the piano, Whitman alludes to "Some fisherman,"
"some carpenter," "some driver," "men rough, [rough], not handsome,
not accomplished." Then he asks,

> Why do I know that the subtle chloro-form of our spirits is affecting each
> other, and though we may [never meet] encounter not again, [we know feel
> that we two] have [pass] exchanged the right [mysterious] [unspoken] pass-
> word [of the night], and [have] are thence free [entrance] comers to [each] the
> guarded tents of each others' [love] most interior love?
>   (What is the [cause] meaning, any how, of my [love attachment] adhe-
> siveness [for] toward others?—What is the cause of theirs [love for] toward
> [for] me?)—(Am I loved by them boundlessly because my love for them is
> more boundless?—) (DBN 3:764–65)

Like "Crossing Brooklyn Ferry" and "Song of the Open Road," this
early notebook entry reworks the problems and promise of male-

homoerotic desire, as experienced by Whitman, who was nothing if not inventive in devising passwords of the night. We have already noted his enthusiasm for stage drivers in previous chapters, and there is a very interesting essay to be written on Whitman and fishermen, whose cooperative virile actions extravagantly enthralled him. Between fishermen, fish rather than women function as mediums of exchange, and there are passages in which Whitman's desire to be a (phallic) fish is palpable, for example at the start of the 1860 "Starting from Paumanok," the birth island he characterizes unexpectedly as "fish-shape." But the pennants of joy that vivify the remarkable notebook entry quoted above have flagged in the 1860 poem "Who is now reading this?" where strangers have neither voice nor heft nor occupation, love is a word, and the speaker finds himself unhappily estranged not only from conventional (hetero)sexual norms but also from himself as a purposefully occupied and socially familiar human being. That sense of playing the same part with the rest is gone, as is his desire to play the part well, as is his ability to realize the cooperative feeling, at first feigned, with which he would like to "imbue [his] soul" (*EPF* 210). There now appears to be a self-destructive element in his "love" which he cannot sublimate; without effective voice and without transcendent vision, he has nothing left but his self-recriminations. Unlike the idealized readers of "Crossing Brooklyn Ferry" and "Song of the Open Road," the shape-shifting addressee of "Who is now reading this?" finally represents an unsympathetic moral perspective which has nothing to teach him. He has heard the voice before, condemning him for "it" and urging him to depress the adhesive nature—all too many times.[39]

In part because of the excessively moralistic language, Whitman deleted "Who is now reading this?" from subsequent editions of his book. Thus one critic contends that "this [poem] is the clearest expression of homosexual guilt ever to appear in *Leaves of Grass*," while another suggests that Whitman internalized the homophobia of his culture.[40] These are good observations, but Whitman talks about loving strangers in other poems (for example *Calamus* 18, "City of my walks and joys!"), about not understanding himself, and about harboring evil impulses. He had already warned readers away in *Calamus* 3 ("Whoever You Are Holding Me Now in Hand"), and to the extent that he was defending himself against official persecution such as he encountered in Washington, D.C., in 1865 and in Boston in 1881, *Calamus* 3 was equally dangerous.[41] Similarly, *Calamus* 12 warns readers in no uncertain terms against idealizing him, and in the rather gruesome *Calamus* 15, he urges his "confession drops" to "Stain every page—stain every song I sing, every word I say, bloody drops, / Let them know your scarlet heat—let them glisten, / Saturate them with yourself, all ashamed and wet, / Glow upon all I have written or shall write, bleeding drops, / Let it all be seen in your light, blushing drops" (*LG* 1860, p. 361). If we are looking for sexual guilt, here it is. And what of *Calamus* 36, in which the phallic speaker likens himself to a volcano, just waiting to explode?

> Earth! my likeness!
> Though you look so impassive, ample and spheric there,
> I now suspect that is not all;
> I now suspect there is something fierce in you, eligible to burst forth;
> For an athlete is enamoured of me—and I of him,
> But toward him there is something fierce and terrible in me, eligible to burst
>   forth,
> I dare not tell it in words—not even in these songs.
>
> (LG 1860, p. 374)

M. Jimmie Killingsworth points out that after the war Whitman considered eliminating other poems from the sequence, as evidenced by the markings in his so-called Blue Book.[42] We can never know for sure why Whitman decided to eliminate *Calamus* 16. But in other poems that link sexual repression and social aggression, Whitman is less critical of himself, and in that sense the split between the public and private Whitmans is less extreme. There are other *Calamus* poems which describe hopelessness, for example *Calamus* 28, "When I peruse the conquered fame of heroes," in which the speaker is filled with the "bitterest envy" when he reads "of the brotherhood of lovers, how it was with them, / How through life, through dangers, odium, unchanging, long and long, / Through youth, and through middle and old age, how unfaltering, how affectionate and faithful they were" (370).[43] But here Whitman is a sympathetic reader of his own troubles. Finally, the spoiling-for-a-fight tone of *Calamus* 16 sets it apart from later statements such as *Calamus* 39, which eventually concluded with the touching parenthesis, "(I loved a certain person ardently and my love was not return'd / Yet out of that I have written these songs)" (*LG*, p. 134). The parenthesis makes all the difference. Whitman could not always believe in himself and he could not always trust his audience. Through writing, he nevertheless hoped to create an enduring erotic community which might justify the psychological and perhaps physical risks he was taking. In the 1860 *Leaves of Grass,* there is always more than one faithful reader, even if there is only one lover. Even in *Calamus* 16, the speaker continues to imagine that "a stranger is reading this who has secretly loved *me*" (emphasis added). But in *Calamus* 16, his faith in his ability to control himself, other people, and his medium has been too deeply threatened. Quite simply, we know this because, following the Civil War, Whitman excised the poem from *Leaves of Grass* and never reprinted it, an action that underscores its significance in his career, in his life, and in the provocatively troubled history of their interrelationship.

We are now in a better position to understand what Whitman meant by "the problems of freedom" in the 1860 *Leaves of Grass,* problems he proposed to solve through male-homoerotic love rather than by "lawyers . . . an agreement on a paper . . . [o]r by arms" (*LG* 1860, p. 349). Whitman, I think, was referring to the freedom of one "modern" person to harm another and to the freedom of any "modern" individual to harm himself. His homosocial, homoerotic, and homosexual "democracy" was a psychological and political construct. It neutralized his characteristic suspicion of male-male intimacy and affirmed the social value of non-coercive, sympathetic affection between men. The boundaries between homosocial, homoerotic, and homosexual relations were constantly redefined by his literary project; he transgressed these historically familiar limits joyfully *and* at his peril. In his attempt to "plant [sexualized] companionship thick as trees along all the rivers of America," Whitman fantasized that he and his comrades would master the world, "under a new power." He also feared that these new masters would master him. Thus he resisted not only the heterosexual "tie[s]" that "band stronger than hoops of iron," but the homoerotic ties that band men together as well. We will never know how Whitman would have desired to "impress" others had homophobia not been part of his world. The poet who "SAW in Louisiana a live-oak growing" and who ironized style as performance was himself mocked by a "real ME" that denigrated his achievements in literature and in love. Despite the power of this depressing specter, which he could not fully overcome, in the 1860 *Leaves of Grass* Whitman's democratic "faith in sex" was emphatically extended to include male-homoerotic love. The first two editions of *Leaves of Grass* had shown the way, and this extraordinary third book revealed a powerfully autobiographical writer who, as he struggled to find happiness for himself, encouraged others to embrace the "real reality" of their own contradictions (*LG* 1860, p. 344).

SIX

Whitman Unperturbed

The Civil War and After

Drum Taps has none of the perturbations of Leaves of Grass.

> *January 6, 1865, to William Douglas O'Connor*
> *(Corr 1:247)*

I feel quite well, perhaps not as completely so as I used to . . . but I think I shall get so this spring—as I did indeed feel yesterday better than I have since I was taken sick last summer.

> *January 30, 1865, to Thomas Jefferson Whitman*
> *(Corr 1:250)*

As you see by the date of this, I am back again in Washington, moving around regularly, but not to excess, among the hospitals. . . . My health is pretty good, but since I was prostrated last July, I have not had that unconscious and perfect health I formerly had. The physician says my system has been penetrated by the malaria—it is tenacious, peculiar and somewhat baffling—but tells it will go over in due time. It is my first appearance in the character of a man not entirely well.

> *February 6, 1865, to John Townsend Trowbridge*
> *(Corr 1:254)*

Could you give me a little further information about my brother Capt. George W. Whitman, 51st New York . . . Why did not he, & the other officers, 51st N. Y., come up with the main body, for exchange? Were the other officers 51st there at Danville [Prison], time you left? Please tell me all you know, or think probable, on this subject of why they did not come? Have they been sent further south, to avoid exchanging them, or are they still at Danville? *Was* my brother *really well* & hearty?. . . . Do you know whether my brother got letters & boxes we sent him? Was he in the attempt to escape, Dec. 10, last? My dear sir, if you could take a leisure half hour & write me, *soon as possible,* what you know on these, or any points relating to my brother, it would deeply oblige me—

> *February 27, 1865, to Captain William Cook*
> *(Corr 1:255)*

I write a few lines to tell you how I find the folks at home—
Both my mother & brother George looked much better than
I expected—Mother is quite well, considering—she goes
about her household affairs pretty much the same as ever,
& is cheerful.

My brother would be in what I would almost call fair
condition, if it were not that his legs are affected—it seems
to me it is rheumatism, following the fever he had—but I
don't know—He goes to bed quite sleepy & falls to sleep—
but then soon wakes, & frequently little or no more sleep
that night—he most always leaves the bed, & comes down-
stairs, & passes the night on the sofa. He goes out most
every day though—some days has to lay by—He is going
to report to Annapolis promptly when his furlough is up—
I told him I had no doubt I could get it extended, but he does
not wish it—

I am feeling finely—& never enjoyed a visit home more
than I am doing this.

March 26, 1865, to William Douglas O'Connor
and Nelly O'Connor (Corr 1:256–57)

I am stopping longer than first intended, as I have decided
to print the book, and am now under way with it. The grand
culminations of past week impress me profoundly of course.
I feel more than ever how America has been entirely re-stated
by them—and they will shape the destinies of the future of
the whole of mankind.

April 7, 1865, to William Douglas O'Connor
(Corr 1:257–58)

After four agonizing years the Civil War was over. Richmond had fallen
on April 3, Lee had surrendered to Grant on April 9, and on April 15
Whitman was in New York seeing his small book *Drum-Taps* through
the press. But what Whitman later called "the foulest crime in history
known in any land or age" had already stained the presidential box at
Ford's Theater (*LG*, p. 339). So on that stupefying Saturday morning,
Whitman and his mother exchanged the papers silently. Neither of them

could say much, and nothing more was eaten that day. "Mother pre-pared breakfast," he later recalled, "and other meals afterward—as usual; but not a mouthful was eaten all day by either of us. We each drank half a cup of coffee; that was all. Little was said. We got every newspaper morning and evening, and the frequent extras of that period, and pass'd them silently to each other" (*SD* 711–12). He further recalled, "I re-member where I was stopping at the time, the season being advanced, there were many lilacs in full bloom. By one of those caprices that enter and give tinge to events without being at all a part of them, I find myself always reminded of the great tragedy of that day by the sight and odor of these blossoms. It never fails." [1]

In Washington the night before, Peter Doyle, who was attracted by celebrities and liked the theater, had gone to see the play, the President, and his wife. For his commemorative Lincoln lectures, which began in 1879, Whitman drew on Doyle's eyewitness account of the shooting, among other sources.[2] Oddly enough, however, the poem he completed by mid-September 1865 omits all direct reference to the violent human intervention that ended Lincoln's life.[3] The symbolism of "When Lilacs Last in the Dooryard Bloom'd"—the broken sprig, for example, that the persona offers to Lincoln's coffin at the end of Section 6—alludes obliquely to a premature ending. But a premature ending is not necessar-ily a historical outrage or a political injustice. Thus until the poem's final climax when, as Ed Folsom notes, Whitman "faces the horrifying results of the war," [4] the imagery seems to be working to exclude vulgar local associations, to exclude the trivial in favor of the exalted.

Critics have tended to assume that in "Lilacs" Whitman sought to avert his gaze and that of his readers from the specifically human deed wrought by John Wilkes Booth. As the "wound-dresser" poet, so the story goes, Whitman was seeking to promote a national psychology of peace. And there was no need for him to restate the obvious. His au-dience knew the unnarratable fact: Lincoln had been brutally assassi-nated.[5] Without denying the validity of this reading, in what follows I would like to suggest that dominant discussions of "the poet's attempts to resolve for himself and the nation the panic-struck vision of Lincoln's assassination as a black horror" have not yet fully accounted for the subtlety of Whitman's griefwork.[6] His cunning omission of the assassin's hand serves to problematize, as do other anti-occasional elements of the poem, the esthetic and erotic complexity of Whitman's bereavement, which includes anger, as we might expect, although the genealogy of this vengeful feeling is perhaps surprising.

With its nostalgia for the unclouded serenity of an earlier political, literary, and spiritual life, "Lilacs" takes its time about its strange revelations.[7] As he memorializes a culture's earlier ways of knowing, including its ways of sexual knowing, Whitman resists the desocialization—in psychoanalytic terms the castration—to which his "comrade lustrous with silver face in the night" (*LG,* p. 337) has been subjected. Michael Moon explains,

> What is perhaps most important to notice about the whole range of modes of relationship represented in *Leaves of Grass* is that the social and the sexual are usually not oppositional categories in them, nor is the social conceived of as being essentially nonerotic while the erotic is consigned to the restricted orbit of what the culture considers the sexual. It is the effect of the entire project not only to eroticize the social realm but also to socialize the culture's construction of the erotic as the highly anxiogenic realm of the intimate, the private, the shameful, the concealed, the destructive.

If, as Moon further argues, "the drama of the speaker's coming to terms (to the degree that he does) with the death of Lincoln and all the losses of the war that Lincoln's death is made to represent is related to the 'drama' of the origins of sexuality in the individual subject," then Whitman's understanding of mourning, and of the relationship between mourning and art, is necessarily pressured by his understanding of sexuality.[8] To a greater degree than Moon cares to acknowledge, however, in "Lilacs," and by extension in the 1867 *Leaves of Grass,* Whitman socializes the realm of grief by depersonalizing the realm of the sexual. Moon stresses "the text's repository of signs drawn from infantile erotic experience": "holding and being held, holding and releasing . . . and a traumatic rupture between the phases of each of these processes."[9] I prefer to emphasize the speaker's pride in his ability as an artist to subjugate his adult trouble and, by extension, to discipline his body. Grief, he informs us, returns each spring following the arrival of certain hopeful natural signs; grief renews itself, but tears do not flow unremittingly. This paradoxical opening is ripe for plunder, and reading the poem now we cannot help but hear the Eliotic echo: April is indeed the cruelest month. Galway Kinnell, however, hears another part of the story when he observes that in "Lilacs" "the grief is too thoroughly consoled before the first line is uttered."[10] Along somewhat similar lines, Christopher Beach contends that the poem "belie[s] Whitman's radical persona: that of a cultural iconoclast seeking to dismantle or overturn the dominant forms and values of the English and European literary traditions."[11]

These objections notwithstanding, "Lilacs" is Whitman's most astutely self-referential poem. As it revisits the esthetic and erotic crises of his career, the interior and exterior geographies of "Lilacs" take us back to all those erotically ambivalent occasions when the Whitman persona entered into and then resisted enduring personal attachments. These include the belated *Calamus* attachments of *Drum-Taps* without its "*Sequel.*" In the volume as completed before Lincoln's death, Whitman, finding his "boy of responding kisses," "buried him where he fell" (*DT* 43). Again, Moon is helpful here. He explains,

> Rather than representing a relational norm in Whitman, the erotic pairings depicted in a number of the "Calamus" poems (for example, "When I Heard at the Close of the Day," or "We Two Boys Together Clinging") are exceptional. They are also highly problematic in the broader context of the project, because they are alternately represented as being so satisfying that they isolate the erotic subject from all but one other person, or so painful that they isolate him altogether.[12]

When Whitman finds his "boy of responding kisses" on the battlefield, he is able to fantasize a relation of lovers and perfect equals that satisfies him completely. As we have seen, finding an adult man was another matter, beginning even before the 1855 *Leaves of Grass*. The point is not that Whitman chronically used or abused the young men who fell in love with him, but rather that, as poet and person, he was working to free himself of heterosexual relational norms based on the anxiety-producing model of the patriarchal family. "Lilacs" thus takes on a formidable challenge. Peter M. Sacks has shrewdly suggested that Whitman did not want to reestablish traditional fatherhood in the text, nor did he intend to affirm "the kind of figure traditionally essential to elegiac consolation," "a highly differentiated, totemic figure of authority and justice."[13] Although a full-scale critique of Whitman's bellicose mode in *Drum-Taps* lies beyond the scope of this chapter, it is evident that the poet who was writing "Lilacs" in the self-conscious character of "a man not entirely well" was seeking to spare himself, as well as the nation, from further suffering.

Suffering takes many forms, however, and as Robert Leigh Davis observes, in Whitman's Civil War writings there are multiple ironic layerings: "'enemies' are at the same time 'brothers,' 'sisters,' 'fathers,' 'friends,' and 'lovers.'"[14] In attempting to distinguish enemies from friends, a project that had been to some extent abandoned in the *Calamus* sequence, Whitman the artist (who claimed that "Drum Taps has none of the perturbations of Leaves of Grass") had begun to minimize the importance of the body. Under the pressure of Civil War, the social and the sex-

ual were becoming oppositional categories. After all, how *could* he
continue to view the body as a socializing agent for his culture when the
Union so insistently demanded its sacrifice? With the advantage of hind-
sight and with seeming inevitability, the bloodlust of battle culminated in
Lincoln's death. Yet if perturbation was a fact of sexual life, it was not the
only fact, and the elegiac voice of "Lilacs" is alert to its own duplicity. The
strain between comic and tragic sexual histories is palpable, and the poem
encourages a resisting reading. Does the lilac sprig, for example, which
the speaker breaks from its flowering bush and places on Lincoln's coffin,
evoke the assassin's or the lover's hand? Should we link the poet's cas-
trative gesture to the already somewhat archaic meaning of "hand" as
"handwriting"? Is it Whitman who engages in the "sexual renunciation"
of his lover, as Sacks contends,[15] or is it Whitman who affirms his own
literary and erotic potency through this tributary gesture? Indirectly,
"Lilacs" exposes the difficulty of distinguishing enemy from friend, and
the self as complete lover from the self as partial aggressor. It implies
many narratives of mutually exclusive desire; they do not fully cohere.

As he sentimentalized the lost leader, the "comrade lustrous with silver face in the night" (*LG*, p. 337), Whitman nevertheless stopped short
of celebrating the instruments of Civil War. This is an important consideration, and I should like to explore its erotic dimension further. Writing for himself and as his own first reader, in "Lilacs" Whitman creates
an idealized community of lovers who for the time being are not enemies. This temporary community is organized by death, since death
alone has the power to interrupt a phallic narrative which identifies the
male gender with social aggression. In the *Calamus* sequence, the poet
of comrades had already written and rewritten a homoerotic pastoral
from which personal aggression had been imperfectly exiled. But whereas
Calamus is mainly pressured by the persona's inconstant affections, together with those of his lover(s), the postwar poet discovers in death the
"Spirit Whose Work is Done." Reluctantly, he finds himself and the
nation eerily empowered by the loss of a leader who, in his absence, can
be reimagined as universally and personally beloved. Thus, as Benedict
Anderson might have predicted, Whitman's imagined community origi-
nates in a powerful repression of memory, the memory of a confused political and sexual life before death.[16] This necessary forgetting facilitates
the emotional reorientation and deep attachment between men and between men and women Whitman had long been seeking. The erotic poet
humbled by loss discovers in shared grief a personal and national bond
that democratizes social and psychological difference. Whitman's pow-

erful and self-reflexive poem represents the nation "draped in black" as a fragile but enduring socioerotic community, and in so doing realizes its true style and subject.

After visiting the White House on October 31, 1863, Whitman recorded in his diary, "Saw Mr. Lincoln standing, talking with a gentleman, apparently a dear friend. His face & manner . . . are inexpressibly sweet— one hand on his friend's shoulder, the other holds his hand. I love the President personally" (*DT* xviii–xix). These are the words of a man who wistfully watches other people's friendships and who romanticizes forbidden loves. Composing a sonorous hymn to endangered devotion that transformed the assassination from a political to a natural and even mythic event, Whitman was writing out of the context of earlier affectional losses, including the failure of his relationship with his father and the probable loss during the late 1850s of more than one idealized *Calamus* lover. He was also writing out of the more immediate failure of his love affair with the American public. His books had not sold, and despite his admiration for the common soldiers whom he encountered during his hospital visits, the fact still rankled. Though in Washington he had some ardent admirers, including John Burroughs to whom he was indebted for his knowledge of the reclusive hermit thrush ("likes shaded, dark, places in swamps— / is very shy / sings in May & June— / not much after June / is our best songster" ["Hermit Thrush," *NUPM* 2:766]), his words were mainly unheard by the nation at large, and Whitman's erotic anxieties were reinforced by his professional marginalization.

As a Lincoln lover, however, Whitman admits no erotic rivals. Living beyond time, under no temporal circumstances can he be displaced by his beloved's beloved, and he celebrates an erotic life inviolable by third parties. This fantasy of imperial selfhood nevertheless proves, is proving, and has proved remarkably unstable. "Lincoln" in death becomes the speaker's permanent possession, but "Lincoln" in death also becomes the speaker's permanent loss. The tenuous balance that Whitman achieves between erotic expression and erotic self-suppression is continually threatened by a number of historical factors, including, in the more or less real world, the demonstrable rivalrous intervention of John Wilkes Booth, who notoriously figures in the poem through his absence. Evidently Whitman is determined to expunge Booth from his text: both his national, political text and his timeless, unconscious text. But here Whitman discovers that silencing Booth is easier said than done. Insofar as "Booth" represents unanchored, free-floating aggression—that which cannot be contained, normalized, or truly forgotten—he also represents a perpetual possibility in the human soul. Although he may not know it, grief is only one of the feelings that threaten the persona's psychic integrity at the poem's inception. Because of the uncanny coincidence between his personal and cultural work—in both spheres his mission is ruthlessly to silence Booth and Booth's impersonators, including himself—the bereaved lover may have trouble distinguishing the nation's mourning, in which he participates, from his own less social, more self-immortalizing project. Ironically, reviewing Whitman's attitudes toward the historical Lincoln may serve to reinforce this point.

Like other ardent Northern Unionists, Whitman had initially entertained substantial and, in the event, realistic reservations about Lincoln's ability to hold the country together. At one time, he hubristically imagined that Lincoln could profit from the benefit of his political advice. "Brochure," he projected: "Two characters as of a dialogue between A. L.——n and W. Whitman.—as in? a dream—or better? Lessons for a President elect—Dialogue between W. W. and 'President elect.'" [17] Commenting on the fabled Lincoln-Douglas debates in August 1858, he observed that "of the two, Mr. Lincoln seems to have had the advantage thus far in the war of words." But he supported Douglas, to whom he looked to reinvigorate the moribund Democratic party. And it was Douglas rather than Lincoln who, Whitman hoped, would organize "a great middle conservative party, neither proscribing slavery . . . nor fostering it." [18] Before the war, then, Lincoln struck him as too extreme in his opposition to the South's peculiar institution.

Moreover, the radically competitive Whitman was prejudiced against the institution of the presidency, disputing as he did the concept of "Supremes." "I praise no eminent man—I rebuke to his face the one that was thought most worthy," he announced in the 1860 consciousness-raising poem "Myself and Mine," a rather transparent example of his envious need to feel good about himself, and a poem in which he vowed "To speak readily and clearly—to feel at home among common people." "It is ended—I dally no more," he wrote,

> After to-day I inure myself to run, leap, swim, wrestle, fight,
> To stand the cold or heat—to take good aim with a gun—to sail a boat—
>   to manage horses—to beget superb children,
> To speak readily and clearly—to feel at home among common people,
> And to hold my own in terrible positions, on land and sea.
>
> (*LG* 1860, p. 224)

Paradoxically, the antebellum Whitman was both a statesrighter and a Unionist, and in the "Proto-Leaf" to the 1860 *Leaves,* he had declared, "I will make a song for the ears of the President, full of weapons with menacing points, / And behind the weapons countless dissatisfied faces" (*LG* 1860, p. 10). With good reason, Whitman hated Buchanan, but his antipresidential diatribes were part of a larger politics in which there had to be room at the top for the ordinary men and women whom he imagined as his readers. "Have you outstript the rest? Are you the President?" he inquired. "It is a trifle—they will more than arrive there every one, and still pass on" (*LG* 1860, p. 50). Thus, he had asked:

> Is it you that thought the President greater than you?
> Or the rich better off than you? or the educated wiser than you?
> . . . .
> The President is there in the White House for you—it is not you who are
>   here for him. . . .
> . . . .
> You workwomen and workmen of These States having your own divine
>   and strong life,
> Looking the President always sternly in the face, unbending, nonchalant,
> Understanding that he is to be kept by you to short and sharp account of
>   himself,
> And all else thus far giving place to men and women like you.
>   (*LG* 1860, pp. 145, 149, 157)

Along with the 1855 "Preface," the first three editions of *Leaves of Grass* are filled with this kind of language: antipatriarchal, anti-establishment, and antipresidential. There is also a self-interested, demagogic edge to Whitman's rhetoric. When the "Presidents shall not be their common referee so much as their poets shall" (*LG* 1860, p. 115), power shall be transferred not just to any poet but to Whitman in particular.

Associating presidents with tyrannical fathers as he does in "Song of the Broad-Axe," where he urges that children are to be "taught from the jump . . . to be laws to themselves, and to depend on themselves" (*LG* 1860, p. 133), Whitman also announced in the "Apostroph" to the "Chants Democratic" of the 1860 *Leaves,* "O you grand Presidentiads! I wait for you!" (*LG* 1860, p. 108), which is not surprising considering that he had always been reluctant to jettison a vocabulary of personal loyalty based on the model of family ties. This model, as we have seen, generated fantasies of perfect brotherhood and fatherhood, included a weeping George Washington, enabled Whitman to address Emerson as "dear Friend and Master", and could accommodate other "supremes," such as God. (On perfect motherhood, see the next chapter.) In any event, the poetically productive contradiction between the anarchic and conservative Whitmans is inscribed in "Lilacs," where the dead president is both a melancholy comrade (not a supreme) and "the sweetest, wisest soul of all my days and lands" (a supreme of a democratic sort).

Whitman first saw Lincoln in person in mid-February 1861. From the top of an omnibus, he observed a silent, sulky crowd observing the black-clad president-elect in front of the Astor House on Broadway. Though Lincoln's life was already being threatened—both Lincoln and his wife feared that he would never return to Springfield alive—at the suggestion of New York Senator William Henry Seward he was deliberately taking a circuitous route on his journey to the capital, so as to rally support in the North. "The crowd that hemm'd around consisted I should think," Whitman recalled in his anniversary lecture,

> of thirty to forty thousand men, not a single one his personal friend—while I have no doubt, (so frenzied were the ferments of the time,) many an assassin's knife and pistol lurk'd in hip or breast-pocket there, ready, soon as break and riot came.
>
> But no break or riot came. The tall figure gave another relieving stretch or two of arms and legs; then with moderate pace, and accompanied by a few unknown looking persons, ascended the portico-steps of the Astor House, disappear'd through its broad entrance—and the dumb-show ended.[19]

So frenzied were the ferments of the time that in the homiletic 1860 poem beginning "Respondez! Respondez!" Whitman had commanded apocalyptically, "Let Death be inaugurated! / Let nothing remain upon the earth except the ashes of teachers, artists, moralists, lawyers, and learned and polite persons! / Let him who is without my poems be assassinated!" (*LG* 1860, p. 168). It was galling to the poet who called himself the Answerer to find his ideas slighted, ignored, or even violently rebuffed by America's thinking elite. Whitman could play a part no longer; he was incensed with a little success.[20]

Following his own move to Washington in December 1862, Whitman was able to observe Lincoln more closely. The two men were never introduced and never spoke, but Whitman often saw the president as he was driven through the streets of Washington in his carriage. And he began to identify with Lincoln's plight. Writing to his friends Nat Bloom and Fred Gray, whom he called his "gossips & darlings," on March 19, 1863, Whitman noted:

> I think well of the President. He has a face like a hoosier Michael Angelo, so awful ugly it becomes beautiful, with its strange mouth, its deep cut, criss-cross lines, and its doughnut complexion. My notion is, too, that

underneath his outside smutched mannerism, and stories from third-class county barrooms, (it is his humor,) Mr. Lincoln keeps a fountain of first-class practical telling wisdom. I do not dwell on the supposed failures of his government; he has shown, I sometimes think, an almost supernatural tact in keeping the ship afloat at all, with head steady, not only not going down, and now certain not to, but with proud and resolute spirit, and flag flying in sight of the world, menacing and high as ever. I say never yet captain, never ruler, had such a perplexing, dangerous task as his, the past two years. I more and more rely upon his idiomatic western genius, careless of court dress or court decorums. (*Corr* 1:82–83)

"I had a good view of the President last evening," the poet, who remained concerned for Lincoln's safety, wrote to his mother on June 30, 1863:

He looks more careworn even than usual—his face with deep cut lines, seams, & his *complexion gray,* through very dark skin, a curious looking man, very sad—I said to a lady who was looking with me, "Who can see that man without losing all wish to be sharp upon him personally? Who can say he has not a good soul?" The lady assented, although she is almost vindictive on the course of the administration, (thinks it wants nerve &c., the usual complaint). (*Corr* 1:113)

This complaint was shared by Whitman's brother Jeff, who found Lincoln indecisive, "not a man for the times, not big enough . . . an old woman." [21] For his part, Whitman tried not to blame Lincoln for Union losses. "I believe fully in Lincoln," he wrote to Abby Price as Meade was unable to slow the Confederate advance across Virginia's Rapidan River; again, Whitman employed the ship of state metaphor that figured prominently in his letters home: "Few know the rocks & quicksands he has to steer through" (*Corr* 1:163–64).

The ship of state metaphor also figured prominently in one of Lincoln's recurrent anxiety dreams, which, despite its murky symbolism, the president himself considered an omen of Union victory. And so it happened that on Good Friday, April 14, 1865, when Lincoln held his last cabinet meeting,

General Grant, who attended the meeting, was asked for late news from Sherman, but had none. Lincoln remarked that it would come soon, and be favorable, for last night he had dreamed a familiar dream. In a strange indescribable ship he seemed to be moving with great rapidity toward a dark and undefined shore. He had this same dream before Sumter, Bull Run, Antietam, Murfreesborough, Vicksburg, and Wilmington. Matter-of-fact Grant remarked that Murfreesborough was no victory—"a few such fights would have ruined us." Lincoln looked at him curiously and said, however that might be, his dream preceded that battle. [22]

So Whitman's fears for Lincoln's safety, as expressed in his most popular poem, "O Captain! My Captain!" and as represented by the thoroughly conventional ship of state metaphor, had a dense history in the poet's thoughts and in the president's. With good reason, then, both Mutlu Konuk Blasing and Kenneth M. Price refer to Lincoln as Whitman's political alter ego.[23] He had not always been so, but so he became. As a political person, however, Whitman was making what Jahan Ramazani calls "the prototypical elegiac leap from particulars to redemptive abstractions."[24] To write his way out of those historically specific divisions and self-divisions we have been examining, Whitman allied himself emotionally with the reclusive hermit thrush who, whatever else he may be, is clearly his *artistic* alter ego in "Lilacs." Whitman addresses this bleeding other as "dear brother," reminding him in somewhat archaic diction, "If thou wast not granted to sing thou would'st surely die." The language recalls the voice of the bereaved mockingbird in "Out of the Cradle Endlessly Rocking," but following the Civil War, Whitman understands even more acutely not only that poetry, in and through communion with others, may forestall spiritual death, but that "song" arises from parting. "Sooner or later," ceremonies of departure epitomize the human condition.

"Must not worry about George, for I hope the worst is over—must keep up a stout heart," Whitman had cautioned himself in a notebook entry written early in 1863. But then he had exploded, "My opinion is *to stop the war now*" (*NUPM* 2:548–49). Whatever his reservations about Lincoln's leadership, by the end of October he explained to his mother, "I have finally made up my mind that Mr. Lincoln has done as good as a human man could do—I still think him a pretty big President" (*Corr* 1:174). Thereafter, he continued to reiterate his support for a beleaguered president, although it could be argued that he was almost equally taken with General Grant, "the most in earnest of any man in command or in the government either" (*Corr* 1:211). "Others may say what they like, I believe in Grant & in Lincoln too" (*Corr* 1:213). By May 6, 1864, he was convinced that

> Grant has taken the reins entirely in his own hands—he is really dictator at present—we shall hear something important within two or three days—Grant is very secretive indeed—he bothers himself very little about sending news even to the President or Stanton—time only can develope his plans—I still think *he is going to take Richmond & soon*, (but I may be mistaken as I have been in past)— (*Corr* 1:219–20)

Many of these contradictory attitudes toward Lincoln and male heroism are exemplified by a letter Whitman wrote to his mother following the assassination. On May 25, he praised the new president, Andrew
Johnson, extolled Grant, who had been instrumental in effecting the exchange of Captain George Whitman from a Confederate prison camp,
as "the noblest Roman of them all," and proffered an oblique dismissal
of both leaders, Johnson and Grant, with the statement, "but the *rank
& file* was the greatest sight of all" (*Corr* 1:261–62). So the point is not
that Whitman was more or less indifferent to Lincoln before John Wilkes
Booth changed history. The seeds of his Lincoln cult had been planted,
as had the seeds of a Grant cult. But following Whitman's attitudes in
his contemporaneous writings, we are far from a vision of Lincoln as "the
grandest figure yet, on all the crowded canvas of the Nineteenth Century," as he became in the somewhat ironically titled "Personal Reminiscences of Abraham Lincoln." [25]

Nevertheless, Whitman's finest Lincoln elegy, "When Lilacs Last in
the Dooryard Bloom'd," is strikingly free of such particularizing detail
as he could have provided from personal observation, from the firsthand
accounts of others, or from his reading—had he wished to memorialize
the historical Lincoln. As Helen Vendler has noted, "Lilacs" does not
really contain "Memories of President Lincoln," which is the title of the
Leaves cluster to which the poem was eventually assigned.[26] Other ele-
gists provided "memories" of President Lincoln, evoking his rise from
obscure origins, early losses, "cunning with the pen" (the phrase is Richard Henry Stoddard's), proverbial honesty, penchant for telling humorous stories, hatred of slavery, clemency toward the South, and political
martyrdom—to name just a few themes in the voluminous Lincoln literature of the postbellum era.[27] Instead, Whitman histrionically fore-
grounded himself as the leading character in Lincoln's drama and dis-
solved the actual Abe into a national panorama of lost men. Given this
dramatic repression of Lincoln's personal history and particular qualities ("the sweetest, wisest soul of all my days and lands" does not really
qualify in the way of particularizing historical detail), and Whitman's almost complete repression of the murder as murder, it is evident that the
poet's literary aggression had targets other than Booth. In short, Whitman's historically conditioned distrust of powerful men was so great as
to covertly determine the structure of any serious poem that he might
write in praise of a fallen leader.

How does one compete with the honored dead, the dead whom one also wishes to honor? To say that Whitman identifies positively or even narcissistically with Lincoln, as to some extent he surely does, is not to suggest that he identifies with a unitary phenomenon. The poet who earlier in his career prided himself on his contradictions knew whereof he spoke. Caught as he is between a regenerative ideal ("fresh as the morning") and the nightstricken actual, the persona is determined to transcend his very representative grief and is committed to his personal, isolating quarrel with what, in his shrewd psychic economy, the dead president also represents: the power of the presidency, the power of the father, the power of the modern, technological, military state. Let's not be foolish here and claim that Whitman is in love with an aristocratic ideal. But just as at one time John Fitzgerald Kennedy seemed to represent a witty and humane alternative to his lackluster predecessor, so too, Lincoln, even as a "hoosier Michael Angelo," accumulated some of the trappings of an imperial presidency.[28] Nor was Whitman unimpressed by imperial presences. From a distance, he had also been starstruck by the handsome young Prince of Wales, the future King Edward VII.[29] And he admired the "Princes of Asia" who visited New York City in June 1860 and whose "swart" cheeks provided a positive model of elegant nonwhiteness. (The Japanese princes are described as "leaning back in their open barouches, bare-headed, impassive" [*DT* 61].) Considered as a democratic performance, then, "Lilacs" brilliantly encapsulates the American fascination with royalty, with "Yous up there" and with "Supremes."

I am suggesting that "Lilacs" has two emotional projects: transcending grief and transmuting aggression. When the speaker praises the dead president as "the sweetest, wisest soul of all my days and lands" or as his "dear," then "dearest" comrade, he is specifically denying Lincoln's political power and robbing him of his phallic force. Vaguely reminiscent of Wordsworth's Lucy, "Fair as a star, when only one / Is shining in the sky," Lincoln is associated with the evening star Whitman later called "voluptuous Venus . . . languid and shorn of her beams, as if from some divine excess" (*SD* 806). Just as in the opening poem of Wordsworth's "Lucy" sequence a dropping moon portends her death ("'O mercy!' to myself I cried, / 'If Lucy should be dead!'"), so too in "Lilacs" the star's disappearance portends the president's death, stagily.[30] In keeping with the poem's ambiguous emotional project, Whitman's "lustrous" orb is both masculinized and feminized, empowered and disempowered, possessing the brilliance of a masculine supreme tempered by the obscurity of the feminized dead.

The persona's need to evade his aggression, to cover it all over with "bouquets of roses . . . with roses and early lilies . . . [and with] the lilac that blooms the first" (*LG*, p. 331), has two main literary consequences. First, in offering Lincoln's coffin his sprig of lilac, he renounces his vision of himself as a romantic rebel, a vision allied with his sense of himself as a primitive phallic force. Second, having renounced this sociopolitical conception of his poetic mission, he is compelled to sing "Death's outlet song of life," "Song of the bleeding throat" (*LG*, p. 330). Glancing obliquely at Lincoln's martyrdom, the self-dramatizing Whitman stages his own demise. Empathetically merging with Lincoln, he defuses "Lincoln's" structural power.

At the same time, however, Whitman's still-powerful need to compete with his beloved, with "Lincoln," erupts in Section 15 when he compares the welfare of the living and the dead. Such comparisons were conventional in sentimental literature, where, as in Susanna Rowson's novel *Charlotte Temple*, they usually functioned as devices to resolve otherwise irreconcilable political and literary conflicts.[31] The belief that the dead are better off than the living also influenced how people thought about hardship. Consider the memoirs of Private Henry Robinson Berkeley, a Confederate soldier who, like Peter Doyle, was a member of a Virginia militia unit when the war began. Unlike Doyle, Berkeley lasted out the entire conflict, although he was captured in March 1865 and imprisoned at Fort Delaware, Delaware. Along with other Southern prisoners, he was released in mid-June on the condition that he take an oath of allegiance to the United States government. Berkeley was a Virginia native, and the son of a farmer. Though his future occupation was schoolteaching, he was not a particularly reflective man and was thoroughly demoralized by the war's conclusion. He was convinced that Lincoln should have been in church rather than at the theater on that fatal Good Friday and was personally embittered by the rough treatment he and other Confederate prisoners received in the weeks following Lincoln's death, when there was talk of a national conspiracy afoot that caused Confederate prisoners to be subjected to further reprisals.

Searching for a way to conclude a diary that had become a record of his humiliations, Berkeley, who was by then waiting in Richmond for a ride back to his home in Hanover County, recorded:

> As I had an hour, I thought I would walk a little way down Main Street and take a look at the burnt district. One could hardly tell where Main Street had been. It was one big pile of ruins from the Custom House to the wharf at Rocketts. At this point, the Yanks had collected all kinds of debris of war: cannon, muskets, bayonets, cartridge boxes, swords, broken guncarriages, broken

wagons, etc. I had never imagined that the Confederacy had one-half as many
siege guns in and around Richmond. As I gazed sadly over all this war wreck-
age for a few moments, my thoughts were with our noble dead, "the unre-
turning brave." Is it better with them or with us? We hope, aye, we almost
know it is well with them. But who knows what the future holds for us; only
God. I turned away and with a sad and gloomy heart bent my steps towards
the Depot.[32]

In the midst of a still unfolding narrative, Berkeley's question—"Is
it better with them or with us?"—cannot be answered. A Yankee-
dominated life may no longer be tolerable for him, and as he steps toward the Depot, his shattered affections lie with the heroic dead. Whitman, with greater freedom to *shape* his narrative, and less deference
to an outcome-determining God, cannily and categorically asserts that
whereas the living remain and suffer, the dead are fully at rest:

I saw battle-corpses, myriads of them,
And the white skeletons of young men, I saw them,
I saw the debris and debris of all the dead soldiers of the war,
But I saw they were not as was thought,
They themselves were fully at rest, they suffer'd not,
The living remain'd and suffer'd, the mother suffer'd,
And the wife and the child and the musing comrade suffer'd,
And the armies that remain'd suffer'd.

                                                            (*LG*, p. 336)[33]

Perhaps, after all, Whitman *did* feel some guilt about not having served
in the war, guilt that provokes an unequal, even inelegant competition
with the dead for primacy of suffering. Although he claims to have fled
forth into "the hiding receiving night that talks not," his flight from language into "unconscious scenery" is countermanded by the evidence of
his text (*LG*, pp. 334, 333). Whitman's marked assertion of subjective
privilege may also be intended to block other memories, specifically
the failure of consciousness to sustain itself under the pressure of trau-
matizing events. Whitman, for example, represses telltale memories of
the hospitals, and of his personal crises in ministering to the wounded
young soldiers whom he tried to comfort, with varying success. Joining
hands with two ambiguously gendered companions, his "comrades in
the night," the oblivion-seeking speaker is prepared by "the song of the
bird" to encounter the unorthodox parent whom he has always feared,
the "*Dark mother always gliding near with soft feet*," and whom he
now welcomes as a "*strong deliveress*" (*LG*, pp. 334, 335).
    As he abandons his "war of words" and bids farewell to the deeply
gendered poetry of the politically marked body, the "Lilacs" elegist

grasps at abstractions and, in Ramazani's terms, "hails a shadowy maternal figure as origin and end." But whereas Ramazani describes Whitman as participating in a patriarchal, homosocial tradition that relegates women to the roles "of ineffectual muses, distracting nymphs, inadequate mothers, and figures of death," [34] we may also see him as turning away from a phallic economy of death not only toward an alliance with his shy and solitary brother, the graybrown hermit thrush, who floats "the carol of death, and a verse for him I love," but toward an even more powerful alliance with the pre-oedipal mother. By reconnecting with her, the poet may turn back toward life.

> Approach strong deliveress,
> When it is so, when thou hast taken them I joyously sing the dead,
> Lost in the loving floating ocean of thee,
> Laved in the flood of thy bliss O death.
> . . . .
> I float this carol with joy, with joy to thee O death.
>
> (LG, p. 335)

In voicing his chant of fullest welcome to the unknown mother, Whitman celebrates both the return to the intersubjective intimacy he associates with a feminine origin ("*And the body gratefully nestling close to thee*") and the heroism of all those who, like him, persist in clinging to the familiar in the face of the unimaginable. Furthermore, in emphasizing that the male dead do not suffer, the poet carves out an important role for the grieving wife and mother, with whom he is unambiguously identified. Faced with devastation, he holds both men and women accountable for their work of memory, "there in the fragrant pines and the cedars dusk and dim." This work proceeds beyond the borders of a brutally phallic economy, taking the Whitman persona, then, into a country he has glimpsed before. Reconnecting with a maternal origin, Whitman seeks to free himself and his nation from the violence engendered by a patriarchal past. This return is, however, as Ramazani and others have suggested, not without its cost, and in the next chapter I examine this matter from a somewhat different perspective.

"The death of the late President," Abraham Lincoln had declared in July 1850, following the sudden death of Zachary Taylor, whom Whitman had seen in New Orleans, "may not be without its use in reminding us that we, too, must die. Death, abstractly considered, is the same with the high as with the low; but practically, we are not so much aroused to the contemplation of our own mortal natures, by the fall of *many* un-

distinguished, as that of one great, and well known name." [35] Lincoln's
death caused Whitman to contemplate the problem of death, "abstractly
considered," just as the deaths of many undistinguished people, including that of his civilian brother Andrew in 1863, contributed to his ambivalently gendered sense of himself as a ghostly survivor.[36] In "Lilacs,"
the poet of the body becomes the poet of the phallic body's tragedies.
Despite Whitman's desire to free himself and the nation from guilty
complicity in the war and in Lincoln's death by naturalizing death as, for
example, "the black murk that hides the star!" and as "the cloud, the
long black trail" (*LG,* p. 334), there linger the guilt-inducing stains of
specifically human and, one imagines, mostly male actions. Perfuming
"the grave of him I love," the speaker seems to blame himself in Section
8 for not having prevented Lincoln's death, and to blame himself in Section 15 for not having fought in the war, with his comrades. Psychically
battle-fatigued, "all splinter'd and broken" (*LG,* p. 336), he finds it necessary to insist, as I have remarked, that the young men who have died
are fully at rest, whereas the remaining men, women, and children remain
to suffer.

While suffering eventually defines the poem's richly complex idiom,
Whitman stresses that life, "The miracle spreading bathing all," emerges
out of death, and that art must accommodate both. Throughout "When
Lilacs Last in the Dooryard Bloom'd," as the speaker confronts both
loss and aggression, there are ebbs and flows in his access to physical
and psychic power. Cruel hands hold him powerless; he uses his hands
to break off a sprig of lilac with its flower; he contributes his sprig of lilac
to the coffin that slowly passes and then to all conceivable coffins, discovering joyously and paradoxically the copiousness of nature in his
feverish efforts to celebrate death; he imagines himself as a tomb deco-
rator hanging pictures on the walls of "the burial-house of him I love"
(*LG,* p. 332); he holds hands with the thought and the knowledge, with
the anticipation and the retrospective awareness of death; he hymns
"the sure-enwinding arms of cool-enfolding Death" in Section 14 (*LG,*
p. 334); and, following his visionary experience in Section 15, he frees
himself from "the hold of my comrades' hands" (*LG,* p. 336). Finally,
in Section 16, his hands are at rest and he leaves the lilac with heart-
shaped leaves "there in the door-yard, blooming, returning with spring"
(*LG,* p. 337). He doesn't need to break it or to use it to smother his grief.
He can afford to leave it alone.

Can it be, then, as Harold Bloom has wickedly suggested, that hands
are more than merely totemistic in "Lilacs" and that the poem is cen-

trally concerned with masturbation? He explains that the sprig of lilac represents what the poet, in Section 25 of "Song of Myself," calls his "live parts," and that "the voice of the bird will represent those ardors so intense, so wrenched from Whitman, that he did not know he possessed them." Moreover, "a failed masturbation is the concealed reference in Section 2 of the *Lilacs* elegy":

> O powerful western fallen star!
> O shades of night—O moody, tearful night!
> O great star disappear'd—O the black murk that hides the star!
> O cruel hands that hold me powerless—O helpless soul of me!
> O harsh surrounding cloud that will not free my soul!
>
> (*LG*, p. 329)

Bloom further explains that "the cruel hands are Whitman's own, as he vainly seeks relief from his repressed guilt, since the death of Father Abraham has rekindled the death, a decade before, of the drunken Quaker carpenter-father, Walter Whitman, Senior."[37]

However implausibly lurid, Bloom's father-centered analysis accounts for the fact that Whitman writes like a man whose social world has collapsed because of his hero's death. This melodramatic perspective, as Bloom hints when he refers to "the supposed elegy for Lincoln" and then, several pages later, to the "elegy for President Lincoln," reinforces our sense of the speaker's covert antagonism toward all undependable lovers—especially those who, like Whitman's father, proved themselves to be merely mortal. Hence, in part, the speaker's willingness to be seduced by death, the "Dark Mother." If "Lilacs" takes as its subject the dream of an enduring socioerotic community, it tests this deeply personal fantasy against public history, and against the tragic history of American slavery. To the extent that this vividly imagined community turns out to be white and male, the dark mother is necessary to complete it. By the same token, the dark mother, the only dark person in the poem, remains a mystery. As a person, she cannot be known. However we choose to read this figure—does she exemplify the Africanist presence?—it is clear that the concept of motherhood in the poem and in nineteenth-century America was subjected to extraordinary stresses. In the next chapter, I would like to consider some of them, as Whitman continued to seek personally gratifying solutions for the problems of democracy and of America, which, in *Democratic Vistas,* he proposed to employ as "convertible terms."

SEVEN

"In Loftiest Spheres"

Whitman's Visionary Feminism

Of these rapidly-sketch'd hiatuses, the two which seem to me
most serious are, for one, the condition, absence, or perhaps
the singular abeyance, of moral conscientious fibre all through
American society; and, for another, the appaling depletion of
women in their powers of sane athletic maternity, their crowning attribute, and ever making the woman, in loftiest spheres,
superior to the man.

Democratic Vistas

This chapter describes Whitman's disruption of his claims to empower
women by situating them in social roles in which they are always potentially subordinated to men.[1] For complex personal and cultural reasons,
Whitman tended to collapse the many possibilities contained in the word
"Woman" into the single word "Mother," and then to extol the preemi-
nence of maternal work over other contributions that women might make
to culture, especially those that depend on self-determining thought and
self-determining language. As we have seen, the erotic idiom of *Leaves
of Grass* is rich and varied, but the idea of motherhood typically suggests a positive identity to the poet who resists "anything better than [his]
own diversity" and who "moisten[s] the roots of all that has grown"
(*LG* 1855, pp. 41, 46). I will argue that however necessary the figure of
the good mother-muse was to Whitman's "scattering" psyche, for women
readers this motherist function can be oppressive as well as empowering.[2] Consequently, this chapter examines both Whitman's feminism and
his antifeminism, his resistance to linguistically totalizing norms and his
reaffirmation of the mid-nineteenth-century American cult of the mother,
which celebrated maternity as any woman's supreme destiny and which,
to a significant degree, depended on a code of silence about the unlofti-
ness of the lives many women were living. The tension between Whitman's embrace of the new (for example, the fully audible female voice)

and his embrace of the old (for example, the institution and practice of idealizing maternity as a depoliticizing, universalizing trope) has, I believe, interpretative power for other vexed issues in Whitman's poetry, all of them having to do with his ambivalence toward the cultural changes that he himself was helping to inaugurate.

Rather than turning to Whitman's biography to explain the personal origins of his conflicted literary feminism, I want to advance this discussion by considering the intersection of race and gender in *Democratic Vistas,* the 1871 prose work in which he repeatedly acknowledges the appeal of what another writer, Henry Clarke Wright, called "the empire of the mother." [3] Participating in the tradition of the American jeremiad that has been eloquently described by Sacvan Bercovitch, Whitman, as we have seen, complained of the "absence . . . of moral conscientious fibre all through American society" and of the "appaling [*sic*] depletion of women in their powers of sane athletic maternity, their crowning attribute . . . ever making the woman, in loftiest spheres, superior to the man." [4] The idea that women were superior to men was not inherent in Whitman's original project. For example, at the conclusion of the second paragraph of the 1855 "Preface," the poet notes that "men beget children upon women." This is the first mention of women in that document and the statement confers agency upon men rather than women. Similarly, in Whitman's 1856 open letter to Emerson, the focus is on male agency, even though any programmatic prose piece of any length written by Whitman is likely to contain references to the maternal role. (An exception is the unpublished *Eighteenth Presidency!*)

I will show that although Whitman's maternal family romance was more or less emphasized at different rhetorical moments, the cultural and psychological work of the Democratic Mother was thoroughly embedded in his original poetic project and was not merely the product of his postwar middle age. Thus, even in the 1855, 1856, and 1860 *Leaves of Grass,* as the poet worked to articulate a radical social vision in which differences might flourish without destroying a national erotic union, his claim to speak *for* women and to understand their experience better than they understand it themselves emerges as the most problematic element of his feminism.

Democratic Vistas was written over the course of several years, beginning shortly after Thomas Carlyle's essay "Shooting Niagara" appeared in the New York *Tribune* on August 16, 1867.[5] Whitman's deeply conflicted defense of the theory if not the practice of American democracy

was, as he freely acknowledged, a "collection of memoranda ... open
to the charge of one part contradicting another," in whose emotional,
moral, and intellectual unity he nevertheless and somewhat miraculously
continued to believe (*DV* 930). Whitman composed the article ("Democracy") which was the first installment of this strongly impassioned
yet disjointed and "wandering ... argument" while on short-term leave
from his moderately lucrative job as a Record Clerk in the Attorney
General's office.[6] Transcribing official documents, answering correspondence, abridging and abstracting legal material, he made at least sixteen
hundred dollars a year while working intermittently from nine to three
in pleasant physical surroundings. This was more money than he had
ever made before or was ever to see again; on a regular basis, he sent
some of it home to his mother, who, as we have seen, depended on him
for financial support.

From New York, where he was taking his annual vacation in September, he wrote back to Ellen O'Connor, the wife of his pen-wielding
"champion," William Douglas O'Connor, "I am well as usual, & go
daily around New York & Brooklyn yet with interest, of course—but
I find the places & crowds & excitements—Broadway, &c—have not
the zest of former times—they have done their work, & now they are to
me as a tale that is told." He added, "I am trying to write a piece, to be
called *Democracy,* for the leading article in the December or January
number of the *Galaxy*—in some sort a counterblast or rejoinder to Carlyle's late piece, *Shooting Niagara,* which you must have read, or at least
heard about" (*Corr* 1:342).

Several months later, Whitman completed his first response to Carlyle's offensive essay, which had condemned the American Civil War as
a useless slaughter. "Half a million ... of excellent White Men," Carlyle
wrote, "full of gifts and faculty, have torn and slashed one another into
horrid death, in a temporary humour, which will leave centuries of
remembrance fierce enough: and three million absurd Blacks, men
and brothers (of a sort), are completely 'emancipated.'" "Essentially the
Nigger Question was one of the smallest," he had written,

> and in itself did not much concern mankind in the present time of struggles
> and hurries. One always rather likes the Nigger; evidently a poor blockhead
> with good dispositions, with affections, attachments,—with a turn for Nig-
> ger Melodies, and the like:—he is the only Savage of all the coloured races
> that doesn't die out on sight of the White Man; but can actually live beside
> him, and work and increase and be merry. The Almighty Maker has appointed
> him to be a Servant.[7]

And so on. The language still hurts. Carlyle's diatribe against American democracy was prompted by the proposed passage of Disraeli's 1867 Reform Bill, which extended the suffrage in Britain to most working-class men. Carlyle likened this extension to "Shooting Niagara," to a headlong leap down Niagara Falls, to cultural suicide.

As we saw in the last chapter, Whitman, too, had expressed reservations about the politics of the War, and in an elegiac passage previously examined, he reluctantly consigned "the white skeletons of young men" to an irrational Dark Mother, death.[8] "I saw battle-corpses, myriads of them," he wrote in "When Lilacs Last in the Dooryard Bloom'd,"

> And the white skeletons of young men, I saw them,
> I saw the debris and debris of all the slain soldiers of the war,
> But I saw they were not as was thought,
> They themselves were fully at rest, they suffer'd not,
> The living remain'd and suffer'd, the mother suffer'd,
> And the wife and the child and the musing comrade suffer'd,
> And the armies that remain'd suffer'd.
>
> (*LG*, p. 336)

This is no vision of meaningful personal sacrifice, since Whitman specifically withholds the "masculine" consolation of effective military martyrdom. For white women, children, mothers, brothers, and brothers-in-arms, the war's legacy is a "feminized" consciousness of collective futility. Focusing on the dramatic and in some ways reassuring binary *life versus death* serves to obscure degrees of vitality and power among the living, as do sentimental appeals to a national family consciousness and to a national family tragedy that suppresses the distinction *North versus South*. Similarly, these depoliticizing tropes function to minimize the importance of race, as well as degrees of whiteness or blackness among persons of the same race (the binary *white versus black* remaining constant). When color is introduced into this scene in the phrase "white skeletons," we tend to experience it as a cliché, but the effect is to reinforce, albeit covertly, the racial status quo. Though it could be argued that whiteness is the universalized color of death, that the human body, deprived of its particularizing fleshly hues, is in fact bleached of its living colors, one effect of Whitman's language in this context is to suppress the contribution of black soldiers and civilians to the war effort.[9] The historian James McPherson observes that without the two hundred thousand blacks who enlisted in the army and navy, thirty-eight thousand of whom were killed, "the North could not have won the war as soon as it did, and perhaps it could not have won at all." According to McPherson, "The enlistment of black soldiers to fight and kill their former masters was by far the most revolutionary dimension of the emancipation policy." [10]

So it may be, as Whitman explained in his 1856 "Poem of the Road," later called "Song of the Open Road," that "The black with his woolly head, the felon, the diseas'd, the illiterate person, are not denied" (*LG,* p.150). But having lived through the War's bloody confusions, he dreaded further strife. "The fear of conflicting and irreconcilable interiors, and the lack of a common skeleton, knitting all close, continually haunts me," he noted in *Vistas* (935). As a war poet, Whitman was reluctant to turn his attention to racial matters.

Although *Drum-Taps* is haunted by a crucial ellipsis, when Whitman revised *Leaves of Grass* in 1871 he added "Ethiopia Saluting the Colors," in which race and gender intersect to produce a grotesquely aged woman who is described as "hardly human." We might expect Whitman to focus on the generativity of her body—as he does in celebrating the humanity of the female slave in the 1855 poem "I Sing the Body Electric"—but the postwar Whitman sidesteps this to-be-expected move. Instead, he grants his "Mammy" a childlike voice of her own, although it is a voice constrained by pidgin English and by the traditional, full-end-rhyme closure, internal rhyme, and stanzaic regularity of Whitman's pre–*Leaves of Grass* verse. The 1867 version of "Ethiopia Saluting the Colors," then called "Ethiopia Commenting," was rejected by *The Galaxy,* despite the fact that Whitman coupled it with his article "Democracy," whose subject he described as "opportune" (*Corr* 1:338). When he offered the poem to the magazine, he reserved the right to use it in a future volume, and in 1871 he included it in *Leaves of Grass* in a section subtitled *Bathed in War's Perfume.* In 1881, it became part of the *Drum-Taps* sequence, where it has remained ever since. Remarkably, Whitman's postsexual woman is the only African American in this Civil War memorial section.

"I will not gloss over the appaling dangers of universal suffrage in the United States," Whitman explained in his reactive *Vistas.* "In fact, it is to admit and face these dangers I am writing" (*DV* 930). Universal male suffrage was a desirable goal but not yet a practical one, he believed. Because he favored gradual rather than immediate extension of the suffrage to freed*men* (italics mine), Whitman opposed the Fifteenth Amendment,[11] which passed in 1870, and which held "the right of citizens of the United States to vote shall not be denied or abridged by the United States or by any State on account of race, color, or previous condition of servitude." [12] On occasion, his letters were peppered with derogatory references to "nigger waiters" (*Corr* 2:109) and to "darkeys." "Dearest Mother," reads one,

> We had the strangest procession here last Tuesday night, about 3000 darkeys, old & young, men & women—I saw them all—they turned out in honor of *their* victory in electing the Mayor, Mr. Bowen—the men were all armed with clubs or pistols—besides the procession in the street, there was a string went along the sidewalk in single file with bludgeons & sticks, yelling & gesticulating like madmen—it was quite comical, yet very disgusting & alarming in some respects—They were very insolent, & altogether it was a strange sight—they looked like so many wild brutes let loose— thousands of slaves from the Southern plantations have crowded up here— many are supported by the Gov't. (*Corr* 2:34–35)[13]

Yet if in the post–Civil War period Whitman's racial prejudice became more pronounced, he was also becoming more open to the possibility of arming white women with the vote. As editor of the Brooklyn *Daily Times* in 1858, he had written contemptuously of the view that "woman ought to be placed politically and industrially on a level with man and to be allowed to swing sledge-hammers, climb the giddy mast, and hit out from the shoulder at primary elections." Reporting on "One of the queerest conventions on record even in this land where all extremes of belief meet upon a common ground and all sorts of odd-fishes do most congregate," he attributed to these antebellum feminists gathered in Rutland, Vermont, whom he characterized as "amiable lunatics," the view that "The marriage relation . . . was a detestable humbug."[14] In *Vistas,* however, he began to revise his earlier prejudice against female suffrage. "The day is coming," he explained, "when the deep questions of woman's entrance amid the arenas of practical life, politics, the suffrage, &c., will not only be argued all around us, but may be put to decision, and real experiment" (*DV* 968). Women might be developed, he affirmed, to be "robust equals, workers, and, it may be, even practical and political deciders with the men." But how their potential careers as practical politicians might be reconciled with "their divine maternity, always their towering, emblematical attribute" (*DV* 955), Whitman left it to the future to decide.[15]

In *Vistas* as published in 1870, Whitman has little to say about the realities of race in the Reconstruction era. Instead, as one critic has noted, "he appears to substitute a lengthy discussion of women's elevation for any mention of racial equality."[16] Searching for "a great moral and religious civilization—the only justification of a great material one," Whitman felt compelled to rehearse his personal discovery of the tragedy of American culture. "Confess," he wrote, returning to the world-weary mood of his letter to Ellen O'Connor,

> that to severe eyes, using the moral microscope upon humanity, a sort of dry and flat Sahara appears, these cities, crowded with petty grotesques, malformations, phantoms, playing meaningless antics. Confess that everywhere, in shop, street, church, theatre, bar-room, official chair, are pervading flippancy and vulgarity, low cunning, infidelity—everywhere the youth puny, impudent, foppish, prematurely ripe—everywhere an abnormal libidinousness, unhealthy forms, male, female, painted, padded, dyed, chignon'd, muddy complexions, bad blood, the capacity for good motherhood deceasing or deceas'd, shallow notions of beauty, with a range of manners, or rather lack of manners, (considering the advantages enjoy'd,) probably the meanest to be seen in the world. (DV 939)

Whitman mentions "the capacity for good motherhood" only in passing, but this capacity is the redemptive focal point of the passage. In the cities, where an "abnormal libidinousness" prevails, colors and forms bleed into each other to produce degeneracy. "Good motherhood" thus functions as a categorical absolute that distinguishes sex from sex and race from race. A return to the traditional preindustrial, rural values signified by this trope will, Whitman hopes, arrest the unhealthy proliferation of sexualities and the allied hybridizations of race that concern him here. In this urban wasteland, morally astute men such as himself are marginalized, whereas women can still aspire to an indispensable social, economic, and biological role. Perhaps, though, if women return to their destined maternal mission, men too will find meaning in living. In short, "good motherhood," an unamplified and I shall argue unamplifiable trope, is the later, more conservative Whitman's solution to the problem of modernity, figured here as the suspension of meaningful sexual, racial, and social norms.

"The capacity for good motherhood" on which so much seems to depend had long been central to Whitman's thinking about women, a subject about which he had once asserted his total ignorance, perhaps in jest. As we recall, in one of his earliest essays, when he was still Walter Whitman Junior, the unhappy schoolteacher, he emphasized his desire to write a "wonderful and ponderous book," surveying "the nature and peculiarities of men." But he added, "I would carefully avoid saying any thing of woman; because it behoves a modest personage like myself not to speak upon a class of beings of whose nature, habits, notions, and ways he has not been able to gather any knowledge, either by experience or observation" (*UPP* 1:37). Subsequently, he made it a point to abandon modesty and to proclaim himself the poet of the woman the same as the man. Since the women in whom he invests himself emotionally often seem so self-contained, he goes some distance toward situating them outside the system of marriage exchange which, as described by Claude Levi-Strauss, Gayle Rubin, and others, subordinates women to men.[17] But just as Whitman could overestimate his access to the experience of Blacks—witness "Ethiopia Saluting the Colors," with its embarrassing approximation of pidgin English—so too when Whitman claimed to speak for women who had been culturally silenced, he reinforced a politics of dependence on the male voice. Thus Joanne Feit Diehl reproves him for chauvinist imperialism when she observes that "essential as the Whitmanian Mother may be, she remains an instrument, as through her the poet reaffirms *his* own priority."[18]

In his own time, however, the poet was not merely anxious about the state of American society, as *Democratic Vistas* might suggest, but anxious about his place within it. When he wrote to Nelly O'Connor in September 1867, telling her about the essay he was trying to write, in addition to describing his boredom in New York ("a tale that is told") he returned instinctively to the internal geography of the 1860 crisis poem, "As I Ebb'd with the Ocean of Life." Comparing his "never placid, never calm" currents of thought and feeling to the "real sea-waters" of his youth, Whitman referred to "this uneasy spirit, Me, that ebbs & flows too all the while, yet gets nowhere, & amounts to nothing" (*Corr* 1:342).[19] The traumatized "I" of "As I Ebb'd" has been quelled by two equally demanding gendered traditions, each of them fiercely unresponsive to the other. His shame and his glory is that he is unwilling to identify exclusively with either one.

Consequently, although Diehl's point is well taken, it is a partial truth. Whitman *always* believed that his career was in crisis, and there were times when he wanted to "retreat from competition [with other men] into a protected female sphere."[20] In the poetry, this female-identified haven in a heartless world is typically exemplified not by a wife but by a mother, and in "As I Ebb'd" we see what happens once the Whitmanic mother abdicates her traditional defensive role. The son, victimized by a harsh and uncaring father *and* rejected by his cruel mother, concludes that he understands nothing and that "no man ever can" (*LG* 1860, p. 197). The poet's dilemma in "As I Ebb'd" is that no woman ever can either. *Neither* exemplary parent is interested in tales not yet told, since such tales threaten both of them with the loss of the status to which each separately and rigidly clings.

Given the authorial Whitman's struggle with aggressive masculinity, we should probably not be surprised that, so often in the poetry, he needs to instantiate a happy mother, a mother exempt from "the politics of male suffering." As he attempts to negotiate between aggressive and feminized masculinities, Whitman is curious about his position in relation to structures of male dominance, but he is understandably wary of being *too* curious. For example, in the 1855 poem "There Was a Child Went Forth," he appears to celebrate the mother at home, "quietly placing the dishes on the suppertable" (*LG* 1855, p. 139). This too-perfect mother has no dissatisfactions, at least none that Whitman is willing to pursue. "Mild," "clean," and "wholesome," she is apparently fulfilled by what he calls, in another 1855 poem, "womanly housework" and "the beautiful maternal cares," as are the even blurrier daughters by whom she is at times surrounded (*LG* 1855, p. 101). This archetypally gratified mother appears throughout the poetry, but in "There Was a Child Went Forth" she does not produce an emotionally resilient son. We will never know what would have happened had she not been associated with "The father, strong, selfsufficient, manly, mean, angered, unjust," for he is her fate, just as it is the son's fate to experience

> The doubts of daytime and the doubts of nighttime . . . the curious whether and how,
> Whether that which appears so is so. . . . Or is it all flashes and specks?
> Men and women crowding fast in the street . . if they are not flashes and specks what are they?
>
> (*LG* 1855, p. 139)

Assuming that this is a poem about Whitman's complicated response to feminization—its appeal, its danger—it is all the more remarkable that he resists the temptation to blame the unavailing mother for his emotional vulnerability. Yet it is probably true—for these are the tears of things—that the poet-hero's identification with his mother's mildness condemns him to what Stephen Gould Axelrod calls "a lonely, bitter struggle for his own strength and self-sufficiency."[21] As Whitman reworks the role of the uncaring father in both his life and poetry—"The blow, the quick loud word, the tight bargain, the crafty lure"—he seeks to reconcile the power positions the poem imagines. The dominant masculine position is unjust, but the "wholesome" feminized position, especially for a man-child, is untenable.

In any event, as Whitman explained to his own mother in 1868, he found writing *Democratic Vistas,* his "little book . . . on political & literary subjects . . . a real pleasure" (*Corr* 2:39), although writing to instantiate a socially acceptable and internally purposeful self was not his first choice. His first choice was to feel real off the page, in his own person, in the nineteenth century—as he did in the hospitals and among his variously wounded young male lovers. But in the crowds and excitements of New York he too often felt *unreal,* and New York (or Brooklyn) remained his home. And so when he ended *Democratic Vistas* with an image of a self-poised mother, swinging her way through time, he was projecting an ego-ideal for himself and for the home-person he consciously loved the best, who, of course, caused him no end of trouble.

We have seen that in the 1860 *Leaves of Grass,* notably in "As I Ebb'd with the Ocean of Life" and in the *Calamus* sequence, a chastened Whitman looked back on his career and seemed to disavow it. Perhaps he was claiming to have abandoned not only the much remarked sexual arrogance of the 1855 and 1856 volumes but also the lesser-known fears which he had expressed in passages such as the following, from "To Think of Time." For if Whitman had restricted himself to this secretly panicked style, he would be a very boring poet indeed.

> To think how much pleasure there is!
> Have you pleasure from looking at the sky? Have you pleasure from
>   poems?
> Do you enjoy yourself in the city? or engaged in business? or planning a
>   nomination and election? or with your wife and family?
> Or with your mother and sisters? or in womanly housework? or the
>   beautiful maternal cares?
>
> These also flow onward to others. . . . you and I flow onward;
> But in due time you and I shall take less interest in them.
>
> (*LG* 1855, p. 101)

Abstracted from time, "motherhood" functions as premature closure, a resolution to social anxieties that are insufficiently voiced. Other critics have hinted that the unreality of Whitman's "good" mothers is related to his sexual love for men. Lewis Hyde, for example, remarks that "as in those churches in which sex is tolerated only as an instrument of procreation, it is a persistent quirk of Whitman's imagination that heterosexual lovemaking always leads to babies. His women are always mothers. No matter how graphically Whitman describes 'the clinch,' 'the merge,' within a few lines out pops a child." [22] Let us grant that Whitman's use of the equation woman/mother to collapse perceived differences between himself and other men can have the opposite effect. But the question remains, in a gender-polarized society, how can relationships develop that nurture the deeper self? and more specifically, can Whitman risk identifying himself with female discontent? As we saw in a previous chapter, listening to his mother's story of erotic frustration in "The Sleepers" makes him intensely uncomfortable, and retelling his mother's story does not resolve his crisis of gender identification.

Given that Whitman saw himself as responding to a spiritual as well as a gender crisis in his time, it is not surprising that his recurrent near-obsession with the maternal body persisted, for he hoped that the trope of the maternal body might provide an alternative to the violence of patriarchal language. According to this line of argument, all men are first "Unfolded out of the folds of the woman," however unique their subsequent sexual and psychological development. Thus, in the programmatic 1856 poem "Unfolded Out of the Folds," Whitman suggests that his poems emerge out of maternal rather than paternal traditions of language. "A man is a great thing upon the earth and through eternity," he writes, "but every jot of the greatness of man is unfolded out of woman; / First the man is shaped in the woman, he can then be shaped in himself" (*LG,* p. 391). In this weirdly logical utterance, whose unfolding seems at first glance abstract and merely schematic, Whitman celebrates an archetypal Poem-Mother who is "brawny," "arrogant," "strong," "well-muscled," but also complete in and of herself. Reworking that moment in "There Was a Child Went Forth" in which he had praised a personal father for propelling the fatherstuff at night, to whom he had given chronological priority over "she that conceived him in her womb and birthed him" (*LG* 1855, pp. 138–39), Whitman now eliminates the difficult partner and expands the idea of conception to include a maternal imaginary.

In "Unfolded Out of the Folds," the fecund Poem-Mother transmits her "friendliest" and most "perfect body" to the disciplined hierophant, "duly obedient." Having written the male symbolic order out of his (psychic) state, Whitman contends that the female dynamo who provides him with "the strong and arrogant man I love" also transmits such utopian social values as superior wisdom, sympathy, and justice. Conventional readings of this highly elliptical 1856 poem, which was then called "Poem of Women," link it to Whitman's interest in eugenics.[23] But as the poet of women, Whitman writes most effectively of himself. The utterance of "*a Person*" (*LG,* p. 573) whose literary politics include his sexual love for other men, here Whitman represents himself as bound to the logic of the "feminine." Beginning in a vaguely pornographic vaginal economy that compels strict obedience to sexual and moral abstractions in which, with his love of shapely particulars, he cannot truly believe, the poet delivers himself to still other realms of abstraction where, while much is "unfolded," much is concealed.

At the very least, then, there are several "dread" mothers whom Whitman, linking his speech and male ejaculate, (re)conceives.[24] One of them testifies to the "athletic" power of maternity, while the other exemplifies a more conventionally "conscientious" and self-effacing social role. These differently gendered personae can merge in the poet's imagination and in his own self-representation. In the 1855 "Preface," for example, the outsetting bard refers to "all the vast sweet love and precious suffering of mothers," to "self-denial that stood steady and aloof on wrecks and saw others take the seats of the boats," and to the furtherance of "fugitives and . . . the escape of slaves" (*LG* 1855, p. 20; ellipsis mine). In these schematic formulations, Mother-love becomes the physical and cultural type of androgynous heroism. Elsewhere, in "Poems bridging the way from Life to Death," Whitman describes a maternal origin and ambiguous end that he needs to contain and dominate. In "Proud Music of the Storm," for example, which was first published in the *Atlantic Monthly* in 1869, he masterfully alludes to "My mother's voice in lullaby or hymn" (*LG*, pp. 410, 405), but his mother's voice, like all the other sounds in this self-regarding tribute to art and artists, is relegated to a footnote in his own career. "The manly strophe of the husbands of the world," he writes, "And all the wives responding" (*LG*, p. 405).

As my examples are intended to suggest, the life of the Democratic Mother is not a topic that Whitman usually explores very deeply, but if he exaggerated her power to restrain male-identified aggression, he did so in part because of his desire to mobilize discontent with, in Christopher Newfield's fine phrase, a "patriarchy constructed by other men."[25] This patriarchy was not a separate sphere, as some would have it, and Whitman did not imagine that he had a stable relationship to its productions. Consider the following famous self-definition:

> I am the poet of the body,
> And I am the poet of the soul.
>
> The pleasures of heaven are with me, and the pains of hell are with me,
> The first I graft and increase upon myself. . . . the latter I translate into a
>   new tongue.
>
> I am the poet of the woman the same as the man,

And I say it is as great to be a woman as to be a man,
And I say there is nothing greater than the mother of men.
(*LG* 1855, p. 44)

As Whitman attempts to translate conventional codes of pleasure and
pain into "a new tongue" and to dissolve the distinction between the here
and the hereafter that organizes other binaries, he goes too far to suit
himself, and in the end his "chant of dilation or pride" reinforces the oppositional pairing (male/female) he seems to wish to deconstruct. "What
is a man anyhow?" the speaker has been asking, "What am I? and what
are you?" (*LG* 1855, p. 43). In this section of "Song of Myself," the "I"
has been describing his own feminization, whose symbolic equivalent is
social powerlessness, or the death of the masculine ego and the hierarchical language that sustains it. While we may honor the poet's desire
to imagine alternatives to the traditional belief that men are the superior sex, what emerges is indeed, as Alicia Ostriker has suggested, one
of Whitman's "crudest statements on gender."[26] Superficially at least,
the new story—that the mothering of men is the supreme goal of any
woman's destiny—has too much in common with the old one, and one
effect of such language, D. H. Lawrence has apocalyptically contended,
is to reduce any woman to a biological function and to objectify her as
a womb.[27]

More recently, however, Betsy Erkkila has urged us to read motherhood as a trope for other forms of creativity, rather than as a purely biological or narrowly familial role. In *Whitman the Political Poet,* she
writes that

> Although Whitman insisted on the superiority of the mother, he did not limit
> the female to a maternal *role,* or trap her in what Simone de Beauvoir would
> later call biological "immanence". . . . Whitman sought to revive the mother
> not as a biological function only but as a creative and intellectual force. . . .
> His mothers do not exist as wives in relation to individual husbands, nor are
> they pious, pure, domestic, or self-sacrificing in any limited sense of the terms.
> Like feminist works ranging from Margaret Fuller's *Woman in the Nine-
> teenth Century* (1845) to Charlotte Perkins Gilman's *Herland* (1915) to Adri-
> enne Rich's *Of Woman Born: Motherhood As Experience and Institution*
> (1976), Whitman sought to remove motherhood from the private sphere and
> release the values of nurturance, love, generativity, and community into the
> culture at large. Exceeding the bounds of home, marriage, and the isolate
> family, Whitman's "perfect motherhood" is motherhood raised to the height
> of solicitude for the future of the race.[28]

In one sense, Erkkila is right, for in such lines as "And I say there is nothing greater than the mother of men," Whitman suggests that culture is

founded on the relationship between sons and mothers, rather than on the more conventionally gendered, patrilineal model of cultural trans-mission from father to son. Certainly, too, mothers *do* transmit some of their values to the future through their sons, though those values cannot automatically be equated with "nurturance, love, generativity, and com-munity." Indeed, in a subsequent work Erkkila herself deconstructs this romanticization of womanhood, as she challenges the historically neu-tral, unifying trope of sisterhood. In *The Wicked Sisters: Women Poets, Literary History, and Discord,* she seeks to reclaim "women's literature and women's literary history as a site of dissension, contingency, and on-going struggle rather than a separate space of some untroubled and es-sentially cooperative accord among women." [29] But these are precisely the sorts of historical and psychological tensions that Whitman's moth-erhood tropes are designed to repress. So even though Whitman at one point described himself as the medium for his own mother's (presum-ably coherent) moral vision and credited Louisa Van Velsor Whitman with generating *Leaves of Grass* (WWWC 2:113–14), many feminist critics will, as Ostriker has done, resist the Whitman who speaks in the passage from "Song of Myself" quoted above.

What are we to make, then, of Ostriker's further contention that even Whitman's most problematic statements on gender "are revolutionary compared to the sentimental conventions of his own time"? [30] Discus-sions of antebellum and postbellum literary sentimentality within the past decade or so have highlighted the antipatriarchal, matrifocal ele-ments contained within the so-called Cult of True Womanhood. Under pressure of such analysis, categorical distinctions between revolution-ary, socially subversive, and socially conservative styles tend not to stand up to close scrutiny. As Robert Leigh Davis notes in his insightful discus-sion of Whitman's Civil War nursing, sentimental writers such as Har-riet Beecher Stowe "had a more profound effect on Whitman than is usu-ally recognized, a fact owing to the poet's determined effort to distinguish himself from a tradition of literary sentimentality." As Davis further notes, "Under his touch, the male body becomes less monumental, less rigidly centered and symbolic." [31] This line of inquiry is fruitful, and male feminization evidently held considerable appeal for Whitman, even though he was inconsistent about what it might mean. Whitman's fa-mously heterodox style—with its extraordinary linguistic, psychologi-cal, and intellectual range—makes it even harder to define definitively the shifting relationships between language, on the one hand, and the in-stitutions that regulate social power, on the other, that attentive readers encounter within any single version of *Leaves of Grass,* let alone within the multiple published versions that constitute his variants.

Contending with this long life, this multigenre career, and these complex textual issues, poet-critic Sandra M. Gilbert, while comparing "The American Sexual Poetics of Walt Whitman and Emily Dickinson," suggests that

> We cannot . . . ignore the fact that both poets assimilated experimental passages . . . into extended sequences whose sexual modalities appear continually to reiterate and reinforce traditional definitions of masculinity and femininity: lapses of gender, indeed, seem to occur because of lapses of genre rather than the other way around. In fact, it is likely that the subversions of stereotypical sexuality which do mark Whitman's and Dickinson's writings are consequences, rather than causes, of these poets' mutual disaffection from stereotypical "poetry," specifically from its coherent "voice," its cohesive "form," and its conventional language, rhyme, and meter. It is arguable, in other words, that for both poets the wellspring of all alienation was a profound literary alienation.[32]

Gilbert's cogent analysis nevertheless leaves unanswered the question of what, other than literature, motivates literary alienation. And for a poet such as Whitman, who identified his body as his inspiration, literature seems an insufficient (though a necessary) source. Whitman's poetry was shaped by his gendered ambivalence to personal, political, and literary history. The effect of such deeply disturbed, creative ambivalence on women readers, including women poets, has been far from uniform.

When Whitman writes, "What exclamations of women taken suddenly, who hurry home and give birth to babes, / What living and buried speech is always vibrating here. . . . what howls restrained by decorum" (*LG* 1855, p. 32), or when he writes "My voice is the wife's voice, the screech by the rail of the stairs, / They fetch my man's body up dripping and drowned" (*LG* 1855, p. 61), is he preempting women's speech or encouraging it? Perhaps, as Adrienne Rich has suggested, "The issue of the writer's power, right, obligation to speak for others denied a voice, or the writer's duty to shut up at times or at least to make room for those who can speak with more immediate authority—these are crucial questions for our time."[33] The line between sympathetic identification and erasure of the other's personhood is a fine one, as is the line between sympathetic identification and living *as* another because one cannot live as oneself. "Carrying the crescent child that carries its own full mother in its belly" (*LG* 1855, p. 60), the Whitman persona carries *us* along in his exuberant wake—representing himself as male and female, impersonating a bridegroom, and then a wife. He "turn[s] the bridegroom out of bed and stay[s] with the bride [himself], / [He] tighten[s] her all night to [his] thighs and lips" (*LG* 1855, p. 65). And then the wife screams. And the husband is lost, as is Whitman's wifely role. Such flights of fancy work best when we understand their interior logic, and this logic is often deeply disguised. As Whitman explained to his not entirely baffled English admirer Edward Carpenter,

> What lies behind "Leaves of Grass" is something that few, very few, only one here and there, perhaps oftenest women, are at all in a position to seize. It lies behind almost every line; but concealed, studiedly concealed; some passages left purposely obscure. There is something in my nature *furtive* like an old hen! You see a hen wandering up and down a hedgerow, looking apparently quite unconcerned, but presently she finds a concealed spot, and furtively lays an egg, and comes away as though nothing had happened! That is how I felt in writing "Leaves of Grass." Sloane Kennedy calls me "artful"—which about hits the mark. I think there are truths which it is necessary to envelop or wrap up.[34]

Despite the fact that Whitman saw himself as the poet of the woman as well as the man, that he once described *Leaves of Grass* as "essentially a woman's book" (*WWWC* 2:331), and that many nineteenth-century women readers such as the Englishwoman Anne Gilchrist were tantalized, encouraged, and fortified by his writings, there were many nineteenth-century American women who ignored, rejected, or otherwise problematized his claims.[35] In April 1862, for example, Emily Dickinson told Thomas Wentworth Higginson, an abolitionist activist, women's rights advocate, and literary critic with whom she had just begun to correspond, "You speak of Mr Whitman—I never read his Book—but was told that he was disgraceful." Possibly she was being ironic in representing herself as the docile recipient of received ideas. Possibly not, for she may also have wanted Higginson to know that she was at least somewhat aware of current big-city literary gossip and not nearly so rusticated as she was pretending to be. As she continued to play the game of ranking writers in her correspondence with Higginson over the years, other names surfaced. "Of Howells and James, one hesitates," she later wrote. This was long after their first meeting in 1870, when she startled him with such comments as "I never had a mother. I suppose a mother is one to whom you hurry when you are troubled," a theme she picked up in a subsequent letter when she explained punningly, "I always ran Home to Awe when a child, if anything befell me. He was an awful Mother, but I liked him better than none."[36] Dickinson enjoyed being

disgraceful herself—or at least playing at disgrace. Possibly this fascination with social, sexual, and linguistic transgression accounts for the
emphasis of her Whitman disclaimer to Higginson in 1862. Possibly not.

In addition to Josiah Gilbert Holland, a close family friend who as the
editor of *Scribner's Monthly* later rejected Whitman's poems with insulting letters, there were many people who might have cautioned Dickinson
against Whitman, including Higginson, a conflicted genteel critic who
eroticized his relations with men but who also repeatedly attacked Whitman's political, sexual, and literary morals in print. So what is surprising
here, in April 1862, is that Higginson appears to have been directing
Dickinson toward Whitman as the forerunner of a new kind of experimental poetry that she herself was engaged in writing. Higginson also
advised her to "delay 'to publish,'" which she did, and when Dickinson's
posthumously published poems began to appear in the 1890s, reviewers were somewhat prepared for her deviations from the genteel norm
by Whitman's innovations and scandalousness. For all her formal and
psychological subversions of the culture's grammar, at least she wasn't
Whitman, they thought. Her rhymes might be off-rhymes, but they were
rhymes nevertheless.[37]

We don't know if Dickinson ever read Whitman's "Book," although
she is likely to have read "As I Ebb'd with the Ocean of Life" when it
appeared in April 1860 in the *Atlantic Monthly,* to which she and her
family subscribed. There, under the title "Bardic Symbols," she would
have encountered that "fierce old mother," the Whitmanic sea, "endlessly" crying for her "castaways," including the corpse of the earlier
poet who believed in his ability to "condense—a Nationality" without
sacrificing his real life to do so.[38] Dickinson almost certainly read brief
excerpts from "As I Ebb'd" and even briefer excerpts from "Song of
Myself" in Holland's paper the *Springfield Daily Republican* in 1860,
as well as a derisive long column entitled "'Leaves of Grass'—Smut in
Them."[39] But she never mentioned Whitman elsewhere in her correspondence and so far as we know there were no *books* by Whitman in
her library at her death or in the library of her sister-in-law and brother
next door.

One of the people who might have warned her against Whitman was
her sister-in-law and best friend, Susan Gilbert Dickinson. Sue advocated
the passionlessness that enabled American Victorian women not to become the mothers of many children, and erotic fondling, at least with
men, made her nervous. At one point in the early 1880s she cast Dickinson herself in the role of a fallen woman, after having stumbled upon

the poet "reclining" at home in the arms of Judge Otis Lord, a widowed suitor and friend. Ironically, Sue warned the sexually venturesome Mabel Loomis Todd to safeguard her husband against the Dickinson sisters, explaining, "They have not, either of them, any idea of morality." [40] Sue's sense of sexual morality was prudish by modern standards and perhaps even by the standards of her day, but in other respects she was an enlightened woman: a thinker and a doer. She participated in an important nineteenth-century social movement, the movement to limit the size of families, which was crucial in liberating women from motherhood as a totalizing social role. In Whitman's poetry, however, fecundity is better.

As I have been suggesting, Whitman too often represents motherhood as a uniform and unifying role. His mothers do not disrupt, challenge, provoke, or disappoint conventional expectations. Although biologically "teeming" (*LG* 1855, p. 122), they represent social limits, whereas the Whitman persona is free to go to self-indulgent extremes. In the 1856 open letter to Emerson, for example, the maternal body potentially resolves the problems of the political body. Despite "the threats and screams of disputants," the maternal body, which is hostile to coteries, including "the owners of slaves," is invested with the power to preserve "the union of These States" (*LG*, pp. 733, 736, 735). As depicted by Whitman, fatherhood is a less all-encompassing role. For instance, "I Sing the Body Electric" collapses the difference between African American male and female bodies, in that both are spiritualized (they are priceless) and valued for their "divine" generativity. In "Electric," there are nevertheless important differences between the imagined occupations of white fathers and mothers. White fathers farm, hunt, fish, sail, build ships, and pursue other trades, whereas for white women, conceiving "daughters as well as sons" is an all-encompassing task. This imputed work-restriction links the white woman to her unacknowledged double, the African American male slave whose only job is to "start . . . populous states and rich republics" (*LG* 1855, p. 122).

If these symmetries and asymmetries accurately reflect some of the realities of Whitman's time, they also reflect Whitman's need to ground his project in a parenting ethic that de-eroticizes his representation of women. As the feminist reformer Elizabeth Cady Stanton noted in her diary in 1883, "He speaks as if the female must be forced to the creative act, apparently ignorant of the great natural fact that a healthy woman has as much passion as a man, that she needs nothing stronger than the law of attraction to draw her to the male." [41] Thus whereas Whitman's vision of a human community in which women might reclaim their self-pride not in spite of but because of their bodies was powerfully persuasive for Gilchrist, Stanton criticized Whitman's understanding of female eroticism, objecting particularly to the "Poem of Procreation," later re-titled "A Woman Waits for Me," in which Whitman seemingly forces himself on "impassive" women, "to start sons and daughters fit for these States" (*LG*, p. 102).[42]

As the self-proclaimed poet of "sane athletic maternity," Whitman aggressively endorsed an ideology of Real Womanhood, modeled somewhat after the radical speeches and writings of his firebrand heroine Frances Wright. In her *Views of Society and Manners in America* (1821), Wright had suggested that "The American women might, with advantage, be taught in early youth to excel in the race, to hit a mark, to swim and in short, to use every exercise which would impart vigor to their frames and independence of their minds."[43] In the scandal-producing "Poem of Procreation," Whitman characterized the women with whom he hoped metaphorically to mate in similar terms:

> They are not one jot less than I am,
> They are tanned in the face by shining suns and blowing winds,
> Their flesh has the old divine suppleness and strength,
> They know how to swim, row, ride, wrestle, shoot, run, strike, retreat,
>   advance, resist, defend themselves,
> They are ultimate in their own right—they are calm, clear, well-possessed
>   of themselves.
>
> (*LG* 1856, p. 241)

Whitman's poem was riddled with ideological inconsistency, for his self-dependent women were clearly dependent on *him* for identity. A coercive heterosexism is both the poem's mode and the target of its satire: the shameless speaker is being shamefully coerced by the situation he is describing. Perhaps Whitman's reference to "semitic milk" in stanza two was not altogether a mistake, since linguistic and sexual *im*purities continued to fascinate him,[44] and the Cult of True Womanhood struck him as an ideological distortion of nature's more inclusive project. Writers who emphasized the difference between men and women and the corresponding difference between their social talents and missions often sought to confine women within the middle-class home, whereas Whitman wanted to bring both men and women out into an atmosphere of freer self-development.[45]

Undraping himself and encouraging readers to do the same, in his 1856 "Clef Poem" he asked, "Do you suppose I wish to enjoy life in other spheres? I say distinctly I comprehend no better sphere than this earth, / I comprehend no better life than the life of my body" (*LG* 1856, p. 249). To prove the point, he included the following lines, which he later deleted:

> I am not uneasy but I am to be beloved by young and old men, and to love them the same,
> I suppose the pink nipples of the breasts of women with whom I shall sleep will taste the same to my lips,
> But this is the nipple of a breast of my mother, always near and always divine to me, her true child and son.
>
> (*LG* 1856, p. 250)[46]

Mortality, he suggests, does not disturb him, for love exists in other spheres. The argument anticipates the closing line of *Calamus* 11 ("And that night I was happy"); the 1856 "Clef Poem" begins "This night I am happy." In both poems, the speaker's happiness depends on a sense of connection with a beloved other, but the 1856 utterance makes the grander assertion that "A vast similitude interlocks all" (*LG* 1856, p. 250). Moving from man to man, breast to breast, nipple to nipple, he has had the key to the universe all along, since his own mother's divinity has been justifying *him*. Whitman is proclaiming his freedom from gender anxiety and gesturing toward a Protestant cult of the Virgin Mary that was embedded in nineteenth-century American literature and exemplified by such canonically central works as *The Scarlet Letter*.[47] Nevertheless, fetishizing his "divine" mother's breast and returning to it is a drastic solution to Whitman's anxiety about "good housing" in the future. To the extent that his body is like a house, with its "studs and rafters," Whitman fears its demise, as well as the death of the fragile loves that have sustained it. "Clef Poem," then, reminds us inadvertently of the whole web of circumstances that separates people from each other, and the "I am not uneasy" lines quoted above produce discomfort because they are the product of discomfort. The poet was right to excise them.

Although the 1856 "Clef Poem" suggests that Whitman experienced considerable sexual guilt, he wants to believe that loving a personal and cultural mother who "span[s]" the "interlocking" spheres will draw generations of men closer. At a less abstract level, the Whitman who was willing to cede women practical and moral authority within the home, as he does, for example, in *Democratic Vistas,* was not always willing to grant them power in the public sphere. If "the best culture will always be that of the manly and courageous instincts" (*DV* 962), then the best culture will tend to silence women. Without necessarily intending this result—his admiration for some women artists was indisputable—Whitman suggests even in the 1855 poem "There Was a Child Went Forth" that domestic morality is woman's special province and that mild words are necessary to her peacekeeping mission. "One genuine woman is worth a dozen Fanny Ferns," he remarked succinctly in 1857, after he had quarreled bitterly with Sara Willis Parton, the popular journalist and satiric novelist who was the first woman to praise *Leaves of Grass* in print. "The majority of people do not want their daughters to be trained to become authoresses and poets," he observed in this Brooklyn *Daily Times* editorial, while he was arguing against "Free Academies at Public Cost." The majority of people, he added, want for their daughters "only that they may receive sufficient education to serve as the basis of life-long improvement and self-cultivation, and which will qualify them to become good and intelligent wives and mothers."[48] He must have been right, but more than a hundred years later it is distressing to hear this antiprogressive message from the poet of *Leaves of Grass*.

At the same time, then, that Whitman was actively championing economic equality for women, deploring their low wages, and representing them in his journalism in a variety of economic roles, in his poetry this larger social context tends to be erased. Except for those rare moments when he identifies with women artists and with women as frustrated lovers, the life of women as he imagines it is simply less various than that of men. They contain fewer multitudes economically, intellectually, and psychologically, though on them, granted, the future of the race is said to depend. Challenging the nineteenth-century cult of domesticity and the allied doctrine of separate spheres, Whitman also tended to reinscribe the emotional power of "the mother at home." Of such fundamental contradictions is his poetry made.

"The direct trial of him who would be the greatest poet is today," Whitman explained in the 1855 "Preface" (*LG* 1855, p. 21), and in this book I have attempted to describe the social generosity of Whitman's vision in relation to the immediate trials by which his life was defined. For example, Whitman wanted to affirm the role of the mother in nineteenth-century America but he also wanted to liberate himself from the anxieties associated with his actual familial role as dutiful son. Similarly, Whitman tried to think of himself as "an example to lovers" but was deeply ambivalent about his erotic experience with men. As a poet who encouraged others to follow his example without emulating it too closely, he urged his readers not to surrender to appearances: to pursue the life beneath the life.

In a late essay on "The Death of Abraham Lincoln," Whitman asked, "Strange, (is it not?), that battles, martyrs, agonies, blood, even assassination, should so condense—perhaps only really, lastingly condense— a Nationality."[49] Throughout the *Leaves of Grass* project, the poet wondered whether the power of love could enable Americans to transcend privatizing traditions of moral worth and what the place of literature might be in this transformation. Walt Whitman did not want to choose between the unities his culture associated with masculinity and the personalisms of the feminine. During the most inspired parts of his career, he tried to imagine alternatives to the violent antagonisms of his age and to open a space for himself as an erotically experimental writer. Whitman did not know what of lasting value would emerge from his language experiments or how "poets to come" would receive him. But he continued to hope that the intimate fears and fears of intimacy that had been for him "the real reality" (*LG* 1860, pp. 186, 344) would be transformed by "a new tongue," one in which, in certain moods, it would be possible to believe that "All goes onward and outward. . . . and nothing collapses, / And to die is different from what any one supposed, and luckier" (*LG* 1855, p. 30).

Notes

PREFACE

    1. On the history of domination as a psychological problem, see Jessica Benjamin, *The Bonds of Love: Psychoanalysis, Feminism, and the Problem of Domination* (New York: Pantheon, 1988). Paraphrasing Freud, she writes that "The injunction to love our neighbor is not a reflection of abiding concern for others, but a testimony to the opposite: our propensity for aggression" (p. 4). Her analysis has furthered my understanding of the relationship between social aggression and sexual love.

    2. As Betsy Erkkila points out in *Whitman the Political Poet* (New York: Oxford University Press, 1989), p. v, the term *politics* may refer to a wide and subtle range of signifying practices, as well as to specific structures of government, though the more general concept of *power* links these usages. In this book, I am most interested in analyzing Whitman's strategies for maximizing personal power and, correspondingly, minimizing gender and sexual anxiety—some of it common to his culture, some of it more uniquely his own.

    3. Whitman composed the 1855 "Preface" after the book of poems had been written.

    4. Kerry C. Larson, *Whitman's Drama of Consensus* (Chicago: University of Chicago Press, 1988), p. xiii.

    5. The quotation is from Larson, *Whitman's Drama of Consensus,* pp. 58–59. See also George B. Hutchinson, *The Ecstatic Whitman: Literary Shamanism and the Crisis of the Union* (Columbus: Ohio State University Press, 1986); Erkkila, *Whitman the Political Poet;* M. Jimmie Killingsworth, *Whitman's Poetry of the Body: Sexuality, Politics, and the Text* (Chapel Hill: University of North Carolina Press, 1989); Michael Moon, *Disseminating Whitman: Revision and Corporeality in "Leaves of Grass"* (Cambridge: Harvard University Press, 1991);

Robert K. Martin, ed., *The Continuing Presence of Walt Whitman: The Life After the Life* (Iowa City: University of Iowa Press, 1992), pp. xi–xxiii; Tenney Nathanson, *Whitman's Presence: Body, Voice, and Writing in "Leaves of Grass"* (New York: New York University Press, 1992); Bryne R. S. Fone, *Masculine Landscapes: Walt Whitman and the Homoerotic Text* (Carbondale: Southern Illinois University Press, 1992); Karen Sánchez-Eppler, "To Stand Between: Walt Whitman's Poetics of Merger and Embodiment," in *Touching Liberty: Abolition, Feminism, and the Politics of the Body* (Berkeley: University of California Press, 1993), pp. 50–82; David S. Reynolds, *Walt Whitman's America: A Cultural Biography* (New York: Alfred A. Knopf, 1995).

6. In recreating Whitman's early life, I am indebted to biographers and cultural historians such as Gay Wilson Allen, Justin Kaplan, Paul Zweig, and David S. Reynolds. See Allen, *The Solitary Singer: A Critical Biography* (1955; reprint, New York: New York University Press, 1967); Kaplan, *Walt Whitman: A Life* (New York: Simon and Schuster, 1980); Zweig, *Walt Whitman: The Making of a Poet* (New York: Basic Books, 1983); and Reynolds, *Walt Whitman's America: A Cultural Biography*. Other biographers and cultural historians whose work has facilitated my project are cited later in the text.

7. Peter Doyle, quoted in *Calamus: A Series of Letters Written during the Years 1868–1880. By Walt Whitman to a Young Friend (Peter Doyle)*, ed. Richard Maurice Bucke (Boston: Laurens Maynard, 1897), p. 25. See also Charles A. Roe, quoted in Allen, *Solitary Singer,* pp. 35–36, and George Washington Whitman, quoted in Allen, p. 33.

8. Whitman described this episode to Ellen M. O'Connor. See Allen, *Solitary Singer,* p. 37, and Reynolds, *Walt Whitman's America,* p. 72.

9. Louis Crompton, *Byron and Greek Love: Homophobia in 19th-Century England* (Berkeley: University of California Press, 1985), p. 6. In "The Biographer's Problem," in *Walt Whitman of Mickle Street: A Centennial Collection,* ed. Geoffrey M. Sill (Knoxville: University of Tennessee Press, 1994), pp. 18–27, Justin Kaplan observes that "Correctly or not, we tend to think of Ralph Waldo Emerson as having the sexual voltage of a day-old corpse. Yet we know that Emerson married twice and fathered four children. To reduce this to simple acts, we know with certainty at least four more things about Emerson's sex life than we have ever been able to find out about Whitman's" (p. 20). On Whitman and homoerotic desire, see my discussion of the letters to Abraham Paul Leech in chapter 1, and of the men described in Whitman's notebooks in chapter 3.

10. See the Introductions and Commentary in Charley Shively, ed., *Calamus Lovers: Walt Whitman's Working-Class Camerados* (San Francisco: Gay Sunshine, 1987), as well as my discussion of these valuable archival materials in chapters 1 and 5. See also *Drum Beats: Walt Whitman's Civil War Boy Lovers* (San Francisco: Gay Sunshine, 1989), though here the sexually insatiable Whitman persona is even less credible.

11. See Reynolds, *Walt Whitman's America,* pp. 70–80, and my discussion of this purported episode in chapter 3.

12. Concurrently, Whitman in Washington had formed a deep and he hoped lasting attachment to the abolitionist writer William Douglas O'Connor and his wife Ellen. "Dear Nelly," he wrote in December 1864, "you & William have nei-

ther of you any idea how I daily & nightly bear you in mind & in love too—I did not know myself that you both had taken such deep root in my heart—few attachments wear & last through life, but ours *must*" (*Corr* 1:244). Before her marriage, Ellen (Tarr) O'Connor had worked on *The Liberator,* William Lloyd Garrison's antislavery journal, and was active in the women's rights movement. Through her sister's husband William F. Channing, a scientist and physician, she was related to the Concord intellectual circle that included Emerson, Thoreau, and Hawthorne, as well as to Thomas Wentworth Higginson—friend of Emily Dickinson, women's rights advocate, and abolitionist hero. Ezra Greenspan notes that "the kind of family [Whitman] did not have in New York he came to believe during the war decade he had found in Washington in the home of the O'Connors." See *Walt Whitman and the American Reader* (New York: Cambridge University Press, 1990), p. 227.

13. On Whitman and the British sex reformers, see chapter 5. See also Eve Kosofsky Sedgwick, "Toward the Twentieth Century: English Readers of Whitman," in *Between Men: English Literature and Male Homosocial Desire* (New York: Columbia University Press, 1985), pp. 201–17.

14. See, for example, the issues raised by Christopher Newfield in "Democracy and Male Homoeroticism," *Yale Journal of Criticism* 6, no. 2 (fall 1993): 29–62. Newfield suggests that "Whitman ties democratic theory and the fluid social arrangements represented, in his view, by male friendship" (42). This is both true and not true, and I amplify the psychology of Whitman's perspective in chapter 5.

15. Whitman did not attempt to integrate Doyle into his Washington circle of writers and artists, where his fondness for Pete's company was acknowledged but not easily understood.

16. For the view that "Whitman extended himself with Peter Doyle farther than he had with any other man and at greater risk to his psychic safety," see Kaplan, *Walt Whitman: A Life,* p. 313. Kaplan further describes Whitman as "mainly objectless in his affections until" falling in love with Doyle, whereas I describe sequential loves whose intensity belies the "objectless" label.

17. See also *Corr* 2:69–70 and 118–19.

18. Peter Doyle, quoted in Shively, *Calamus Lovers,* p. 106.

19. *The Correspondence* contains a total of forty-six letters written by Whitman to Doyle beginning in September 1868 and continuing until mid-June 1873. Beginning in the spring of 1874, Whitman's letters were more perfunctory. Doyle visited Camden in May but Whitman became increasingly depressed and debilitated during the summer and fall and described himself as too ill to write. See *Corr* 2:312, 316. By November 1875, Whitman was able to travel to Washington, where he boarded with Pete's relatives.

20. On Whitman and Stafford, see *Corr* 3:2–9. Following his multiple strokes in 1873, Whitman never fully recovered his health, but at the Stafford Farm in Kirkwood, New Jersey, which he describes rhapsodically in *Specimen Days,* his health improved markedly. Throughout their loving friendship, Stafford and Whitman quarreled repeatedly, and by 1878 both men had begun to go their separate ways.

21. On war and remasculinization, see Susan Jeffords, *The Remasculiniza-*

tion of America: Gender and the Vietnam War (Bloomington: Indiana University Press, 1989). An alternative though not necessarily antithetical view is that both masculinity and femininity unsettle in historical crisis. See *Behind the Lines: Gender and the Two World Wars,* ed. Margaret Randolph Higonnet, Jane Jenson, Sonya Michel, and Margaret Collins Weitz (New Haven: Yale University Press, 1987); *Arms and the Woman: War, Gender, and Literary Representation,* ed. Helen M. Cooper, Adrienne Auslander Munich, and Susan Merrill Squier (Chapel Hill: University of North Carolina Press, 1989); Susan Schweik, *"A Gulf So Deeply Cut": American Women Poets and the Second World War* (Madison: University of Wisconsin Press, 1991).

CHAPTER ONE

1. Horace Traubel (1858–1919), son of a Quaker mother and German Jewish immigrant father, produced *With Walt Whitman in Camden,* the most important biography of Whitman's later years. Compliments to Whitman's mother proliferate throughout the poet's conversations with Traubel, who visited him almost daily during the last four years of his life. Whitman's revisionary personal history took a decisive turn in 1867, however, when he described himself not only as "Well-begotten" but as "rais'd by a perfect mother." See "Starting from Paumanok," *LG* 1867, in *"Leaves of Grass": A Textual Variorum of the Printed Poems,* ed. Sculley Bradley, Harold W. Blodgett, Arthur Golden, and William White, 3 vols. (New York: New York University Press, 1980), 2:273.

2. On Traubel as "the last of the young men with whom the poet developed a strong emotional attachment," see Gary Schmidgall, *Walt Whitman: A Gay Life* (New York: Dutton, 1997), p. 226.

3. See Quentin Anderson, "Whitman's New Man," in *Walt Whitman's Autograph Revision of the Analysis of "Leaves of Grass" (For Dr. R. M. Bucke's Walt Whitman),* ed. Stephen Railton (New York: New York University Press, 1974), p. 29.

4. The notebooks had other purposes as well. For an analysis of their various functions that concentrates mainly on the late 1870s and 1880s, see *DBN* 1:xi–xix.

5. On the Van Velsors and war, see also Whitman's notebook entry for August 11, 1864: "Mother was telling me at dinner to-day, how glad she was when peace was declared, after the war of 1812 &c. She said her father told them he hoped they never would be compelled to see the horrors of war, as he had seen them in the Revolution. Mother's brothers were in the army at Brooklyn in 1812. She told me that her father came down to visit them and bring them some things, and she came with him. The camp must have been somewhere in the neighborhood of what is now Washington Park" (*NUPM* 2:523–24).

6. For example, "In dress she was rather Quakerish" (*NUPM* 1:6); "the last of Quaker training" (*NUPM* 1:31); "my grandmother Amy's sweet old face in its Quaker cap" (*SD* 694); "Amy Williams, of the Friends' or Quakers' denomination" (*SD* 694); "The maternal one (Amy Williams before marriage) was a Friend, or Quakeress, of sweet, sensible character, housewifely proclivities, and deeply intuitive and spiritual" (*SD* 695).

In 1867, Whitman attributed the stirring battle narrative in Section 35 of "Song of Myself" to "my grandmother's father the sailor," though in 1855 he had asked, "Did you read in the seabooks of the oldfashioned frigate-fight?" This yarn-telling great-grandfather is described by the editors of the Norton Critical Edition of *Leaves of Grass* as Amy Williams Van Velsor's father, Captain John Williams, assumed to have served under John Paul Jones when the *Bonhomme Richard* defeated the *Serapis*. Whitman does not mention this "fact" in any of his prose genealogies, which is curious given his hunger for any scrap of ancestral glory. And Quakers, of course, were not supposed to participate in military engagements.

7. This passage is introduced by a countertype "who sprang in crimson youth from the white froth and the water-blue." Probably this exotic figure is Aphrodite, the ancient mother-goddess of the eastern Mediterranean.

8. In ferreting out evidence of physical and moral corruption in "Faces," Whitman looks back to William Cullen Bryant's emblematic catalogue technique in "The Crowded Street" (1843). He also mobilizes a furious energy that anticipates the psychological, sexual, and spiritual dislocation of T. S. Eliot's *The Waste Land*. On "Faces" as a city poem, and on its historical and literary sources, see Christopher Beach, *The Politics of Distinction: Whitman and the Discourses of Nineteenth-Century America* (Athens: University of Georgia Press, 1996), pp. 111, 128, 130, 133–40, 142–43, 147, 154, 184.

9. Whitman was vague about his maternal aunts and uncles, and it is unclear how many ways the estate was likely to have been divided, assuming that something remained after his stepgrandmother's death. Cornelius Van Velsor may have wanted some of his estate to go to Amy's children, but he had a son, Alonzo, by his second wife. Given Alonzo's comparative youth, there may have been nothing left over for the others.

10. Bronson Alcott, *The Journals of Bronson Alcott,* ed. Odell Shepard (Boston: Little, Brown, 1938), p. 289.

11. John Burroughs in a letter to his wife, June 1868, as quoted in Clara Barrus, *Whitman and Burroughs: Comrades* (Boston: Houghton Mifflin, 1931), p. 57.

12. Louisa Whitman, quoted in *Mattie: The Letters of Martha Mitchell Whitman,* ed. Randall H. Waldron (New York: New York University Press, 1977), pp. 19–20.

13. Louisa Whitman, from the Trent Collection, William R. Perkins Library, Duke University. Except as otherwise indicated, Louisa Van Velsor Whitman's letters are paraphrased or quoted from this source.

14. See Carroll Smith-Rosenberg, "The Female World of Love and Ritual: Relations Between Women in Nineteenth-Century America," *Signs* 1 (autumn 1975), 1–29.

15. Josephine Barkeloo, quoted in *Dear Brother Walt: The Letters of Thomas Jefferson Whitman,* ed. Dennis Berthold and Kenneth Price (Kent, Ohio: Kent State University Press, 1984), p. 149 n.

16. Louisa Whitman, quoted in Bliss Perry, *Walt Whitman* (Boston: Houghton Mifflin, 1906), p. 19.

17. See Sandra Tomc, "An Idle Industry: Nathaniel Parker Willis and the

Workings of Literary Leisure," *American Quarterly* 49, no. 4 (December 1997): 780–805.

18. On Walter Senior's body, see Whitman, quoted in Barrus, p. 281.

19. On Jesse's intelligence, see Katherine Molinoff, *Some Notes on Whitman's Family* (Brooklyn: Comet Press, 1941), p. 19. Walt never discussed Jesse with Traubel or, so far as we can tell, with any of his friends.

20. Jeff also believed that Jesse had contracted syphilis from her. See *Dear Brother Walt*, pp. 85, 86. On Jesse's injuries, see *Civil War Letters of George Washington Whitman*, ed. Jerome M. Loving (Durham, N.C.: Duke University Press, 1975), pp. 9–10.

21. See the Record of the Kings County Lunatic Asylum, quoted in Gay Wilson Allen, *The Solitary Singer: A Critical Biography of Walt Whitman* (1955; reprint, New York: New York University Press, 1967), p. 318.

22. See the letter written by Fred Vaughan after his visit on April 29, 1860, in *Calamus Lovers: Walt Whitman's Working Class Camerados,* ed. Charley Shively (San Francisco: Gay Sunshine Press, 1987), p. 87. Vaughan provides a careful accounting of the whereabouts of all family members then living at home. Jesse is not among them.

23. The extent of Edward's retardation is puzzling. Family letters show that as an adult he attended church by himself every night, successfully ran errands, and transmitted messages. Louisa Whitman quotes his comments in her letters to Walt and they are almost always apt. On at least one occasion, she provides a long account of a disturbing situation based on Ed's reporting and it is perfectly coherent, even graphic. (He had met an escapee from the asylum where Jesse was being detained who claimed that "it was too damned bad to keep him there." Mrs. Whitman became alarmed that Jesse might try to escape as well. See the letter of April 7, 1869, in Allen, *Solitary Singer,* pp. 407–8. The escapee was Henry Rome, who was related to the printers of the first edition of *Leaves of Grass*.)

24. See the two letters in *Faint Clews & Indirections: Manuscripts of Walt Whitman and His Family,* ed. Clarence Gohdes and Rollo G. Silver (Durham, N.C.: Duke University Press, 1949), pp. 184–90. This volume reprints sixteen of her letters to Walt, along with a selection of letters written by other family members: the sisters, cheerful Mary Elizabeth Whitman Van Nostrand and disturbed Hannah Whitman Heyde; the vicious brother-in-law Charles Heyde; and the faithful George—these last written during his service in the Civil War. Walt saved approximately one hundred and seventy of his mother's letters.

25. See her letter of November 14, 1865, in *Faint Clews,* p. 192.

26. See Horace L. Traubel, "Notes from Conversations with George W. Whitman, 1893: Mostly in His Own Words," in *In Re Walt Whitman,* ed. Horace L. Traubel, Richard Maurice Bucke, and Thomas Harned (Philadelphia: David McKay, 1893), pp. 35–36.

In a paper presented at the 1984 Modern Language Association Convention in Washington, D.C., "Out of Her Cradle: Walt and Louisa Van Velsor Whitman," Kenneth M. Price further explains,

Louisa's letters show . . . that she strongly supported Walt's work. . . . She kept up with reviews of his poetry and commented on one written by Henry James ["a long one with flourishes"]. . . . She expressed concern over whether Walt would succeed in placing his essay "Democracy" in *The Galaxy.* She read much of the early criticism on her son, expressing a preference for William Douglas O'Connor's *The Good Gray Poet* over John Burroughs's *Notes on Walt Whitman, as Poet and Person.* She concluded, however, that Anne Gilchrist's essay "A Woman's Estimate of Walt Whitman" was the best piece written on her son because Gilchrist understood Walt "better than ever any one did before as if she could see right through you." Unquestionably, Louisa offered the poet important emotional support and demonstrated a sustained and genuine interest in Walt's literary endeavors.

Price cogently points out that critics who emphasize Louisa's illiteracy are wide of the mark. See, for example, Larzer Ziff, in *Literary Democracy: The Declaration of Cultural Independence in America* (New York: Viking, 1981), p. 33:

> Whitman's mother was his gentle sustenance throughout his young manhood, but she was illiterate, and Whitman's love for her, even adoration of her, could not be communicated to her in his poems. If he would have addressed anybody in a lyric it would have been she, as say Wordsworth addressed Dorothy, but this outlet was closed by her inability to read, although he could, of course, recite his verses to her. To this circumstance must in some small part be attributed the public as opposed to the lyric nature of his verse.

At the other extreme, Michael Moon explains that Whitman "remained a loyal partisan of the romances for which he had shared a passion with his mother in his boyhood—books like Scott's *Ivanhoe,* Cooper's *The Wept of Wish-ton-Wish,* and George Sand's *Consuelo.*" See "Disseminating Whitman," *South Atlantic Quarterly* 88, no. 1 (winter 1989), 262. A happy fantasy, but untrue, in that Louisa Whitman is not known to have read any novels during Whitman's boyhood, let alone to have read them with him. In later life she was an avid newspaper reader who was especially interested in politics.

27. Richard Maurice Bucke, *Walt Whitman* (Philadelphia: David McKay, 1883), p. 15.

28. David S. Reynolds notes that the house, which had been built in 1810, "was on a tract of sixty acres that Walter Whitman at first leased and then bought at sheriff's sale . . . on April 21, 1821, three years before taking the family to Brooklyn." See *Walt Whitman's America: A Cultural Biography* (New York: Alfred A. Knopf, 1995), p. 25.

29. See Berthold and Price, *Dear Brother Walt,* p. 28.

30. Louisa Whitman, November 1863, from the Trent Collection.

31. For a discussion of Whitman Senior as tavernkeeper, see chapter 4.

32. Louisa Whitman's letters quoted in this paragraph are in the Trent Collection.

33. Alternatively, Kenneth M. Price observes, "It is possible that Louisa consciously echoed Walt's language, but the artless way she worked the phrase into her letter suggests that she was not trying to allude to her son's poem. Instead this was probably one of her pet locutions that Walt weaves into his verse." Price, "Out of Her Cradle," p. 6. Louisa's letter is dated June 20, 1867, and is in the Trent Collection; further citations in this paragraph are from the same letter.

34. There are many directions in which this topic could be pursued. For example, we might turn to Donald Grant Mitchell's *Reveries of a Bachelor* (1850) and other classics of the sentimental genre that Ann Douglas brilliantly

recanonized (in spite of herself) in *The Feminization of American Culture* (New York: Alfred A. Knopf, 1977). Or we might consider the figure of the flaneur in nineteenth-century urban literature, as reflected in the Knickerbocker school of New York journalism with which Whitman was intimately familiar, and as discussed by Dana Brand in *The Spectator and the City in Nineteenth-Century American Literature* (New York: Cambridge University Press, 1991). Brand describes the bachelor as an "urban spectator detached from ordinary social, familial, or economic obligations" (p. 28). Or we might want to look further at tropes of pastoral lounging in Romantic poetry, as described by Willard Spiegelman in *Majestic Indolence: English Romantic Poetry and the Work of Art* (New York: Oxford University Press, 1995). Spiegelman's discussion of Keats's addiction to a "wise passivity," in chapter 4, is especially valuable. Or to the extent that Whitman's loafer is mainly a symbol of sexual freedom, we should consult Eve Kosofsky Sedgwick, *Epistemology of the Closet* (Berkeley: University of California Press, 1990), pp. 188–212. Sedgwick theorizes the relationship between the urban bachelor figure in the Victorian context and the larger topos of male homosexual panic. For further thoughts on the bachelor as deviant, see Vincent J. Bertolini, "Fireside Chastity: The Erotics of Sentimental Bachelorhood in the 1850s," *American Literature* 63, no. 4 (December 1996): 707–37. Bertolini argues that "the bachelor represented the transgressive triple threat of masturbation, whoremongering, and that nameless horror—homosexual sex" (708). As my text is intended to demonstrate, Whitman's loaferish bachelor persona is also shaped by a very specific psychological and domestic environment.

35. Louisa Whitman, August 19, 1868, from the Trent Collection. Louisa was referring to the dog of the Brown family, who occupied the lower part of her house. She disliked them.

36. On Walter Senior as a "natural mechanic," see Jeff Whitman's obituary, quoted in *Dear Brother Walt*, p. 189. The obituary was based on information supplied by Walt.

37. Whitman, "Elias Hicks," in *November Boughs*, in *Walt Whitman: Complete Poetry and Collected Prose*, ed. Justin Kaplan (New York: Literary Classics of the United States, 1982), p. 1232. In speaking to Traubel, Whitman suggested that it was his mother rather than his father who first introduced him to Hicks's teachings, but many of the original Long Island Whitmans had been Quakers, and Hicks (1748–1830) had been a friend of Whitman's paternal grandfather. As a young man on Long Island, Walt Whitman considered converting to Quakerism, and in his last years, he kept a large bust of Hicks in his room in Camden. See Perry, *Walt Whitman*, p. 257.

For an analysis of Hicksite Quakerism, see Robert W. Doherty, *The Hicksite Separation: A Sociological Analysis of Religious Schism in Early Nineteenth Century America* (New Brunswick, N.J.: Rutgers University Press, 1967). Doherty notes that "in an age which witnessed the decline in status of people who performed physical labor and at the same time saw the development of economic specialization under the merchant capitalist," Hicks's rural-based opposition to "Orthodox" leaders who were "wealthy, refined, urban-dwelling businessmen" was powerful indeed (pp. 42, 27). In Philadelphia, for example, forty percent of Hicks's followers were artisans, as was Walter Senior, who would have been part of the "natural" constituency for Hicks's antiurbanism. For the life of Hicks, who died several months after Whitman may have heard him preach, see Bliss Forbush, *Elias Hicks: Quaker Liberal* (New York: Columbia University Press, 1956). The term "liberal" is, however, misleading, in that Hicks mainly opposed changes in traditional modes of behavior and belief.

38. Hicks, quoted in *November Boughs*, p. 1226.

39. "Elias Hicks," in *November Boughs*, p. 1233. At the time of Hicks's speech in the ballroom at Morrison's Hotel in Brooklyn Heights in November 1829, Louisa was nine months pregnant and was about to give birth several days later.

40. For a genealogy of the Whitman family, see Allen, *Solitary Singer*, p. 595. Walter Whitman Senior was born on July 14, 1789 (Bastille Day), and Jesse Whitman died in February 1803.

41. M. Wynn Thomas, *The Lunar Light of Whitman's Poetry* (Cambridge: Harvard University Press, 1987), pp. 28–29. The internal quote is Sean Wilentz, *Chants Democratic: New York City and the Rise of the American Working Class, 1788–1850* (New York: Oxford University Press, 1984), p. 55. For further analysis of the expanding market as it pressured the urban artisan class in antebellum America, see Charles Sellers, *The Market Revolution in Jacksonian America: 1815–1846* (New York: Oxford University Press, 1991), and Stuart M. Blumin, *The Emergence of the Middle Class: Social Experience in the American City, 1760–1900* (New York: Cambridge University Press, 1989). Thomas's perspective, however, overstates the solidity of class boundaries in Jacksonian America and in Walter Senior's life. Because class boundaries were unstable, Walter Senior's various occupations (as farmer, craftsman, and small entrepreneur) were important in defining his social status. For Walter Senior as small entrepreneur, see chapter 4. On masculinity as constructed by professional competence, see E. Anthony Rotundo, *American Manhood: Transformations in Masculinity from the Revolution to the Modern Era* (New York: Basic Books, 1993), chapter 8, "Work and Identity." And for a sensitive analysis of the poet's anomalous class position, see David Leverenz, *Manhood and the American Renaissance* (Ithaca: Cornell University Press, 1989), passim. He suggests that Whitman's public voice combines "an artisan's insouciance with entrepreneurial brag" (p. 106).

42. Betsy Erkkila probably overstates the case for Whitman's father as a reader in *Whitman the Political Poet* (New York: Oxford University Press, 1989), when she asserts that "copies of the major freethinking texts—Volney's *The Ruins* (1791), Paine's *The Age of Reason* (1791), and Wright's *A Few Days in Athens* (1822)—were cherished books in the Whitman household" (p. 15). Whitman does not claim that his father was a reader of anything except the *Free Enquirer* (*WWWC* 2:205), and his statement "Books were scarce" aptly applies not only to the home of his paternal grandparents but also to the home in which he was raised. Erkkila makes a compelling case, however, for *Walt* Whitman's responsiveness to Volney's critique of religious orthodoxy as "a primary source of human oppression" (p. 113).

43. According to Clara Barrus, "Burroughs once told me that he understood Walt's father had at one time been addicted to alcohol, and that Walt thought

this habit might have been responsible for Ed's condition. He [Burroughs] in-
stanced a line in 'Faces' as referring to this—'I knew [of] the agents that emp-
tied and broke my brother.'" See Barrus, *Whitman and Burroughs,* p. 254.

44. The relationship between Whitman's formal schooling and his youthful
work needs to be further explored. Intuitively, I agree with the analysis offered
by Floyd Stovall, in *The Foreground of "Leaves of Grass"* (Charlottesville: University of Virginia Press, 1974), pp. 23–24. Stovall speculates that Whitman continued to attend school intermittently after he began working for the Clarkes
and that "this and his first jobs in newspaper offices in 1831 and 1832 occupied
all his time throughout the year. There were two or three school terms during
the year, each usually lasting only three or four months. It seems probable that
Whitman continued to attend school in Brooklyn for a few months each year until the summer of 1833, when his family moved back to the country." Stovall further suggests, following Bucke's lead in *Walt Whitman,* that Whitman attended
the (Union Hall) Academy in Jamaica.

45. Allen, *Solitary Singer,* p. 17.

46. On apprenticeship as an exclusively male institution, "a system of education and job training by which important practical information was passed from
one generation to the next," "a mechanism by which youths could model themselves on socially approved adults," "an institution devised to insure proper
moral development through the master's fatherly responsibility for the behavior
of his apprentice," and "a means of social control imposed upon potentially
disruptive male adolescents," see W. J. Rorabaugh, *The Craft Apprentice: From
Franklin to the Machine Age in America* (New York: Oxford University Press,
1986), pp. vii-viii and passim. Rorabaugh notes that "although printing attracted boys who had some fascination for the written word, such apprentices
came from the same sorts of backgrounds as other apprentices and entered a
craft that stood socially and economically on a par with or only modestly above
other crafts."

47. Possibly some of these moves were due to his father's restlessness. And
some of them reflected bad luck. See Whitman's wistful and angry comments in
NUPM 1:10–11. In *Walt Whitman's America,* Reynolds suggests that "the restlessness and unhappiness Whitman associated with his childhood had less to do
with a uniformly hostile relationship with his father than with his unstable position in a changing economic and social order. . . . Previous biographers have
described a 'buy, build, and sell' pattern in Walter Whitman's business dealings,
suggesting that through speculation he at least kept his head above water. Real
estate records show that the picture was not that rosy." See this richly contex-
tualized discussion on pp. 24–25 and passim. So far as I know, however, no informed biographer has suggested that Whitman's relationship with his father
was uniformly hostile.

48. Whitman, quoted in Charles I. Glicksberg, *Walt Whitman and the Civil
War* (Philadelphia: University of Pennsylvania Press, 1933), pp. 53–54.

49. This was probably the period during which there were "stormy scenes"
with his father who, "when aroused," was "capable of memorable vehemence."
See "Introduction," in *Complete Writings of Walt Whitman,* ed. Richard Maurice Bucke, Thomas B. Harned, and Horace L. Traubel, 10 vols. (New York:

G. P. Putnam, 1902), 1:xvi. But Whitman resisted Walter Senior's attempts to get him to help with the farm work, and was teaching in Norwich beginning in June. Apparently the Whitmans moved to Babylon, further out on the Island, in the summer of 1836 where they remained until May 1840. See *UPP* 2:87. Whitman was teaching "west of Babylon" during the winter of 1836–37. His living arrangements during this time are not clear. For a helpful map of Long Island geography and of Whitman's whereabouts during these unsettled years, see Allen, *Solitary Singer,* p. 27.

The family's economic fortunes had probably improved by 1836, however, when Walter Senior sold land that he had inherited from his mother and his brother for $2,250, which was the equivalent of three or four years' salary for the average carpenter at that time. See Joseph Jay Rubin, *The Historic Whitman* (University Park: Penn State University Press, 1973), pp. 32–33, and Reynolds, *Walt Whitman's America,* p. 55. There are discrepancies between these two accounts, but both Rubin and Reynolds agree that land played a role in Walter Senior's fortunes. Reynolds further notes that he had been able to hold onto the sixty acres he purchased in 1821 and to add to them, so that in 1836 he sold more than a hundred acres to the farmer Richard Colyer, whose wife, Hannah, was the daughter of Walter's sister Sarah. These inheritances, purchases, and sales are relevant in assessing the class identification of Walter Senior, which was more complicated than descriptions of him as a dissatisfied artisan might suggest.

50. Emory Holloway suggests that "Archie's unusually confiding attitude toward his mother parallels Whitman's affection for his 'perfect mother'" (*UPP* 1:232 n). But the story contains a good mother (the victim-confidante) and a bad mother (the repulsive spinster who teaches him the meaning of hard work). These figures are united in that Archie's mother fears that he won't "'excel.'" "Ah, for how many the morose habit which Archie rooted *out* from his nature," Whitman concludes, "becomes by long usage and indulgence rooted *in,* and spreads its bitterness over their existence, and darkens the peace of their families, and carries them through the spring and early summer of life with no inhalement of sweets, and no plucking of flowers!" (*EPF* 330). The "ancient, bony, yellow-faced maiden . . . who seem[s] to be on good terms with everybody" but whose driving ambition shrivels "all other passions," is probably a displaced version of Louisa herself. Although Archie is a passive-aggressive hero who feels "this [clever] old maid's doings as a rebuke—a sharp-pointed moral to himself and his infirmity of purpose," his sympathy, and Whitman's, for "the small payment which is given to female labor" is genuine. Nevertheless, hostility that might have been directed toward the father's fecklessness is projected onto the bad, hard-driving mother, of whom it was said that she had been "handsome" in her youth.

51. This was the period, as Whitman recalled in an 1887 article, in which he was legally exonerated for thrashing a neighbor's boy who interfered with his fishing. He triumphed in court, speaking in his own defense. See Justin Kaplan, *Walt Whitman: A Life* (New York: Simon and Schuster, 1980), pp. 84, 135, and Reynolds, *Walt Whitman's America,* pp. 58–59.

52. Whitman, quoted in Grace Gilchrist, "Chats with Walt Whitman," *Temple Bar Magazine* 113 (February 1898): 208.

53. Herbert Bergman and William White, "Walt Whitman's Lost 'Sun-Down Papers,' Nos. 1–3," *American Book Collector* 20 (January 1970): 18–19.

54. "Sun-Down Papers," in *UPP* 1:37.

55. Katherine Molinoff, *An Unpublished Whitman Manuscript: The Record of the Smithtown Debating Society, 1837–38* (Brooklyn: Comet Press, 1941).

56. There have been a number of interesting studies of Whitman and William Cullen Bryant. In *Whitman and Tradition: The Poet in His Century,* Kenneth M. Price notes that "Our Future Lot" echoes lines and phrases from "Thanatopsis" (pp. 56–57), as it surely does. On McDonald Clarke, see Reynolds, *Walt Whitman's America,* pp. 88–90. The so-called "Mad Poet of Broadway" died in a New York City prison on March 5, 1842; Whitman memorialized him in the *Aurora* several days later. In "The Death and Burial of McDonald Clarke. A Parody" (*EPF* 25–26), Whitman imitates the form of Charles Wolfe's "The Burial of Sir John Moore at Corunna" (1817). (Wolfe was an Anglo-Irish curate; Sir John Moore was a military leader in the British campaign against Napoleon.) Thomas L. Brasher notes, "Whitman's parody is identical in meter, and in the form and number of stanzas, with Wolfe's poem. Whitman borrowed verbatim one line from Wolfe, which appears as the second line of his fourth stanza. For the rest he was content with a general parallel of Wolfe's ideas" (*EPF* 25 n). Whitman seized the occasion of Clarke's death to condemn the hypocrisy and hardheartedness of the reading public.

57. Orvetta Hall Brenton, in *UPP* 1:xxxiii-iv n. 1.

58. James J. Brenton, in Rubin, *The Historic Whitman,* pp. 223, 244.

59. As Carroll Smith-Rosenberg notes in "Davy Crockett as Trickster," in *Disorderly Conduct: Visions of Gender in Victorian America* (New York: Alfred A. Knopf, 1985), "The nation extolled ambition, change, and individualism at the same time that it continued to praise the family and traditional social order" (p. 99). "Tomb Blossoms" slyly exemplifies this conflict. "Men of cities!" a tricksterish Whitman writes, "what is there in all your boasted pleasure—your fashions, parties, balls, and theatres, compared to the simplest of the delights we country folk enjoy?" (*EPF* 88).

60. Ellen Moers, *Literary Women* (Garden City, N.Y.: Doubleday, 1976).

61. Whitman, as quoted in Arthur Golden, "Nine Early Whitman Letters, 1840–1841," *American Literature* 58, no. 3 (October 1986): 347–48.

62. Whitman, in Golden, "Nine Early Letters," 349–50. Mosher is unidentified.

63. Whitman, in Golden, "Nine Early Letters," 351–52.

64. Henry James, in *CH,* p. 260. James's review of *Calamus,* ed. R. M. Bucke (Boston: Laurens Maynard, 1897), appeared as an "American Letter" in *Literature* on April 16, 1898.

65. Golden, "Nine Early Letters," 352–53 n. 22. Golden adds that "this would not have been an early expression of the 'Calamus' sentiment on Whitman's part." For a related contemporary context, see "Youth and Male Intimacy," in Rotundo, *American Manhood,* pp. 56–91. He describes "intimate attachments that verged on romance" (p. 75) and suggests that "most young men enjoyed at least one strong friendship" (p. 76). Rotundo further argues that these "romantic friendships of male youth closely resembled the intense bonds

between women first portrayed by Carroll Smith-Rosenberg in her landmark article, 'The Female World of Love and Ritual,'" but that "the intimate ties between young men of the nineteenth century differed from those described by Smith-Rosenberg in at least one fundamental way. Among males, romantic friendship was largely a product of a distinct phase in the life cycle—youth" (p. 76). See also Donald Yacovone, "Abolitionists and the 'Language of Fraternal Love,'" in *Meanings for Manhood: Constructions of Masculinity in Victorian America,* ed. Mark C. Carnes and Clyde Griffen (Chicago: University of Chicago Press, 1990), pp. 85–95. Yacovone argues, "The freedom with which many abolitionists expressed their love and devotion, and the open ritualistic nature of their relationships, calls for a reconsideration of the commonplace view that Victorian men were emotionally inexpressive and hypermasculine" (p. 85). He further contends that although antebellum Americans accepted no single definition of manhood, "They displayed a variety of phases or types of masculinity which sometimes blurred gender distinctions in ways that would disturb contemporary Americans. This modern reaction to intimate male friendships underscores the profound changes which have occurred in the culture's perception of masculinity. To a surprising degree, mid-nineteenth-century social attitudes permitted great liberty in personal relations, largely untainted by homophobia" (p. 86). Thus, whereas Rotundo emphasizes life cycle effects, Yacovone purports to have identified a more lasting pattern of socially unproblematic male-male intimacy. Whitman's confidential relationship with Leech does, however, appear to be restricted to youth.

66. Whitman, in Golden, "Nine Early Letters," 353.

67. This association surfaces again in the tenth "Sun-Down Paper," published a year later. Whitman describes a pleasure party on the South Bay during which he observed, "One of us, a married man, had come from home without his breakfast; whereupon an inquiry was instituted that resulted in bringing out the astounding fact that every married man in the company was in the like predicament. An evil-disposed character among us was ungallant enough to say that the fact was a fair commentary on matrimonial comfort." Ungallant or not, Whitman's observation stuck. Married men get no breakfast. See *UPP* 1:48–51.

68. His business correspondence was more extensive. The 1857 letter to the Philadelphia abolitionist Sarah Tyndale combines business and pleasure; see *Corr* 1:42–43.

69. Leech's drafts are in the Feinberg Collection of the Library of Congress, Washington, D.C.

70. For more on Leech's political and temperance activities, and for a fascinating reading of him as an educated and religious person, see Jerome Loving, *Walt Whitman: The Song of Himself* (Berkeley: University of California Press, 1999), pp. 71–72, 41–42. The Whitman quotation is from "Sun-Down Paper," no. 5, in *UPP* 1:33. The essay was published in Brenton's *Long Island Democrat* on April 28, 1840.

71. On drinking as a male prerogative and on temperance as an attack on masculine culture, see Mary Ann Clawson, *Constructing Brotherhood: Class, Gender, and Fraternalism* (Princeton: Princeton University Press, 1989), chapter 5, "Social Fraternalism and the Artisanal Ideal," pp. 145–177. Much of what

Clawson observes about emerging bourgeois sociability is relevant to my discussion of temperance fiction in the next chapter.

72. Whitman, in Golden, "Nine Early Letters," 355–56.

CHAPTER TWO

1. See "Bamboozle and Benjamin," reprinted in *Walt Whitman of the New York Aurora: Editor at Twenty-Two,* ed. Joseph Jay Rubin and Charles H. Brown (State College, Pa.: Bald Eagle Press, 1950), pp. 110–11. The essay begins, "We have in America many literary quacks." "Bamboozle and Benjamin" also attacks the contemporary feminist Frances Wright, whom Whitman subsequently claimed to have revered.

2. On the *Democratic Review,* see Frank Luther Mott, *A History of American Magazines 1741–1850* (New York: D. Appleton, 1930), pp. 677–84. The 20,000-copy figure for *Franklin Evans* was first advanced by Henry Bryan Binns, in *A Life of Walt Whitman* (London: Methuen, 1905), p. 35, and is thoroughly in keeping with the sales of comparable works described by Mott. Whitman described his payment to Horace Traubel and Thomas Harned in 1888. The gist of the conversation is reprinted in *EPF* 125.

3. Lowell's remark is quoted in Esther Shephard, "Walt Whitman's Whereabouts in the Winter of 1842–1843," *American Literature* 29, no. 3 (November 1957): 291.

4. Sophia Hawthorne is quoted in Mott, *A History,* p. 680.

5. Whitman's letter to Nathan Hale, Jr., editor of the *Miscellany,* is included in *Corr* 1:25.

6. In *A Dictionary of Slang and Unconventional English* (New York: Macmillan, 1984), Eric Partridge lists 1920 as the earliest date for the use of "queer" to mean homosexual. But the history of this word is still being written. See, for example, George Chauncey, *Gay New York: Gender, Urban Culture, and the Making of the Gay Male World, 1890–1940* (New York: Basic Books, 1994), pp. 13–22, 24–25, 101, 125.

7. Stephen A. Black combines these lines of thinking. See *Whitman's Journeys into Chaos: A Psychoanalytic Study of the Poetic Process* (Princeton: Princeton University Press, 1975), in which Black explains, "The fiction fails because when Whitman employed stock situations and devices of characterization his own unconscious attitudes and assumptions intruded upon the material. Unconscious forces conflicted with the intent to be conventional; Whitman's narcissism confused the fictional world he was trying to create" (p. 17).

8. For a fuller discussion of Whitman's attitudes toward Indians and for the view that "like many Americans who lived through this period, Whitman never stopped struggling with the insoluble 'Indian problem,'" see Ed Folsom, *Walt Whitman's Native Representations* (New York: Cambridge University Press, 1994), chapter 3. For the view that Whitman did not struggle enough, see Steven B. Shively, "Prejudice and Praise: Walt Whitman's Portrayal of the American Indian," *Nebraska English Journal* 38, no. 2 (1993): 28–39, and Maurice Kenny, "Whitman's Indifference to Indians," in *The Continuing Presence of Walt*

Whitman, ed. Robert K. Martin (Iowa City: University of Iowa Press, 1992), pp. 28–38.

9. For Whitman's relation to this debate, see Florence Bernstein Freedman, *Walt Whitman Looks at the Schools* (New York: King's Crown, 1950), especially pp. 70–71, 73–79, 83–85, 89–90, 92–93, 107–8, 114–19, 133–34, 137–39, 171, 190–93, 196–200. Freedman reprints articles Whitman wrote for the *Brooklyn Evening Star* and the *Brooklyn Daily Eagle* between 1845 and 1848 that show him as an educational reformer, campaigning vigorously for the abolition of corporal punishment.

For speculation that Whitman was publicly accused of sodomy while teaching school on Long Island, that he was denounced from the pulpit and tarred and feathered and run out of the town of Southold by a mob of enraged parents, see David S. Reynolds, *Walt Whitman's America: A Cultural Biography* (New York: Alfred A. Knopf, 1995), chapter 3. On the whole, I find Reynolds's provocative discussion unpersuasive, though I agree that such an accusation, coupled with public disgrace, would clarify some of the murkier passages in Whitman's biography.

For a superb article on the broader cultural significance of flogging scenes, see Richard H. Brodhead, "Sparing the Rod: Discipline and Fiction in Antebellum America," *Representations* 21 (winter 1988): 67–96. Brodhead argues that "in the 1830s, then even more prominently in the 1840s and early 1850s, the picturing of scenes of physical correction emerges as a major form of imaginative activity in America, and arguing the merits of such discipline becomes a major item on the American public agenda" (p. 67).

10. See David Leverenz, *Manhood and the American Renaissance* (Ithaca: Cornell University Press, 1989), p. 5.

11. For a reading of "The Child's Champion" that treats the end of the story as a "pure expression of a homoerotic utopian dream," see Byrne R. S. Fone, "The Fountains of Love: Poetry and Fiction, 1838–1850," in *Masculine Landscapes: Walt Whitman and the Homoerotic Text* (Carbondale: Southern Illinois University Press, 1992), p. 61. Fone's reading of this story and of the early fiction as "muted testimony to a life beneath the life" (p. 38) has many points of similarity to my own analysis, though he goes too far when he writes, "Langton and Charles, at least the implied fantasy hopes, will spend the rest of their days in a very nearly mystical and certainly spiritually uplifting union" (p. 61), since Whitman's fantasy of meaningful male bonding seeks to accommodate heterosexual marriage as well. To this end, Whitman seems to be working more with a "stages of development" model of sexuality, in which homoerotic desire among men eventually forms the basis of a manlier, that is heterosexual, identity. Charles and Langton are presented as emotionally immature; when Langton grows up he marries. What remains underdeveloped in the story's ending is the life beneath the life of their subsequent friendship, especially from Charles's narratively-collapsed perspective. We are led to believe that Langton gets it all (the friend and the wife and the family) but that Charles, second first and second always, remains excluded from the full range of power relations that Langton organizes. As I read it, their relationship is far from egalitarian, which is one of its more believable fea-

tures. Charles remains dependent on Langton, whereas Langton, the good father/brother/lover, continues to have access to a wider range of erotic empowerments.

12. In a now classic analysis of this story, "Rendering the Text and the Body Fluid: The Cases of 'The Child's Champion' and the 1855 *Leaves of Grass*," in *Disseminating Whitman: Revision and Corporeality in "Leaves of Grass"* (Cambridge: Harvard University Press, 1991), Michael Moon considers "the clear traces of self-censorship, a highly specialized form of writerly substitution, to be found in the successive editions of [t]his very early story" (p. 26). As I do, Moon sees Whitman as "both practicing and evading self-censorship" and further suggests that Whitman's strategies of "simultaneous extreme literality and extreme indeterminacy have a formative effect on the representation of the fluidity of selves, bodies, and texts which are central to the 1855 *Leaves of Grass*" (p. 26). Moon further explains,

> The most persuasive evidence that Whitman was aware of the strong homoerotic quality of "The Child's Champion" is that when he came to revise it for republication in 1844 . . . , he did so by censoring it of a number of the pronounced and recurrent homoerotic references which the first version of the story foregrounded. . . . Censorship and self-censorship were crucial elements—were in a sense formative—of Whitman's literary practice from very early on. (pp. 29–30)

13. *Franklin Evans* has been mistakenly praised as the first or one of the first temperance novels, but as Jean Romig Kirkpatrick points out in "The Temperance Movement and Temperance Fiction 1820–1860" (Ph.D. diss., University of Pennsylvania, 1970), "At least 70 temperance novels were published before Whitman's *Franklin Evans* and certainly 8 were published in New York City during the ten year period prior to 1840" (p. 21 n. 1). There is an extensive literature on the history of temperance, but temperance fiction awaits the full scale treatment it deserves. See, however, "Ten Thousand and One Nights in a Barroom," in Herbert Ross Brown, *The Sentimental Novel in America 1789–1860* (Durham, N.C.: Duke University Press, 1940), pp. 201–41. Valuable specialized studies of *Franklin Evans* in its historical context include Barton L. St. Armand, "*Franklin Evans*: A Sportive Temperance Novel," in *Books at Brown* 24 (1971): 134–47, and Anne Dalke, "Whitman's Literary Intemperance: *Franklin Evans*, or The Power of Love," *Walt Whitman Quarterly Review* 2, no. 3 (winter 1984): 17–22. For the larger context of reform literature and for a brief but stimulating look at temperance fiction, see David S. Reynolds, *Beneath the American Renaissance: The Subversive Imagination in the Age of Emerson and Melville* (New York: Alfred A. Knopf, 1988). For Reynolds's discussion of *Franklin Evans* in the context of the Washingtonian temperance movement, see his *Walt Whitman's America,* chapter 4. And for more on the "Literary Uses of Temperance and Alcohol," see Reynolds, "Black Cats and Delirium Tremens: Temperance and the American Renaissance," in *The Serpent in the Cup: Temperance in American Literature,* ed. David S. Reynolds and Debra J. Rosenthal (Amherst: University of Massachusetts Press, 1997), pp. 22–59. This volume also contains valuable material on the sociological and medical debates to which Whitman was responding.

14. For an insightful discussion of this novel as an example of the litera-

ture of addiction, see Michael Warner, "Whitman Drunk," in *Breaking Bounds: Whitman and American Cultural Studies,* ed. Betsy Erkkila and Jay Grossman (New York: Oxford University Press, 1996), pp. 30–43.

15. The word *gay* was not used to signify homosexual identity until the twentieth century, but Whitman seems to be on the verge of developing this new range of linguistic and affective associations.

16. On Walter Whitman Senior's financial failures, see Justin Kaplan, *Walt Whitman: A Life* (New York: Simon and Schuster, 1980), pp. 64–65, as well as the discussion in my chapter 1. See too Whitman's remarks about his father's swindling in *NUPM* 1:10, 10 n. 30, 98, and 98 n. 12.

17. Walt Whitman, "New York Boarding Houses," in Rubin and Brown, *Walt Whitman of the New York Aurora,* pp. 22–24.

18. In *The Solitary Singer: A Critical Biography of Walt Whitman* (1955; reprint, New York: New York University Press, 1967), Gay Wilson Allen explains that "M—could hardly have been any one except his mother" (p. 216). Yet why code his mother's name? Emory Holloway (*UPP* 2:91) suggests "a lover, or perhaps Whitman's mother or sister Mary." Roger Asselineau suggests a male lover, in *The Evolution of Walt Whitman,* 2 vols. (Cambridge: Harvard University Press, 1960), 1:106 ff. Given Whitman's close identification with his brother Jeff, another possibility is his sister-in-law Mattie, whom he adored. His sister Mary seems implausible.

19. See *NUPM* 1:401–3, 2:876, 3:1269–70. On "Song of Myself" as a spiritual novel, see *DBN* 3:774–75.

20. As Marjorie Perloff has argued, "Genre, far from being a normative category, is always culture-specific and, to a high degree, historically determined." In this chapter I have been suggesting that genre is also biographically determined. See *Postmodern Genres,* ed. Marjorie Perloff (Norman: University of Oklahoma Press, 1989), p. 7.

21. Large and passionate, she was originally "Ruth Anderson, a Quaker's daughter," and there was to be "An old Quaker lady—good—sensible." Whitman wondered "how to intertwine [her] with Antoinette's affairs," and we too may wonder how he would have done it. For more historical context, see Timothy J. Gilfoyle, *City of Eros: New York City, Prostitution, and the Commercialization of Sex, 1790–1920* (New York: W. W. Norton, 1992).

22. Whitman attended Emerson's lecture on "Poetry and the Times" on March 5, 1842, as a reporter for the *New York Aurora.* A version of the lecture was published in *Essays: Second Series* (1844) as "The Poet."

23. For the view that metaphors are pernicious in that they obliterate particularity and can make distinct exploitations appear identical, see Karen Sánchez-Eppler, "Bodily Bonds," in *Touching Liberty: Abolition, Feminism, and the Politics of the Body* (Berkeley: University of California Press, 1993), p. 20. See also her discussion of the Virginia section of *Franklin Evans* in the context of Whitman's depictions of slavery, pp. 57–63 and following, in chapter 2, "To Stand Between: Whitman's Poetics of Merger and Embodiment." Sánchez-Eppler argues that "the same politically grounded conception of miscegenation informs both *Franklin Evans* and the 1855 *Leaves of Grass*" (p. 63).

CHAPTER THREE

1. For other photographs of Whitman, see the special double issue of the *Walt Whitman Quarterly Review* 2–3 (1986–87), which brings together all known photographs of the poet for the first time—some 130 in number, ranging from the early 1840s to 1891.

2. See Richard Rorty, *Achieving Our Country: Leftist Thought in Twentieth-Century America* (Cambridge: Harvard University Press, 1998), p. 18. Rorty provides a brief and insightful discussion of body-worship as an alternative to God-worship in *Leaves of Grass*. In directing attention toward Whitman's inner life, I do not mean to minimize the importance of those cultural roughnesses inflicted on him by the cruelly intolerant "priests" who authored the "logic and sermons" he was seeking to disavow. Rather, I am attempting to describe the analogies between these inner and outer systems of emotion and belief.

3. For a philosophical approach to Whitman and the uses of compassion, see Martha Nussbaum, "Poets as Judges," in *Poetic Justice: The Literary Imagination and Public Life* (Boston: Beacon Press, 1995), 74–121 and passim. She praises Whitman as a poet "whose commitment both to narrative and to the conscious depiction of different ways of life brings him into close contact with the novel" (p. 7).

4. See Dana Brand, *The Spectator and the City in Nineteenth-Century American Literature* (New York: Cambridge University Press, 1991), p. 179. I draw on his lively and astute discussion of Whitman and the Knickerbocker journalists in the discussion that follows.

5. Rorty, *Achieving Our Country*, p. 24.

6. I exaggerate here to make a point, since we can't rule out the possibility that Whitman recorded his meeting with Emerson in a notebook now missing or subsequently destroyed by him. My hunch, however, is that if he kept a record, it wasn't a detailed one.

7. See, for example, Fanny Fern's titillating praise of Whitman's broad shoulders, exposed "muscular throat," and "ample chest" in "Peeps from under a Parasol," a newspaper column in which she attacked the "*pretty*" gentleman who defined the New York literary establishment, which notoriously included several of her own brothers, by reversing the male gaze. Her satiric appropriation of Whitman as a sex object in her effort to sponsor a more democratic literary culture is reprinted in *Ruth Hall and Other Writings,* ed. Joyce W. Warren (New Brunswick, N.J.: Rutgers University Press, 1986), pp. 272–73. Fern later became the first woman to praise *Leaves of Grass* in print, calling it "Well baptized: fresh, hardy, and grown for the masses" (p. 274).

8. Walt Whitman, quoted in Joseph Jay Rubin, *The Historic Whitman* (University Park: Pennsylvania State University Press, 1973), p. 222.

9. Rubin, *Historic Whitman*, p. 376.

10. From late December 1849 to late February 1850, for example, Whitman edited the first issues of the *New York Daily News,* but the paper was unable to attract enough subscribers to remain in business. Whitman lost his job when the paper folded.

11. In 1850, Whitman published three poems experimenting with a new free-verse line. "Blood-Money" appeared in the *New York Tribune Supplement* on March 22 and again in the *Evening Post* on April 30; "The House of Friends" in the *New York Tribune* on June 14; and "Resurgemus" in the *Tribune* on June 21 and again in the *Dispatch* on August 28. A fourth poem, "Song for Certain Congressmen," later titled "Dough-Face Song," appeared in the *Post* on March 2, but it is a doggerel piece employing strict rhythms and rhymes. "Resurgemus" was untitled in *Leaves of Grass* 1855, called "Poem of The Dead Young Men of Europe, the 72nd and 73rd Years of These States" in 1856, and titled "Europe" in 1860. This title stuck.

12. "My Boys and Girls" is part of Whitman's bachelor-persona group. Published in 1844, it asks, "What would you say, dear reader, were I to claim the nearest relationship to George Washington, Thomas Jefferson and Andrew Jackson?" He mentions little Louisa, a composite of his mother and sister Hannah Louisa, and a sexually precocious fourteen-year-old apparently modeled on his sister Mary. But he omits the most troublesome two brothers, Jesse and Ed. See *EPF* 248–50.

13. Richard Maurice Bucke, *Walt Whitman* (Philadelphia: David McKay, 1883), p. 18 n.

14. Helen E. Price, "Reminiscences of Walt Whitman," *New York Evening Post,* May 31, 1919, p. 2: "When we first knew him, before the contraction of his first name became so common, he told us of a stranger who came up to him, and clapping him on the shoulder said: 'Well, Walt, how are you?' He evidently resented the familiarity, and one of us asked him if he liked being called by his first name or its contraction. 'No,' he said, 'not by strangers, but I want my friends to call me so: you all and the girls also.' My sister was only thirteen at the time. Incidentally I will add that I never heard his mother call him 'Walt.' To her he was always 'Walter.'" Reprinted in *Walt Whitman in His Own Time: A Biographical Chronicle of His Life, Drawn from Recollections, Memoirs, and Interviews by Friends and Associates,* ed. Joel Myerson (Detroit: Omnigraphics, 1991), pp. 274–82.

15. See, for example, a letter of April 4, 1860, which begins, "Walter it is so strange you have not got my letter I sent one last friday morning and should have written more particularly but Jeff said he would write to you the first of last week but when he was home on sunday he said he had not written. . . . Walt there was A letter come from Boston wanted A Book and I made a mistake and put some other in the letter I sent you, so I will send it in this. . . . Jesse is working he wants to come home I told him I had hired so much of the house out he would have to hire his board write Walt if you got my letter." The original, along with 141 other autograph letters from Louisa to Walt that were written from 1860 to 1873, is in the Trent Collection, William R. Perkins Library, Duke University. See also a letter written on October 26, 1863, which reads in part, "My dear walt i was sorry my being so late last week with my letter caused you any uneaseness if any thing was the matter with me more than common you would be advised of it my dear walter so if any thing occurs that i dont write as usual you must not think any thing unusual is the matter) i got the order walter last saturday and was going down to day to get the money but the wind blew so hard i

was afraid to venture it rained here last night very hard). . . . not one word have i had from Jeff or matt or han or mary you are my whole dependance."

16. After Whitman addressed the Brooklyn Art Union on the evening of March 31, 1851, the *Brooklyn Daily Advertizer* reprinted the speech on April 3 under the title "Art and Artists." According to Emory Holloway, *UPP* 1:241, the subcaption reads, "Remarks of Walt Whitman, before the Brooklyn Art Union, on the evening of March 31, 1851." However, Holloway's reprint turns out to be inaccurate. The *Brooklyn Daily Advertizer* reads "Walter," not "Walt."

See also Whitman's letter to his coworker Andrew Kerr, written on August 25, 1866 in which he satirizes the "original & solemn advice, 'Be *virtuous*—& you will be happy,'" signing himself "from your Christian friend—*Walter*" (*Corr* 1:284).

17. Thomas Jefferson Whitman, as quoted in *Dear Brother Walt: The Letters of Thomas Jefferson Whitman,* ed. Dennis Berthold and Kenneth M. Price (Kent, Ohio: Kent State University Press, 1984), p. 15.

18. "I suppose I shall not be a true Whitman," Jeff wrote to Walt in 1863, "if I dont get dis-heartened." He had been explaining his "'real estate' scheme." See *Dear Brother Walt,* p. 25.

19. For a reading of this passage as a "toast" to the nation's health, see Joan Burbick, "Biodemocracy in *Leaves of Grass,*" in *Healing the Republic: The Language of Health and the Culture of Nationalism in Nineteenth-Century America* (New York: Cambridge University Press, 1994), p. 114. She further suggests that Whitman's "poetic language represents the United States by privileging the human body as the key to democratic meaning. If the body can be expressed in language, the democratic experiment can be known."

20. See, for example, Arthur Golden, "The Ending of the 1855 Version of 'Song of Myself,'" *Walt Whitman Quarterly Review* 3, no. 4 (spring 1986): 27–30. Golden comes down on the side of a chance misprint.

21. For further discussion of the venerable New Orleans romance theory, which Whitman helped to foster, see chapter 5. The myth dies hard. See, for example, Yusef Komunyakaa: "that octoroon in New Orleans / Who showed you how passion / Ignited dogwoods, how it came / From inside the singing sap," in "Kosmos," *Walt Whitman: 19 Poets on His Work & Influence, Massachusetts Review* 33, no. 1 (spring 1992): 87.

22. As David Cavitch explains in *My Soul and I: The Inner Life of Walt Whitman* (Boston: Beacon Press, 1985), in New Orleans Whitman was "farther from the center of his life than he could expect to endure except as an exile":

> Whitman may have been stimulated by the cosmopolitan, Southern culture of New Orleans in the feverish military atmosphere right after the Mexican War, but whatever attractions he found in the city did not reach deep or hold him long. This single venture far away from home ended in an abrupt disappointment that has never been fully explained, though the utter unlikelihood of Whitman thriving in such a remote place may be enough to account for his return to Brooklyn in just three months. He was too uneasy over the distance between himself and his home life. (p. 17)

On Whitman's quarrel with his employers J. E. McClure and A. H. Hayes, publishers of the *New Orleans Crescent,* see, for example, Gay Wilson Allen, *The*

Solitary Singer: A Critical Biography of Walt Whitman (1955; reprint, New York: New York University Press, 1967), pp. 98–99.

23. Whitman was using an 1846 London translation of Bernhard Ingemann's 1828 novel, which he proposed to retitle *The Sleeptalker*. Set in thirteenth century Denmark and chronicling struggles for national unity, *The Childhood of King Erik Menved: An Historical Romance* describes conflicts between personal love and patriotic duty which are, in the end, cheerfully resolved. The defiant trances of one of the leading female characters evidently caught Whitman's attention and may have contributed to the dream-vision frame of "The Sleepers."

24. For an excellent discussion of Whitman's 1856 letter to Emerson, see Kenneth M. Price, "Whitman on Emerson: New Light on the 1856 Letter," *American Literature* 56, no. 1 (March 1984), 83–87. For the larger context of Whitman's relationship to Emerson, see Jerome Loving, *Emerson, Whitman, and the American Muse* (Chapel Hill: University of North Carolina Press, 1982).

25. Among the many passing notices of Whitman's links to the Young America movement, there is a particularly thorough discussion offered by Thomas Bender, in *New York Intellect: A History of Intellectual Life in New York City, from 1750 to the Beginnings of Our Own Time* (New York: Alfred A. Knopf, 1987), pp. 147–55. Bender concludes, "In time, however, Whitman did diverge in an important way from the political and cultural principles of the *Democratic Review*. As we have noted, Young America believed that political reform, especially equal rights, represented the fundamental reform, the one that would bring social improvement and the flowering of a democratic culture. Whitman eventually rejected that vision, believing, increasingly, that cultural reform, not politics, would be the path to a fulfilled American democracy" (p. 155).

26. See *The Letters of Emily Dickinson*, ed. Thomas H. Johnson, 3 vols. (Cambridge: Harvard University Press, 1958), 2:333, 373–74, 391–92. On Dickinson and Susan, see Vivian R. Pollak, *Dickinson: The Anxiety of Gender* (Ithaca: Cornell University Press, 1984); Martha Nell Smith, *Rowing in Eden: Rereading Emily Dickinson* (Austin: University of Texas Press, 1992); *Open Me Carefully: Emily Dickinson's Intimate Letters to Susan Huntington Dickinson,* ed. Ellen Louise Hart and Martha Nell Smith (Ashfield, Mass.: Paris Press, 1998). See also *The Master Letters of Emily Dickinson,* ed. R. W. Franklin (Amherst, Mass.: Amherst College Press, 1986). Franklin changes the order of the sequence established by Johnson, but Johnson's psychology is more believable and I am not persuaded that Franklin's textual evidence in this instance is compelling.

27. Whitman is referring to the poet's younger brother *Samuel* Longfellow, pastor of the Second Unitarian Church in Brooklyn, whom he met during the summer of 1855 after *Leaves of Grass* was published. Samuel Longfellow was acquainted with Emerson, Alcott, and Thoreau, among others; in late December 1856, Alcott's *Journal* describes meeting Whitman there. Henry Kirke Brown (1814–1886) is perhaps best known for his equestrian statue of George Washington at Union Square in New York. According to the *Dictionary of American Biography,* "He was the first of our sculptors to make any serious attempt to shake off the 'real chains' of the contemporary Italianate pseudo-

classicism, but he came too early to profit by the vigorous new naturalism taught in the French schools" (p. 124). See also the excellent discussion in Kirk Savage, *Standing Soldiers, Kneeling Slaves: Race, War, and Monument in Nineteenth-Century America* (Princeton: Princeton University Press, 1997), chapter 2 and passim. Brown, an abolitionist, is credited with extraordinary attempts to represent slavery in public places during the antebellum era.

28. Ward was Brown's favorite pupil. See Savage, *Race, War, and Monument,* chapter 3. On Ward and Symonds, see *WWWC* 2:277–78. Traubel reprints Symonds's letter of 1871, beginning, "When a man has ventured to dedicate his work to another without authority or permission, I think he is bound to make confession of the liberty he has taken. This must be my excuse for sending you the crude poem in which you may perchance detect some echo, faint and feeble, of your Calamus." After linking Symonds, Ward, and his own army experience, Whitman moved on to Oscar Wilde. Wilde, he explained, "has extraordinary brilliancy of genius with perhaps rather too little root in eternal soils. Wilde gives up too much to the extrinsic decorative values in art" (*WWWC* 2:279).

29. In an 1858 article entitled "The Moral Effect of the [Atlantic] Cable," reprinted in *I Sit and Look Out: Editorials from the Brooklyn Daily Times by Walt Whitman,* ed. Emory Holloway and Vernolian Schwarz (New York: Columbia University Press, 1932), pp. 159–61, Whitman explained,

> When Beranger, the French Poet of Freedom, wrote the great lyric of his ["La Sainte Alliance des Peuples"], calling upon the nations to "join hands" in amity and with prophetic vision told them of the day when international quarrels should cease and the lion should lie down with the lamb, he must have had some dim foresight, which for ought we know, is vouchsafed to the bards sublime, of the great triumph of man's ingenuity and skill which has just set our people wild with joy and excitement.

Pierre-Jean de Béranger (1780–1857) was more than a passing enthusiasm. During the post–Civil War period, Whitman clipped four magazine articles on the French poet. See *Notes and Fragments,* ed. Richard Maurice Bucke (London, Ontario, Canada: 1899), p. 81. For further discussion of Whitman and Béranger, see Betsy Erkkila, *Walt Whitman Among the French: Poet and Myth* (Princeton: Princeton University Press, 1980), pp. 32–34. She plausibly suggests that Whitman's use of the word "song" in his titles may have been influenced by Béranger, and describes Whitman's early response to Béranger as "a prelude to his later and much more interesting relationship to Victor Hugo."

30. See Edward Carpenter, *Days with Walt Whitman: With Some Notes on His Life and Work* (London: G. Allen, 1906; reprint, New York: AMS Press, 1983), p. 47.

31. There now exists a considerable literature on Whitman and painters, sculptors, architects, and photographers. See, for example, the various essays in *Walt Whitman and the Visual Arts,* ed. Geoffrey M. Sill and Roberta K. Tarbell (New Brunswick, N.J.: Rutgers University Press, 1992), with a foreword by David S. Reynolds. Of special interest for my purposes is the essay by Ruth L. Bohan, "'The Gathering of the Forces': Walt Whitman and the Visual Arts in Brooklyn in the 1850s," pp. 1–27. The volume includes a useful bibliography ranging from an 1896 essay by Edward Carpenter on "Wagner, Millet and Whitman: In Relation to Art and Democracy" through F. O. Matthiessen's *American Renais-*

sance (1941) and on to such classics of contemporary art criticism as Elizabeth Johns, *Thomas Eakins: The Heroism of Modern Life* (Princeton: Princeton University Press, 1983). Whitman was nominated for president of the Brooklyn Art Union shortly before it was forced to go out of business early in 1852. The Union, like the American Art Union in New York that was its model, depended on prize-giving to stimulate membership. Admission was free, and when the state banned these art lotteries as a form of gambling, both the New York and the Brooklyn Unions folded.

32. Edwin H. Miller suggests that "this is too disingenuous, even for Whitman." But Whitman's focus here seems to be on the institutionalization of homosexuality in classical Greece rather than on passions as such. Miller speculates that the notebook manuscript dates from the 1860s. See *Walt Whitman's Poetry: A Psychological Journey* (Boston: Houghton Mifflin, 1968), p. 146. On Greek sexual customs, see, among other sources, David M. Halperin, *One Hundred Years of Homosexuality: And Other Essays on Greek Love* (New York: Routledge, 1990). On the way Greek studies operated as a "homosexual code" in England, see Linda Dowling, *Hellenism and Homosexuality in Victorian Oxford* (Ithaca: Cornell University Press, 1994). I know of no comparable study for the nineteenth-century United States, but the British context may be relevant for someone as widely read in British literature as Whitman. On subsequent developments in New York City, see George Chauncey, *Gay New York: Gender, Urban Culture, and the Making of the Gay Male World, 1890–1940* (New York: Basic Books, 1994). I find this study invaluable for its descriptions of the public places that in effect authorized sexual contact between men.

33. See Robert K. Martin, *The Homosexual Tradition in American Poetry* (Austin: University of Texas Press, 1979). Martin begins with Whitman and includes such poets as Hart Crane, Fitz-Greene Halleck, Bayard Taylor, George Santayana, Allen Ginsberg, Robert Duncan, Thom Gunn, Edward Field, Richard Howard, James Merrill, and Alfred Corn. For Whitman's influence in England, see Eve Kosofsky Sedgwick's "Coda" in *Between Men: English Literature and Male Homosocial Desire* (New York: Columbia University Press, 1985). More generally, Whitman's influence on continental homosexual literature and consciousness has been the subject of a number of specialized studies, some of them appearing in the *Walt Whitman Quarterly Review*. See, for example, Robert K. Martin, "Walt Whitman and Thomas Mann," *Walt Whitman Quarterly Review* 4, no. 1 (summer 1986): 1–6. See also Walter Grünzweig, *Constructing the German Walt Whitman* (Iowa City: University of Iowa Press, 1995), chapter 19 and passim.

34. For a thorough discussion of "Pictures" as part of Whitman's dialogue with British romanticism, see Kenneth M. Price, *Whitman and Tradition: The Poet in His Century* (New Haven: Yale University Press, 1990), pp. 28–34. Price effectively critiques Grier's dating of the notebook, and I agree with his conclusion.

35. As quoted in Allen, *Solitary Singer,* pp. 151–52. Allen examined a transcript of the missing original, which was made by Clifton J. Furness. Its present location is unknown. The transcript further stated that a Baptist minister presided, which is surprising given Walter Whitman Senior's freethinking religious

views during the 1820s and 1830s. But perhaps he had become more conservative in his old age, or perhaps the minister was known to someone in the family and available on short notice.

A very different funeral is described in Whitman's 1855 poem, "To Think of Time." The burial of a forty-one-year-old stage driver who "grew lowspirited toward the last . . sickened . . [and] was helped by a contribution" is noticeably lacking in clerical presence. The driver is surrounded by friends, not family, for whom he was unambiguously "ready with life or death." All this under "A gray discouraged sky overhead. . . . the short last daylight of December" (*LG* 1855, p. 100).

36. For a discussion of these receipts, see Justin Kaplan, *Walt Whitman: A Life* (New York: Simon and Schuster, 1980), pp. 160–61.

37. Kaplan, *Walt Whitman,* p. 184.

38. As quoted in Ellen M. [O'Connor] Calder, "Personal Recollections of Walt Whitman," *Atlantic Monthly* 99, June 1907, 832.

39. Walt Whitman, in *Notes and Fragments,* p. 116.

40. Allen, *Solitary Singer,* p. 120.

41. Whitman, however, continued to associate "brutality of utterance" with strong creators, with "the initiators and inspirers." See his comment to Traubel about Symonds, whom he considered "always gentle" and "dangerously near the superfine in his weaker moments" (*WWWC* 2:276–77).

CHAPTER FOUR

1. Whitman used this very public document to conclude the 1856 *Leaves of Grass.* He also used the famous sentence from Emerson's 1855 letter on the book's spine ("I greet you at the beginning of a great career, which yet must have had a long foreground somewhere, for such a start"), but without Emerson's permission. Neither Emerson nor his friends were pleased by this appropriation.

2. On Whitman as lecturer, see C. Carroll Hollis, *Language and Style in "Leaves of Grass"* (Baton Rouge: Louisiana State University Press, 1983). And on the importance of Whitman's "presence," which Hollis also stresses, see Tenney Nathanson, *Whitman's Presence: Body, Voice, and Writing in "Leaves of Grass"* (New York: New York University Press, 1992). Nathanson suggests, and I concur, that "at its best [Whitman's] work does bear on us with an immediacy not ordinarily associated with poetry: the figure who is said to rise up and appear to us in the poet's direct addresses to his audience seems to overflow the boundaries of the very work that conveys him to us, to shuck off his status as a fictive character existing in a literary representation and impinge on us personally and directly" (p. 2).

3. Timothy Morris also suggests that Whitman's poetry has succeeded in part because the poet-hero can seem so fully present in his work. See *Becoming Canonical in American Poetry* (Urbana: University of Illinois Press, 1995), in which he suggests that "the belief that a work of art conveys the living presence of the artist, and the implied value that a work is better as the artist is more present in it" (p. xi), emerged as one of the central tenets of the American Renaissance. Morris analyzes the critical mandates for an authentically American

literature that preceded the 1855 *Leaves of Grass,* as well as the canon-making metanarratives that determined the course of American Studies in the twentieth century. He finds that "the poetics of presence, by valuing those texts that most directly and immediately present the writer as a living voice, came to be a guarantee of the nationalism of canonical texts: an American writer sufficiently present in a work would automatically deliver the greatest amount of Americanism in that work" (p. xi). Writing against the canon, Morris suggests that Americanism was associated with the privilege of the white, Anglo-Saxon, heterosexual male voice, and with (now incredible) principles of originality (p. 9).

4. Benedict Anderson, *Imagined Communities: Reflections on the Origin and Spread of Nationalism* (London: Verso, 1991), pp. 202–3.

5. See David S. Reynolds, *Beneath the American Renaissance: The Subversive Imagination in the Age of Emerson and Melville* (New York: Alfred A. Knopf, 1988). See also his *Walt Whitman's America: A Cultural Biography* (New York: Alfred A. Knopf, 1995), chapters 4, 6, and passim.

6. There are many discussions of childhood that have been helpful to me in thinking about Whitman and his family. Especially useful were the following. John Bowlby, *Attachment and Loss. Volume 2: Separation, Anxiety, and Anger* (New York: Basic Books, 1973), p. 235, quoted in Cindy Hazan and Phillip R. Shaver, "Romantic Love Conceptualized as an Attachment Process," *Journal of Psychology and Social Personality* 52, no. 3 (March 1987): 512. Hazan and Shaver provide a succinct overview of attachment theory, as well as an empirical study supporting some of their claims about the continuity of an individual's attachment patterns over the life cycle. See also Bowlby, *A Secure Base: Parent-Child Attachment and Healthy Human Development* (New York: Basic Books, 1988), for a fuller working out of the conceptual framework of attachment theory, which is based on three personality types: secure, anxious-ambivalent, and avoidant. Whitman exhibits characteristics of all three of them.

7. On the newly emerging languages of the Jacksonian era, see Marvin Meyers, *The Jacksonian Persuasion: Politics and Belief* (Stanford: Stanford University Press, 1960).

8. Anderson, *Imagined Communities,* p. 203.

9. For a stimulating and different reading of this dynamic among men, see Donald E. Pease, "Walt Whitman and the Vox Populi of the American Masses," in *Visionary Compacts: American Renaissance Writings in Cultural Context* (Madison: University of Wisconsin Press, 1987), pp. 155–56. Pease suggests that "the power in this scenario derives from the unusual work to which Whitman puts this young woman's loneliness and longing. For she does not indulge in regret for what she cannot have. Her longing does not, as it would in Hawthorne or Poe, intensify our sense of her separateness. Instead the intensity of her longing fills in the distance between these young men. She fills the spaces separating the men with the fullness of her longing for all of them equally. As her eyes touch and caress the men, her vision claims an intimacy with the bathers greater than the intimacy with each other disclosed by their nakedness." Pease concludes that "'unseen' relations, the intimate compact the men did not know they shared, becomes visible only through her sight."

10. Michel Foucault, *The History of Sexuality. Volume 1: An Introduction*

(New York: Random House, 1978), pp. 4–5. For an interesting analysis of common misreadings of Foucault's repressive hypothesis, in which *The History of Sexuality* is understood as "the charter for so much current writing about homosexuality," see Linda Dowling, *Hellenism and Homosexuality in Victorian England* (Ithaca: Cornell University Press, 1994), pp. xi–xiii.

11. Louise Pound, "Whitman and the French Language," *American Speech* 1 (May 1926): 421–30; F. O. Matthiessen, *American Renaissance: Art and Expression in the Age of Emerson and Whitman* (New York: Oxford University Press, 1941), pp. 528–31; Roger Asselineau, *The Evolution of Walt Whitman: The Creation of a Book* (Cambridge: Harvard University Press, 1962), pp. 225–38; Betsy Erkkila, *Walt Whitman Among the French: Poet and Myth* (Princeton: Princeton University Press, 1980), pp. 10–11, 105, 231. See also Erkkila, "Walt Whitman: The Politics of Language," *American Studies* 29 (spring 1984): 21–34.

12. In *Majestic Indolence: English Romantic Poetry and the Work of Art* (New York: Oxford University Press, 1995), Willard Spiegelman offers a brilliant, extended reading of this passage, in which he points out that "watching and wondering at it" is not an exact parallel for "Both in and out of the game." Participant and spectator, the speaker participates most continuously by watching. Spiegelman rewrites the passage to read, "'Although I play the game by coming into and going out of it alternately, I *also* simply stand in the audience as a perpetual spectator.'" He concludes that "from such passages we may hope for a final balance, but they disorient us, never permitting us certain knowledge of where or when Whitman may reenter the lists from the sidelines" (pp. 147–48).

13. For Crane's quotation of "Passage to India," see the "Cape Hatteras" section of *The Bridge*, in *The Poems of Hart Crane*, ed. Marc Simon (New York: Liveright, 1986), pp. 75–84.

14. For "Home Burial," see *The Poetry of Robert Frost: The Collected Poems, Complete and Unabridged*, ed. Edwin Connery Lathem (New York: Holt, Rinehart and Winston, 1975), pp. 51–55. On Frost as the inheritor of Whitman's need for loafing, see Spiegelman, "Our American Cousins," in *Majestic Indolence*, p. 150.

15. For other uses of these words, see Harold Edwin Eby, *A Concordance of Walt Whitman's "Leaves of Grass" and Selected Prose Writings* (Seattle: University of Washington Press, 1949). The word "mullen," whose spelling Whitman changed after 1871, appears only one other time, in the posthumously published poem "Supplement Hours" (1897). "Sullen," on the other hand, appears with comparative frequency, as in the *Calamus* line "Sullen and suffering hours! (I am ashamed—but it is useless—I am what I am)" (*LG* 1860, p. 355). Whitman subsequently deleted the entire poem. Contrary to what we might expect, however, the incidence of words used only once in Whitman's poetry is high. See Asselineau, *Evolution of Walt Whitman*, p. 231.

Eby's pre-computer concordance does not attempt to index *Specimen Days*, and so misses Whitman's charming vignette on "Mulleins and Mulleins" (*SD* 805). Here the much maligned mullein figures as an emblem of peace. "Every object has its lesson," the poet writes, "enclosing the suggestion of everything else—and lately I sometimes think all is concentrated for me in these hardy, yellow-flower'd weeds."

16. *Webster's New International Dictionary*, 3d ed., s.v. "worm fence."

17. See Paul Zweig, *Walt Whitman: The Making of the Poet* (New York: Basic Books, 1984), especially chapter 1, in which he describes Walter Whitman Senior as the muse of the new language of *Leaves of Grass* (p. 39).

18. On the tragic element in Whitman's erotic nature, see Edward Carpenter, *Days with Walt Whitman: With Some Notes on his Life and Work* (London: G. Allen, 1906), p. 47. He describes the poet as self-confident and outgoing, but also as moody, fixed, silent, unquestionable.

19. Christopher Bollas, *The Shadow of the Object: Psychoanalysis of the Unthought Known* (New York: Columbia University Press, 1987), p. 4. See also chapter 5, "The Trisexual," pp. 82–96, in which Bollas moves beyond Freud's account of "an innate bisexual disposition in man" to posit a third position, occupied by "a person who 'seduces' members of each sex in order to gain the other's desire of his self. The object of desire is the person's own self, but a self hypercathected as part of an erotic family triangle" (82). As a narcissist, Whitman has something in common with this figure, who gratifies others without being able to gratify himself.

20. Jorie Graham, "The Geese," in *The Dream of the Unified Field: Selected Poems 1974–1994* (Hopewell, N.J.: Ecco Press, 1995), p. 12.

21. For Dickinson's correspondence with Susan Gilbert Dickinson, see *The Poems of Emily Dickinson*, ed. Thomas H. Johnson, 3 vols. (Cambridge: Harvard University Press, 1955), 1: 151–55. The poem in question was "Safe in their Alabaster Chambers."

22. Helen Price recalled that Whitman read the manuscript aloud in "1858, I think." See her account in Richard Maurice Bucke, *Walt Whitman* (Philadelphia: David McKay, 1883), p. 29. She stresses his diffidence. On Abby Price and her circle, see Sherry Ceniza, "Abby Hills Price," in *Walt Whitman and 19th-Century Women Reformers* (Tuscaloosa: University of Alabama Press, 1998), pp. 45–95. George B. Arnold was the father of the "Bohemian" poet George Arnold and a former president of the Raritan Bay Union (1853–56), a reform community with which the Prices were also associated.

23. Helen E. Price, "Reminiscences of Walt Whitman," *New York Evening Post,* May 31, 1919, p. 2.

24. Whitman, quoted by Helen Price in Bucke, *Walt Whitman,* p. 29.

25. Emerson lectured on "Manners" at the New York Christian Union on Friday, March 23, 1860, and this is presumably the place Vaughan refers to as "Fr. Chapins church." For Vaughan's letters to Whitman, see *Calamus Lovers: Walt Whitman's Working Class Camerados,* ed. Charley Shively (San Francisco: Gay Sunshine, 1987), pp. 41–50. The passages I quote are on p. 43. During the two months that Whitman was in Boston in 1860, Vaughan wrote seven extant letters to him, but Whitman's letters from what Vaughan calls "the *City of Notions*" have not been found.

26. Father Chapin is the Universalist minister Edwin Hubbell Chapin (1814–80), who spoke at a Crystal Palace dinner organized by the New York Publishers' Association in September 1855. He was the author of popular advice books such as *True Manliness* (1854) and, according to Ezra Greenspan, his speech praised the power of the printing press in an age of "steam and electric-

ity." See *Walt Whitman and the American Reader* (New York: Cambridge University Press, 1990), p. 6. See also *UPP* 1:252.

27. Vaughan, letter of November 16, 1874, quoted in *Calamus Lovers,* pp. 49–50.

28. See Vaughan's references to "the Press" and to the "Brooklyn Daily Times" in his letter of November 16, 1874. The context suggests that "the Press" was one of his jobs.

29. The "now praying now cursing" quote is from Vaughan's letter of November 16, 1874, in *Calamus Lovers,* p. 50. His career was unsuccessful, his marriage unhappy, his alcoholism difficult to control. Fred felt that he was untrue to his wife and children, apparently because of his desire for other men, and that his intimate relationship with Walt, however it ended, was the one great success of his life.

30. Emily Dickinson, *Poems,* 1: 199–200.

31. D. H. Lawrence has perhaps written most memorably on the death cult in Whitman. See *Studies in Classic American Literature* (1923; reprint, New York: Viking, 1964), pp. 163–77. For a provocative contemporary reading, see David Lawrence Karp, "Death at the Birth of 'Leaves of Grass': Domestic and Morbid Imaginings in Walt Whitman's Writings, 1839–1856" (Ph.D. diss., University of Washington, 1991). Karp describes the sentimental tradition of comparative bodiliness from which, he argues, Whitman could not wholly escape.

32. In this much revised poem, which also concludes all future editions, the persona departs "as one disembodied, triumphant, dead." The neologism "Camerado" was not introduced until 1867.

33. Greenspan, *Whitman and the American Reader,* pp. 109–10. He further notes that "Whitman's need for 'contact' with his readers . . . was an obsession" and that "at times, in fact, the early poems seem addressed less to impersonal readers outside the reaches of the poem than to unidentified friends and lovers located within the imaginary plane of the poem."

34. For a discussion of homophobia and phobias about equality in Whitman's time, see Christopher Newfield, "Democracy and Male Homoeroticism," *Yale Journal of Criticism* 6, no. 2 (fall 1993): 29–62.

35. Here I borrow from Alicia Ostriker, "Desire Gratified and Ungratified: William Blake and Sexuality," in *Critical Essays on William Blake,* ed. Hazard Adams (Boston: G. K. Hall, 1991), p. 107. She writes that "if 'Unity is the cloke of Folly' in a work of art, we might make it our business as critics not only to discover, but also to admire, a large poet's large inconsistencies—particularly in an area like the meaning of sex, where the entire culture, and probably each of us, in the shadows of our chambers, feels profound ambivalence."

36. See M. Wynn Thomas, *The Lunar Light of Whitman's Poetry* (Cambridge: Harvard University Press, 1987), pp. 13, 14. Thomas's extended reading of this poem is one of the finest I have encountered, though he presents Whitman as a more psychologically transcendent figure than I do. He argues that if the effect of Whitman's language is to violate the reader's privacy, this effect is perhaps intentional, "since in such privacy Whitman finds evidence of the disengagement of vital emotions from the activities of a public life that must therefore become increasingly bankrupt of serious human content" (pp. 14–15).

Here Thomas intends to have it both ways. The poem appeals to the authenticity of private life and seeks to abolish such life. His passionate and witty commentary is premised on the observation that "there is, on the face of it, something faintly ludicrous and even offensive about the way Whitman thrusts his unwanted attention upon these intimate situations. Two's company, three's a crowd, and he seems always to be insisting on being just that one person too many, whose presence is bound to alter the color and tone of the occasion" (p. 14).

For an analysis of the poem as "kinky," an example of "cultivated perversity" in making sex public—"pubic hairs on the ink rollers and so on"—see Michael Warner, "Whitman Drunk," in *Breaking Bounds: Whitman and American Cultural Studies,* ed. Betsy Erkkila and Jay Grossman (New York: Oxford University Press, 1996), p. 42.

37. For a further discussion of interdependent public and private languages of love in *Leaves of Grass,* see Betsy Erkkila, "Whitman and the Homosexual Republic," in *Walt Whitman: The Centennial Essays,* ed. Ed Folsom (Iowa City: University of Iowa Press, 1994), pp. 153–71. She argues that "the languages of sexuality and spirituality, same-sex love and love between men and women, private and public, intersect and flow into each other in Whitman's work" (p. 158). And for an insightful discussion of "The Politics of Labor and the Poet's Work: A Reading of 'A Song for Occupations,'" see Alan Trachtenberg, in *Walt Whitman: The Centennial Essays,* pp. 120–52. Trachtenberg sees "a vicious circularity" at work in the poem, since for Whitman "politics itself often seems a literary rather than a political activity" (p. 123). Although Trachtenberg's terms and mine are far from identical, we share some of the same concerns about Whitman and "closeness" and "the necessity of artifice for the sake of the common life" (p. 127).

38. Nathanson adds, "It is particularly useful to do so in a critical climate inclined to privilege the sort of public concerns that can be adduced in support of the claim that the poet's body figures the body politic. That body also staves off fears and satisfies desires of a more intimate order." See *Whitman's Presence,* p. 494.

39. *An American Primer by Walt Whitman: With Facsimiles of the Original Manuscripts,* ed. Horace L. Traubel (1904; reprint, with an afterword by Gay Wilson Allen, Stevens Point, Wisc.: Holy Cow! Press, 1987), p. 15. Subsequent quotations are included in parentheses in the text. The *Primer* is a collection of notes that remained unpublished in Whitman's lifetime. His original title was "The Primer of Words," and he told Traubel that these one hundred and ten separate notes were first intended for a lecture he was planning to deliver in the mid-1850s. The excerpted quote was probably written in 1856 or later. For another presentation of the text, see *DBN* 3:728–54. On the *Primer* as a program for expanding the lexicon, see Ed Folsom, *Walt Whitman's Native Representations* (New York: Cambridge University Press, 1994), pp. 20–21.

40. Justin Kaplan describes Jeff as "for years the chief support of [Whitman's] homoerotic fantasy of 'two boys together clinging.'" See *Walt Whitman: A Life* (New York: Simon and Schuster, 1980), p. 236.

41. In one of his notebooks, the poet suggested that masturbation and inor-

dinate "going with women" rot the voice, but that "no man can have a great vocalism . . . who has no experience of love." He then crossed out the word "love"
and wrote "woman" (*DBN* 3:737). The next entry associates the great Italian
singers with "Mannahatta young men, especially the drivers of horses, and all
whose work leads to free loud calling and commanding." Fred Vaughan was
such a driver and it seems likely that Whitman had more emotional space in his
life because Jeff Whitman was less available as an "ardent" and approving companion. Jeff played the guitar and sang pleasantly, and Walt bought him a piano
in 1852. See the male-homoerotic reverie in *DBN* 3:765, composed while Jeff
was playing the piano.

42. Mattie turned twenty-one in September 1857 and was engaged to Jeff before then. See the account of her lost inheritance in *Dear Brother Walt: The Letters of Thomas Jefferson Whitman,* ed. Dennis Berthold and Kenneth Price (Kent,
Ohio: Kent State University Press, 1984), pp. xviii–xix n. 14. Her father was
dead and her stepmother, who was her guardian, absconded with the funds after Mattie announced that she planned to marry Jeff when she came of age.

43. Justin Kaplan suggests that "Walt loved Mattie as if she were a sister—
she and Louisa Whitman were 'the two best and sweetest women I have ever
seen or known or ever expect to see.' Still, his cherished and exclusive relationship with Jeff had been fractured along with his understanding of 'adhesiveness,'
now divested of its sanctions in brotherly love." See *Walt Whitman,* p. 236.

44. Trachtenberg notes in "The Politics of Labor," p. 128, that this line
echoes Emerson's "wise man in 'Politics,' who needs 'no money, for he is value.'"

45. *The Eighteenth Presidency!* in *Walt Whitman: Complete Poetry and Collected Prose,* ed. Justin Kaplan (New York: Literary Classics of the United States,
1982), pp. 1323–24. In *Whitman the Political Poet,* Erkkila notes that "although Whitman was closest in his views to Fremont's Free-Soil platform, in *The
Eighteenth Presidency!* he refuses to identify with any particular political party"
(p. 130). For further discussion of Whitman's contradictory attitudes toward
slavery in *The Eighteenth Presidency!* see my chapter 7.

46. Mark Maslan has directed our attention to analogies between Whitman's hand and his handwriting. See "Whitman's 'Strange Hand': Body as Text
in *Drum-Taps,*" *ELH* 58, no. 4 (winter 1991): 935–55.

47. The reviewer was objecting to the "female form" passage in "I Sing the
Body Electric," which includes the description of orgasm as "Limitless limpid
jets of love hot and enormous. . . . quivering jelly of love. . . . white-blow and
delirious juice" (*LG* 1855, p. 119).

48. Evidently Whitman is also suggesting that, with his rude American
tongue, he deliberately ignores the models of the past. On nation-building as dependent on such fierce forgettings, see Benedict Anderson, *Imagined Communities,* passim. Anderson's phrase "the amnesias of nationalism" (p. xv) is especially felicitous.

49. Letter of September 11, 1865. Except as otherwise indicated, Louisa Van
Velsor Whitman's unpublished letters are paraphrased or quoted from the Trent
Collection, William R. Perkins Library, Duke University.

50. The editorial is dated June 22, 1859, and is reprinted in *I Sit and Look
Out: Editorials from the Brooklyn Daily Times by Walt Whitman,* ed. Emory

Holloway and Vernolian Schwarz (New York: Columbia University Press, 1932), 120–22. On the chronology of *Calamus,* see the next chapter. Evidently the answer to the question "Can All Marry?" is an emphatic no, though the reasons Whitman advances are not appealing. He contends that some women are too ugly to marry, while granting that plenty of "hard-featured visages lighted up by no redeeming ray of intellect . . . preside at 'good men's feasts.'"

51. Hannah's obituary is included in Katherine Molinoff, *Some Notes on Whitman's Family: Mary Elizabeth Whitman, Edward Whitman, Andrew and Jesse Whitman, Hannah Louisa Whitman* (New York: Comet Press, 1941), pp. 41–43. This work contains other useful information on Hannah, especially pp. 24–43. Molinoff presents the boarding school story uncritically, but see below for my discussion of Hannah's feelings of inferiority because of her lack of education.

52. Molinoff, *Notes,* p. 39.

53. The quotation from Hannah's obituary in the *Burlington Free Press and Times* is from Molinoff, *Notes,* p. 42. The writer was Hannah's friend William Hassett, who later served on Franklin D. Roosevelt's White House staff. "In her earlier years she enjoyed a wide acquaintance with contemporary artists and literary people," Hassett explained in a letter to Molinoff, "and knew intimately many of the celebrities of a generation ago" (Molinoff, *Notes,* p. 25). Though in chronic ill health, Hannah, the last surviving member of Whitman's immediate family, was eighty-five when she died in 1908.

54. George Whitman, quoted in "Notes from Conversations with George W. Whitman, 1893," in *In Re Walt Whitman,* ed. Horace L. Traubel, Richard Maurice Bucke, and Thomas B. Harned (Philadelphia: David McKay, 1893), p. 37.

55. *Faint Clews & Indirections: Manuscripts of Walt Whitman and His Family,* ed. Clarence Gohdes and Rollo G. Silver (Durham, N.C.: Duke University Press, 1949), p. 209. Subsequent citations to this collection of source material will be cited parenthetically in the text.

56. Jerome M. Loving, ed., *Civil War Letters of George Washington Whitman* (Durham, N.C.: Duke University Press, 1975), p. 11.

57. Molinoff, *Notes,* p. 25. For more on Heyde's poetry, see Jerome Loving, *Walt Whitman: The Song of Himself* (Berkeley: University of California Press, 1998), pp. 344–45. And for more on Heyde's career as an artist, see pp. 170, 385, 506 nn. 76, 77.

58. For the "sexual" quote, see *Dear Brother Walt,* p. 114 n. 8. For the "she devil" quote, see *Dear Brother Walt,* p. 114 n. 9. For the "pleasure" quote, see Louisa's letter of June 7, 1866, Trent Collection. For speculation that Louisa relished Heyde's aggressive language, see Eve Kosofsky Sedgwick, "Confusion of Tongues," in Erkkila and Grossman, *Breaking Bounds,* p. 28. Sedgwick further suggests that Louisa was insulting Walt by transmitting Heyde's trenchant abuse of him. My sense of Louisa is that she was genuinely distressed and had no intention of insulting Walt.

59. The "no talents" quote is from an unpublished letter in the Hannah Whitman Heyde Collection, Library of Congress. Pathetically, Hannah adds, "I often wish I was more like him," that is, more like her husband.

60. Hannah extended many invitations that were not accepted, but Heyde,

who censored her letters, was threatened by the prospect of family visits. From Boston in 1860, Walt wrote to Jeff, "Oh how much I would like to see her once more—and I *must,* this summer—After I recruit a while home, I shall very likely take a tour, partly business and partly for edification, through all the N[ew] E[ngland] states—then I shall see Han" (*Corr* 1:54). The 1860 tour never happened and it was not until June 1872, when he was reading at Dartmouth College, that Walt visited Burlington, never seeing his sister again. He continued to send books and money when he could, and his last letter was to her. See *Corr* 5:277.

61. For Louisa Whitman, the issue was not one of theory but of practice. See the 1869 letter in which she compares Hannah unfavorably to a neighbor who dealt with her abusive husband more successfully. After a terrible fight, "young Chapells wife up stairs here . . . was singing and lively as usual she says he has an awful temper but it goes in one ear and out the other." Quoted in Ceniza, *Whitman and 19th-Century Women Reformers,* p. 20. Ceniza makes the point that Louisa admired women who resisted domination.

62. See her letter of July 21, 1861, Hannah Whitman Heyde Collection. Hannah was often frustrated by the fact that Heyde could be so amiable with others and hateful to her. As she explains it, he had been laughing outside her windows with a man who was a fellow boarder in the hotel where they were staying. "I said cheerfully how much I would like it if he could be pleasant so with me. He said he and that young man were of an equality. I laughed and said well is not a husband and wife one as good as another. He as usual got angry[,] said we were not." And then he tried to choke her.

63. On the "uppertendom," see Hannah's unpublished letter dated Monday Morning, Burlington, Oct., beginning "My dear Mother, I have not written in so long because Charlie is most of the time so terrible cross." She repeatedly describes feelings of inferiority when comparing herself to other women. By 1881, however, she was attracting attention as "Walt Whitman's sister" and the "uppertendom" was seeking her out. Her November 1881 letter to Walt is heartening and is written from a better place. Hannah Whitman Heyde Collection, Library of Congress.

64. The quotations are from the letter in the Hannah Whitman Heyde Collection, beginning "My dear Mother," cited above.

CHAPTER FIVE

1. "All About a Mocking-Bird" appeared in the New York *Saturday Press* on January 7, 1860. See *Walt Whitman: The Contemporary Reviews,* ed. Kenneth M. Price (New York: Cambridge University Press, 1996), pp. 74–76. The *Saturday Press* was edited by Whitman's friend Henry Clapp.

2. As early as December 28, 1859, the *Cincinnati Daily Commercial* had lambasted "A Child's Reminiscence" in a sneering review beginning, "The author of *Leaves of Grass* has perpetrated another 'poem.'" See *Contemporary Reviews,* pp. 71–73.

3. Before Thayer and Eldridge went bankrupt during the winter of 1860–61, they printed an edition of about a thousand copies. Whitman's book enjoyed a steady but modest sale, though not of course "going off in a rocket way, (like

'Uncle Tom's Cabin')" (*Corr* 1:52). Subsequently, Charles Eldridge continued to interest himself in Whitman as poet and person, helping him get to Fredericksburg, Virginia, to see his wounded brother George in December 1862, and then to find work as a copyist in the Army Paymaster's Office, where Eldridge was also employed. Eldridge formed part of the social and intellectual Washington circle loosely organized by William Douglas O'Connor and his wife Nellie, which supported Whitman emotionally and in certain respects materially in 1863, easing his transition out of Brooklyn and making it possible for Whitman to pursue his career as a freelance journalist, poet, and minor government functionary.

4. See Sigmund Freud, "Family Romances" (1908), *Standard Edition of the Complete Psychological Works of Sigmund Freud,* trans. James Strachey, 24 vols. (London: Hogarth, 1975), 9:235–41. Other usages may be found in "Fliess Paper" (1902), "Three Essays on the Theory of Sexuality" (1905), "A Special Type of Choice of Object Made by Men" (1910), and "Moses and Monotheism" (1937).

5. The poem, after all, was published a mere twenty-two days after the abolitionist martyr John Brown was executed at Charleston, (West) Virginia. On his way to the scaffold, Brown had prophesied that "the crimes of this *guilty, land: will* never be purged *away;* but with Blood." See Stephen B. Oates, *To Purge This Land with Blood: A Biography of John Brown* (New York: Harper & Row, 1970), p. 351. See also Whitman's rendition of this scene in "Year of Meteors" (*LG,* p. 238), in which he describes himself as standing by with clenched teeth. Whitman, as we have seen, was not wholly averse to the use of physical or psychological force. Mainly, however, he sought to "bind in words" (*LG,* p. 238), preferring unities bloodlessly achieved. For all his conflation of language and body, Whitman knew and respected the difference.

6. Whitman drew on the phrenological term "adhesiveness" to amplify the male friendship tradition he inherited from the fathers of the American Revolution. On the derivation and queering of this term, see, for example, Michael Lynch, "'Here Is Adhesiveness': From Friendship to Homosexuality," *Victorian Studies* 29 (autumn 1985): 67–96. See also Eve Kosofsky Sedgwick, "Toward the Twentieth Century: English Readers of Whitman," in *Between Men: English Literature and Male Homosocial Desire* (New York: Columbia University Press, 1985), p. 204 and passim.

7. An exception here was the *New York Times,* which called the *Enfans d'Adam* section "humanitary." See *Contemporary Reviews,* p. 83.

8. Accounting for Whitman's more positive reception in England, Sedgwick speculates that "the sexual-ideological packages sent by the Kosmic American were very different from the ones unpacked" by "cosmopolitan" Englishmen. "The most important differences lay in the assumed class contexts in which the sexual ideology was viewed, and in the standing of women—both of 'femininity' and of actual women—in the two visions. These very differences made for Whitman's adaptability as an English (far more than as an American) prophet of sexual politics for the nineteenth century." Sedgwick further emphasizes Whitman's iconic status as a working-class figure and suggests that he embodied "contradictory and seductive attributes that would not have been combined in an Englishman." See *Between Men,* p. 204.

9. This wonderful language, quoted in *Corr* 1:4, is taken from an 1867 letter Whitman prepared for William Douglas O'Connor to send to William Michael Rossetti, who was preparing judiciously chosen selections of *Leaves of Grass* for the English market. Rossetti was at work on the Introduction and Whitman was prepared to help him out.

10. Hector Tyndale seems to have dropped out of Whitman's immediate sphere of interest by May 1860, when he visited Louisa Whitman and complained that Walt was not answering his letters. During the Washington years, Whitman mentions him as a repeat visitor in 1866 (*Corr* 1:279). Whitman also visited him in Philadelphia in 1876, but was displeased with his tone of "settled morbidity" and "*ennui*" (*Corr* 3:25, 26). Tyndale had been seriously wounded during the war. Sarah Tyndale, Hector's mother, was an abolitionist friend of Abby Price's. She died not long before Hector's visit to Brooklyn in 1860.

11. So far as we can tell, Whitman refused to heed Emerson's advice, which has been variously described. See *Prose Writings of Walt Whitman,* ed. Floyd Stovall (New York: New York University Press, 1964), 1:281–82 and 2:494, and *WWWC* 3:439. Jerome Loving indicates that Emerson wanted Whitman to remove the sequence as a whole, rather than to modify or eliminate selected parts. See Loving, *Emerson, Whitman, and the American Muse* (Chapel Hill: University of North Carolina Press, 1982), pp. 105–108. M. Jimmie Killingsworth notes that since Emerson himself kept no record of the meeting, "we cannot definitely know which poems he suggested Whitman drop" from the 1860 volume. See *Whitman's Poetry of the Body: Sexuality, Politics, and the Text* (Chapel Hill: University of North Carolina Press, 1989), p. 68. Killingsworth suggests that "A Woman Waits for Me" (first published in 1856 as "Poem of Procreation") was viewed by Emerson and his circle as particularly offensive. More generally, the subject of Whitman's revisions as a form of self-censorship in response to actual and anticipated public criticism, both in 1860 and subsequently, needs further work. Jeff Whitman, writing to his brother in 1860, views the actual attacks of the "Yam" writers as an opportunity for family fun, noting, "I dont suppose you will mind it any more than you did in the days of your editorship of the B[rooklyn] Eagle when the Advertiser['s] Lees used to go at you so roughly." I am less sure that Walt shared Jeff's enthusiasm for such "jolly times." See *Dear Brother Walt: The Letters of Thomas Jefferson Whitman,* ed. Dennis Berthold and Kenneth Price (Kent, Ohio: Kent State University Press, 1984), p. 15.

12. There is also a syntactically less obvious reading of these lines in which Whitman is Eve: "Eve following" functions as an appositive and modifies "me," while the phrase "her just the same" emphasizes a common bond, if not a degendering.

13. In 1856, the untitled poem later called "Great Are the Myths" had been revised and given the more modest title "Poem of a Few Greatnesses." It appeared in the 1856 volume immediately before "I Sing the Body Electric," with its uncanny interest in "defil[ing] the dead," and after the new "Broad-Axe Poem," in which the self and its language are figured as weapons. The closural force of allusions to death obviously appealed to Whitman, as did unifying and psychologically evasive allusions to immortality. The 1856 *Leaves of Grass* ends

with a "Burial Poem" that brings together both of these tropes. (The poem had been untitled in 1855 and was later called "To Think of Time.") On the closural force of allusions to death, see Barbara Herrnstein Smith, *Poetic Closure: A Study of How Poems End* (Chicago: University of Chicago Press, 1968).

14. I don't mean to suggest, however, that Whitman is always optimistic about language. In "Burial Poem," for example, "Slow-moving and black lines creep over the whole earth—they never cease—they are the burial lines," and they may be read as the lines of text moving across Whitman's pages (*LG* 1856, p. 334, partially repeated on p. 339). These quotations prefigure the funeral-train scene in "When Lilacs Last in the Dooryard Bloom'd," but even in 1856, Whitman was reminding readers, "He that was President was buried, and he that is now President shall surely be buried."

15. Kerry C. Larson describes "the empowering of a compulsive eros" in *Whitman's Drama of Consensus* (Chicago: University of Chicago Press, 1988), pp. 160, 157, 159.

16. Here I disagree with James E. Miller, Jr., who argued in *A Critical Guide to "Leaves of Grass"* (Chicago: University of Chicago Press, 1957) that "although [Emory] Holloway's discovery [of the original manuscript] may be biographically revealing, the poem has the 'meaning,' surely, of its final version" (p. 50 n).

I have never been able to warm up to "I Sing the Body Electric" (*LG* 1860, pp. 291–302), which in 1860 had not yet acquired its memorable first line. The poem, the longest in the sequence, seems to me ethically admirable in its concern for racial and sexual justice, but also hysterical in its attack on fools who corrupt their own live bodies, pretentious in its feminism, and overall somewhat inert. Predictably, Section 3, a self-contained lyric vignette beginning "I knew a man, a common farmer, the father of five sons" (*LG*, p. 95) appeals to me as the poem's emotional center. Following this personal and intimate scene, with its unmistakable note of (white) male-male longing, Whitman backs away into a sea of generalities, attempting to constitute a new religion of the variegated body as the basis for American democracy. The poem demonstrates the difficulty of doing so, since the exemplary but also indignant speaker, who delights in taking others apart, is out of touch with his own social aggression. I find the suspension of this aggression in Section 3 refreshing, but it is not clear how this nostalgic lyric episode contains or is related to all the rest. Betsy Erkkila, for example, praises the poem as an "ominous political prophecy" without mentioning this scene. See *Whitman the Political Poet* (New York: Oxford University Press, 1989), p. 125.

17. For a facsimile of the heavily revised manuscript, see Fredson Bowers, *Whitman's Manuscripts: "Leaves of Grass" (1860), A Parallel Text* (Chicago: University of Chicago Press, 1955), p. v. For versions of the text that differ slightly in matters of punctuation, see Gay Wilson Allen, *The Solitary Singer: A Critical Biography of Walt Whitman* (1955; reprint, New York: New York University Press, 1967), p. 252; Bowers, p. 64; and Justin Kaplan, *Walt Whitman: A Life* (New York: Simon and Schuster, 1980), p. 142. For a discussion of the politics of Holloway's discovery, see Robert K. Martin, *The Homosexual Tradition in American Poetry* (Austin: University of Texas Press, 1979), p. 4. He notes that though Holloway discovered the manuscript in 1920, by 1926 he was citing "the

revised version to prove Whitman's heterosexuality." I consider both the manuscript and the versions printed by Whitman as part of a single metastory.

18. Emory Holloway, "Walt Whitman's Love Affairs," *The Dial* (November 1920), 473–483. Luce Irigaray celebrates the inherent autoeroticism of woman's sexuality, "two lips which embrace continually," in "This Sex Which Is Not One" ["Ce sexe qui n'en est pas un"], in *New French Feminisms,* ed. Elaine Marks and Isabelle de Courtivron (New York: Schocken Books, 1981), pp. 99–106. According to Irigaray, woman's sexual pleasure disrupts the dominant, single-mindedly instrumental phallic economy. "Thus, for example, woman's autoeroticism is very different from man's. He needs an instrument in order to touch himself: his hand, woman's genitals, language," whereas the biologically gifted woman, who " 'touches herself' " constantly without anyone being able to forbid her to do so" (p. 100), is inherently self-stimulating. Evidently Whitman's woman is constructed as a socially and emotionally dependent figure. For female autoeroticism in Whitman, see "Spontaneous Me," in *Enfans d'Adam, LG* 1860, p. 306.

19. The word "youth" appears in the Bowers facsimile, though it is crossed out, at the point where the language "rude and ignorant" is inserted above the line. On the legend of Whitman's encounter with a New Orleans woman of "higher social rank," see also Henry Bryan Binns, *A Life of Walt Whitman* (New York: E. P. Dutton, 1905), chapter 4, "Romance (1848)," p. 51, as well as "Appendix B," pp. 349–50.

20. Martin, *Homosexual Tradition*, p. 5. He emphasizes the poet's "joy at sexual experiences with other men," whereas I hear a more self-conscious (in the sense of conflicted) voice.

21. We've already seen a live oak with moss in *Calamus* 4, "These I Singing in Spring," in which the speaker takes out of his pocket "some moss which I pulled off a live-oak in Florida, as it hung trailing down" (*LG* 1860, p. 348). This poem first introduces the figure of the calamus root.

22. Whitman was fond of the figure of glistening and used it memorably. In addition to the swimmers in Section 11 of "Song of Myself," their beards glistening with wet, he immortalized the "glistening yellow" that partially lights the bodies of the oscillating sea-gulls in "Crossing Brooklyn Ferry," as well as "the scallop-edged waves in the twilight, the ladled cups, the frolicsome crests and glistening" (*LG* 1860, pp. 381, 382). See also the effective conjunction of glistening waters and rustling leaves in "To a Common Prostitute," *LG* 1860, p. 399.

23. But what are we to think of the Whitman who seemingly genders intelligence in "I Sing the Body Electric"? Although he writes that "The female contains all qualities, and tempers them—she is in her place, and moves with perfect balance," he specifically identifies knowledge with men, knowledge that enables the male with his gender-specific qualifies of "action and power" to bring "everything to the test of himself, / Whatever the survey, whatever the sea and the sail, he strikes soundings at last only here, / Where else does he strike soundings, except here?" (*LG* 1860, pp. 296, 297). I consider Whitman's construction of maternity at length in chapter 7, and in earlier chapters we have noted that Whitman often described his personal mother not only as his father's intellectual equal but as his father's superior.

24. Whitman's poetry rarely ascribes color to eyes. But see the heroic general in *Drum-Taps:* "(Old as he was, his gray eyes yet shone out in battle like stars)" (*LG*, p. 316). For more on eyes in *Calamus,* see below. And see also his description of himself on Broadway in August 1856, in which he features "singular eyes, of a semi-transparent, indistinct light blue." From *New York Dissected: A Sheaf of Recently Discovered Newspaper Articles by the Author of "Leaves of Grass,"* ed. Emory Holloway and Ralph Adimari (New York: Rufus Rockwell Wilson, 1936), p. 130.

25. The genre of the antebellum Northern secession poem was not unique to Whitman. See Dickinson's "I'm ceded—I've stopped being Their's" and "I'm Nobody! Who are you" for interesting analogues, in *The Poems of Emily Dickinson,* ed. Thomas H. Johnson, 3 vols. (Cambridge: Harvard University Press, 1955), 2:389–90, 1:206–7. For fuller publication history and a different textual transcription, see also *The Poems of Emily Dickinson: Variorum Edition,* ed. R. W. Franklin, 3 vols. (Cambridge: Harvard University Press, 1998), 1:279–80, 377–78.

26. According to Phyllis Grosskurth, "Symonds sat transfixed. Here was the voice of his own heart, speaking of things he dared not say aloud. Here was a voice celebrating the beauty of a love which he could not confess." See *The Woeful Victorian: A Biography of John Addington Symonds* (New York: Holt, Rinehart and Winston, 1965), p. 120. Like Symonds, Myers was a poet and at that time a classical lecturer at Trinity College. Yet Symonds and Myers never physically consummated their loving friendship, and according to Grosskurth, Symonds envied Myers's ability to find sexual pleasure with women, while he himself languished in what he described in his *Memoirs* as an emotionally companionate, yet sexually passionless marriage. See Grosskurth, "Introduction," in *The Memoirs of John Addington Symonds* (New York: Random House, 1984), pp. 27–28. Some of Symonds's friends and acquaintances, however, took a dimmer view of his marriage and of Catherine North Symonds in particular. Henry James, for example, used the Symonds marriage as the basis for his unsympathetic characterization of the wife in "The Author of Beltraffio." "Narrow, cold, Calvinistic . . . a rigid moralist," he called her, in the notebook entry which forms the germ of the story (quoted in Grosskurth, *Woeful Victorian,* p. 270).

27. Whitman was nothing if not persistent, however, and in describing plans for his tomb to his friend Richard Maurice Bucke, he explained in May 1891, "I have two deceased children (young man & woman—illegitimate of course) that I much desired to bury here with me—but have ab't abandon'd the plan on acc't of angry litigation & fuss generally & disinterment f'm down south" (*Corr* 5:203).

28. John Addington Symonds, "Democratic Art. With Special Reference to Walt Whitman," in *Essays Speculative and Suggestive,* 3d ed. (London: Smith, Elder, & Co., 1907), p. 242. While quoting extensively and sympathetically from *Democratic Vistas,* Symonds expressed deep reservations about Whitman's "grotesqueness" and "contempt for history." See also Whitman's formal response, "An Old Man's Rejoinder," in *Walt Whitman: Complete Poetry and Collected Prose,* ed. Justin Kaplan (New York: Literary Classics of the United States, 1982), pp. 1249–52, together with Whitman's informal response to Richard

Maurice Bucke, "I guess there is meat in the vols. but I doubt whether he has gripp'd 'democratic art' by the nuts, or L of G. either" (*Corr* 5:63–64).

29. It would be good to know when "Long I Thought" was written. According to Fredson Bowers, it was one of the original cluster of twelve poems called "Live Oak with Moss," which seems to have come together as a grouping by the late spring of 1859, when Whitman quit his position at the *Brooklyn Daily Times*. This sequence consisted of the following, as numbered in the 1860 *Leaves of Grass*: Calamus 14, 20, 11, 23, 8, 32, 10, 9, 34, 43, 36, 42. Bowers suggests that these twelve notebook poems "appear to be highly unified and to make up an artistically complete story of attachment, crisis, and renunciation." He further notes that "the calamus symbol is nowhere mentioned in these poems." See *Whitman's Manuscripts*, pp. lxiv, lxvi, lxvii. There already existed, however, thirteen other poems that became part of the *Calamus* cluster by the time the book was published. Apparently the idea of the groupings came to Whitman late in the process of composition. Because these thirteen appear on pink paper, Bowers has been able to identify them as having been written by June 20, 1857, when Whitman, in a long letter to his Philadelphia supporter Mrs. Sarah Tyndale, discussed bringing out a third edition and noted that "I have now a *hundred* poems ready" (*Corr* 1:44). One of these thirteen early poems ("Calamus taste") does indeed introduce the symbol later adopted for the expanded, revised, and blended sequence. The original thirteen are as follows: 12 ("Are you the new person"); 13 ("Calamus taste"); 15 ("O Drops of me!"); 16 ("Who is now reading this?"); 17 ("Of him I love day and night"); 21 ("Music always round me"); 22 ("Passing stranger!"); 25 ("The prairie-grass dividing"); 26 ("We two boys together clinging"); 30 ("A promise and gift to California"); 31 ("What ship, puzzled at sea"); 41 ("Among the men and women, the multitude"); 45 ("Full of life"). Apparently the homoerotic portions of "Starting from Paumanok," the longest new poem of the 1860 *Leaves,* had also been composed by June 1857.

Whitman had been unemployed during the winter of 1856–57, but financial pressures drove him back to work as editor of the *Brooklyn Daily Times*. (The country was in the throes of a terrible economic recession, and he was forced to borrow money from James Parton at this time.) When he began editing the *Times* in June 1857, the last such post he was ever to hold, he apparently put his poetry aside, returning to it in the spring of 1859, shortly before he resigned or lost his position. And so despite his good intentions, as an employee of the *Times* he was diverted from "*The Great Construction* of the *New Bible* . . . the principal object—the main life work" which in June 1857 he had projected as "Three Hundred & Sixty-five" poems which "ought to be read[y] in 1859.—(June '57)" (*NUPM* 1:353).

30. The role Whitman renounces has been variously understood. Whereas M. Jimmie Killingsworth suggests that Whitman withdraws from "traditional male sexual politics and poetics" rather than from "poetry per se" (*Whitman's Poetry of the Body,* p. 104), Michael Moon suggests that Whitman considers giving up his career elsewhere in the sequence, that writing male-male desire may be "corrosive" as well as "therapeutic," and that there is a "partial denigration of [proscribed] desire" in at least some of these poems, as Whitman seeks

to return intense male-homoerotic desire to what Moon calls "the orbit of the political 'real.'" See Michael Moon, *Disseminating Whitman: Revision and Corporeality in "Leaves of Grass"* (Cambridge: Harvard University Press, 1991), pp. 166, 167. An excellent discussion is also offered by Alan Helms, who concentrates on a pattern of transgression and retreat he sees as basic to the sequence as a whole. Helms further suggests that the "capitol" begins to invade Whitman's bower, while the "'One who loves me' (the ostensible subject of the poem) hardly appears." See "'Live Oak with Moss,'" in *The Continuing Presence of Walt Whitman: The Life After the Life,* ed. Robert K. Martin (Iowa City: University of Iowa Press, 1992), p. 189.

31. Symonds wrote to Whitman about *Calamus* 8 on December 9, 1889, as follows. "When I read your Bible, I miss—and I have missed for many years in new editions—the poem which first thrilled me like a trumpet-call to you. It was called: 'Long I thought that knowledge alone would suffice me.' Why have you so consistently omitted this in the canon of your works?" Whitman never answered his question, though he wrote to Richard Maurice Bucke, "J A Symonds from Switzerland has sent the warmest & (I think sh'd be call'd) the most *passionate* testimony letter to L of G, & me yet" (*Corr* 4:408). See *The Letters of John Addington Symonds,* 3 vols., ed. Herbert M. Schueller and Robert L. Peters (Detroit: Wayne State University Press, 1969), 3:425. The other two *Calamus* poems omitted from later editions are 9 ("Hours continuing long, sore and heavy-hearted") and 16 ("Who is now reading this?"). There appears to be an element of arbitrariness in Whitman's omissions, for other poems are just as hostile to the public sphere, just as depressed, and just as self-doubting. Symonds rightly linked *Calamus* 28 ("When I peruse the conquered fame of heroes") to *Calamus* 16 ("Long I Thought"), and it remains unclear why Whitman would remove one poem and not the other, though "Long I Thought" is arguably more emphatic in its antinationalism. Perhaps Whitman's initial elation, as represented by *Calamus* 8, was followed by the depressions of the later poems, and perhaps all three poems were inspired by the same love affair. If so, then *Calamus* 9 demonstrates that Whitman has not found his beloved companion in the jealous lover of *Calamus* 8, and I pursue this psychologically later reading in my text.

32. I do not mean to suggest that Whitman's vision of America as a nation of lovers in the *Calamus* sequence and elsewhere was merely a screen for homoerotic desire, but rather that recalcitrant elements in the poems can create this effect. For another view of this matter, see Jay Grossman, "'The Evangel-Poem of Comrades and of Love': Revising Whitman's Republicanism," *ATQ* 4 (September 1990): 201–18. Grossman writes that in the antebellum period Whitman was "deeply committed to resolving the crisis of the republic, even and especially when he appears to us to be 'only' profoundly sexual" (p. 215).

33. Elizabeth Bishop, "One Art," in *The Complete Poems 1927–1979* (New York: Farrar, Straus and Giroux, 1983), p. 178. Whitman also echoes 1 Corinthians 15:8, "By the grace of God I am what I am," seeking to humanize its message. On Whitman and St. Paul, see also his August 1890 letter to Bucke, *Corr* 5:75.

34. Whitman altered "bards" to the more neutral "recorders" in 1867 and eliminated the opening reference to himself as the poet who "prophesied of The

States, and led them the way of their glories." The original language suggests that while most readers will not understand Whitman's pride in loving men, poets may.'

35. For an analysis of *undemocratic* social meetings in antebellum American cities, including New York and Brooklyn, see Edward Pessen, *Riches, Class, and Power Before the Civil War* (Lexington, Mass.: D. C. Heath, 1973), especially chapters 9, "The Streets Where They Lived: The Residential Patterns of the Rich and Elite," 10, "The Marital Theory and Practice of the Rich and Elite," and 11, "The Private World and the Social Circle of the Rich and Elite." Pessen argues that rich people socialized with and married each other, and that their residences were clustered in affluent parts of the city. His analysis of the social position of writers, on pp. 239–40, suggests how anomalous Whitman's class status truly was.

36. Moon, *Disseminating Whitman*, p. 217.

37. Richard Rorty, *Achieving Our Country: Leftist Thought in Twentieth-Century America* (Cambridge: Harvard University Press, 1998), p. 26.

38. Rorty, *Achieving Our Country*, p. 26.

39. We may choose to read the unavowed "it" of "Who is now reading this?" (*LG* 1860, pp. 361–62) as evidence of further conflict between the homoerotic Whitman and the streets of New York, which threaten to reduce him to an "it" and from which perspective the unending tides of humanity—described in the journalism of, say, the summer of 1856—appear not only unlovely but contemptible. "A big, heavy, overgrown man, with a face like a raw beef-steak," he noted, "little piggy eyes, queer, dry, straight, harsh, coarse hair, 'of a speckled color,' made up of brownish red and gray, rather dirty clothes, and quite dirty, yellow dogskin gloves. He goes rolling along in an elephantine style, and for fear of being trod on, probably, people get out of the way. That is George Law, who never will be President. Those people, and many more, go about the streets of New York." See *New York Dissected*, p. 132. Law, known as "Live Oak George," was a wealthy investor and aspirant for the Democratic nomination for the Presidency in 1856. (The live oak was favored in shipbuilding because of its exceptional strength, and Law was a shipping magnate.) The son of a poor Irishman, Law had also acquired a real estate fortune. Perhaps some of Whitman's special animus against him derives not only from Law's financial success but also from his start as an engineer and contractor, a start close to the Whitman family trade but with a very different monetary end. On Law, see *New York Dissected*, pp. 236–37.

40. Killingsworth, *Whitman's Poetry of the Body*, p. 148. In *Whitman the Political Poet*, Erkkila notes that "Whitman internalized the homophobia of his culture" but that "there is no reason to assume that he deleted *Calamus* poems nos. 8, 9, and 16 in order to erase their personal homoerotic signature." She further suggests that "Whitman's decision to drop three of his more confessional *Calamus* poems in the 1867 *Leaves* was probably . . . motivated by his desire to fuse the poet and the lover in a single national persona who would project the unitary figure of a reconstructed self and a reconstructed nation" (pp. 182, 261). As I see it, in the 1860 *Leaves of Grass*, Whitman was trying both to express and to erase his personal erotic signature. Part of him wanted to fuse the poet and the

lover into a single national persona but part of him knew that he needed to transform his personal erotic signature into a less idiosyncratic style. To suggest that his loyalties were divided and his ambitions complex is to understate the case.

41. While working for the Interior Department, Whitman left the copy of *Leaves of Grass* he was revising in his desk. He was suddenly fired on June 30, 1865, by Secretary of the Interior James Harlan and rehired by Attorney General J. Hubley Ashton the next day. There are various accounts of this episode, including Jerome Loving, *Walt Whitman's Champion: William Douglas O'Connor* (College Station: Texas A & M University Press, 1978), pp. 56–65. Loving emphasizes a general move to economize in the Interior Department, but the moral outrage of Harlan, formerly an Iowa Senator, college president, and Methodist minister, was genuine. See also the account of this incident in Allen, *Solitary Singer,* pp. 344–350. For a succinct analysis of what happened when *Leaves of Grass* was banned in Boston and classified as obscene literature, see Allen, pp. 496–500; Erkkila, *Whitman the Political Poet,* pp. 308–9; Killingsworth, *Whitman's Poetry of the Body,* pp. 68, 147, 163–64. The short-term effect of the publicity generated by the Boston Attorney General was to boost the sales of the 1881–82 edition, which was later published in Philadelphia by Rees Welsh & Co., rather than by James R. Osgood, one of America's leading (Boston) publishers, as originally planned.

42. Killingsworth, *Whitman's Poetry of the Body,* p. 149. See also *Walt Whitman's Blue Book: The 1860–61 "Leaves of Grass" Containing His Manuscript Additions and Revisions,* ed. Arthur Golden, 2 vols. (New York: New York Public Library, 1968).

43. Symonds noted this poem in particular as a confirmation of Whitman's lived homoerotic identity.

CHAPTER SIX

1. See "Death of Abraham Lincoln," in *Walt Whitman: Complete Poetry and Collected Prose,* ed. Justin Kaplan (New York: Literary Classics of the United States, 1982), p. 1041. Lilacs were also in full bloom in Washington outside the Peterson House where Lincoln was taken after the shooting. For a detailed account of these and other historical matters, see Dorothy Meserve Kunhardt and Philip B. Kunhardt, *Twenty Days: A Narrative in Text and Pictures of the Assassination of Abraham Lincoln and the Twenty Days and Nights that Followed—The Nation in Mourning, The Long Trip Home to Springfield* (New York: Harper and Row, 1965).

2. Doyle is quoted to this effect in *Calamus: A Series of Letters Written during the Years 1868–1880 by Walt Whitman to a Young Friend (Peter Doyle),* ed. Richard Maurice Bucke (Boston: Laurens Maynard, 1897), pp. 25–26. Whitman had not yet made his acquaintance while writing "When Lilacs Last in the Dooryard Bloom'd." In subsequent correspondence with Whitman, Doyle's love of the theater, including burlesque, is evident. For more on Doyle, see Martin G. Murray, "'Pete the Great': A Biography of Peter Doyle," *Walt Whitman Quarterly Review* 12, no. 1 (summer 1994): 1–51.

3. Exactly when Whitman first drafted "Lilacs" is unknown. Presumably the

poem was written and rewritten. In mid-September, John Burroughs wrote to his friend Myron Benton, "Walt's book will be out in a week or two. . . . He is deeply interested in what I tell him of the Hermit Thrush, and says he has used largely the information I have given him in one of his principal poems." Quoted in Clara Barrus, *Whitman and Burroughs: Comrades* (Boston: Houghton Mifflin, 1931), p. 24. Probably the poem had been completed by the end of August.

4. Ed Folsom, *Walt Whitman's Native Representations* (New York: Cambridge University Press, 1994), p. 115.

5. For an eloquent description of "the specter of a reign of terror in which violence would become the primary means of effecting political change," see Betsy Erkkila, *Whitman the Political Poet* (New York: Oxford University Press, 1989), p. 227. And on the volume as a whole, see, for example, John Burroughs's claim in "Walt Whitman and His *Drum-Taps*": "His aim does not permit of the slightest expression of partisan or sectional feeling, or any exultation over a fallen foe" (*Galaxy* 2 [December 1, 1866]: 128). About "Lilacs," Burroughs continues: "By that curious indirect method which is always the method of nature, the poet makes no reference to the mere facts of Lincoln's death—neither describes it, or laments it, or dwells upon its unprovoked atrocity, or its political aspects, but quite beyond the possibilities of the art of the ordinary versifier, he seizes upon three beautiful facts of nature which he weaves into a wreath for the dead President's tomb" (p. 129).

6. Erkkila, *Whitman the Political Poet*, p. 227.

7. A strong reading challenging the usual unified-poem tradition is offered by Kerry C. Larson in *Whitman's Drama of Consensus* (Chicago: University of Chicago Press, 1988), pp. 231–243. He describes multiple, provisional beginnings; a static, nonincremental mode of development; and a centerless point of view. Though I admire Larson's alertness to fragmentation within the poem, his reading distances the poet's emotional and sexual ambivalence toward figures of male authority, whereas I try to use that ambivalence to explain the poet's (and the poem's) strategic omissions.

8. Michael Moon, *Disseminating Whitman: Revision and Corporeality in "Leaves of Grass"* (Cambridge: Harvard University Press, 1991), pp. 217, 218.

9. Moon, *Disseminating Whitman*, p. 218.

10. Galway Kinnell, "Whitman's Indicative Words," in *Walt Whitman: Walt Whitman's Autograph Revision of the Analysis of "Leaves of Grass" (For Dr. R. M. Bucke's Walt Whitman)*, ed. Stephen Railton (New York: New York University Press, 1974), p. 58.

11. Christopher Beach, *The Politics of Distinction: Whitman and the Discourses of Nineteenth-Century America* (Athens: University of Georgia Press, 1996), p. 23. See also pp. 99–100, on Whitman's turning away from a discourse "of direct personal and political engagement" as a result of his "firsthand experience of a terribly costly war."

12. Moon, *Disseminating Whitman*, p. 217.

13. In *The English Elegy: Studies in the Genre from Spenser to Yeats* (Baltimore: Johns Hopkins University Press, 1985), p. 316, Peter M. Sacks describes the poem's supposed stylistics of sexual sacrifice. I am indebted to Michael

Moon's rich counterreading for calling this discussion to my attention. See *Disseminating Whitman,* pp. 215–16.

14. Robert Leigh Davis, *Whitman and the Romance of Medicine* (Berkeley: University of California Press, 1997), p. 71.

15. Sacks, *English Elegy,* p. 317.

16. Benedict Anderson, *Imagined Communities: Reflections on the Origin and Spread of Nationalism* (London: Verso, 1991).

17. Charles I. Glicksberg, ed., *Walt Whitman and the Civil War* (Philadelphia: University of Pennsylvania Press, 1933), p. 174.

18. *I Sit and Look Out: Editorials from the Brooklyn Daily Times by Walt Whitman,* ed. Emory Holloway and Vernolian Schwarz (New York: Columbia University Press, 1932), pp. 96, 98.

19. "Death of Abraham Lincoln," in *Complete Poetry and Collected Prose,* p. 1039.

20. According to Henry B. Rankin, had Whitman only known it, one of his readers was none other than the prepresidential lawyer himself. In *Personal Recollections of Abraham Lincoln* (New York: G. P. Putnam's Sons, 1916), Rankin writes that "Lincoln . . . who had been . . . in the unapproachable depths of one of his glum moods . . . took up *Leaves of Grass* for his first reading of it. After half an hour or more of devotion to it, he turned back to the first pages and, to our general surprise, began to read aloud. . . . His rendering revealed a charm of new life in Whitman's versification. Save for a few comments on some broad allusions that Lincoln suggested could have been veiled, or left out, he commended the new poet's verses for their virility, freshness, unconventional sentiments, and unique forms of expression, and claimed that Whitman gave promise of a new school of poetry" (p. 91). Alas, the tale is a hoax, according to William E. Barton. In *Abraham Lincoln and Walt Whitman* (Indianapolis: Bobbs-Merrill, 1928), Barton claims that Rankin was never one of Lincoln's law clerks (pp. 90–94). For a more neutral and in that sense encouraging reading, see Merrill D. Peterson, *Lincoln in American Memory* (New York: Oxford University Press, 1994).

21. *Dear Brother Walt: The Letters of Thomas Jefferson Whitman,* ed. Dennis Berthold and Kenneth M. Price (Kent, Ohio: Kent State University Press, 1984), pp. 59, 61.

22. Samuel Eliot Morison and Henry Steele Commager, *The Growth of the American Republic* (New York: Oxford University Press, 1934), p. 613.

23. See Mutlu Konuk Blasing, "Whitman's 'Lilacs' and the Grammars of Time," *PMLA* 97 (January 1982): 31; Kenneth M. Price, *Whitman and Tradition: The Poet in His Century* (New Haven: Yale University Press, 1990), p. 77. On differences between Whitman and Lincoln as the "Beloved Companion," see Allen Grossman, "The Poetics of Union in Whitman and Lincoln: An Inquiry toward the Relationship of Art and Policy," in *The American Renaissance Reconsidered,* ed. Walter Benn Michaels and Donald E. Pease (Baltimore: Johns Hopkins University Press, 1985), pp. 183–208.

24. Jahan Ramazani, *Poetry of Mourning: The Modern Elegy from Hardy to Heaney* (Chicago: University of Chicago Press, 1994), p. 219.

25. *North American Review* (1886), reprinted in Barton, *Abraham Lincoln*

and Walt Whitman, pp. 83–89. The essay is also reprinted with the title "Abraham Lincoln" in *November Boughs,* in *Complete Poetry and Collected Prose,* pp. 1196–99.

26. Helen Vendler, "Whitman's 'When Lilacs Last in the Dooryard Bloom'd,'" in *Textual Analysis: Some Readers Reading,* ed. Mary Ann Caws (New York: Modern Language Association of America, 1986), pp. 132–143.

27. Richard Henry Stoddard, "An Horatian Ode," in *The Praise of Lincoln,* ed. A. Dallas Williams (Indianapolis: Bobbs-Merrill, 1911), pp. 102–108. In addition to Whitman, the authors represented in this volume include Thomas Bailey Aldrich, William Cullen Bryant, Alice Cary, Phoebe Cary, Rose Terry Cooke, Richard Watson Gilder, Oliver Wendell Holmes, Lucy Larcom, James Russell Lowell, John James Piatt (Whitman's Washington friend), Edmund Clarence Stedman, Bayard Taylor, John Townsend Trowbridge, Jones Very, and John Greenleaf Whittier. For a study of Lincoln mythology that is a bit dated but still very helpful, see Roy P. Basler, *The Lincoln Legend: A Study in Changing Conceptions* (Boston: Houghton Mifflin, 1935). Basler lists other anthologies of Lincolniana. Further, for the kind of material that Whitman censored, see "A Lincoln Reminiscence," beginning, "As is well known, story-telling was often with President Lincoln a weapon which he employ'd with great skill" (*Complete Poetry and Prose,* p. 1072).

28. According to Don E. Fehrenbacher, "Serious scholars have applied the word 'dictator' more often to Lincoln than to any other president. The list of his presidential actions inspiring such judgments is a rather long one. With Congress, by his arrangement, not in session, he responded to the attack on Fort Sumter by enlarging the army, proclaiming a blockade of Southern ports, suspending the writ of habeas corpus in certain areas, authorizing arbitrary arrests and imprisonments on a large scale, and spending public funds without legal warrant. He never yielded the initiative seized at this time, and, in later bold assertions of executive authority, he introduced conscription, proclaimed emancipation and inaugurated a program of reconstruction." See "Lincoln and the Constitution," in *The Public and the Private Lincoln: Contemporary Perspectives,* ed. Cullom Davis, Charles B. Strozier, Rebecca Monroe Veach, and Geoffrey C. Ward (Carbondale: Southern Illinois University Press, 1979), p. 127.

29. The love letter to the future King Edward VII that Whitman embedded within "Year of Meteors (1859–60)" is possibly the most embarrassing vignette in *Leaves of Grass.*

> Remember you surging Manhattan's crowds, as you passed with your cortege
>   of nobles?
> There in the crowds stood I, and singled you out with attachment;
> I know not why, but I loved you . . . (and so go forth little song,
> Far over sea speed like an arrow, carrying my love all folded,
> And find in his palace the youth I love, and drop these lines at his feet).
>   (*DT* 51–52)

See also "A Broadway Pageant" in the same volume (pp. 61–65).

30. William Wordsworth, "She dwelt among the untrodden ways" and "Strange fits of passion have I known," in *Poems, Volume I,* ed. John O. Hayden (New York: Penguin Books, 1977), pp. 366–67.

31. According to Cathy N. Davidson, "*Charlotte Temple* became America's first best-selling novel in the earliest years of the Republic, when the fledgling nation was yet defining its own cultural and political identity, and it remained a best-seller well into the beginning of the twentieth century and America's ascendancy as a world power." See Susanna Rowson, *Charlotte Temple,* ed. Cathy N. Davidson (New York: Oxford University Press, 1986), p. xi.

32. *Four Years in the Confederate Artillery: The Diary of Private Henry Robinson Berkeley,* ed. William H. Runge (Chapel Hill: University of North Carolina Press, 1961), p. 144.

33. Vendler sees this passage as an example of Whitman's great delicacy of feeling. She writes, "It is, as the poem says, the living who remain and suffer. Only the dead are excused from suffering, insanity, and the gross inflictions of war. With characteristic delicacy, Whitman puts himself in a minor place in the list of survivors: for each dead soldier 'the mother suffer'd, / And the wife and child and musing comrade suffer'd / And the armies that remain'd suffer'd.' . . . The thrice-repeated 'suffer'd' is paired inextricably with the twice-repeated 'remain'd' until the two verbs become synonymous: to remain is to suffer" ("Whitman's 'Lilacs,'" p. 140).

34. Ramazani, *Poetry of Mourning,* pp. 525–26, 264.

35. *The Collected Works of Abraham Lincoln,* ed. Roy P. Basler, 9 vols. (New Brunswick, N.J.: Rutgers University Press, 1953), 2:90. The address was delivered at City Hall in Chicago.

36. On May 28, 1862, Andrew enlisted as a private in the 13th Regiment, New York State Militia, Heavy Artillery. He was mustered in on June 16, 1862, in Suffolk, Virginia, and served for three months without seeing any serious action. His health declined rapidly after he returned to civilian life in September. For more on Andrew Whitman's military status, see Martin G. Murray, "Bunkum *Did* Go Sogering," *Walt Whitman Quarterly Review* 10, no. 3 (winter 1993): 142–48.

37. Harold Bloom, "Whitman's Image of Voice: To the Tally of My Soul," in *Agon: Towards a Theory of Revisionism* (New York: Oxford University Press, 1982), pp. 179–199. The quoted passages are from pp. 188–190.

CHAPTER SEVEN

1. An earlier version of this chapter appeared in *Breaking Bounds: Whitman and American Cultural Studies,* ed. Betsy Erkkila and Jay Grossman (New York: Oxford University Press, 1996), pp. 92–111. I hope that this revision is less theory-driven and more closely attentive to the emotional complexities of Whitman's social experience. References to *Democratic Vistas* are to the edition given in the Citation Note.

2. For an overview of motherist movements, see Elaine Tuttle Hansen, *Mother Without Child: Contemporary Fiction and the Crisis of Motherhood* (Berkeley: University of California Press, 1997). She summarizes "the prolific and still growing feminist critique of motherhood that has evolved over the past three decades" (p. 5).

3. See Henry Clarke Wright, *The Empire of the Mother Over the Character*

and Destiny of the Race (Boston: B. Marsh, 1863). As the feminist historian Mary Ryan explains in her similarly named book, *The Empire of the Mother: American Writing about Domesticity 1830–1860* (New York: Haworth Press, 1982), "Despite the incongruity between the domestic mystique and the realities of an industrializing society, the cult of the mother's empire continued to gain converts during the 1850s. Even the fledgling women's rights movement succumbed to its seductions. This process is illustrated by the women's rights journal founded by Amelia Bloomer and titled, ominously, *The Lily*. In its early issues, *The Lily* printed adamant proposals for sexual equality, and sarcastically reviewed the 'namby pamby sort of articles on women and wives.' By the mid-1850s, however, *The Lily* enthusiastically endorsed a thoroughly domestic image of woman: 'Not in the whole world . . . is there a character as heroic as the home mother.' While she was to remain in her isolated domestic sphere, the ideal woman was invested with incomparable power. *The Lily* maintained that 'Without home, without the domestic relations, the love, the cares, the responsibilities which bind men's hearts to the one treasury of their precious things, the world would be a chaos, without order, or beauty; without patriotism, or social regulation, without public or private virtue'" (pp. 111–12). Part of Whitman would have agreed.

4. Sacvan Bercovitch refers to *Democratic Vistas* as Whitman's "towering state-of-the-covenant address," yet he argues that the work "has proved disappointing as political or social commentary because it is a work of symbolic interpretation. Its terms are doomsday or millennium." He further notes that a "determination not to surrender the dream, because the dream was the only option to despair, informs Whitman's work." See *The American Jeremiad* (Madison: University of Wisconsin Press, 1978), p. 198.

5. *Democratic Vistas* was based on three installments that Whitman compared to a "serial story" (*Corr* 2:33). His "small volume in prose" was issued as an eighty-four page pamphlet in 1870, though the title page read 1871 (*Corr* 2:100). There was a new introduction for this edition. For additional publication history, see Edward F. Grier, "Walt Whitman, The *Galaxy,* and *Democratic Vistas,*" *American Literature* 23, no. 3 (November 1951): 322–50. For "Shooting Niagara: And After?" see Thomas Carlyle, *Critical and Miscellaneous Essays,* ed. H. D. Traill, 5 vols. (New York: Scribner's, 1901), 5:1–48.

6. The quote is from F. O. Matthiessen, *American Renaissance: Art and Expression in the Age of Emerson and Whitman* (New York: Oxford University Press, 1941), p. 591.

7. Carlyle, "Shooting Niagara," pp. 7, 5.

8. Whatever her virtues, the Dark Mother in "Lilacs" perpetuates a sexist association between the womanly and the unworldly. Even if to capitulate to the Real power of the mother is to escape from the artificially structured and psychologically coercive male symbolic order, this capitulation does not effectively challenge gender or racial binaries. The mystical Dark Mother emerges as that which is not-language. Ironically, then, Whitman's democratic elegy in some measure reproduces the system of gendered and racialized thinking that he intends to unsettle.

9. For a reading of this passage that draws attention to its historical evasiveness while concentrating on the decomposing materiality of the (presumably white) corpse, see Timothy Sweet, *Traces of War: Poetry, Photography, and the Crisis of the Union* (Baltimore: Johns Hopkins University Press, 1990), pp. 75–76. Sweet observes that the scene "is conceived in such a way as to demonstrate that effacing the history of death in war and achieving the ideological significance that makes sense of death in war are a single operation."

10. James McPherson, *The Negro's Civil War: How American Negroes Felt and Acted During the War for the Union* (New York: Pantheon, 1965), pp. ix–x; *Abraham Lincoln and the Second American Revolution* (New York: Oxford University Press, 1991), p. 35.

11. Gay Wilson Allen, *The Solitary Singer* (1955; reprint, New York: New York University Press, 1967), pp. 444–45.

12. Howard Zinn, *A People's History of the United States* (New York: Harper, 1980), p. 194.

13. Several years later he was to break with his champion William Douglas O'Connor, author of the pugilistic "Good Gray Poet," over just this issue. During the heated presidential campaign of 1872 in which Horace Greeley vied openly for the black vote, O'Connor accused Whitman of bigotry. Whitman, who was supporting Grant, responded recklessly, and the damage was done. The friends did not speak again for more than a decade, though Whitman extended his hand when they met by chance on the street the following day. For the most thorough study of the Whitman-O'Connor relationship, see Jerome Loving, *Walt Whitman's Champion: William Douglas O'Connor* (College Station: Texas A & M University Press, 1978). For the view that erotic complications determined the rupture, see David Cavitch, *My Soul and I: The Inner Life of Walt Whitman* (Boston: Beacon Press, 1985), pp. 173–85.

On slaveowning in Whitman's family background, see Justin Kaplan, *Walt Whitman: A Life* (New York: Simon and Schuster, 1980), pp. 131–32, and Allen, *Solitary Singer,* p. 15. On family attitudes toward African Americans, see also George Washington Whitman, *Civil War Letters,* ed. Jerome M. Loving (Durham, N.C: Duke University Press, 1975), pp. 4–5, 127, 156, and passim. In the late 1880s, when Horace Traubel was questioning Whitman about his racial attitudes, he conceded, "After all I may have been tainted a bit, just a little bit, with the New York feeling with regard to anti-slavery" (*WWWC* 3:76).

14. "The Radicals in Council," in *I Sit and Look Out: Editorials from the Brooklyn Daily Times by Walt Whitman,* ed. Emory Holloway and Vernolian Schwarz (New York: Columbia University Press, 1932), pp. 45–46.

15. Needless to say, women today continue to negotiate these issues. In the state of Washington in 1992, where I was then living and working, Senator Patty Murray was elected as "just a mom in tennis shoes." She proudly adopted this slogan after it had been derisively coined by a male colleague in the Washington legislature. But when it was announced early in her Senate term that Murray had canceled her appointments for a day to stay home with a sick child, several of my hardworking "mom" colleagues at the University of Washington were indignant. They didn't cancel classes when their children had the flu; why should she?

16. Robert Weisbuch, "Whitman's Personalism, Arnold's Culture," in *Atlantic Double-Cross: American Literature and British Influence in the Age of Emerson* (Chicago: University of Chicago Press, 1986), p. 85.

17. See Gayle Rubin, "The Traffic in Women: Notes on the 'Political Economy' of Sex," reprinted in *The Second Wave: A Reader in Feminist Theory,* ed. Linda Nicholson (New York: Routledge, 1997), pp. 27–62.

18. Joanne Feit Diehl, "From Emerson to Whitman," *Women Poets and the American Sublime* (Bloomington: Indiana University Press, 1990), p. 11.

19. M. Wynn Thomas observes that "in *Democratic Vistas* Whitman explicitly compares destructive natural forces with widespread social upheaval in terms of their disruptive effects on human life." For a fuller discussion of Whitman's "dissenting anger," jeering tone, and generalized violent impulse, see *The Lunar Light of Whitman's Poetry* (Cambridge: Harvard University Press, 1987), pp. 24, 6–7, and passim. Thomas, however, is uncomfortable with what he calls "the peculiarities of Whitman's own psychology" and suggests that Whitman "is accurately recording objective features of contemporary social relationships" (pp. 19, 20).

20. See Christopher Newfield, "The Politics of Male Suffering: Masochism and Hegemony in the American Renaissance," *Differences* 1, no. 3 (fall 1989): 55–87. He argues that "the first half of the nineteenth century seems to find white American men in a protracted celebration of aggressive masculinity," but that "aggression is only half the story."

21. For a lovely reading of "There Was a Child Went Forth" in the context of family poems, see Stephen Gould Axelrod, in *Sylvia Plath: The Wound and the Cure of Words* (Baltimore: Johns Hopkins University Press, 1990), pp. 59–61. He describes the illusion of self-sufficiency as a "harmful self-deception."

22. See Lewis Hyde, *The Gift: Imagination and the Erotic Life of Property* (New York: Random House, 1983), pp. 185–86.

23. For a reading of this poem in the context of nineteenth-century eugenics, see M. Jimmie Killingsworth, *Whitman's Poetry of the Body* (Chapel Hill: University of North Carolina Press, 1989), pp. 62–65. He suggests that "enfolding and effusing—the actions of the female genitalia—become the model for ideal creative power," but does not fully persuade himself that this is the case. More generally, in the chapter "Procreation and Perfectibility: 1856," Killingsworth argues that "Whitman's woman—rather than developing fully as the archetypal model for creative power—becomes something of a cog in the eugenic machine" (p. 73).

24. See, for example, the gigantic, but also consumptive new-world spirit-mother who suffers from breast cancer in "Thou Mother with Thy Equal Brood," an 1872 poem in which "The livid cancer spread its hideous claws, clinging upon thy breasts, seeking to strike thee deep within" (*LG,* p. 460). Describing this "Emblem of general maternity lifted above all, / Sacred shape of the bearer of daughters and sons," out of whose "teeming womb . . . giant babes in ceaseless procession issu[e]," Whitman writes, "I but thee name, thee prophesy, as now, / I merely thee ejaculate!" (*LG,* pp. 458–59).

25. Newfield, "The Politics of Male Suffering," p. 56.

26. Alicia Ostriker, "Loving Walt Whitman and the Problem of America,"

in *The Continuing Presence of Walt Whitman: The Life After the Life,* ed. Robert K. Martin (Iowa City: University of Iowa Press, 1992), p. 227. See also Michael Moon's superb reading, which emphasizes Whitman's nongeneric use of the word "men," as well as his devaluation of women who are not mothers, in *Disseminating Whitman: Revision and Corporeality in "Leaves of Grass"* (Cambridge: Harvard University Press, 1991), p. 78.

27. D. H. Lawrence, "Whitman," in *A Century of Whitman Criticism,* ed. Edwin Haviland Miller (Bloomington: Indiana University Press, 1969), p. 157.

28. Betsy Erkkila, *Whitman the Political Poet* (New York: Oxford University Press, 1989), pp. 258–59.

29. Betsy Erkkila, *The Wicked Sisters: Women Poets, Literary History, and Discord* (New York: Oxford University Press, 1992), p. 4.

30. Ostriker, "Loving Walt Whitman," p. 227.

31. Robert Leigh Davis, *Whitman and the Romance of Medicine* (Berkeley: University of California Press, 1997), pp. 75, 44.

32. Sandra M. Gilbert, "The American Sexual Poetics of Walt Whitman and Emily Dickinson," in *Reconstructing American Literary History,* ed. Sacvan Bercovitch (Cambridge: Harvard University Press, 1986), pp. 130–31. Gilbert views Whitman as the more socially conservative writer.

33. Adrienne Rich, "The Eye of the Outsider: Elizabeth Bishop's *Complete Poems 1927–1979,*" in *Blood, Bread, and Poetry: Selected Prose 1979–1985* (New York: Norton, 1986), p. 131. The context for her remark is a critique of Bishop's "Songs for a Colored Singer."

34. See Edward Carpenter, *Days with Walt Whitman: With Some Notes on his Life and Work* (London: George Allen, 1906), p. 43. "Sloane Kennedy" was the journalist William Sloane Kennedy, who published "A Study of Whitman" in 1881.

35. The classic nineteenth-century feminist appreciation of Whitman is by Gilchrist—his most influential contemporary woman reader. For a useful study of Gilchrist's often tormented life, see Marion Walker Alcaro, *Walt Whitman's Mrs. G: A Biography of Anne Gilchrist* (Rutherford, N.J.: Fairleigh Dickinson University Press, 1991).

36. Quotations in this paragraph are from Emily Dickinson, *The Letters of Emily Dickinson,* ed. Thomas H. Johnson, 3 vols. (Cambridge: Harvard University Press, 1958), 2:404, 649, 475, 405.

37. See Willis J. Buckingham, *Emily Dickinson's Reception in the 1890s: A Documentary History* (Pittsburgh: University of Pittsburgh Press, 1989), p. 280 and passim.

38. The quotation is from "The Death of Abraham Lincoln," in *Complete Poetry and Collected Prose,* p. 1046.

39. See Walter H. Eitner, "Emily Dickinson's Awareness of Whitman: A Reappraisal," *Walt Whitman Review* 22, no. 3 (September 1976): 111–15; and Karl Keller, "The Sweet Wolf Within: Emily Dickinson and Walt Whitman," in *The Only Kangaroo among the Beauty: Emily Dickinson and America* (Baltimore: Johns Hopkins University Press, 1979), pp. 251–93.

40. Susan Gilbert Dickinson, quoted in Millicent Todd Bingham, *Emily Dickinson: A Revelation* (New York: Harper, 1954), p. 59.

41. *Elizabeth Cady Stanton As Revealed in her Letters, Diary and Reminiscences,* ed. Theodore Stanton and Harriet Stanton Blatch, 2 vols. (New York: Harper, 1902), 2:210.

42. See my discussion of this poem in chapter 4, in which I offer a less familiar reading.

43. Frances Wright, quoted in M. Jimmie Killingsworth, *Whitman's Poetry of the Body* (Chapel Hill: University of North Carolina Press, 1989), p. 66.

44. Whitman did not change "semitic" to "seminal" until 1871, when he also revised "By Blue Ontario's Shore" to read "his seminal muscle" (*LG,* p. 344). See also the reference to the greatest poet's "semitic muscle" in the 1855 "Preface" (*LG* 1855, p. 21). For a reading of Whitman that preserves the association between semen and breast milk, see Sharon Olds, "Nurse Whitman," in *Satan Says* (Pittsburgh: University of Pittsburgh Press, 1980), p. 13.

45. The classic account of this ideology is Barbara Welter, "The Cult of True Womanhood, 1820–1860" (1966), reprinted in her *Dimity Convictions: The American Woman in the Nineteenth Century* (Athens: Ohio State University Press, 1976). The opposing ideology of Real Womanhood is set forth in Frances B. Cogan, *All-American Girl: The Ideal of Real Womanhood in Mid-Nineteenth-Century America* (Athens: University of Georgia Press, 1989).

Both Erkkila, in *Whitman the Political Poet,* pp. 257–59, and Sherry Ceniza, in "Walt Whitman and Abby Price," *Walt Whitman Quarterly Review* 7, no. 2 (fall 1989): 51–52, describe Whitman's women as moving out of the home rather than remaining confined within it. Erkkila makes the valuable point that the conflict between Whitman's emphasis on the power of motherhood and his admiration for women such as "Frances Wright, George Sand, Margaret Fuller, Anne Gilchrist, Lucretia Mott, and Delia Bacon—all women who had challenged traditional women's roles"—is "a contradiction at the root not only of nineteenth-century American culture but of feminism itself" (pp. 315–16).

46. "Clef Poem" was retitled "On the Beach at Night Alone" in 1871, but Whitman was already reworking the nipple-tasting lines in 1860. They were altered to read, "I suppose the pink nipples of the breasts of women with whom I shall sleep will touch the side of my face the same, / But this is the nipple of a breast of my mother, always near and always divine to me, her true child and son, whatever comes" (*LG* 1860, p. 230). The entire passage was abandoned in 1867.

47. See John Gatta, *American Madonna: Images of the Divine Woman in Literary Culture* (New York: Oxford University Press, 1997). Among the writers he considers are Nathaniel Hawthorne, Margaret Fuller, Harriet Beecher Stowe, Harold Frederic, Henry Adams, and T. S. Eliot.

48. "Free Academies at Public Cost," in *I Sit and Look Out,* pp. 53–54. For an account of Whitman's quarrel with Fern, which accuses him of blatant sexism, see Joyce W. Warren, *Fanny Fern: An Independent Woman* (New Brunswick, N.J.: Rutgers University Press, 1992). For a critique of this account, see Sherry Ceniza, review of *Fanny Fern: An Independent Woman, Walt Whitman Quarterly Review* 11, no. 2 (fall 1993): 89–95.

49. "The Death of Abraham Lincoln," in *Complete Poetry and Collected Prose,* p. 1046.

50. "The Death of Abraham Lincoln," p. 1046.

Index

Walt Whitman is sometimes referred to as WW.

compassion, xv, 68, 212n 3; of Louisa
    Whitman, 9
competition: and denial of authority,
    160–161; in erotic exchange, 91; ho-
    moerotic love as dismantling, 68; as
    impediment to male bonding, 136–
    137, 138; with Lincoln, 160, 165–
    166, 167; retreat from, 179; and suf-
    fering, 168. See also fathers; patriar-
    chy; power
compulsory heterosexuality. See hetero-
    sexuality, compulsory
contact, need for, 96, 105–106, 222n 33
contradiction, commitment to, 147–148,
    152, 166
control, fear of loss of, 91, 93, 96
Cooper, James Fenimore, 61
corporal punishment, 46, 209n 9
country life: involuntary, 23–24, 25, 30–
    35, 206n 59; as temporary idyll, 91.
    See also urban life
Crane, Hart, 94
criticism: of arrogance, 59; in England
    vs. United States, 127–128, 227n 8; by
    Fern, 212n 7; of fiction, 38, 208n 7; on
    gender supplanting race, 177; gentle-
    man persona ignored in, 57; Hannah
    Whitman Heyde as ignored in, 116; by
    Heyde, 119; on homosexual guilt, 150;
    on language and morals, 111–112,
    188, 224n 47; on letters, 33; by Louisa
    Whitman, 13; racial themes ignored in,
    124; renunciation by WW and, 140;
    self-reviews, 58, 65–66, 111, 112,
    122–124, 126, 128; startled critics,
    xv; warnings in, 188; WW's relation to,
    58, 96, 123, 226n 2. See also audience
"Crossing Brooklyn Ferry," 102, 145–
    146, 148, 230n 22
Cult of True Womanhood, 185, 190,
    244n 45

Dalke, Anne, 210n 13
Dana, Charles A., 111
Davidson, Cathy N., 239n 31
Davis, Robert Leigh, 157, 185
death: acceptance of, 191, 193; child-
    hood and, 117; closural force of allu-
    sions to, 228n 13; cult of, 89, 103–
    104, 222n 31; Dark Mother as, 168–
    169, 171, 175, 240n 8; escape from,
    103; grieving (see grief); guilt follow-
    ing, 168, 170, 171; as integral, 131,
    228n 13; vs. life, suffering of, 167–
    168, 169, 170, 175, 239n 33; Lincoln
    on, 169–170, 239n 35; morbidity
    charges vs. symbol of, 123, 127; as po-

etic power, 123; protection of children
    against, 110–111. See also sexuality
"Death and Burial of McDonald Clarke.
    A Parody," 206n 56
"Death in the School-Room (A Fact),"
    41–42, 46
debating, 25, 32
"Democracy," 176
democracy: affection and, 109, 125–126,
    141–142, 152; ambivalence toward,
    173–174; "America" as convertible
    term with, 126–127; body-in-process
    as symbol of, 63, 214n 19; as contain-
    ing WW, 126–127; conversion of in-
    timacy fears and, xvii; cultural vs.
    political reform and, 215n 25; and ho-
    moerotic culture, 123–127, 141–142,
    143, 147–148, 152, 158–159, 233n
    32, 234n 40; imperfections in textual
    practice of, xvii–xix; male friendship
    and, xxii; maternal body and, 173; the
    personal vs. the ideal and, xvii; person-
    hood and, xiv; pluralism, 126, 229n
    16; and "rough" persona, 57. See also
    faith in sex; freedom; politics; United
    States
"Democratic Art" (Symonds), 140
Democratic Party: Brenton and WW and,
    26, 30; and Free-Soil movement, 68–
    69; George Law and, 234n 39; Loco-
    focos, 32
Democratic Review, 37–38, 41, 215n 25
Democratic Vistas, 126–127, 147, 172,
    173–176, 180–181, 191, 240nn 4–5,
    242n 19
departures: dynamic of, 91–92, 220n 12;
    as human condition, 164
Dickinson, Emily: on death and rebirth,
    103, 104; editing of poems, 98; literary
    alienation of, 186, 187–188; northern
    secession poems of, 231n 25; romances
    of, 74–75, 215n 26; sexuality and,
    188–189; WW and, xix, 187–188
Dickinson, Susan Gilbert, 75, 98, 188–
    189
Diehl, Joanne Feit, 179
Disraeli, Benjamin, 175
Doherty, Robert W., 202n 37
domesticity, xiv–xv; ambivalence toward,
    190, 192, 244n 45; Louisa Whitman
    and, 2, 15; resistance to, 107–108;
    Woodbury critique of, 30–35. See also
    marriage; middle-class values
domestic violence, 226n 62
domination: as intrinsic, 195n 1; Louisa
    Whitman and resistance to, 226n 61;
    struggle with, of WW, xv–xvi; as un-

male-homoerotic desire (*continued*)
91, 93, 96; democracy and, 123–127,
141–142, 143, 147–148, 152, 158–
159, 233n 32, 234n 40; erotic coerciveness and, 106; as excessive, xxi;
family relationships as model for, 88;
and female, identification with, 89–
90, 93, 116, 129–130, 132–134, 184,
228n 12; as fluid, xxii–xxiii; grief and,
158–159; ideal family as constituted
by, 46; and low-class other, 134–135;
physical expression of, xx–xxii; privileging of, xiii; renunciation of, 105,
135, 138–152, 181, 228n 11, 230n 17,
231nn 27–28, 232n 30, 233nn 31, 34,
234n 40, 235n 41; subculture of, 75;
tensions of WW in expression/self-
suppression of, 159; as undemocratic,
127, 140; women's roles in culture
of, 125. *See also* feminization; male
bonding; male friendship; romantic
friendships
Man-Love poems. See *Calamus*
marriage: bad food and, 207n 67; dis-
mantling of, 130–131; early, as coun-
seled, 47, 49, 53; feminist view of, according to WW, 177; male-homoerotic
desire as stage toward, 209n 11; male-
male, 140, 142; pledge to, as rapidly
exhausted, 132–133; sexism of, 179;
social attitudes and, 206n 59; transgression of WW toward, 29–30, 206n
59; as unavailable to all, 85, 225n 50;
as unhappy, 52. *See also* domesticity;
middle-class values; sexuality
Martin, Robert K., xvii, 135, 217n 33,
229n 17, 230n 20
masculinity: aggression of, retreat from,
179–180, 242n 20; authorship and,
xvi–xvii; disaffection from, xix; drinking and, 207n 71; hypermasculinity,
as defense, 57, 70–71; Louisa Whitman's ideals of, 3; romantic friendship and, 207n 65; war and, xxiii, 15,
197n 21. *See also* femininity; feminization; gender
Maslan, Mark, 224n 46
master narrative, 46
masturbation. *See* autoeroticism
Matthiessen, F. O., 220n 11
McClure, J. E., 214n 22
McPherson, James, 175–176
Melville, Herman, 69
memory: grief and, 168, 169; poet's
mission and, 97; repression of, 158,
168
men: single, sexuality and, 85, 115; as

term, 183, 243n 26. *See also* fathers;
gender; mothers; women
metaphor, 211n 23
Meyers, Marvin, 219n 7
middle-class values, xiv–xv; domesticity
(*see* domesticity); food and, 30–31,
32–34, 35, 207n 67; marriage (*see*
marriage); and publication of work,
97; racializing in fiction of, 39; Woodbury critique of, 30–35. *See also* class;
working class
Miller, Edwin H., 217n 32
Miller, James E., 229n 16
mind, and body as lost vs. found, 97
Mitchell, Donald Grant, 201n 34
modernity, maternity as answer to problem of, 178
Moers, Ellen, 30
Molinoff, Katherine, 118, 200n 19,
225nn 51, 53
Moon, Michael, xvii, 146, 156, 157,
201n 26, 210n 12, 232n 30, 236n 13,
243n 26
"Moral Effect of the [Atlantic] Cable,
The," 216n 29
morbidity, charges of, 123, 127, 228n 10.
See also death
Morris, Timothy, 218n 3
mothers: absence of, violence and, 39–
40; agency of, males and, 173, 179,
190; ambivalence of WW and, 172–
173, 178–183, 189–192; careers of,
177, 192, 241n 15, 244n 45; creativity
as symbolized by, 184–185, 242n 23;
Dark Mother, 168–169, 171, 175,
240n 8; as de-eroticized, 189–190;
divine, 177, 191; "good motherhood,"
178, 192; and healthy sexuality, 109;
ideal, 137; in ideal family, 46; identity
and, 179–180; inadequate, as patriarchal role, 169; motherist movement/
cult, 172–173, 239nn 2–3; as muse, 1,
2, 8, 19, 172, 185, 201n 33; as nurtur-
ant, 41; perfect, xviii–xix, 180–181;
Poem-Mother, 182–183; as political
problem solver, 189; poverty of, 46; as
programmatic, 173; as supreme goal,
184–185, 189–192. *See also* family;
fathers; Whitman, Louisa Van Velsor
mother-surrogates, 7
Mott, Frank Luther, 208n 2
Muchmore, W. M., 73
Murray, Patty, 241n 15
muscle: offset hoped for, 56; semitic/semi-
nal, 244n 44; as symbol, 66, 212n 7;
and tenderness, 60
muses, 1, 2, 8, 19, 169, 172, 185, 201n 33

Designer:	Nicole Hayward
Compositor:	G & S Typesetters, Inc.
Text:	10/13 Sabon
Display:	Sabon
Printer and Binder:	Thomson-Shore, Inc.